Western Philosophy

The Journey

Revised Printing

Thanassis Samaras
University of Georgia

Kendall Hunt
publishing company

www.kendallhunt.com
Send all inquiries to:
4050 Westmark Drive
Dubuque, IA 52004-1840

Copyright 2006 by Kendall/Hunt Publishing Company

ISBN: 978-1-4652-6846-4

Printed in the United States of America

Contents

Preface

What is philosophy? There are probably as many answers to this question as there are philosophers, and this hardly encourages the average student to embark on a serious study of philosophy.

But although it may be difficult to provide a definition of philosophy that covers all its various facets, there is one thing all philosophers and all philosophical currents have in common: the desire to explain reality, the world that we live in. As Aristotle puts it, 'human beings by nature desire to philosophize.' For the ancient Greeks, who inaugurated Western philosophy, the term meant 'love of wisdom.' It is this love which motivated them to examine the mysteries of the natural world and of the human mind, and to lay the foundations for everything that followed.

The fundamental question for the Greeks was the question of change. Is change real or only apparent? And what is it that remains the same underneath the faзade of change? These questions, along with practical considerations and political aspirations led the Pre-Socratics to create the first philosophical works of the Western tradition.

But they did not stop there. While trying to discover the one entity which underlies all the changes that we observe around us, they came up with the concept of universal principles which govern the world. Anaximander's *apeiron*, which can be translated as either unlimited or indefinite (and probably includes the meanings of both these English terms) was the first abstract notion intended to explicate reality as a whole. From the evolution of this simple concept to the elaborate metaphysical schemes of Plato and Aristotle it was a question of time.

The desire to explain the world is not unique to the Greeks. In fact, it is a common characteristic of mankind. What made the Greeks go beyond the magical and religious thought that characterized other civilizations, was a unique set of social and political circumstances, but also the fact that for the first time, with the emergence of democracy, it was the best argument, rather than sheer force, which decided an issue. The Greek democracy provided a unique venue for the exchange of ideas, and it also made self-evident the importance of lucid and clear argumentation.

As Christianity gradually developed into the major spiritual force of the last part of antiquity, philosophy got incorporated into the theological teaching of the Catholic Church. For almost a millennium, philosophy became indistinguishable from theology. It is the giants of Christian thought, men like Augustine and Aquinas, who not only reinterpreted Greek thought, but also provided the link between this thought and modernity. Although the first indications of a trend towards the secularization of philosophy can be clearly traced in the thirteenth century, it would take Descartes' radical questioning of all authority, as well as the supersession of Aristotelian physics by Newton, for philosophy to become secular again. The question of whether human knowledge is innate or comes from experience, addressed by Plato and Aristotle, now comes once more to the fore and dominates Western thinking until Kant's synthesis of the two puts the matter to, at least a temporary, rest. At the same time, the social changes which follow the industrial revolution give rise to the treatises of thinkers like Hobbes and Locke. Both of these British philosophers attempt, in distinctly different ways, to express the aspirations of a rising industrial/commercial class, which will later be identified as the "middle" class or the *bourgeoisie*. By the nineteenth century industrialization had proceeded enough for a new class to develop its own ideology and to challenge the worldview of the middle class, which had succeeded the medieval understanding of the world. The working class finds its aspirations expressed in the works of Marx and his epigones. But liberalism will remain politically dominant, and it will be invigorated by the works of John Stuart Mill. Mill also offers an alternative to the rigorous Kantian duty ethics. His utilitarianism, a refined version of a notion previously advanced by Bentham, is based on the idea that what is moral is what gives the greatest satisfaction to the greatest number of people. A post-Kantian duty ethics with strong emphasis on the concept of rights and Utilitarianism remain the two most influential moral theories in the West today.

There is another current of thought which appears in the nineteenth century and flourishes even further on the twentieth. The existentialists turn to philosophy not necessarily for an understanding of the world as a whole, but for personal non-religious salvation. Kierkegaard and Nietzsche pave the way for the thinking of Heidegger and Sartre. But with the end of the relative complacency which existed in Western Europe in previous decades and with the problems of globalization and the conflict between recent civilizations becoming more acute in different years, traditional existentialism is not as dominant in academic circles as it used to be.

It is not possible, in an introductory course, to cover all aspects of Western philosophy. This book, and the course, follow a historical order and concentrate on some major thinkers and issues in its history. Metaphysics (ontology and epistemology) on the one hand, and ethics and politics on the other, are the two areas in which most emphasis is placed. With some exceptions, the texts selected for this volume are short. No memorization of any kind is expected from the students. It is rather the case that we will use these texts as a springboard to a better understanding of the world we live in and of the way the thinkers of the past understood it.

Western philosophy is a journey in history and in understanding. Let's enjoy it!

1. Introduction to the Pre-Socratics

Western philosophy, as we know it, begins with the Pre-Socratics. This term has come to designate a large number of philosophers, some of whom actually lived later than Socrates.

The Pre-Socratics initiate Western philosophy by doing, mainly, two things: (1) they move away from the 'magico-religious' explanations of the world which permeate Greek poetry (especially Homer and Hesiod) and they substitute religious thinking with rationalism; (2) for the first time in the history of our civilization, they try to explain the world as a whole, and they come up with the notion of the 'first principle' (*archē*), which is supposed to explain everything that there is. Ontology, a Greek term which means speech about being (*to on*), thus becomes for the first time possible.

Although the Pre-Socratics are a varied group of thinkers who cover the whole Greek world geographically and most of the sixth and fifth centuries BC chronologically, most of them share some fundamental characteristics:

1. They replace magico-religious explanation by rational thinking and argument.
2. They attempt to explain nature without reference to anything other than nature itself.
3. They attempt to produce a principle which will explain everything in the physical universe.
4. They are what we would today call 'scientists'—excellent astronomers, biologists and mathematicians.

Anaximander, in my opinion the first great Greek philosopher, was born in the Asia Minor city of Miletus and was probably the student of the distinguished astronomer and philosopher Thales. Thales thought of water as the principle out of which all things come, but Anaximander reached a much higher level of abstraction by claiming that the first principle is the *apeiron*, the indefinite and limitless. The question of what he means with *apeiron* we will address in the class. But Anaximander also has a theory according to which in the world there is—or there should be—both cosmic and political balance. Cosmic balance is here used as an argument

1

for the sharing of power between the traditional landed aristocracy of birth and a rising non-aristocratic farming and commercial class. Anaximander argues that the permanent domination of one element over another constitutes injustice: this is a thinly disguised attack on the monolithic control of the city-state by the aristocrats. His concept of justice as balance expresses the aspirations of the economically successful non-aristocrats who strive to be included in the political system.

In addition to Thales and Anaximander, the ranks of the Pre-Socratics include metaphysicians like Parmenides and Heraclitus, mathematicians like Pythagoras, and Democritus, who created a materialistic physics and an atomic theory remarkably similar in its fundamental concept to twentieth century AD atomic physics.

We have nothing that the Pre-Socratics wrote themselves. All our information comes from subsequent sources, sometimes writing a long time after them. Simplicius, who gives us Anaximander's famous fragment B12, and who is a very good source on the Pre-Socratics, writes in the sixth century AD, more than a thousand years after Anaximander's death!

Anaximander

Anaximander, the son of Praxiades, was the student and successor of Thales. He claimed that the *apeiron* was the principle (*archēn*) and element (*stoicheion*) of existing things (*tōn ontōn*), and he was the first to give this name to the principle. He claims that this principle is neither water nor any other of the so-called elements, but some other *apeiron* nature. Everything that exists in the heavens and in all the worlds that exist in them came from it. The existing things (*tois ousi*) are generated from the same things into which their destruction takes place according to necessity (*kata to chreōn*), because they pay penalty and they offer retribution (*didonai ... dikēn kai tisin*) to each other for their injustice (*adikias*), in accordance with the order of time (*kata tēn tou chronou taxin*), as he says about them in rather poetical terms.

Simplicius, *Commentary on Aristotle's Physics* 24.13–21; DK12A9

2. Introduction to Socrates and Plato's *Apology*

Socrates is credited with turning philosophy's focus from metaphysics to ethics. He lived in Athens from 469 BC to 399 BC. In 399 BC he was indicted for corrupting the young and for not believing in the gods of Athens. He was convicted and executed.

Socrates never wrote anything, but he played a major part in the history of Western philosophy by asking some of the ethical and metaethical questions that his famous student, Plato, later addressed. Soon after his death many authors began writing 'Socratic dialogues,' philosophical works with Socrates as the main speaker. It was Plato's dialogues, however, who decisively shaped the path of Western thought.

Socrates was brought to trial four years after Athens' defeat in the Peloponnesian War and the oligarchic coup which followed it. The junta of the so-called Thirty Tyrants lasted for only eight months, but led to the assassination of 1,500 citizens, a vast number given that the citizen population of Athens after the war was probably less than 20,000. Although Socrates never got involved in practical politics, he associated himself with Critias, the leader of the Thirty, and he was known to be critical of the democracy. Socrates argued, in particular, that in political issues it is expertise, not the opinion of the majority, that matters. In the political climate which followed the Thirty's downfall, what looked earlier as innocuous criticism became, to the Athenian democrats, a real danger to majority rule in Athens. The principal accuser of Socrates was Anytus, a leader of the democratic party, and, interestingly enough, by all accounts a moderate.

Socrates was essentially convicted because of his constant, even if implicit, criticisms of the democracy and because of his association with the Athenian aristocratic youth, one prominent member of which had betrayed the city twice during the Peloponnesian War (Alcibiades). By unceasingly questioning the ability of the many to make the right moral and political decisions, Socrates undercut the foundations of common Greek morality. In a moment of crisis, the Athenians decided that they could not allow this kind of public behavior any longer.

Although Socrates' conviction is often described as an inexcusable crime against freedom of speech, it is actually better understood as a collision between a philosophical and individualistic theory and a conventional and community-based moral theory. This interpretation, which was for the first time offered by Hegel, catches well the essence of what happened in Athens in 399 BC.

Plato's *Apology* is written with the single-minded purpose of proving Socrates' innocence. It is also a rhetorical masterpiece. It is impossible for us to know how close it is to the actual speech that Socrates delivered in his trial, because it is certainly not a stenographic reproduction of that speech. What emerges most clearly from the *Apology* is Socrates' strict devotion to his principles. In another dialogue, the *Crito*, Plato describes how Socrates refused to escape from prison after his conviction, because if he did he would harm his city.

[Handwritten margin note top-left: Read for 8/30. In 60 words, is Socrates guilty or not]

Apology

Plato

Translated by Benjamin Jowett

[Handwritten: disrespectful]

How you, O Athenians, have been affected by my accusers, I cannot tell; but I know that they almost made me forget who I was—so persuasively did they speak; and yet they have hardly uttered a word of truth. But of the many falsehoods told by them, there was one which quite amazed me;—I mean when they said that you should be upon your guard and not allow yourselves to be deceived by the force of my eloquence. To say this, when they were certain to be detected as soon as I opened my lips and proved myself to be anything but a great speaker, did indeed appear to me most shameless—unless by the force of eloquence they mean the force of truth; for is such is their meaning, I admit that I am eloquent. But in how different a way from theirs! Well, as I was saying, they have scarcely spoken the truth at all; but from me you shall hear the whole truth: not, however, delivered after their manner in a set oration duly ornamented with words and phrases. No, by heaven! but I shall use the words and arguments which occur to me at the moment; for I am confident in the justice of my cause (Or, I am certain that I am right in taking this course.): at my time of life I ought not to be appearing before you, O men of Athens, in the character of a juvenile orator—let no one expect it of me. And I must beg of you to grant me a favour:—If I defend myself in my accustomed manner, and you hear me using the words which I have been in the habit of using in the agora, at the tables of the money-changers, or anywhere else, I would ask you not to be surprised, and not to interrupt me on this account. For I am more than seventy years of age, and appearing now for the first time in a court of law, I am quite a stranger to the language of the place; and therefore I would have you regard me as if I were really a stranger, whom you would excuse if he spoke in his native tongue, and after the fashion of his country:—Am I making an unfair request of you? Never mind the manner, which may or may not be good; but think only of the truth of my words, and give heed to that: let the speaker speak truly and the judge decide justly.

[Handwritten: talking plainly]

[Handwritten: trying to play it as he is not a good speaker]

[Handwritten: all common things defenders say]

And first, I have to reply to the older charges and to my first accusers, and then I will go on to the later ones. For of old I have had many accusers, who have accused me falsely to you during many years; and I am more afraid of them than of Anytus and his associates, who are dangerous, too, in their own way. But far more dangerous are the others, who began when you were children, and took possession of your minds with their falsehoods, telling of one Socrates, a wise man, who speculated about the heaven above, and searched into the earth beneath, and made the worse appear the better cause. The disseminators of this tale are the accusers whom I dread; for their hearers are apt to fancy that such enquirers do not believe in the existence of the gods. And they are many, and their charges against me are of ancient date, and they were made by them in the days when you were more impressible than you are now—in childhood, or it may have been in youth—and the cause when heard went by default, for there was none to answer. And hardest of all, I do not know and cannot tell the names of my accusers; unless in the chance case of a Comic poet. All who from envy and malice have persuaded you—some

[Handwritten: poets have moral authority]

of them having first convinced themselves—all this class of men are most difficult to deal with; for I cannot have them up here, and cross-examine them, and therefore I must simply fight with shadows in my own defence, and argue when there is no one who answers. I will ask you then to assume with me, as I was saying, that my opponents are of two kinds; one recent, the other ancient: and I hope that you will see the propriety of my answering the latter first, for these accusations you heard long before the others, and much oftener.

Well, then, I must make my defence, and endeavour to clear away in a short time, a slander which has lasted a long time. May I succeed, if to succeed be for my good and yours, or likely to avail me in my cause! The task is not an easy one; I quite understand the nature of it. And so leaving the event with God, in obedience to the law I will now make my defence.

I will begin at the beginning, and ask what is the accusation which has given rise to the slander of me, and in fact has encouraged Meletus to proof this charge against me. Well, what do the slanderers say? They shall be my prosecutors, and I will sum up their words in an affidavit: 'Socrates is an evil-doer, and a curious person, who searches into things under the earth and in heaven, and he makes the worse appear the better cause; and he teaches the aforesaid doctrines to others'. Such is the nature of the accusation: it is just what you have yourselves seen in the comedy of Aristophanes (Aristoph., Clouds.), who has introduced a man whom he calls Socrates, going about and saying that he walks in air, and talking a deal of nonsense concerning matters of which I do not pretend to know either much or little—not that I mean to speak disparagingly of any one who is a student of natural philosophy. I should be very sorry if Meletus could bring so grave a charge against me. But the simple truth is, O Athenians, that I have nothing to do with physical speculations. Very many of those here present are witnesses to the truth of this, and to them I appeal. Speak then, you who have heard me, and tell your neighbours whether any of you have ever known me hold forth in few words or in many upon such matters. You hear their answer. And from what they say of this part of the charge you will be able to judge of the truth of the rest.

As little foundation is there for the report that I am a teacher, and take money; this accusation has no more truth in it than the other. Although, if a man were really able to instruct mankind, to receive money for giving instruction would, in my opinion, be an honour to him. There is Gorgias of Leontium, and Prodicus of Ceos, and Hippias of Elis, who go the round of the cities, and are able to persuade the young men to leave their own citizens by whom they might be taught for nothing, and come to them whom they not only pay, but are thankful if they may be allowed to pay them. There is at this time a Parian philosopher residing in Athens, of whom I have heard; and I came to hear of him in this way:—I came across a man who has spent a world of money on the Sophists, Callias, the son of Hipponicus, and knowing that he had sons, I asked him: 'Callias', I said, 'if your two sons were foals or calves, there would be no difficulty in finding some one to put over them; we should hire a trainer of horses, or a farmer probably, who would improve and perfect them in their own proper virtue and excellence; but as they are human beings, whom are you thinking of placing over them? Is there any one who understands human and political virtue? You must have thought about the matter, for you have sons; is there any one?' 'There is', he said. 'Who is he?' said I; 'and of what country? and what does he charge?' 'Evenus the Parian', he replied; 'he is the man, and his charge is five minae.' Happy is Evenus, I said to myself, if he really has this wisdom, and teaches at such a moderate charge. Had I the same, I should have been very proud and conceited; but the truth is that I have no knowledge of the kind.

I dare say, Athenians, that some one among you will reply, 'Yes, Socrates, but what is the origin of these accusations which are brought against you; there must have been something strange which you have been doing? All these rumours and this talk about you would never have arisen if you had been like other men: tell us, then, what is the cause of them, for we should be sorry to judge hastily of you.' Now I regard this as a fair challenge, and I will endeavour to explain to you the reason why I am called wise and have such an evil fame. Please to attend then. And although some of you may think that I am joking, I declare that I will tell you the entire truth. Men of Athens, this reputation of mine has come of a certain sort of wisdom which I possess. If you ask me what kind of wisdom, I reply, wisdom such as may perhaps be attained by man, for to that extent I am inclined to believe that I am wise; whereas the persons of whom I was speaking have a superhuman wisdom which I may fail to describe, because I have it not myself; and he who says that I have, speaks falsely, and is taking away my character. And here, O men of Athens, I must beg you not to interrupt me, even if I seem to say something extravagant. For the word which I will speak is not mine. I will refer you to a witness who is worthy of credit; that witness shall be the God of Delphi—he will tell you about my wisdom, if I have any, and of what sort it is. You must have known Chaerephon; he was early a friend of mine, and also a friend of yours, for he shared in the recent exile of the people, and returned with you. Well, Chaerephon, as you know, was very impetuous in all his doings, and he went to Delphi and boldly asked the oracle to tell him whether—as I was saying, I must beg you not to interrupt—he asked the oracle to tell him whether anyone was wiser than I was, and the Pythian prophetess answered, that there was no man wiser. Chaerephon is dead himself; but his brother, who is in court, will confirm the truth of what I am saying.

Why do I mention this? Because I am going to explain to you why I have such an evil name. When I heard the answer, I said to myself, What can the god mean? and what is the interpretation of his riddle? for I know that I have no wisdom, small or great. What then can he mean when he says that I am the wisest of men? And yet he is a god, and cannot lie; that would be against his nature. After long consideration, I thought of a method of trying the question. I reflected that if I could only find a man wiser than myself, then I might go to the god with a refutation in my hand. I should say to him, 'Here is a man who is wiser than I am; but you said that I was the wisest.' Accordingly I went to one who had the reputation of wisdom, and observed him—his name I need not mention; he was a politician whom I selected for examination—and the result was as follows: When I began to talk with him, I could not help thinking that he was not really wise, although he was thought wise by many, and still wiser by himself; and thereupon I tried to explain to him that he thought himself wise, but was not really wise; and the consequence was that he hated me, and his enmity was shared by several who were present and heard me. So I left him, saying to myself, as I went away: Well, although I do not suppose that either of us knows anything really beautiful and good, I am better off than he is,—for he knows nothing, and thinks that he knows; I neither know nor think that I know. In this latter particular, then, I seem to have slightly the advantage of him. Then I went to another who had still higher pretensions to wisdom, and my conclusion was exactly the same. Whereupon I made another enemy of him, and of many others besides him.

Then I went to one man after another, being not unconscious of the enmity which I provoked, and I lamented and feared this: but necessity was laid upon me,—the word of God, I thought, ought to be considered first. And I said to myself, Go I must to all who appear to know, and find out the meaning of the oracle. And I swear to you, Athenians, by the dog I swear!—for I must tell you the truth—the result of my mission was just this: I found that the men most in repute were all but the most foolish; and that others less esteemed were really wiser and better. I will tell you the tale of my wanderings and of the 'Herculean' labours, as I may call them, which I endured only to find at last the oracle irrefutable. After the politicians, I went to the poets; tragic, dithyrambic, and all sorts. And there, I said to myself, you will be instantly detected; now you will find out that you are more ignorant than they are. Accordingly, I took them some of the most elaborate passages in their own writings, and asked what was the meaning of them—thinking that they would teach me something. Will you believe me? I am almost ashamed to confess the truth, but I must say that there is hardly a person present who would not have talked better about their poetry than they did themselves. Then I knew that not by wisdom do poets write poetry, but by a sort of genius and inspiration; they are like diviners or soothsayers who also say many fine things, but do not understand the meaning of them. The poets appeared to me to be much in the same case; and I further observed that upon the strength of their poetry they believed themselves to be the wisest of men in other things in which they were not wise. So I departed, conceiving myself to be superior to them for the same reason that I was superior to the politicians.

At last I went to the artisans. I was conscious that I knew nothing at all, as I may say, and I was sure that they knew many fine things; and here I was not mistaken, for they did know many things of which I was ignorant, and in this they certainly were wiser than I was. But I observed that even the good artisans fell into the same error as the poets;—because they were good workmen they thought that they also knew all sorts of high matters, and this defect in them overshadowed their wisdom; and therefore I asked myself on behalf of the oracle, whether I would like to be as I was, neither having their knowledge nor their ignorance, or like them in both; and I made answer to myself and to the oracle that I was better off as I was.

This inquisition has led to my having many enemies of the worst and most dangerous kind, and has given occasion also to many calumnies. And I am called wise, for my hearers always imagine that I myself possess the wisdom which I find wanting in others: but the truth is, O men of Athens, that God only is wise; and by his answer he intends to show that the wisdom of men is worth little or nothing; he is not speaking of Socrates, he is only using my name by way of illustration, as if he said, He, O men, is the wisest, who, like Socrates, knows that his wisdom is in truth worth nothing. And so I go about the world, obedient to the god, and search and make enquiry into the wisdom of any one, whether citizen or stranger, who appears to be wise; and if he is not wise, then in vindication of the oracle I show him that he is not wise; and my occupation quite absorbs me, and I have no time to give either to any public matter of interest or to any concern of my own, but I am in utter poverty by reason of my devotion to the god.

There is another thing: young men of the richer classes, who have not much to do, come about me of their own accord; they like to hear the pretenders examined, and they often imitate me, and proceed to examine others; there are plenty of persons, as they quickly discover, who think that they know something, but really know little or nothing; and then those who are examined by them instead of being angry with themselves are angry with me: This confounded Socrates, they say; this villainous misleader of youth!—and then if somebody asks them, Why, what evil does he practise or teach? they do not know, and cannot tell; but in order that they may not appear to be at a loss, they repeat the ready-made charges which are used against all philosophers about teaching things up in the clouds and under the earth, and having no gods, and making the worse appear the better cause; for they do not like to confess that their pretence of knowledge has been detected—which is the truth; and as they are numerous and ambitious and energetic, and are drawn up in battle array and have persuasive tongues, they have filled your ears with their loud and inveterate calumnies. And this is the reason why my three accusers, Meletus and Anytus and Lycon, have set upon me; Meletus, who has a quarrel with me on behalf of the poets; Anytus, on behalf of the craftsmen and politicians; Lycon, on behalf of the rhetoricians: and as I said at the beginning, I cannot expect to get rid of such a mass of calumny all in a moment. And this, O men of Athens, is the truth and the whole truth; I have concealed nothing, I have dissembled nothing. And yet, I know that my plainness of speech makes them hate me, and what is their hatred but a proof that I am speaking the truth?—Hence has arisen the prejudice against me; and this is the reason of it, as you will find out either in this or in any future enquiry.

I have said enough in my defence against the first class of my accusers; I turn to the second class. They are headed by Meletus, that good man and true lover of his country, as he calls himself. Against these, too, I must try to make a defence:—Let their affidavit be read: it contains something of this kind: It says that Socrates is a doer of evil, who corrupts the youth; and who does not believe in the gods of the state, but has other new divinities of his own. Such is the charge; and now let us examine the particular counts. He says that I am a doer of evil, and corrupt the youth; but I say, O men of Athens, that Meletus is a doer of evil, in that he pretends to be in earnest when he is only in jest, and is so eager to bring men to trial from a pretended zeal and interest about matters in which he really never had the smallest interest. And the truth of this I will endeavour to prove to you.

Come hither, Meletus, and let me ask a question of you. You think a great deal about the improvement of youth?   *questions him but only really embarress* *(youth)*

Yes, I do.

Tell the judges, then, who is their improver; for you must know, as you have taken the pains to discover their corrupter, and are citing and accusing me before them. Speak, then, and tell the judges who their improver is.—Observe, Meletus, that you are silent, and have nothing to say. But is not this rather disgraceful, and a very considerable proof of what I was saying, that you have no interest in the matter? Speak up, friend, and tell us who their improver is.

The laws.

But that, my good sir, is not my meaning. I want to know who the person is, who, in the first place, knows the laws.

The judges, Socrates, who are present in court.

What, do you mean to say, Meletus, that they are able to instruct and improve youth?

Certainly they are.

What, all of them, or some only and not others?

All of them.

By the goddess Here, that is good news! There are plenty of improvers, then. And what do you say of the audience,—do they improve them?

Yes, they do.

And the senators?

Yes, the senators improve them.

But perhaps the members of the assembly corrupt them?—or do they too improve them?

They improve them.

Then every Athenian improves and elevates them; all with the exception of myself; and I alone am their corrupter? Is that what you affirm?

That is what I stoutly affirm.

I am very unfortunate if you are right. But suppose I ask you a question: How about horses? Does one man do them harm and all the world good? Is not the exact opposite the truth? One man is able to do them good, or at least not many;—the trainer of horses, that is to say, does them good, and others who have to do with them rather injure them? Is not that true, Meletus, of horses, or of any other animals? Most assuredly it is; whether you and Anytus say yes or no. Happy indeed would be the condition of youth if they had one corrupter only, and all the rest of the world were their improvers. But you, Meletus, have sufficiently shown that you never had a thought about the young: your carelessness is seen in your not caring about the very things which you bring against me.

And now, Meletus, I will ask you another question—by Zeus I will: Which is better, to live among bad citizens, or among good ones? Answer, friend, I say; the question is one which may be easily answered. Do not the good do their neighbours good, and the bad do them evil?

Certainly.

And is there anyone who would rather be injured than benefited by those who live with him? Answer, my good friend, the law requires you to answer—does any one like to be injured?

Certainly not.

And when you accuse me of corrupting and deteriorating the youth, do you allege that I corrupt them intentionally or unintentionally?

Intentionally, I say.

But you have just admitted that the good do their neighbours good, and the evil do them evil. Now, is that a truth which your superior wisdom has recognized thus early in life, and am I, at my age, in such darkness and ignorance as not to know that if a man with whom I have to live is corrupted by me, I am very likely to be harmed by him; and yet I corrupt him, and intentionally, too—so you say, although neither I nor any other human being is ever likely to be convinced by you. But either I do not corrupt them, or I corrupt them unintentionally; and on either view of the case you lie. If my offence is unintentional, the law has no cognizance of unintentional offences: you ought to have taken me privately, and warned and admonished me; for if I had been better advised, I should have left off doing what I only did unintentionally—no doubt I should; but you would have nothing to say to me and refused to teach me. And now you bring me up in this court, which is a place not of instruction, but of punishment.

It will be very clear to you, Athenians, as I was saying, that Meletus has no care at all, great or small, about the matter. But still I should like to know, Meletus, in what I am affirmed to corrupt the young. I suppose you mean, as I infer from your indictment, that I teach them not to acknowledge the gods which the state acknowledges, but some other new divinities or spiritual agencies in their stead. These are the lessons by which I corrupt the youth, as you say.

Yes, that I say emphatically.

Then, by the gods, Meletus, of whom we are speaking, tell me and the court, in somewhat plainer terms, what you mean! for I do not as yet understand whether you affirm that I teach other men to acknowledge some gods, and therefore that I do believe in gods, and am not an entire atheist—this you do not lay to my charge,—but only you say that they are not the same gods which the city recognizes—the charge is that they are different gods. Or, do you mean that I am an atheist simply, and a teacher of atheism?

I mean the latter—that you are a complete atheist.

What an extraordinary statement! Why do you think so, Meletus? Do you mean that I do not believe in the godhead of the sun or moon, like other men?

I assure you, judges, that he does not: for he says that the sun is stone, and the moon earth.

Friend Meletus, you think that you are accusing Anaxagoras: and you have but a bad opinion of the judges, if you fancy them illiterate to such a degree as not to know that these doctrines are found in the books of Anaxagoras the Clazomenian, which are full of them. And so, forsooth, the youth are said to be taught them by Socrates, when there are not unfrequently exhibitions of them at the theatre (Probably in allusion to Aristophanes who caricatured, and to Euripides who borrowed the notions of Anaxagoras, as well as to other dramatic poets.) (price of admission one drachma at the most); and they might pay their money, and laugh at Socrates if he pretends to father these extraordinary views. And so, Meletus, you really think that I do not believe in any god?

I swear by Zeus that you believe absolutely in none at all.

Nobody will believe you, Meletus, and I am pretty sure that you do not believe yourself. I cannot help thinking, men of Athens, that Meletus is reckless and impudent, and that he has written this indictment in a spirit of mere wantonness and youthful bravado. Has he not compounded a riddle,

thinking to try me? He said to himself:—I shall see whether the wise Socrates will discover my facetious contradiction, or whether I shall be able to deceive him and the rest of them. For he certainly
does appear to me to contradict himself in the indictment as much as if he said that Socrates is guilty of
not believing in the gods, and yet of believing in them—but this is not like a person who is in earnest.

I should like you, O men of Athens, to join me in examining what I conceive to be his inconsistency; and do you, Meletus, answer. And I must remind the audience of my request that they would
not make a disturbance if I speak in my accustomed manner:

Did ever man, Meletus, believe in the existence of human things, and not of human beings? I
wish, men of Athens, that he would answer, and not be always trying to get up an interruption. Did
ever any man believe in horsemanship, and not in horses? or in flute-playing, and not in flute-players?
No, my friend; I will answer to you and to the court, as you refuse to answer for yourself. There is
no man who ever did. But now please to answer the next question: Can a man believe in spiritual and
divine agencies, and not in spirits or demigods?

He cannot.

How lucky I am to have extracted that answer, by the assistance of the court! But then you swear
in the indictment that I teach and believe in divine or spiritual agencies (new or old, no matter for
that); at any rate, I believe in spiritual agencies,—so you say and swear in the affidavit; and yet if I
believe in divine beings, how can I help believing in spirits or demigods;—must I not? To be sure I
must; and therefore I may assume that your silence gives consent. Now what are spirits or demigods?
Are they not either gods or the sons of gods?

Certainly they are.

But this is what I call the facetious riddle invented by you: the demigods or spirits are gods, and
you say first that I do not believe in gods, and then again that I do believe in gods; that is, if I believe
in demigods. For if the demigods are the illegitimate sons of gods, whether by the nymphs or by any
other mothers, of whom they are said to be the sons—what human being will ever believe that there are
no gods if they are the sons of gods? You might as well affirm the existence of mules, and deny that
of horses and asses. Such nonsense, Meletus, could only have been intended by you to make trial of
me. You have put this into the indictment because you had nothing real of which to accuse me. But no
one who has a particle of understanding will ever be convinced by you that the same men can believe
in divine and superhuman things, and yet not believe that there are gods and demigods and heroes.

I have said enough in answer to the charge of Meletus: any elaborate defence is unnecessary, but
I know only too well how many are the enmities which I have incurred, and this is what will be my
destruction if I am destroyed;—not Meletus, nor yet Anytus, but the envy and detraction of the world,
which has been the death of many good men, and will probably be the death of many more; there is
no danger of my being the last of them.

Some one will say: And are you not ashamed, Socrates, of a course of life which is likely to bring
you to an untimely end? To him I may fairly answer: There you are mistaken: a man who is good for *Is*
anything ought not to calculate the chance of living or dying; he ought only to consider whether in *Achilles*
doing anything he is doing right or wrong—acting the part of a good man or of a bad. Whereas, upon ~~Pericles~~
your view, the heroes who fell at Troy were not good for much, and the son of Thetis above all, who
altogether despised danger in comparison with disgrace; and when he was so eager to slay Hector, his
goddess mother said to him, that if he avenged his companion Patroclus, and slew Hector, he would
die himself—'Fate', she said, in these or the like words, 'waits for you next after Hector;' he, receiving this warning, utterly despised danger and death, and instead of fearing them, feared rather to live
in dishonour, and not to avenge his friend. 'Let me die forthwith', he replies, 'and be avenged of my
enemy, rather than abide here by the beaked ships, a laughing-stock and a burden of the earth.' Had

Achilles any thought of death and danger? For wherever a man's place is, whether the place which he has chosen or that in which he has been placed by a commander, there he ought to remain in the hour of danger; he should not think of death or of anything but of disgrace. And this, O men of Athens, is a true saying.

   Strange, indeed, would be my conduct, O men of Athens, if I who, when I was ordered by the generals whom you chose to command me at Potidaea and Amphipolis and Delium, remained where they placed me, like any other man, facing death—if now, when, as I conceive and imagine, God orders me to fulfil the philosopher's mission of searching into myself and other men, I were to desert my post through fear of death, or any other fear; that would indeed be strange, and I might justly be arraigned in court for denying the existence of the gods, if I disobeyed the oracle because I was afraid of death, fancying that I was wise when I was not wise. For the fear of death is indeed the pretence of wisdom, and not real wisdom, being a pretence of knowing the unknown; and no one knows whether death, which men in their fear apprehend to be the greatest evil, may not be the greatest good. Is not this ignorance of a disgraceful sort, the ignorance which is the conceit that a man knows what he does not know? And in this respect only I believe myself to differ from men in general, and may perhaps claim to be wiser than they are:—that whereas I know but little of the world below, I do not suppose that I know: but I do know that injustice and disobedience to a better, whether God or man, is evil and dishonourable, and I will never fear or avoid a possible good rather than a certain evil. And therefore if you let me go now, and are not convinced by Anytus, who said that since I had been prosecuted I must be put to death; (or if not that I ought never to have been prosecuted at all); and that if I escape now, your sons will all be utterly ruined by listening to my words—if you say to me, Socrates, this time we will not mind Anytus, and you shall be let off, but upon one condition, that you are not to enquire and speculate in this way any more, and that if you are caught doing so again you shall die;—if this was the condition on which you let me go, I should reply: Men of Athens, I honour and love you; but I shall obey God rather than you, and while I have life and strength I shall never cease from the practice and teaching of philosophy, exhorting any one whom I meet and saying to him after my manner: You, my friend,—a citizen of the great and mighty and wise city of Athens,—are you not ashamed of heaping up the greatest amount of money and honour and reputation, and caring so little about wisdom and truth and the greatest improvement of the soul, which you never regard or heed at all? And if the person with whom I am arguing, says: Yes, but I do care; then I do not leave him or let him go at once; but I proceed to interrogate and examine and cross-examine him, and if I think that he has no virtue in him, but only says that he has, I reproach him with undervaluing the greater, and overvaluing the less. And I shall repeat the same words to every one whom I meet, young and old, citizen and alien, but especially to the citizens, inasmuch as they are my brethren. For know that this is the command of God; and I believe that no greater good has ever happened in the state than my service to the God. For I do nothing but go about persuading you all, old and young alike, not to take thought for your persons or your properties, but first and chiefly to care about the greatest improvement of the soul. I tell you that virtue is not given by money, but that from virtue comes money and every other good of man, public as well as private. This is my teaching, and if this is the doctrine which corrupts the youth, I am a mischievous person. But if any one says that this is not my teaching, he is speaking an untruth. Wherefore, O men of Athens, I say to you, do as Anytus bids or not as Anytus bids, and either acquit me or not; but whichever you do, understand that I shall never alter my ways, not even if I have to die many times.

   Men of Athens, do not interrupt, but hear me; there was an understanding between us that you should hear me to the end: I have something more to say, at which you may be inclined to cry out; but I believe that to hear me will be good for you, and therefore I beg that you will not cry out. I would have you know, that if you kill such an one as I am, you will injure yourselves more than you will injure me. Nothing will injure me, not Meletus nor yet Anytus—they cannot, for a bad man is not permitted to injure a better than himself. I do not deny that Anytus may, perhaps, kill him, or drive him into exile, or deprive him of civil rights; and he may imagine, and others may imagine, that he is inflicting a great injury upon him: but there I do not agree. For the evil of doing as he is doing—the evil of unjustly taking away the life of another—is greater far.

And now, Athenians, I am not going to argue for my own sake, as you may think, but for yours, that you may not sin against the God by condemning me, who am his gift to you. For if you kill me you will not easily find a successor to me, who, if I may use such a ludicrous figure of speech, am a sort of gadfly, given to the state by God; and the state is a great and noble steed who is tardy in his motions owing to his very size, and requires to be stirred into life. I am that gadfly which God has attached to the state, and all day long and in all places am always fastening upon you, arousing and persuading and reproaching you. You will not easily find another like me, and therefore I would advise you to spare me. I dare say that you may feel out of temper (like a person who is suddenly awakened from sleep), and you think that you might easily strike me dead as Anytus advises, and then you would sleep on for the remainder of your lives, unless God in his care of you sent you another gadfly. When I say that I am given to you by God, the proof of my mission is this:—if I had been like other men, I should not have neglected all my own concerns or patiently seen the neglect of them during all these years, and have been doing yours, coming to you individually like a father or elder brother, exhorting you to regard virtue; such conduct, I say, would be unlike human nature. If I had gained anything, or if my exhortations had been paid, there would have been some sense in my doing so; but now, as you will perceive, not even the impudence of my accusers dares to say that I have ever exacted or sought pay of any one; of that they have no witness. And I have a sufficient witness to the truth of what I say—my poverty.

Some one may wonder why I go about in private giving advice and busying myself with the concerns of others, but do not venture to come forward in public and advise the state. I will tell you why. You have heard me speak at sundry times and in divers places of an oracle or sign which comes to me, and is the divinity which Meletus ridicules in the indictment. This sign, which is a kind of voice, first began to come to me when I was a child; it always forbids but never commands me to do anything which I am going to do. This is what deters me from being a politician. And rightly, as I think. For I am certain, O men of Athens, that if I had engaged in politics, I should have perished long ago, and done no good either to you or to myself. And do not be offended at my telling you the truth: for the truth is, that no man who goes to war with you or any other multitude, honestly striving against the many lawless and unrighteous deeds which are done in a state, will save his life; he who will fight for the right, if he would live even for a brief space, must have a private station and not a public one.

I can give you convincing evidence of what I say, not words only, but what you value far more—actions. Let me relate to you a passage of my own life which will prove to you that I should never have yielded to injustice from any fear of death, and that 'as I should have refused to yield' I must have died at once. I will tell you a tale of the courts, not very interesting perhaps, but nevertheless true. The only office of state which I ever held, O men of Athens, was that of senator: the tribe Antiochis, which is my tribe, had the presidency at the trial of the generals who had not taken up the bodies of the slain after the battle of Arginusae; and you proposed to try them in a body, contrary to law, as you all thought afterwards; but at the time I was the only one of the Prytanes who was opposed to the illegality, and I gave my vote against you; and when the orators threatened to impeach and arrest me, and you called and shouted, I made up my mind that I would run the risk, having law and justice with me, rather than take part in your injustice because I feared imprisonment and death. This happened in the days of the democracy. But when the oligarchy of the Thirty was in power, they sent for me and four others into the rotunda, and bade us bring Leon the Salaminian from Salamis, as they wanted to put him to death. This was a specimen of the sort of commands which they were always giving with the view of implicating as many as possible in their crimes; and then I showed, not in word only but in deed, that, if I may be allowed to use such an expression, I cared not a straw for death, and that my great and only care was lest I should do an unrighteous or unholy thing. For the strong arm of that oppressive power did not frighten me into doing wrong; and when we came out of the rotunda the other four went to Salamis and fetched Leon, but I went quietly home. For which I might have lost my life, had not the power of the Thirty shortly afterwards come to an end. And many will witness to my words.

Now do you really imagine that I could have survived all these years, if I had led a public life, supposing that like a good man I had always maintained the right and had made justice, as I ought, the first thing? No indeed, men of Athens, neither I nor any other man. But I have been always the same in all my actions, public as well as private, and never have I yielded any base compliance to those who are slanderously termed my disciples, or to any other. Not that I have any regular disciples. But if any one likes to come and hear me while I am pursuing my mission, whether he be young or old, he is not excluded. Nor do I converse only with those who pay; but any one, whether he be rich or poor, may ask and answer me and listen to my words; and whether he turns out to be a bad man or a good one, neither result can be justly imputed to me; for I never taught or professed to teach him anything. And if any one says that he has ever learned or heard anything from me in private which all the world has not heard, let me tell you that he is lying.

But I shall be asked, Why do people delight in continually conversing with you? I have told you already, Athenians, the whole truth about this matter: they like to hear the cross-examination of the pretenders to wisdom; there is amusement in it. Now this duty of cross-examining other men has been imposed upon me by God; and has been signified to me by oracles, visions, and in every way in which the will of divine power was ever intimated to any one. This is true, O Athenians, or, if not true, would be soon refuted. If I am or have been corrupting the youth, those of them who are now grown up and have become sensible that I gave them bad advice in the days of their youth should come forward as accusers, and take their revenge; or if they do not like to come themselves, some of their relatives, fathers, brothers, or other kinsmen, should say what evil their families have suffered at my hands. Now is their time. Many of them I see in the court. There is Crito, who is of the same age and of the same deme with myself, and there is Critobulus his son, whom I also see. Then again there is Lysanias of Sphettus, who is the father of Aeschines—he is present; and also there is Antiphon of Cephisus, who is the father of Epigenes; and there are the brothers of several who have associated with me. There is Nicostratus the son of Theosdotides, and the brother of Theodotus (now Theodotus himself is dead, and therefore he, at any rate, will not seek to stop him); and there is Paralus the son of Demodocus, who had a brother Theages; and Adeimantus the son of Ariston, whose brother Plato is present; and Aeantodorus, who is the brother of Apollodorus, whom I also see. I might mention a great many others, some of whom Meletus should have produced as witnesses in the course of his speech; and let him still produce them, if he has forgotten—I will make way for him. And let him say, if he has any testimony of the sort which he can produce. Nay, Athenians, the very opposite is the truth. For all these are ready to witness on behalf of the corrupter, of the injurer of their kindred, as Meletus and Anytus call me; not the corrupted youth only—there might have been a motive for that—but their uncorrupted elder relatives. Why should they too support me with their testimony? Why, indeed, except for the sake of truth and justice, and because they know that I am speaking the truth, and that Meletus is a liar.

Well, Athenians, this and the like of this is all the defence which I have to offer. Yet a word more. Perhaps there may be some one who is offended at me, when he calls to mind how he himself on a similar, or even a less serious occasion, prayed and entreated the judges with many tears, and how he produced his children in court, which was a moving spectacle, together with a host of relations and friends; whereas I, who am probably in danger of my life, will do none of these things. The contrast may occur to his mind, and he may be set against me, and vote in anger because he is displeased at me on this account. Now if there be such a person among you,—mind, I do not say that there is,—to him I may fairly reply: My friend, I am a man, and like other men, a creature of flesh and blood, and not 'of wood or stone', as Homer says; and I have a family, yes, and sons, O Athenians, three in number, one almost a man, and two others who are still young; and yet I will not bring any of them hither in order to petition you for an acquittal. And why not? Not from any self-assertion or want of respect for you. Whether I am or am not afraid of death is another question, of which I will not now speak. But, having regard to public opinion, I feel that such conduct would be discreditable to myself, and to you, and to the whole state. One who has reached my years, and who has a name for wisdom, ought not to demean himself. Whether this opinion of me be deserved or not, at any rate the world has decided that Socrates is in some way superior to other men. And if those among you who are said to be superior in wisdom and courage, and any other virtue, demean themselves in this way, how shameful is their conduct! I have seen men of reputation, when they have been condemned, behaving in the strangest manner: they seemed to fancy that they were going to suffer something dreadful if they died, and that they could be immortal if you only allowed them to live; and I think that such are a dishonour to the state, and that any stranger coming in would have said of them that the most eminent men of Athens, to whom the Athenians themselves give honour and command, are no better than women. And I say that these things ought not to be done by those of us who have a reputation; and if they are done, you ought not to permit them; you ought rather to show that you are far more disposed to condemn the man who gets up a doleful scene and makes the city ridiculous, than him who holds his peace.

But, setting aside the question of public opinion, there seems to be something wrong in asking a favour of a judge, and thus procuring an acquittal, instead of informing and convincing him. For his duty is, not to make a present of justice, but to give judgment; and he has sworn that he will judge according to the laws, and not according to his own good pleasure; and we ought not to encourage you, nor should you allow yourselves to be encouraged, in this habit of perjury—there can be no piety in that. Do not then require me to do what I consider dishonourable and impious and wrong, especially now, when I am being tried for impiety on the indictment of Meletus. For if, O men of Athens, by force of persuasion and entreaty I could overpower your oaths, then I should be teaching you to believe that there are no gods, and in defending should simply convict myself of the charge of not believing in them. But that is not so—far otherwise. For I do believe that there are gods, and in a sense higher than that in which any of my accusers believe in them. And to you and to God I commit my cause, to be determined by you as is best for you and me.

***

There are many reasons why I am not grieved, O men of Athens, at the vote of condemnation. I expected it, and am only surprised that the votes are so nearly equal; for I had thought that the majority against me would have been far larger; but now, had thirty votes gone over to the other side, I should have been acquitted. And I may say, I think, that I have escaped Meletus. I may say more; for without the assistance of Anytus and Lycon, any one may see that he would not have had a fifth part of the votes, as the law requires, in which case he would have incurred a fine of a thousand drachmae.

And so he proposes death as the penalty. And what shall I propose on my part, O men of Athens? Clearly that which is my due. And what is my due? What return shall be made to the man who has never had the wit to be idle during his whole life; but has been careless of what the many care for—wealth, and family interests, and military offices, and speaking in the assembly, and magistracies, and plots, and parties. Reflecting that I was really too honest a man to be a politician and live, I did not go where I could do no good to you or to myself; but where I could do the greatest good privately to every one of you, thither I went, and sought to persuade every man among you that he must look to himself, and seek virtue and wisdom before he looks to his private interests, and look to the state before he looks to the interests of the state; and that this should be the order which he observes in all his actions. What shall be done to such an one? Doubtless some good thing, O men of Athens, if he has his reward; and the good should be of a kind suitable to him. What would be a reward suitable to a poor man who is your benefactor, and who desires leisure that he may instruct you? There can be no reward so fitting as maintenance in the Prytaneum, O men of Athens, a reward which he deserves far more than the citizen who has won the prize at Olympia in the horse or chariot race, whether the chariots were drawn by two horses or by many. For I am in want, and he has enough; and he only gives you the appearance of happiness, and I give you the reality. And if I am to estimate the penalty fairly, I should say that maintenance in the Prytaneum is the just return.

Perhaps you think that I am braving you in what I am saying now, as in what I said before about the tears and prayers. But this is not so. I speak rather because I am convinced that I never intentionally wronged any one, although I cannot convince you—the time has been too short; if there were a law at Athens, as there is in other cities, that a capital cause should not be decided in one day, then I believe that I should have convinced you. But I cannot in a moment refute great slanders; and, as I am convinced that I never wronged another, I will assuredly not wrong myself. I will not say of myself that I deserve any evil, or propose any penalty. Why should I? because I am afraid of the penalty of death which Meletus proposes? When I do not know whether death is a good or an evil, why should I propose a penalty which would certainly be an evil? Shall I say imprisonment? And why should I live in prison, and be the slave of the magistrates of the year—of the Eleven? Or shall the penalty be a fine, and imprisonment until the fine is paid? There is the same objection. I should have to lie in prison, for money I have none, and cannot pay. And if I say exile (and this may possibly be the penalty which you will affix), I must indeed be blinded by the love of life, if I am so irrational as to expect that when you, who are my own citizens, cannot endure my discourses and words, and have found them so grievous and odious that you will have no more of them, others are likely to endure me. No indeed, men of Athens, that is not very likely. And what a life should I lead, at my age, wandering from city to city, ever changing my place of exile, and always being driven out! For I am quite sure that wherever I go, there, as here, the young men will flock to me; and if I drive them away, their elders will drive me out at their request; and if I let them come, their fathers and friends will drive me out for their sakes.

Some one will say: Yes, Socrates, but cannot you hold your tongue, and then you may go into a foreign city, and no one will interfere with you? Now I have great difficulty in making you understand my answer to this. For if I tell you that to do as you say would be a disobedience to the God, and therefore that I cannot hold my tongue, you will not believe that I am serious; and if I say again that daily to discourse about virtue, and of those other things about which you hear me examining myself and others, is the greatest good of man, and that the unexamined life is not worth living, you are still less likely to believe me. Yet I say what is true, although a thing of which it is hard for me to persuade you. Also, I have never been accustomed to think that I deserve to suffer any harm. Had I money I might have estimated the offence at what I was able to pay, and not have been much the worse. But I have none, and therefore I must ask you to proportion the fine to my means. Well, perhaps I could afford a mina, and therefore I propose that penalty: Plato, Crito, Critobulus, and Apollodorus, my friends here, bid me say thirty minae, and they will be the sureties. Let thirty minae be the penalty; for which sum they will be ample security to you.

***

Not much time will be gained, O Athenians, in return for the evil name which you will get from the detractors of the city, who will say that you killed Socrates, a wise man; for they will call me wise, even although I am not wise, when they want to reproach you. If you had waited a little while, your desire would have been fulfilled in the course of nature. For I am far advanced in years, as you may perceive, and not far from death. I am speaking now not to all of you, but only to those who have condemned me to death. And I have another thing to say to them: you think that I was convicted because I had no words of the sort which would have procured my acquittal—I mean, if I had thought fit to leave nothing undone or unsaid. Not so; the deficiency which led to my conviction was not of words—certainly not. But I had not the boldness or impudence or inclination to address you as you would have liked me to do, weeping and wailing and lamenting, and saying and doing many things which you have been accustomed to hear from others, and which, as I maintain, are unworthy of me. I thought at the time that I ought not to do anything common or mean when in danger: nor do I now repent of the style of my defence; I would rather die having spoken after my manner, than speak in your manner and live. For neither in war nor yet at law ought I or any man to use every way of escaping death. Often in battle there can be no doubt that if a man will throw away his arms, and fall on his knees before his pursuers, he may escape death; and in other dangers there are other ways of escaping death, if a man is willing to say and do anything. The difficulty, my friends, is not to avoid death, but to avoid unrighteousness; for that runs faster than death. I am old and move slowly, and the slower runner has overtaken me, and my accusers are keen and quick, and the faster runner, who is unrighteousness, has overtaken them. And now I depart hence condemned by you to suffer the penalty of death,—they too go their ways condemned by the truth to suffer the penalty of villainy and wrong; and I must abide by my award—let them abide by theirs. I suppose that these things may be regarded as fated,—and I think that they are well.

And now, O men who have condemned me, I would fain prophesy to you; for I am about to die, and in the hour of death men are gifted with prophetic power. And I prophesy to you who are my murderers, that immediately after my departure punishment far heavier than you have inflicted on me will surely await you. Me you have killed because you wanted to escape the accuser, and not to give an account of your lives. But that will not be as you suppose: far otherwise. For I say that there will be more accusers of you than there are now; accusers whom hitherto I have restrained: and as they are younger they will be more inconsiderate with you, and you will be more offended at them. If you think that by killing men you can prevent some one from censuring your evil lives, you are mistaken; that is not a way of escape which is either possible or honourable; the easiest and the noblest way is not to be disabling others, but to be improving yourselves. This is the prophecy which I utter before my departure to the judges who have condemned me.

Friends, who would have acquitted me, I would like also to talk with you about the thing which has come to pass, while the magistrates are busy, and before I go to the place at which I must die. Stay then a little, for we may as well talk with one another while there is time. You are my friends, and I should like to show you the meaning of this event which has happened to me. O my judges—for you I may truly call judges—I should like to tell you of a wonderful circumstance. Hitherto the divine faculty of which the internal oracle is the source has constantly been in the habit of opposing me even about trifles, if I was going to make a slip or error in any matter; and now as you see there has come upon me that which may be thought, and is generally believed to be, the last and worst evil. But the oracle made no sign of opposition, either when I was leaving my house in the morning, or when I was on my way to the court, or while I was speaking, at anything which I was going to say; and yet

I have often been stopped in the middle of a speech, but now in nothing I either said or did touching the matter in hand has the oracle opposed me. What do I take to be the explanation of this silence? I will tell you. It is an intimation that what has happened to me is a good, and that those of us who think that death is an evil are in error. For the customary sign would surely have opposed me had I been going to evil and not to good.

Let us reflect in another way, and we shall see that there is great reason to hope that death is a good; for one of two things—either death is a state of nothingness and utter unconsciousness, or, as men say, there is a change and migration of the soul from this world to another. Now if you suppose that there is no consciousness, but a sleep like the sleep of him who is undisturbed even by dreams, death will be an unspeakable gain. For if a person were to select the night in which his sleep was undisturbed even by dreams, and were to compare with this the other days and nights of his life, and then were to tell us how many days and nights he had passed in the course of his life better and more pleasantly than this one, I think that any man, I will not say a private man, but even the great king will not find many such days or nights, when compared with the others. Now if death be of such a nature, I say that to die is gain; for eternity is then only a single night. But if death is the journey to another place, and there, as men say, all the dead abide, what good, O my friends and judges, can be greater than this? If indeed when the pilgrim arrives in the world below, he is delivered from the professors of justice in this world, and finds the true judges who are said to give judgment there, Minos and Rhadamanthus and Aeacus and Triptolemus, and other sons of God who were righteous in their own life, that pilgrimage will be worth making. What would not a man give if he might converse with Orpheus and Musaeus and Hesiod and Homer? Nay, if this be true, let me die again and again. I myself, too, shall have a wonderful interest in there meeting and conversing with Palamedes, and Ajax the son of Telamon, and any other ancient hero who has suffered death through an unjust judgment; and there will be no small pleasure, as I think, in comparing my own sufferings with theirs. Above all, I shall then be able to continue my search into true and false knowledge; as in this world, so also in the next; and I shall find out who is wise, and who pretends to be wise, and is not. What would not a man give, O judges, to be able to examine the leader of the great Trojan expedition; or Odysseus or Sisyphus, or numberless others, men and women too! What infinite delight would there be in conversing with them and asking them questions! In another world they do not put a man to death for asking questions: assuredly not. For besides being happier than we are, they will be immortal, if what is said is true.

Wherefore, O judges, be of good cheer about death, and know of a certainty, that no evil can happen to a good man, either in life or after death. He and his are not neglected by the gods; nor has my own approaching end happened by mere chance. But I see clearly that the time had arrived when it was better for me to die and be released from trouble; wherefore the oracle gave no sign. For which reason, also, I am not angry with my condemners, or with my accusers; they have done me no harm, although they did not mean to do me any good; and for this I may gently blame them.

Still I have a favour to ask of them. When my sons are grown up, I would ask you, O my friends, to punish them; and I would have you trouble them, as I have troubled you, if they seem to care about riches, or anything, more than about virtue; or if they pretend to be something when they are really nothing,—then reprove them, as I have reproved you, for not caring about that for which they ought to care, and thinking that they are something when they are really nothing. And if you do this, both I and my sons will have received justice at your hands.

The hour of departure has arrived, and we go our ways—I to die, and you to live. Which is better God only knows.

3. Introduction to the Sophists and Plato's *Protagoras*

Plato's *Protagoras* is both an important philosophical dialogue and, in my opinion, the best work of literature that we have from Classical Greece.

Protagoras is the most famous sophist of his time, and a great thinker in his own right. The sophists were a group with widely different views, but they all had in common the fact that they were teachers of rhetoric and that they were mainly preoccupied with ethical and political questions. Although their works did not survive, their theories provided Plato with a philosophical 'enemy,' and helped him in the formulation of his own theory.

The encounter between Protagoras and Socrates is imaginary, but Plato uses it to make some crucial philosophical points. Protagoras advances a relativistic point of view, according to which there is no absolute standard of truth. Because of this, in political matters, the best course is to follow the wishes of the majority. Protagoras therefore comes up with an argument in support of conventional morality, as well as of the Athenian democracy.

Socrates responds by claiming that correct moral and political decision-making require expertise and that one needs the 'measuring art' if one is to act rightly in these matters. This view is incompatible both with the assumption that common practice makes something morally correct and with majority rule: if the majority lacks knowledge, they cannot reach the right decision.

The subject is still of vital significance today. In the dealings of the West with other cultures, should Westerners respect the worldview of other communities as equally valid with their own, even if it involves elements with which they disagree, such as violations of human rights or an inferior social role for women? To this question, Protagoras would answer by promoting non-interference, whereas Socrates could provide a basis for adopting the opposite point of view.

Protagoras

Plato
Translated by Benjamin Jowett

PERSONS OF THE DIALOGUE:
Socrates, who is the narrator of the Dialogue to his Companion.
Hippocrates, Alcibiades and Critias.
Protagoras, Hippias and Prodicus (Sophists).
Callias, a wealthy Athenian.

SCENE: The House of Callias.

COMPANION: Where do you come from, Socrates? And yet I need hardly ask the question, for I know that you have been in chase of the fair Alcibiades. I saw him the day before yesterday; and he had got a beard like a man,—and he is a man, as I may tell you in your ear. But I thought that he was still very charming.

SOCRATES: What of his beard? Are you not of Homer's opinion, who says 'Youth is most charming when the beard first appears'? And that is now the charm of Alcibiades.

COMPANION: Well, and how do matters proceed? Have you been visiting him, and was he gracious to you?

SOCRATES: Yes, I thought that he was very gracious; and especially to-day, for I have just come from him, and he has been helping me in an argument. But shall I tell you a strange thing? I paid no attention to him, and several times I quite forgot that he was present.

COMPANION: What is the meaning of this? Has anything happened between you and him? For surely you cannot have discovered a fairer love than he is; certainly not in this city of Athens.

SOCRATES: Yes, much fairer.

COMPANION: What do you mean—a citizen or a foreigner?

SOCRATES: A foreigner.

COMPANION: Of what country?

SOCRATES: Of Abdera.

COMPANION: And is this stranger really in your opinion a fairer love than the son of Cleinias?

SOCRATES: And is not the wiser always the fairer, sweet friend?

COMPANION: But have you really met, Socrates, with some wise one?

SOCRATES: Say rather, with the wisest of all living men, if you are willing to accord that title to Protagoras.

COMPANION: What! Is Protagoras in Athens?

SOCRATES: Yes; he has been here two days.

COMPANION: And do you just come from an interview with him?

SOCRATES: Yes; and I have heard and said many things.

COMPANION: Then, if you have no engagement, suppose that you sit down and tell me what passed, and my attendant here shall give up his place to you.

SOCRATES: To be sure; and I shall be grateful to you for listening.

COMPANION: Thank you, too, for telling us.

SOCRATES: That is thank you twice over. Listen then: —Last night, or rather very early this morning, Hippocrates, the son of Apollodorus and the brother of Phason, gave a tremendous thump with his staff at my door; some one opened to him, and he came rushing in and bawled out: Socrates, are you awake or asleep?

I knew his voice, and said: Hippocrates, is that you? and do you bring any news?

Good news, he said; nothing but good.

Delightful, I said; but what is the news? and why have you come hither at this unearthly hour?

He drew nearer to me and said: Protagoras is come.

Yes, I replied; he came two days ago: have you only just heard of his arrival?

Yes, by the gods, he said; but not until yesterday evening.

At the same time he felt for the truckle-bed, and sat down at my feet, and then he said: Yesterday quite late in the evening, on my return from Oenoe whither I had gone in pursuit of my runaway slave Satyrus, as I meant to have told you, if some other matter had not come in the way;—on my return, when we had done supper and were about to retire to rest, my brother said to me: Protagoras is come. I was going to you at once, and then I thought that the night was far spent. But the moment sleep left me after my fatigue, I got up and came hither direct.

I, who knew the very courageous madness of the man, said: What is the matter? Has Protagoras robbed you of anything?

He replied, laughing: Yes, indeed he has, Socrates, of the wisdom which he keeps from me.

But, surely, I said, if you give him money, and make friends with him, he will make you as wise as he is himself.

Would to heaven, he replied, that this were the case! He might take all that I have, and all that my friends have, if he pleased. But that is why I have come to you now, in order that you may speak to him on my behalf; for I am young, and also I have never seen nor heard him; (when he visited Athens before I was but a child;) and all men praise him, Socrates; he is reputed to be the most accomplished of speakers. There is no reason why we should not go to him at once, and then we shall find him at home. He lodges, as I hear, with Callias the son of Hipponicus: let us start.

I replied: Not yet, my good friend; the hour is too early. But let us rise and take a turn in the court and wait about there until day-break; when the day breaks, then we will go. For Protagoras is generally at home, and we shall be sure to find him; never fear.

Upon this we got up and walked about in the court, and I thought that I would make trial of the strength of his resolution. So I examined him and put questions to him. Tell me, Hippocrates, I said, as you are going to Protagoras, and will be paying your money to him, what is he to whom you are going? and what will he make of you? If, for example, you had thought of going to Hippocrates of Cos, the Asclepiad, and were about to give him your money, and some one had said to you: You are paying money to your namesake Hippocrates, O Hippocrates; tell me, what is he that you give him money? how would you have answered?

I should say, he replied, that I gave money to him as a physician.

And what will he make of you?

A physician, he said.

And if you were resolved to go to Polycleitus the Argive, or Pheidias the Athenian, and were intending to give them money, and some one had asked you: What are Polycleitus and Pheidias? and why do you give them this money?—how would you have answered?

I should have answered, that they were statuaries.

And what will they make of you?

A statuary, of course.

Well now, I said, you and I are going to Protagoras, and we are ready to pay him money on your behalf. If our own means are sufficient, and we can gain him with these, we shall be only too glad; but if not, then we are to spend the money of your friends as well. Now suppose, that while we are thus enthusiastically pursuing our object some one were to say to us: Tell me, Socrates, and you Hippocrates, what is Protagoras, and why are you going to pay him money,—how should we answer? I know that Pheidias is a sculptor, and that Homer is a poet; but what appellation is given to Protagoras? how is he designated?

They call him a Sophist, Socrates, he replied.

Then we are going to pay our money to him in the character of a Sophist?

Certainly.

But suppose a person were to ask this further question: And how about yourself? What will Protagoras make of you, if you go to see him?

He answered, with a blush upon his face (for the day was just beginning to dawn, so that I could see him): Unless this differs in some way from the former instances, I suppose that he will make a Sophist of me.

By the gods, I said, and are you not ashamed at having to appear before the Hellenes in the character of a Sophist?

Indeed, Socrates, to confess the truth, I am.

But you should not assume, Hippocrates, that the instruction of Protagoras is of this nature: may you not learn of him in the same way that you learned the arts of the grammarian, or musician, or trainer, not with the view of making any of them a profession, but only as a part of education, and because a private gentleman and freeman ought to know them?

Just so, he said; and that, in my opinion, is a far truer account of the teaching of Protagoras.

I said: I wonder whether you know what you are doing?

And what am I doing?

You are going to commit your soul to the care of a man whom you call a Sophist. And yet I hardly think that you know what a Sophist is; and if not, then you do not even know to whom you are committing your soul and whether the thing to which you commit yourself be good or evil.

I certainly think that I do know, he replied.

Then tell me, what do you imagine that he is?

I take him to be one who knows wise things, he replied, as his name implies.

And might you not, I said, affirm this of the painter and of the carpenter also: Do not they, too, know wise things? But suppose a person were to ask us: In what are the painters wise? We should answer: In what relates to the making of likenesses, and similarly of other things. And if he were further to ask: What is the wisdom of the Sophist, and what is the manufacture over which he presides?—how should we answer him?

How should we answer him, Socrates? What other answer could there be but that he presides over the art which makes men eloquent?

Yes, I replied, that is very likely true, but not enough; for in the answer a further question is involved: Of what does the Sophist make a man talk eloquently? The player on the lyre may be supposed to make a man talk eloquently about that which he makes him understand, that is about playing the lyre. Is not that true?

Yes.

Then about what does the Sophist make him eloquent? Must not he make him eloquent in that which he understands?

Yes, that may be assumed.

And what is that which the Sophist knows and makes his disciple know?

Indeed, he said, I cannot tell.

Then I proceeded to say: Well, but are you aware of the danger which you are incurring? If you were going to commit your body to some one, who might do good or harm to it, would you not carefully consider and ask the opinion of your friends and kindred, and deliberate many days as to whether you should give him the care of your body? But when the soul is in question, which you hold to be of far more value than the body, and upon the good or evil of which depends the well-being of your all,—about this you never consulted either with your father or with your brother or with any one of us who are your companions. But no sooner does this foreigner appear, than you instantly commit your soul to his keeping. In the evening, as you say, you hear of him, and in the morning you go to him, never deliberating or taking the opinion of any one as to whether you ought to intrust yourself to him or not;—you have quite made up your mind that you will at all hazards be a pupil of Protagoras, and are prepared to expend all the property of yourself and of your friends in carrying out at any price this determination, although, as you admit, you do not know him, and have never spoken with him: and you call him a Sophist, but are manifestly ignorant of what a Sophist is; and yet you are going to commit yourself to his keeping.

When he heard me say this, he replied: No other inference, Socrates, can be drawn from your words.

I proceeded: Is not a Sophist, Hippocrates, one who deals wholesale or retail in the food of the soul? To me that appears to be his nature.

And what, Socrates, is the food of the soul?

Surely, I said, knowledge is the food of the soul; and we must take care, my friend, that the Sophist does not deceive us when he praises what he sells, like the dealers wholesale or retail who sell the food of the body; for they praise indiscriminately all their goods, without knowing what are really beneficial or hurtful: neither do their customers know, with the exception of any trainer or physician who may happen to buy of them. In like manner those who carry about the wares of knowledge, and make the round of the cities, and sell or retail them to any customer who is in want of them, praise them all alike; though I should not wonder, O my friend, if many of them were really ignorant of their effect upon the soul; and their customers equally ignorant, unless he who buys of them happens to be a physician of the soul. If, therefore, you have understanding of what is good and evil, you may safely buy knowledge of Protagoras or of any one; but if not, then, O my friend, pause, and do not hazard your dearest interests at a game of chance. For there is far greater peril in buying knowledge than in buying meat and drink: the one you purchase of the wholesale or retail dealer, and carry them away in other vessels, and before you receive them into the body as food, you may deposit them at home and call in any experienced friend who knows what is good to be eaten or drunken, and what not, and how much, and when; and then the danger of purchasing them is not so great. But you cannot buy the wares of knowledge and carry them away in another vessel; when you have paid for them you must receive them into the soul and go your way, either greatly harmed or greatly benefited; and therefore we should deliberate and take counsel with our elders; for we are still young—too young to determine such a matter. And now let us go, as we were intending, and hear Protagoras; and when we have heard what he has to say, we may take counsel of others; for not only is Protagoras at the house of Callias, but there is Hippias of Elis, and, if I am not mistaken, Prodicus of Ceos, and several other wise men.

To this we agreed, and proceeded on our way until we reached the vestibule of the house; and there we stopped in order to conclude a discussion which had arisen between us as we were going along; and we stood talking in the vestibule until we had finished and come to an understanding. And I think that the door-keeper, who was a eunuch, and who was probably annoyed at the great inroad of the Sophists, must have heard us talking. At any rate, when we knocked at the door, and he opened and saw us, he grumbled: They are Sophists—he is not at home; and instantly gave the door a hearty bang with both his hands. Again we knocked, and he answered without opening: Did you not hear me say that he is not at home, fellows? But, my friend, I said, you need not be alarmed; for we are not Sophists, and we are not come to see Callias, but we want to see Protagoras; and I must request you to announce us. At last, after a good deal of difficulty, the man was persuaded to open the door.

When we entered, we found Protagoras taking a walk in the cloister; and next to him, on one side, were walking Callias, the son of Hipponicus, and Paralus, the son of Pericles, who, by the mother's side, is his half-brother, and Charmides, the son of Glaucon. On the other side of him were Xanthippus, the other son of Pericles, Philippides, the son of Philomelus; also Antimoerus of Mende, who of all the disciples of Protagoras is the most famous, and intends to make sophistry his profession. A train of listeners followed him; the greater part of them appeared to be foreigners, whom Protagoras had brought with him out of the various cities visited by him in his journeys, he, like Orpheus, attracting them with his voice, and they following (Compare Rep.). I should mention also that there were some Athenians in the company. Nothing delighted me more than the precision of their movements: they never got into his way at all; but when he and those who were with him turned back, then the band of listeners parted regularly on either side; he was always in front, and they wheeled round and took their places behind him in perfect order.

After him, as Homer says (Od.), 'I lifted up my eyes and saw' Hippias the Elean sitting in the opposite cloister on a chair of state, and around him were seated on benches Eryximachus, the son of Acumenus, and Phaedrus the Myrrhinusian, and Andron the son of Androtion, and there were strangers whom he had brought with him from his native city of Elis, and some others: they were putting to Hippias certain physical and astronomical questions, and he, ex cathedra, was determining their several questions to them, and discoursing of them.

Also, 'my eyes beheld Tantalus (Od.);' for Prodicus the Cean was at Athens: he had been lodged in a room which, in the days of Hipponicus, was a storehouse; but, as the house was full, Callias had cleared this out and made the room into a guest-chamber. Now Prodicus was still in bed, wrapped up in sheepskins and bedclothes, of which there seemed to be a great heap; and there was sitting by him on the couches near, Pausanias of the deme of Cerameis, and with Pausanias was a youth quite young, who is certainly remarkable for his good looks, and, if I am not mistaken, is also of a fair and gentle nature. I thought that I heard him called Agathon, and my suspicion is that he is the beloved of Pausanias. There was this youth, and also there were the two Adeimantuses, one the son of Cepis, and the other of Leucolophides, and some others. I was very anxious to hear what Prodicus was saying, for he seems to me to be an all-wise and inspired man; but I was not able to get into the inner circle, and his fine deep voice made an echo in the room which rendered his words inaudible.

No sooner had we entered than there followed us Alcibiades the beautiful, as you say, and I believe you; and also Critias the son of Callaeschrus.

On entering we stopped a little, in order to look about us, and then walked up to Protagoras, and I said: Protagoras, my friend Hippocrates and I have come to see you.

Do you wish, he said, to speak with me alone, or in the presence of the company?

Whichever you please, I said; you shall determine when you have heard the purpose of our visit. And what is your purpose? he said.

I must explain, I said, that my friend Hippocrates is a native Athenian; he is the son of Apollodorus, and of a great and prosperous house, and he is himself in natural ability quite a match for anybody of his own age. I believe that he aspires to political eminence; and this he thinks that conversation with you is most likely to procure for him. And now you can determine whether you would wish to speak to him of your teaching alone or in the presence of the company.

Thank you, Socrates, for your consideration of me. For certainly a stranger finding his way into great cities, and persuading the flower of the youth in them to leave company of their kinsmen or any other acquaintances, old or young, and live with him, under the idea that they will be improved by his conversation, ought to be very cautious; great jealousies are aroused by his proceedings, and he is the subject of many enmities and conspiracies. Now the art of the Sophist is, as I believe, of great antiquity; but in ancient times those who practised it, fearing this odium, veiled and disguised themselves under various names, some under that of poets, as Homer, Hesiod, and Simonides, some, of hierophants and prophets, as Orpheus and Musaeus, and some, as I observe, even under the name of gymnastic-masters, like Iccus of Tarentum, or the more recently celebrated Herodicus, now of Selymbria and formerly of Megara, who is a first-rate Sophist. Your own Agathocles pretended to be a musician, but was really an eminent Sophist; also Pythocleides the Cean; and there were many others; and all of them, as I was saying, adopted these arts as veils or disguises because they were afraid of the odium which they would incur. But that is not my way, for I do not believe that they effected their purpose, which was to deceive the government, who were not blinded by them; and as to the people, they have no understanding, and only repeat what their rulers are pleased to tell them. Now to run away, and to be caught in running away, is the very height of folly, and also greatly increases the exasperation of mankind; for they regard him who runs away as a rogue, in addition to any other objections which they have to him; and therefore I take an entirely opposite course, and acknowledge myself to be a Sophist and instructor of mankind; such an open acknowledgment appears to me to be a better sort of caution than concealment. Nor do I neglect other precautions, and therefore I hope, as I may say, by the favour of heaven that no harm will come of the acknowledgment that I am a Sophist. And I have been now many years in the profession—for all my years when added up are many: there is no one here present of whom I might not be the father. Wherefore I should much prefer conversing with you, if you want to speak with me, in the presence of the company.

As I suspected that he would like to have a little display and glorification in the presence of Prodicus and Hippias, and would gladly show us to them in the light of his admirers, I said: But why should we not summon Prodicus and Hippias and their friends to hear us?

Very good, he said.

Suppose, said Callias, that we hold a council in which you may sit and discuss.—This was agreed upon, and great delight was felt at the prospect of hearing wise men talk; we ourselves took the chairs and benches, and arranged them by Hippias, where the other benches had been already placed. Meanwhile Callias and Alcibiades got Prodicus out of bed and brought in him and his companions.

When we were all seated, Protagoras said: Now that the company are assembled, Socrates, tell me about the young man of whom you were just now speaking.

I replied: I will begin again at the same point, Protagoras, and tell you once more the purport of my visit: this is my friend Hippocrates, who is desirous of making your acquaintance; he would like to know what will happen to him if he associates with you. I have no more to say.

Protagoras answered: Young man, if you associate with me, on the very first day you will return home a better man than you came, and better on the second day than on the first, and better every day than you were on the day before.

When I heard this, I said: Protagoras, I do not at all wonder at hearing you say this; even at your age, and with all your wisdom, if any one were to teach you what you did not know before, you would become better no doubt: but please to answer in a different way—I will explain how by an example. Let me suppose that Hippocrates, instead of desiring your acquaintance, wished to become acquainted with the young man Zeuxippus of Heraclea, who has lately been in Athens, and he had come to him as he has come to you, and had heard him say, as he has heard you say, that every day he would grow and become better if he associated with him: and then suppose that he were to ask him, 'In what shall I become better, and in what shall I grow?'—Zeuxippus would answer, 'In painting.' And suppose that he went to Orthagoras the Theban, and heard him say the same thing, and asked him, 'In what shall I become better day by day?' he would reply, 'In flute-playing.' Now I want you to make the same sort of answer to this young man and to me, who am asking questions on his account. When you say that on the first day on which he associates with you he will return home a better man, and on every day will grow in like manner,—in what, Protagoras, will he be better? and about what?

When Protagoras heard me say this, he replied: You ask questions fairly, and I like to answer a question which is fairly put. If Hippocrates comes to me he will not experience the sort of drudgery with which other Sophists are in the habit of insulting their pupils; who, when they have just escaped from the arts, are taken and driven back into them by these teachers, and made to learn calculation, and astronomy, and geometry, and music (he gave a look at Hippias as he said this); but if he comes to me, he will learn that which he comes to learn. And this is prudence in affairs private as well as public; he will learn to order his own house in the best manner, and he will be able to speak and act for the best in the affairs of the state.

Do I understand you, I said; and is your meaning that you teach the art of politics, and that you promise to make men good citizens?

That, Socrates, is exactly the profession which I make.

Then, I said, you do indeed possess a noble art, if there is no mistake about this; for I will freely confess to you, Protagoras, that I have a doubt whether this art is capable of being taught, and yet I know not how to disbelieve your assertion. And I ought to tell you why I am of opinion that this art cannot be taught or communicated by man to man. I say that the Athenians are an understanding people, and indeed they are esteemed to be such by the other Hellenes. Now I observe that when we are met together in the assembly, and the matter in hand relates to building, the builders are summoned as advisers; when the question is one of ship-building, then the ship-wrights; and the like of other arts which they think capable of being taught and learned. And if some person offers to give them advice who is not supposed by them to have any skill in the art, even though he be good-looking, and rich, and noble, they will not listen to him, but laugh and hoot at him, until either he is clamoured down and retires of himself; or if he persists, he is dragged away or put out by the constables at the command of the prytanes. This is their way of behaving about professors of the arts. But when the question is an affair of state, then everybody is free to have a say—carpenter, tinker, cobbler, sailor, passenger; rich and poor, high and low—any one who likes gets up, and no one reproaches him, as in the former case, with not having learned, and having no teacher, and yet giving advice; evidently because they are under the impression that this sort of knowledge cannot be taught. And not only is this true of the state, but of individuals; the best and wisest of our citizens are unable to impart their political wisdom to others: as for example, Pericles, the father of these young men, who gave them excellent instruction in all that could be learned from masters, in his own department of politics neither taught them, nor gave them teachers; but they were allowed to wander at their own free will in a sort of hope that they would light upon virtue of their own accord. Or take another example: there was Cleinias the younger brother of our friend Alcibiades, of whom this very same Pericles was the guardian; and he being in fact under the apprehension that Cleinias would be corrupted by Alcibiades, took him away, and placed him in the house of Ariphron to be educated; but before six months had elapsed, Ariphron sent him back, not knowing what to do with him. And I could mention numberless other instances of persons who were good themselves, and never yet made any one else good, whether friend or stranger. Now I, Protagoras, having these examples before me, am inclined to think that virtue cannot be taught. But then again, when I listen to your words, I waver; and am disposed to think that there must be something in what you say, because I know that you have great experience, and learning, and invention. And I wish that you would, if possible, show me a little more clearly that virtue can be taught. Will you be so good?

That I will, Socrates, and gladly. But what would you like? Shall I, as an elder, speak to you as younger men in an apologue or myth, or shall I argue out the question?

To this several of the company answered that he should choose for himself.

Well, then, he said, I think that the myth will be more interesting.

Once upon a time there were gods only, and no mortal creatures. But when the time came that these also should be created, the gods fashioned them out of earth and fire and various mixtures of both elements in the interior of the earth; and when they were about to bring them into the light of day, they ordered Prometheus and Epimetheus to equip them, and to distribute to them severally their proper qualities. Epimetheus said to Prometheus: 'Let me distribute, and do you inspect.' This was agreed, and Epimetheus made the distribution. There were some to whom he gave strength without swiftness, while he equipped the weaker with swiftness; some he armed, and others he left unarmed; and devised for the latter some other means of preservation, making some large, and having their size as a protection, and others small, whose nature was to fly in the air or burrow in the ground; this was to be their way of escape. Thus did he compensate them with the view of preventing any race from becoming extinct. And when he had provided against their destruction by one another, he contrived also a means of protecting them against the seasons of heaven; clothing them with close hair and thick skins sufficient to defend them against the winter cold and able to resist the summer heat, so that they might have a natural bed of their own when they wanted to rest; also he furnished them with hoofs and hair and hard and callous skins under their feet. Then he gave them varieties of food,—herb of the soil to some, to others fruits of trees, and to others roots, and to some again he gave other animals as food. And some he made to have few young ones, while those who were their prey were very prolific; and in this manner the race was preserved. Thus did Epimetheus, who, not being very wise, forgot that he had distributed among the brute animals all the qualities which he had to give,—and when he came to man, who was still unprovided, he was terribly perplexed. Now while he was in this perplexity, Prometheus came to inspect the distribution, and he found that the other animals were suitably furnished, but that man alone was naked and shoeless, and had neither bed nor arms of defence. The appointed hour was approaching when man in his turn was to go forth into the light of day; and Prometheus, not knowing how he could devise his salvation, stole the mechanical arts of Hephaestus and Athene, and fire with them (they could neither have been acquired nor used without fire), and gave them to man. Thus man had the wisdom necessary to the support of life, but political wisdom he had not; for that was in the keeping of Zeus, and the power of Prometheus did not extend to entering into the citadel of heaven, where Zeus dwelt, who moreover had terrible sentinels; but he did enter by stealth into the common workshop of Athene and Hephaestus, in which they used to practise their favourite arts, and carried off Hephaestus' art of working by fire, and also the art of Athene, and gave them to man. And in this way man was supplied with the means of life. But Prometheus is said to have been afterwards prosecuted for theft, owing to the blunder of Epimetheus.

Now man, having a share of the divine attributes, was at first the only one of the animals who had any gods, because he alone was of their kindred; and he would raise altars and images of them. He was not long in inventing articulate speech and names; and he also constructed houses and clothes and shoes and beds, and drew sustenance from the earth. Thus provided, mankind at first lived dispersed, and there were no cities. But the consequence was that they were destroyed by the wild beasts, for they were utterly weak in comparison of them, and their art was only sufficient to provide them with the means of life, and did not enable them to carry on war against the animals: food they had, but not as yet the art of government, of which the art of war is a part. After a while the desire of self-preservation gathered them into cities; but when they were gathered together, having no art of government, they evil intreated one another, and were again in process of dispersion and destruction. Zeus feared that the entire race would be exterminated, and so he sent Hermes to them, bearing reverence and justice to be the ordering principles of cities and the bonds of friendship and conciliation. Hermes asked Zeus how he should impart justice and reverence among men:—Should he distribute them as the arts are distributed; that is to say, to a favoured few only, one skilled individual having enough of medicine or of any other art for many unskilled ones? 'Shall this be the manner in which I am to distribute justice and reverence among men, or shall I give them to all?' 'To all,' said Zeus; 'I should like them all to have a share; for cities cannot exist, if a few only share in the virtues, as in the arts. And further, make a law by my order, that he who has no part in reverence and justice shall be put to death, for he is a plague of the state.'

And this is the reason, Socrates, why the Athenians and mankind in general, when the question relates to carpentering or any other mechanical art, allow but a few to share in their deliberations; and when any one else interferes, then, as you say, they object, if he be not of the favoured few; which, as I reply, is very natural. But when they meet to deliberate about political virtue, which proceeds only by way of justice and wisdom, they are patient enough of any man who speaks of them, as is also natural, because they think that every man ought to share in this sort of virtue, and that states could not exist if this were otherwise. I have explained to you, Socrates, the reason of this phenomenon.

And that you may not suppose yourself to be deceived in thinking that all men regard every man as having a share of justice or honesty and of every other political virtue, let me give you a further proof, which is this. In other cases, as you are aware, if a man says that he is a good flute-player, or skilful in any other art in which he has no skill, people either laugh at him or are angry with him, and his relations think that he is mad and go and admonish him; but when honesty is in question, or some other political virtue, even if they know that he is dishonest, yet, if the man comes publicly forward and tells the truth about his dishonesty, then, what in the other case was held by them to be good sense, they now deem to be madness. They say that all men ought to profess honesty whether they are honest or not, and that a man is out of his mind who says anything else. Their notion is, that a man must have some degree of honesty; and that if he has none at all he ought not to be in the world.

I have been showing that they are right in admitting every man as a counsellor about this sort of virtue, as they are of opinion that every man is a partaker of it. And I will now endeavour to show further that they do not conceive this virtue to be given by nature, or to grow spontaneously, but to be a thing which may be taught; and which comes to a man by taking pains. No one would instruct, no one would rebuke, or be angry with those whose calamities they suppose to be due to nature or chance; they do not try to punish or to prevent them from being what they are; they do but pity them. Who is so foolish as to chastise or instruct the ugly, or the diminutive, or the feeble? And for this reason. Because he knows that good and evil of this kind is the work of nature and of chance; whereas if a man is wanting in those good qualities which are attained by study and exercise and teaching, and has only the contrary evil qualities, other men are angry with him, and punish and reprove him—of these evil qualities one is impiety, another injustice, and they may be described generally as the very opposite of political virtue. In such cases any man will be angry with another, and reprimand him,—clearly because he thinks that by study and learning, the virtue in which the other is deficient may be acquired. If you will think, Socrates, of the nature of punishment, you will see at once that in the opinion of mankind virtue may be acquired; no one punishes the evil-doer under the notion, or for the reason, that he has done wrong,—only the unreasonable fury of a beast acts in that manner. But he who desires to inflict rational punishment does not retaliate for a past wrong which cannot be undone; he has regard to the future, and is desirous that the man who is punished, and he who sees him punished, may be deterred from doing wrong again. He punishes for the sake of prevention, thereby clearly implying that virtue is capable of being taught. This is the notion of all who retaliate upon others either privately or publicly. And the Athenians, too, your own citizens, like other men, punish and take vengeance on all whom they regard as evil doers; and hence, we may infer them to be of the number of those who think that virtue may be acquired and taught. Thus far, Socrates, I have shown you clearly enough, if I am not mistaken, that your countrymen are right in admitting the tinker and the cobbler to advise about politics, and also that they deem virtue to be capable of being taught and acquired.

There yet remains one difficulty which has been raised by you about the sons of good men. What is the reason why good men teach their sons the knowledge which is gained from teachers, and make them wise in that, but do nothing towards improving them in the virtues which distinguish themselves? And here, Socrates, I will leave the apologue and resume the argument. Please to consider: Is there or is there not some one quality of which all the citizens must be partakers, if there is to be a city at all? In the answer to this question is contained the only solution of your difficulty; there is no other. For if there be any such quality, and this quality or unity is not the art of the carpenter, or the smith, or the potter, but justice and temperance and holiness and, in a word, manly virtue—if this is the quality of which all men must be partakers, and which is the very condition of their learning or doing anything else, and if he who is wanting in this, whether he be a child only or a grown-up man or woman, must be taught and punished, until by punishment he becomes better, and he who rebels against instruction and punishment is either exiled or condemned to death under the idea that he is incurable—if what I am saying be true, good men have their sons taught other things and not this, do consider how extraordinary their conduct would appear to be. For we have shown that they think virtue capable of being taught and cultivated both in private and public; and, notwithstanding, they have their sons taught lesser matters, ignorance of which does not involve the punishment of death: but greater things, of which the ignorance may cause death and exile to those who have no training or knowledge of them—aye, and confiscation as well as death, and, in a word, may be the ruin of families—those things, I say, they are supposed not to teach them,—not to take the utmost care that they should learn. How improbable is this, Socrates!

Education and admonition commence in the first years of childhood, and last to the very end of life. Mother and nurse and father and tutor are vying with one another about the improvement of the child as soon as ever he is able to understand what is being said to him: he cannot say or do anything without their setting forth to him that this is just and that is unjust; this is honourable, that is dishonourable; this is holy, that is unholy; do this and abstain from that. And if he obeys, well and good; if not, he is straightened by threats and blows, like a piece of bent or warped wood. At a later stage they send him to teachers, and enjoin them to see to his manners even more than to his reading and music; and the teachers do as they are desired. And when the boy has learned his letters and is beginning to understand what is written, as before he understood only what was spoken, they put into his hands the works of great poets, which he reads sitting on a bench at school; in these are contained many admonitions, and many tales, and praises, and encomia of ancient famous men, which he is required to learn by heart, in order that he may imitate or emulate them and desire to become like them. Then, again, the teachers of the lyre take similar care that their young disciple is temperate and gets into no mischief; and when they have taught him the use of the lyre, they introduce him to the poems of other excellent poets, who are the lyric poets; and these they set to music, and make their harmonies and rhythms quite familiar to the children's souls, in order that they may learn to be more gentle, and harmonious, and rhythmical, and so more fitted for speech and action; for the life of man in every part has need of harmony and rhythm. Then they send them to the master of gymnastic, in order that their bodies may better minister to the virtuous mind, and that they may not be compelled through bodily weakness to play the coward in war or on any other occasion. This is what is done by those who have the means, and those who have the means are the rich; their children begin to go to school soonest and leave off latest. When they have done with masters, the state again compels them to learn the laws, and live after the pattern which they furnish, and not after their own fancies; and just as in learning to write, the writing-master first draws lines with a style for the use of the young beginner, and gives him the tablet and makes him follow the lines, so the city draws the laws, which were the invention of good lawgivers living in the olden time; these are given to the young man, in order to guide him in his conduct whether he is commanding or obeying; and he who transgresses them is to be corrected, or, in other words, called to account, which is a term used not only in your country, but also in many others, seeing that justice calls men to account. Now when there is all this care about virtue private and public, why, Socrates, do you still wonder and doubt whether virtue can be taught? Cease to wonder, for the opposite would be far more surprising.

But why then do the sons of good fathers often turn out ill? There is nothing very wonderful in this; for, as I have been saying, the existence of a state implies that virtue is not any man's private possession. If so—and nothing can be truer—then I will further ask you to imagine, as an illustration, some other pursuit or branch of knowledge which may be assumed equally to be the condition of the existence of a state. Suppose that there could be no state unless we were all flute-players, as far as each had the capacity, and everybody was freely teaching everybody the art, both in private and public, and reproving the bad player as freely and openly as every man now teaches justice and the laws, not concealing them as he would conceal the other arts, but imparting them—for all of us have a mutual interest in the justice and virtue of one another, and this is the reason why every one is so ready to teach justice and the laws;—suppose, I say, that there were the same readiness and liberality among us in teaching one another flute-playing, do you imagine, Socrates, that the sons of good flute-players would be more likely to be good than the sons of bad ones? I think not. Would not their sons grow up to be distinguished or undistinguished according to their own natural capacities as flute-players, and the son of a good player would often turn out to be a bad one, and the son of a bad player to be a good one, all flute-players would be good enough in comparison of those who were ignorant and unacquainted with the art of flute-playing? In like manner I would have you consider that he who appears to you to be the worst of those who have been brought up in laws and humanities, would appear to be a just man and a master of justice if he were to be compared with men who had no education, or courts of justice, or laws, or any restraints upon them which compelled them to practise virtue— with the savages, for example, whom the poet Pherecrates exhibited on the stage at the last year's Lenaean festival. If you were living among men such as the man-haters in his Chorus, you would be only too glad to meet with Eurybates and Phrynondas, and you would sorrowfully long to revisit the rascality of this part of the world. You, Socrates, are discontented, and why? Because all men are teachers of virtue, each one according to his ability; and you say Where are the teachers? You might as well ask, Who teaches Greek? For of that too there will not be any teachers found. Or you might ask, Who is to teach the sons of our artisans this same art which they have learned of their fathers? He and his fellow-workmen have taught them to the best of their ability,—but who will carry them further in their arts? And you would certainly have a difficulty, Socrates, in finding a teacher of them; but there would be no difficulty in finding a teacher of those who are wholly ignorant. And this is true of virtue or of anything else; if a man is better able than we are to promote virtue ever so little, we must be content with the result. A teacher of this sort I believe myself to be, and above all other men to have the knowledge which makes a man noble and good; and I give my pupils their money's-worth, and even more, as they themselves confess. And therefore I have introduced the following mode of payment:—When a man has been my pupil, if he likes he pays my price, but there is no compulsion; and if he does not like, he has only to go into a temple and take an oath of the value of the instructions, and he pays no more than he declares to be their value.

Such is my Apologue, Socrates, and such is the argument by which I endeavour to show that virtue may be taught, and that this is the opinion of the Athenians. And I have also attempted to show that you are not to wonder at good fathers having bad sons, or at good sons having bad fathers, of which the sons of Polycleitus afford an example, who are the companions of our friends here, Paralus and Xanthippus, but are nothing in comparison with their father; and this is true of the sons of many other artists. As yet I ought not to say the same of Paralus and Xanthippus themselves, for they are young and there is still hope of them.

Protagoras ended, and in my ear

'So charming left his voice, that I the while Thought him still speaking; still stood fixed to hear (Borrowed by Milton, "Paradise Lost".).'

At length, when the truth dawned upon me, that he had really finished, not without difficulty I began to collect myself, and looking at Hippocrates, I said to him: O son of Apollodorus, how deeply grateful I am to you for having brought me hither; I would not have missed the speech of Protagoras for a great deal. For I used to imagine that no human care could make men good; but I know better now. Yet I have still one very small difficulty which I am sure that Protagoras will easily explain, as he has already explained so much. If a man were to go and consult Pericles or any of our great speakers about these matters, he might perhaps hear as fine a discourse; but then when one has a question to ask of any of them, like books, they can neither answer nor ask; and if any one challenges the least particular of their speech, they go ringing on in a long harangue, like brazen pots, which when they are struck continue to sound unless some one puts his hand upon them; whereas our friend Protagoras can not only make a good speech, as he has already shown, but when he is asked a question he can answer briefly; and when he asks he will wait and hear the answer; and this is a very rare gift. Now I, Protagoras, want to ask of you a little question, which if you will only answer, I shall be quite satisfied. You were saying that virtue can be taught;—that I will take upon your authority, and there is no one to whom I am more ready to trust. But I marvel at one thing about which I should like to have my mind set at rest. You were speaking of Zeus sending justice and reverence to men; and several times while you were speaking, justice, and temperance, and holiness, and all these qualities, were described by you as if together they made up virtue. Now I want you to tell me truly whether virtue is one whole, of which justice and temperance and holiness are parts; or whether all these are only the names of one and the same thing: that is the doubt which still lingers in my mind.

There is no difficulty, Socrates, in answering that the qualities of which you are speaking are the parts of virtue which is one.

And are they parts, I said, in the same sense in which mouth, nose, and eyes, and ears, are the parts of a face; or are they like the parts of gold, which differ from the whole and from one another only in being larger or smaller?

I should say that they differed, Socrates, in the first way; they are related to one another as the parts of a face are related to the whole face.

And do men have some one part and some another part of virtue? Or if a man has one part, must he also have all the others?

By no means, he said; for many a man is brave and not just, or just and not wise.

You would not deny, then, that courage and wisdom are also parts of virtue?

Most undoubtedly they are, he answered; and wisdom is the noblest of the parts.

And they are all different from one another? I said.

Yes.

And has each of them a distinct function like the parts of the face;—the eye, for example, is not like the ear, and has not the same functions; and the other parts are none of them like one another, either in their functions, or in any other way? I want to know whether the comparison holds concerning the parts of virtue. Do they also differ from one another in themselves and in their functions? For that is clearly what the simile would imply.

Yes, Socrates, you are right in supposing that they differ.

Then, I said, no other part of virtue is like knowledge, or like justice, or like courage, or like temperance, or like holiness?

No, he answered.

Well then, I said, suppose that you and I enquire into their natures. And first, you would agree with me that justice is of the nature of a thing, would you not? That is my opinion: would it not be yours also?

Mine also, he said.

And suppose that some one were to ask us, saying, 'O Protagoras, and you, Socrates, what about this thing which you were calling justice, is it just or unjust?'—and I were to answer, just: would you vote with me or against me?

With you, he said.

Thereupon I should answer to him who asked me, that justice is of the nature of the just: would not you?

Yes, he said.

And suppose that he went on to say: 'Well now, is there also such a thing as holiness?'—we should answer, 'Yes,' if I am not mistaken?

Yes, he said.

Which you would also acknowledge to be a thing—should we not say so?

He assented.

'And is this a sort of thing which is of the nature of the holy, or of the nature of the unholy?' I should be angry at his putting such a question, and should say, 'Peace, man; nothing can be holy if holiness is not holy.' What would you say? Would you not answer in the same way?

Certainly, he said.

And then after this suppose that he came and asked us, 'What were you saying just now? Perhaps I may not have heard you rightly, but you seemed to me to be saying that the parts of virtue were not the same as one another.' I should reply, 'You certainly heard that said, but not, as you imagine, by me; for I only asked the question; Protagoras gave the answer.' And suppose that he turned to you and said, 'Is this true, Protagoras? and do you maintain that one part of virtue is unlike another, and is this your position?'—how would you answer him?

I could not help acknowledging the truth of what he said, Socrates.

Well then, Protagoras, we will assume this; and now supposing that he proceeded to say further, 'Then holiness is not of the nature of justice, nor justice of the nature of holiness, but of the nature of unholiness; and holiness is of the nature of the not just, and therefore of the unjust, and the unjust is the unholy': how shall we answer him? I should certainly answer him on my own behalf that justice is holy, and that holiness is just; and I would say in like manner on your behalf also, if you would allow me, that justice is either the same with holiness, or very nearly the same; and above all I would assert that justice is like holiness and holiness is like justice; and I wish that you would tell me whether I may be permitted to give this answer on your behalf, and whether you would agree with me.

He replied, I cannot simply agree, Socrates, to the proposition that justice is holy and that holiness is just, for there appears to me to be a difference between them. But what matter? if you please I please; and let us assume, if you will I, that justice is holy, and that holiness is just.

Pardon me, I replied; I do not want this 'if you wish' or 'if you will' sort of conclusion to be proven, but I want you and me to be proven: I mean to say that the conclusion will be best proven if there be no 'if.'

Well, he said, I admit that justice bears a resemblance to holiness, for there is always some point of view in which everything is like every other thing; white is in a certain way like black, and hard is like soft, and the most extreme opposites have some qualities in common; even the parts of the face which, as we were saying before, are distinct and have different functions, are still in a certain point of view similar, and one of them is like another of them. And you may prove that they are like one another on the same principle that all things are like one another; and yet things which are like in some particular ought not to be called alike, nor things which are unlike in some particular, however slight, unlike.

And do you think, I said in a tone of surprise, that justice and holiness have but a small degree of likeness?

Certainly not; any more than I agree with what I understand to be your view.

Well, I said, as you appear to have a difficulty about this, let us take another of the examples which you mentioned instead. Do you admit the existence of folly?

I do.

And is not wisdom the very opposite of folly?

That is true, he said.

And when men act rightly and advantageously they seem to you to be temperate?

Yes, he said.

And temperance makes them temperate?

Certainly.

And they who do not act rightly act foolishly, and in acting thus are not temperate?

I agree, he said.

Then to act foolishly is the opposite of acting temperately?

He assented.

And foolish actions are done by folly, and temperate actions by temperance?

He agreed.

And that is done strongly which is done by strength, and that which is weakly done, by weakness?

He assented.

And that which is done with swiftness is done swiftly, and that which is done with slowness, slowly?

He assented again.

And that which is done in the same manner, is done by the same; and that which is done in an opposite manner by the opposite?

He agreed.

Once more, I said, is there anything beautiful?

Yes.

To which the only opposite is the ugly?

There is no other.

And is there anything good?

There is.

To which the only opposite is the evil?

There is no other.

And there is the acute in sound?

True.

To which the only opposite is the grave?

There is no other, he said, but that.

Then every opposite has one opposite only and no more?

He assented.

Then now, I said, let us recapitulate our admissions. First of all we admitted that everything has one opposite and not more than one?

We did so.

And we admitted also that what was done in opposite ways was done by opposites?

Yes.

And that which was done foolishly, as we further admitted, was done in the opposite way to that which was done temperately?

Yes.

And that which was done temperately was done by temperance, and that which was done foolishly by folly?

He agreed.

And that which is done in opposite ways is done by opposites?

Yes.

And one thing is done by temperance, and quite another thing by folly?

Yes.

And in opposite ways?

Certainly.

And therefore by opposites:—then folly is the opposite of temperance?

Clearly.

And do you remember that folly has already been acknowledged by us to be the opposite of wisdom?

He assented.

And we said that everything has only one opposite?

Yes.

Then, Protagoras, which of the two assertions shall we renounce? One says that everything has but one opposite; the other that wisdom is distinct from temperance, and that both of them are parts of virtue; and that they are not only distinct, but dissimilar, both in themselves and in their functions, like the parts of a face. Which of these two assertions shall we renounce? For both of them together are certainly not in harmony; they do not accord or agree: for how can they be said to agree if everything is assumed to have only one opposite and not more than one, and yet folly, which is one, has clearly the two opposites—wisdom and temperance? Is not that true, Protagoras? What else would you say?

He assented, but with great reluctance.

Then temperance and wisdom are the same, as before justice and holiness appeared to us to be nearly the same. And now, Protagoras, I said, we must finish the enquiry, and not faint. Do you think that an unjust man can be temperate in his injustice?

I should be ashamed, Socrates, he said, to acknowledge this, which nevertheless many may be found to assert.

And shall I argue with them or with you? I replied.

I would rather, he said, that you should argue with the many first, if you will.

Whichever you please, if you will only answer me and say whether you are of their opinion or not. My object is to test the validity of the argument; and yet the result may be that I who ask and you who answer may both be put on our trial.

Protagoras at first made a show of refusing, as he said that the argument was not encouraging; at length, he consented to answer.

Now then, I said, begin at the beginning and answer me. You think that some men are temperate, and yet unjust?

Yes, he said; let that be admitted.

And temperance is good sense?

Yes.

And good sense is good counsel in doing injustice?

Granted.

If they succeed, I said, or if they do not succeed?

If they succeed.

And you would admit the existence of goods?

Yes.

And is the good that which is expedient for man?

Yes, indeed, he said: and there are some things which may be inexpedient, and yet I call them good.

I thought that Protagoras was getting ruffled and excited; he seemed to be setting himself in an attitude of war. Seeing this, I minded my business, and gently said:—

When you say, Protagoras, that things inexpedient are good, do you mean inexpedient for man only, or inexpedient altogether? and do you call the latter good?

Certainly not the last, he replied; for I know of many things—meats, drinks, medicines, and ten thousand other things, which are inexpedient for man, and some which are expedient; and some which are neither expedient nor inexpedient for man, but only for horses; and some for oxen only, and some for dogs; and some for no animals, but only for trees; and some for the roots of trees and not for their branches, as for example, manure, which is a good thing when laid about the roots of a tree, but utterly destructive if thrown upon the shoots and young branches; or I may instance olive oil, which is mischievous to all plants, and generally most injurious to the hair of every animal with the exception of man, but beneficial to human hair and to the human body generally; and even in this application (so various and changeable is the nature of the benefit), that which is the greatest good to the outward parts of a man, is a very great evil to his inward parts: and for this reason physicians always forbid their patients the use of oil in their food, except in very small quantities, just enough to extinguish the disagreeable sensation of smell in meats and sauces.

* * * * * * *

So I said: Do not imagine, Protagoras, that I have any other interest in asking questions of you but that of clearing up my own difficulties. For I think that Homer was very right in saying that

'When two go together, one sees before the other (Il.),'
for all men who have a companion are readier in deed, word, or thought; but if a man
'Sees a thing when he is alone,'

he goes about straightway seeking until he finds some one to whom he may show his discoveries, and who may confirm him in them. And I would rather hold discourse with you than with any one, because I think that no man has a better understanding of most things which a good man may be expected to understand, and in particular of virtue. For who is there, but you?—who not only claim to be a good man and a gentleman, for many are this, and yet have not the power of making others good—whereas you are not only good yourself, but also the cause of goodness in others. Moreover such confidence have you in yourself, that although other Sophists conceal their profession, you proclaim in the face of Hellas that you are a Sophist or teacher of virtue and education, and are the first who demanded pay in return. How then can I do otherwise than invite you to the examination of these subjects, and ask questions and consult with you? I must, indeed. And I should like once more to have my memory refreshed by you about the questions which I was asking you at first, and also to have your help in considering them. If I am not mistaken the question was this: Are wisdom and temperance and courage and justice and holiness five names of the same thing? or has each of the names a separate underlying essence and corresponding thing having a peculiar function, no one of them being like any other of them? And you replied that the five names were not the names of the same thing, but that each of them had a separate object, and that all these objects were parts of virtue, not in the same way that the parts of gold are like each other and the whole of which they are parts, but as the parts of the face are unlike the whole of which they are parts and one another, and have each of them a distinct function. I should like to know whether this is still your opinion; or if not, I will ask you to define your meaning, and I shall not take you to task if you now make a different statement. For I dare say that you may have said what you did only in order to make trial of me.

I answer, Socrates, he said, that all these qualities are parts of virtue, and that four out of the five are to some extent similar, and that the fifth of them, which is courage, is very different from the other four, as I prove in this way: You may observe that many men are utterly unrighteous, unholy, intemperate, ignorant, who are nevertheless remarkable for their courage.

Stop, I said; I should like to think about that. When you speak of brave men, do you mean the confident, or another sort of nature?

Yes, he said; I mean the impetuous, ready to go at that which others are afraid to approach.

In the next place, you would affirm virtue to be a good thing, of which good thing you assert yourself to be a teacher.

Yes, he said; I should say the best of all things, if I am in my right mind.

And is it partly good and partly bad, I said, or wholly good?

Wholly good, and in the highest degree.

Tell me then; who are they who have confidence when diving into a well?

I should say, the divers.

And the reason of this is that they have knowledge?

Yes, that is the reason.

And who have confidence when fighting on horseback—the skilled horseman or the unskilled? The skilled.

And who when fighting with light shields—the peltasts or the nonpeltasts?

The peltasts. And that is true of all other things, he said, if that is your point: those who have knowledge are more confident than those who have no knowledge, and they are more confident after they have learned than before.

And have you not seen persons utterly ignorant, I said, of these things, and yet confident about them?

Yes, he said, I have seen such persons far too confident.

And are not these confident persons also courageous?

In that case, he replied, courage would be a base thing, for the men of whom we are speaking are surely madmen.

Then who are the courageous? Are they not the confident?

Yes, he said; to that statement I adhere.

And those, I said, who are thus confident without knowledge are really not courageous, but mad; and in that case the wisest are also the most confident, and being the most confident are also the bravest, and upon that view again wisdom will be courage.

Nay, Socrates, he replied, you are mistaken in your remembrance of what was said by me. When you asked me, I certainly did say that the courageous are the confident; but I was never asked whether the confident are the courageous; if you had asked me, I should have answered 'Not all of them': and what I did answer you have not proved to be false, although you proceeded to show that those who have knowledge are more courageous than they were before they had knowledge, and more courageous than others who have no knowledge, and were then led on to think that courage is the same as wisdom. But in this way of arguing you might come to imagine that strength is wisdom. You might begin by asking whether the strong are able, and I should say 'Yes'; and then whether those who know how to wrestle are not more able to wrestle than those who do not know how to wrestle, and more able after than before they had learned, and I should assent. And when I had admitted this, you might use my admissions in such a way as to prove that upon my view wisdom is strength; whereas in that case I should not have admitted, any more than in the other, that the able are strong, although I have admitted that the strong are able. For there is a difference between ability and strength; the former is given by knowledge as well as by madness or rage, but strength comes from nature and a healthy state of the body. And in like manner I say of confidence and courage, that they are not the same; and I argue that the courageous are confident, but not all the confident courageous. For confidence may be given to men by art, and also, like ability, by madness and rage; but courage comes to them from nature and the healthy state of the soul.

I said: You would admit, Protagoras, that some men live well and others ill?

He assented.

And do you think that a man lives well who lives in pain and grief?

He does not.

But if he lives pleasantly to the end of his life, will he not in that case have lived well?

He will.

Then to live pleasantly is a good, and to live unpleasantly an evil?

Yes, he said, if the pleasure be good and honourable.

And do you, Protagoras, like the rest of the world, call some pleasant things evil and some painful things good?—for I am rather disposed to say that things are good in as far as they are pleasant, if they have no consequences of another sort, and in as far as they are painful they are bad.

I do not know, Socrates, he said, whether I can venture to assert in that unqualified manner that the pleasant is the good and the painful the evil. Having regard not only to my present answer, but also to the whole of my life, I shall be safer, if I am not mistaken, in saying that there are some pleasant things which are not good, and that there are some painful things which are good, and some which are not good, and that there are some which are neither good nor evil.

And you would call pleasant, I said, the things which participate in pleasure or create pleasure?

Certainly, he said.

Then my meaning is, that in as far as they are pleasant they are good; and my question would imply that pleasure is a good in itself.

According to your favourite mode of speech, Socrates, 'Let us reflect about this,' he said; and if the reflection is to the point, and the result proves that pleasure and good are really the same, then we will agree; but if not, then we will argue.

And would you wish to begin the enquiry? I said; or shall I begin?

You ought to take the lead, he said; for you are the author of the discussion.

May I employ an illustration? I said. Suppose some one who is enquiring into the health or some other bodily quality of another:—he looks at his face and at the tips of his fingers, and then he says, Uncover your chest and back to me that I may have a better view:—that is the sort of thing which I desire in this speculation. Having seen what your opinion is about good and pleasure, I am minded to say to you: Uncover your mind to me, Protagoras, and reveal your opinion about knowledge, that I may know whether you agree with the rest of the world. Now the rest of the world are of the opinion that knowledge is a principle not of strength, or of rule, or of command: their notion is that a man may have knowledge, and yet that the knowledge which is in him may be overmastered by anger, or pleasure, or pain, or love, or perhaps by fear,—just as if knowledge were a slave, and might be dragged about anyhow. Now is that your view? or do you think that knowledge is a noble and commanding thing, which cannot be overcome, and will not allow a man, if he only knows the difference of good and evil, to do anything which is contrary to knowledge, but that wisdom will have strength to help him?

I agree with you, Socrates, said Protagoras; and not only so, but I, above all other men, am bound to say that wisdom and knowledge are the highest of human things.

Good, I said, and true. But are you aware that the majority of the world are of another mind; and that men are commonly supposed to know the things which are best, and not to do them when they might? And most persons whom I have asked the reason of this have said that when men act contrary to knowledge they are overcome by pain, or pleasure, or some of those affections which I was just now mentioning.

Yes, Socrates, he replied; and that is not the only point about which mankind are in error.

Suppose, then, that you and I endeavour to instruct and inform them what is the nature of this affection which they call 'being overcome by pleasure,' and which they affirm to be the reason why they do not always do what is best. When we say to them: Friends, you are mistaken, and are saying what is not true, they would probably reply: Socrates and Protagoras, if this affection of the soul is not to be called 'being overcome by pleasure,' pray, what is it, and by what name would you describe it?

But why, Socrates, should we trouble ourselves about the opinion of the many, who just say anything that happens to occur to them?

I believe, I said, that they may be of use in helping us to discover how courage is related to the other parts of virtue. If you are disposed to abide by our agreement, that I should show the way in which, as I think, our recent difficulty is most likely to be cleared up, do you follow; but if not, never mind.

You are quite right, he said; and I would have you proceed as you have begun.

Well then, I said, let me suppose that they repeat their question, What account do you give of that which, in our way of speaking, is termed being overcome by pleasure? I should answer thus: Listen, and Protagoras and I will endeavour to show you. When men are overcome by eating and drinking and other sensual desires which are pleasant, and they, knowing them to be evil, nevertheless indulge in them, would you not say that they were overcome by pleasure? They will not deny this. And suppose that you and I were to go on and ask them again: 'In what way do you say that they are evil,—in that they are pleasant and give pleasure at the moment, or because they cause disease and poverty and other like evils in the future? Would they still be evil, if they had no attendant evil consequences, simply because they give the consciousness of pleasure of whatever nature?'—Would they not answer that they are not evil on account of the pleasure which is immediately given by them, but on account of the after consequences—diseases and the like?

I believe, said Protagoras, that the world in general would answer as you do.

And in causing diseases do they not cause pain? and in causing poverty do they not cause pain;—they would agree to that also, if I am not mistaken?

Protagoras assented.

Then I should say to them, in my name and yours: Do you think them evil for any other reason, except because they end in pain and rob us of other pleasures:—there again they would agree?

We both of us thought that they would.

And then I should take the question from the opposite point of view, and say: 'Friends, when you speak of goods being painful, do you not mean remedial goods, such as gymnastic exercises, and military service, and the physician's use of burning, cutting, drugging, and starving? Are these the things which are good but painful?'—they would assent to me?

He agreed.

'And do you call them good because they occasion the greatest immediate suffering and pain; or because, afterwards, they bring health and improvement of the bodily condition and the salvation of states and power over others and wealth?'—they would agree to the latter alternative, if I am not mistaken?

He assented.

'Are these things good for any other reason except that they end in pleasure, and get rid of and avert pain? Are you looking to any other standard but pleasure and pain when you call them good?'—they would acknowledge that they were not?

I think so, said Protagoras.

'And do you not pursue after pleasure as a good, and avoid pain as an evil?'

He assented.

'Then you think that pain is an evil and pleasure is a good: and even pleasure you deem an evil, when it robs you of greater pleasures than it gives, or causes pains greater than the pleasure. If, however, you call pleasure an evil in relation to some other end or standard, you will be able to show us that standard. But you have none to show.'

I do not think that they have, said Protagoras.

'And have you not a similar way of speaking about pain? You call pain a good when it takes away greater pains than those which it has, or gives pleasures greater than the pains: then if you have some standard other than pleasure and pain to which you refer when you call actual pain a good, you can show what that is. But you cannot.'

True, said Protagoras.

Suppose again, I said, that the world says to me: 'Why do you spend many words and speak in many ways on this subject?' Excuse me, friends, I should reply; but in the first place there is a difficulty in explaining the meaning of the expression 'overcome by pleasure'; and the whole argument turns upon this. And even now, if you see any possible way in which evil can be explained as other than pain, or good as other than pleasure, you may still retract. Are you satisfied, then, at having a life of pleasure which is without pain? If you are, and if you are unable to show any good or evil which does not end in pleasure and pain, hear the consequences:—If what you say is true, then the argument is absurd which affirms that a man often does evil knowingly, when he might abstain, because he is seduced and overpowered by pleasure; or again, when you say that a man knowingly refuses to do what is good because he is overcome at the moment by pleasure. And that this is ridiculous will be evident if only we give up the use of various names, such as pleasant and painful, and good and evil. As there are two things, let us call them by two names—first, good and evil, and then pleasant and painful. Assuming this, let us go on to say that a man does evil knowing that he does evil. But some one will ask, Why? Because he is overcome, is the first answer. And by what is he overcome? the enquirer will proceed to ask. And we shall not be able to reply 'By pleasure,' for the name of pleasure has been exchanged for that of good. In our answer, then, we shall only say that he is overcome. 'By what?' he will reiterate. By the good, we shall have to reply; indeed we shall. Nay, but our questioner will rejoin with a laugh, if he be one of the swaggering sort, 'That is too ridiculous, that a man should do what he knows to be evil when he ought not, because he is overcome by good. Is that, he will ask, because the good was worthy or not worthy of conquering the evil'? And in answer to that we shall clearly reply, Because it was not worthy; for if it had been worthy, then he who, as we say, was overcome by pleasure, would not have been wrong. 'But how,' he will reply, 'can the good be unworthy of the evil, or the evil of the good'? Is not the real explanation that they are out of proportion to one another, either as greater and smaller, or more and fewer? This we cannot deny. And when you speak of being overcome—'what do you mean,' he will say, 'but that you choose the greater evil in exchange for the lesser good?' Admitted. And now substitute the names of pleasure and pain for good and evil, and say, not as before, that a man does what is evil knowingly, but that he does what is painful knowingly, and because he is overcome by pleasure, which is unworthy to overcome. What measure is there of the relations of pleasure to pain other than excess and defect, which means that they become greater and smaller, and more and fewer, and differ in degree? For if any one says: 'Yes, Socrates, but immediate pleasure differs widely from future pleasure and pain'—To that I should reply: And do they differ in anything but in pleasure and pain? There can be no other measure of them. And do you, like a skilful weigher, put into the balance the pleasures and the pains, and their nearness and distance, and weigh them, and then say which outweighs the other. If you weigh pleasures against pleasures, you of course take the more and greater; or if you weigh pains against pains, you take the fewer and the less; or if pleasures against pains, then you choose that course of action in which the painful is exceeded by the pleasant, whether the distant by the near or the near by the distant; and you avoid that course of action in which the pleasant is exceeded by the painful. Would you not admit, my friends, that this is true? I am confident that they cannot deny this.

He agreed with me.

Well then, I shall say, if you agree so far, be so good as to answer me a question: Do not the same magnitudes appear larger to your sight when near, and smaller when at a distance? They will acknowledge that. And the same holds of thickness and number; also sounds, which are in themselves equal, are greater when near, and lesser when at a distance. They will grant that also. Now suppose happiness to consist in doing or choosing the greater, and in not doing or in avoiding the less, what would be the saving principle of human life? Would not the art of measuring be the saving principle; or would the power of appearance? Is not the latter that deceiving art which makes us wander up and down and take the things at one time of which we repent at another, both in our actions and in our choice of things great and small? But the art of measurement would do away with the effect of appearances, and, showing the truth, would fain teach the soul at last to find rest in the truth, and would thus save our life. Would not mankind generally acknowledge that the art which accomplishes this result is the art of measurement?

Yes, he said, the art of measurement.

Suppose, again, the salvation of human life to depend on the choice of odd and even, and on the knowledge of when a man ought to choose the greater or less, either in reference to themselves or to each other, and whether near or at a distance; what would be the saving principle of our lives? Would not knowledge?—a knowledge of measuring, when the question is one of excess and defect, and a knowledge of number, when the question is of odd and even? The world will assent, will they not?

Protagoras himself thought that they would.

Well then, my friends, I say to them; seeing that the salvation of human life has been found to consist in the right choice of pleasures and pains,—in the choice of the more and the fewer, and the greater and the less, and the nearer and remoter, must not this measuring be a consideration of their excess and defect and equality in relation to each other?

This is undeniably true.

And this, as possessing measure, must undeniably also be an art and science?

They will agree, he said.

The nature of that art or science will be a matter of future consideration; but the existence of such a science furnishes a demonstrative answer to the question which you asked of me and Protagoras. At the time when you asked the question, if you remember, both of us were agreeing that there was nothing mightier than knowledge, and that knowledge, in whatever existing, must have the advantage over pleasure and all other things; and then you said that pleasure often got the advantage even over a man who has knowledge; and we refused to allow this, and you rejoined: O Protagoras and Socrates, what is the meaning of being overcome by pleasure if not this?—tell us what you call such a state:—if we had immediately and at the time answered 'Ignorance,' you would have laughed at us. But now, in laughing at us, you will be laughing at yourselves: for you also admitted that men err in their choice of pleasures and pains; that is, in their choice of good and evil, from defect of knowledge; and you admitted further, that they err, not only from defect of knowledge in general, but of that particular knowledge which is called measuring. And you are also aware that the erring act which is done without knowledge is done in ignorance. This, therefore, is the meaning of being overcome by pleasure;—ignorance, and that the greatest. And our friends Protagoras and Prodicus and Hippias declare that they are the physicians of ignorance; but you, who are under the mistaken impression that ignorance is not the cause, and that the art of which I am speaking cannot be taught, neither go yourselves, nor send your children, to the Sophists, who are the teachers of these things—you take care of your money and give them none; and the result is, that you are the worse off both in public and private life: — Let us suppose this to be our answer to the world in general: And now I should like to ask you, Hippias, and you, Prodicus, as well as Protagoras (for the argument is to be yours as well as ours), whether you think that I am speaking the truth or not?

They all thought that what I said was entirely true.

Then you agree, I said, that the pleasant is the good, and the painful evil. And here I would beg my friend Prodicus not to introduce his distinction of names, whether he is disposed to say pleasurable, delightful, joyful. However, by whatever name he prefers to call them, I will ask you, most excellent Prodicus, to answer in my sense of the words.

Prodicus laughed and assented, as did the others.

Then, my friends, what do you say to this? Are not all actions honourable and useful, of which the tendency is to make life painless and pleasant? The honourable work is also useful and good?

This was admitted.

Then, I said, if the pleasant is the good, nobody does anything under the idea or conviction that some other thing would be better and is also attainable, when he might do the better. And this inferiority of a man to himself is merely ignorance, as the superiority of a man to himself is wisdom.

They all assented.

And is not ignorance the having a false opinion and being deceived about important matters?

To this also they unanimously assented.

Then, I said, no man voluntarily pursues evil, or that which he thinks to be evil. To prefer evil to good is not in human nature; and when a man is compelled to choose one of two evils, no one will choose the greater when he may have the less.

All of us agreed to every word of this.

Well, I said, there is a certain thing called fear or terror; and here, Prodicus, I should particularly like to know whether you would agree with me in defining this fear or terror as expectation of evil.

Protagoras and Hippias agreed, but Prodicus said that this was fear and not terror.

Never mind, Prodicus, I said; but let me ask whether, if our former assertions are true, a man will pursue that which he fears when he is not compelled? Would not this be in flat contradiction to the admission which has been already made, that he thinks the things which he fears to be evil; and no one will pursue or voluntarily accept that which he thinks to be evil?

That also was universally admitted.

Then, I said, these, Hippias and Prodicus, are our premises; and I would beg Protagoras to explain to us how he can be right in what he said at first. I do not mean in what he said quite at first, for his first statement, as you may remember, was that whereas there were five parts of virtue none of them was like any other of them; each of them had a separate function. To this, however, I am not referring, but to the assertion which he afterwards made that of the five virtues four were nearly akin to each other, but that the fifth, which was courage, differed greatly from the others. And of this he gave me the following proof. He said: You will find, Socrates, that some of the most impious, and unrighteous, and intemperate, and ignorant of men are among the most courageous; which proves that courage is very different from the other parts of virtue. I was surprised at his saying this at the time, and I am still more surprised now that I have discussed the matter with you. So I asked him whether by the brave he meant the confident. Yes, he replied, and the impetuous or goers. (You may remember, Protagoras, that this was your answer.)

He assented.

Well then, I said, tell us against what are the courageous ready to go — against the same dangers as the cowards?

No, he answered.

Then against something different?

Yes, he said.

Then do cowards go where there is safety, and the courageous where there is danger?

Yes, Socrates, so men say.

Very true, I said. But I want to know against what do you say that the courageous are ready to go—against dangers, believing them to be dangers, or not against dangers?

No, said he; the former case has been proved by you in the previous argument to be impossible.

That, again, I replied, is quite true. And if this has been rightly proven, then no one goes to meet what he thinks to be dangers, since the want of self-control, which makes men rush into dangers, has been shown to be ignorance.

He assented.

And yet the courageous man and the coward alike go to meet that about which they are confident; so that, in this point of view, the cowardly and the courageous go to meet the same things.

And yet, Socrates, said Protagoras, that to which the coward goes is the opposite of that to which the courageous goes; the one, for example, is ready to go to battle, and the other is not ready.

And is going to battle honourable or disgraceful? I said.

Honourable, he replied.

And if honourable, then already admitted by us to be good; for all honourable actions we have admitted to be good.

That is true; and to that opinion I shall always adhere.

True, I said. But which of the two are they who, as you say, are unwilling to go to war, which is a good and honourable thing?

The cowards, he replied.

And what is good and honourable, I said, is also pleasant?

It has certainly been acknowledged to be so, he replied.

And do the cowards knowingly refuse to go to the nobler, and pleasanter, and better?

The admission of that, he replied, would belie our former admissions.

But does not the courageous man also go to meet the better, and pleasanter, and nobler?

That must be admitted.

And the courageous man has no base fear or base confidence?

True, he replied.

And if not base, then honourable?

He admitted this.

And if honourable, then good?

Yes.

But the fear and confidence of the coward or foolhardy or madman, on the contrary, are base?

He assented.

And these base fears and confidences originate in ignorance and uninstructedness?

True, he said.

Then as to the motive from which the cowards act, do you call it cowardice or courage?

I should say cowardice, he replied.

And have they not been shown to be cowards through their ignorance of dangers?

Assuredly, he said.

And because of that ignorance they are cowards?

He assented.

And the reason why they are cowards is admitted by you to be cowardice?

He again assented.

Then the ignorance of what is and is not dangerous is cowardice?

He nodded assent.

But surely courage, I said, is opposed to cowardice?

Yes.

Then the wisdom which knows what are and are not dangers is opposed to the ignorance of them?

To that again he nodded assent.

And the ignorance of them is cowardice?

To that he very reluctantly nodded assent.

And the knowledge of that which is and is not dangerous is courage, and is opposed to the ignorance of these things?

At this point he would no longer nod assent, but was silent.

And why, I said, do you neither assent nor dissent, Protagoras?

Finish the argument by yourself, he said.

I only want to ask one more question, I said. I want to know whether you still think that there are men who are most ignorant and yet most courageous?

You seem to have a great ambition to make me answer, Socrates, and therefore I will gratify you, and say, that this appears to me to be impossible consistently with the argument.

My only object, I said, in continuing the discussion, has been the desire to ascertain the nature and relations of virtue; for if this were clear, I am very sure that the other controversy which has been carried on at great length by both of us—you affirming and I denying that virtue can be taught—would also become clear. The result of our discussion appears to me to be singular. For if the argument had a human voice, that voice would be heard laughing at us and saying: 'Protagoras and Socrates, you are strange beings; there are you, Socrates, who were saying that virtue cannot be taught, contradicting yourself now by your attempt to prove that all things are knowledge, including justice, and temperance, and courage,—which tends to show that virtue can certainly be taught; for if virtue were other than knowledge, as Protagoras attempted to prove, then clearly virtue cannot be taught; but if virtue is entirely knowledge, as you are seeking to show, then I cannot but suppose that virtue is capable of being taught. Protagoras, on the other hand, who started by saying that it might be taught, is now eager to prove it to be anything rather than knowledge; and if this is true, it must be quite incapable of being taught.' Now I, Protagoras, perceiving this terrible confusion of our ideas, have a great desire that they should be cleared up. And I should like to carry on the discussion until we ascertain what virtue is, whether capable of being taught or not, lest haply Epimetheus should trip us up and deceive us in the argument, as he forgot us in the story; I prefer your Prometheus to your Epimetheus, for of him I make use, whenever I am busy about these questions, in Promethean care of my own life. And if you have no objection, as I said at first, I should like to have your help in the enquiry.

Protagoras replied: Socrates, I am not of a base nature, and I am the last man in the world to be envious. I cannot but applaud your energy and your conduct of an argument. As I have often said, I admire you above all men whom I know, and far above all men of your age; and I believe that you will become very eminent in philosophy. Let us come back to the subject at some future time; at present we had better turn to something else.

By all means, I said, if that is your wish; for I too ought long since to have kept the engagement of which I spoke before, and only tarried because I could not refuse the request of the noble Callias. So the conversation ended, and we went our way.

4.   Introduction to Plato's *Republic*

The *Republic* is a complex dialogue, in which Plato advances and ties together a number of distinct but intertwined philosophical theories. It is a colossal undertaking, the historical importance of which is not diminished by the fact that both its metaphysical and its ethical and political doctrines are demonstrably untenable.

The *Republic* includes an ontological theory and a theory of knowledge (together they constitute Plato's metaphysics), an ethical theory, a political one, a complex moral psychology scheme, a theory of education and a theory of art.

In this chapter, we will discuss Plato's metaphysical construction, the so-called theory of the Forms. Plato believes that all human knowledge is *a priori*, meaning that it comes before sense experience. Our souls, which are separable from our bodies, spend the time between their successive entrances into bodies in the 'realm of the Forms.' This realm consists of the gods, the souls and the Forms. The Forms are what may be called 'universals' or concepts. Plato asserts, for example, that in order for someone to be able to recognize and correctly identify a table (and not to confuse it with, say, a coach), one must know the Form of the table first. But only very few people, the philosophers, ever achieve knowledge of the Forms. The rest go about by using their 'opinions,' which are unreliable.

Since all souls lose their previous knowledge at birth, the 'recollection' of this knowledge is the ultimate aim of the philosopher. A life of abstention from bodily pleasures and intense study of philosophy and mathematics is presupposed for the soul to 'recollect' what it knew before. But even such a life is no guarantee of success. Ultimately, achieving knowledge of the Forms is a mystical experience which cannot be completely rationalized.

Plato's theory attempts to explain where our knowledge comes from, as well as how it is possible to know for certain that the object in front of me is a table and not a T-Rex. In the part of the *Republic* that follows, Plato tries to establish that there is a realm of the Forms and a realm of particular, sensible things (the physical world), by arguing that the Forms are the object of knowledge and particular things the object of opinion and that these two realms are separate.

Plato's theory of the Forms was devastatingly criticized by Aristotle and was never accepted in its entirety by any philosopher after that. The main problems are that for the theory to work Plato must make the 'Form of the table' completely independent of any particular table and that only the Forms fully exist, whereas material things come between existence and non-existence. Both claims are very strongly counterintuitive.

Republic

Book V (473C–480A)

Plato
Translated by Benjamin Jowett

I said: Until philosophers are kings, or the kings and princes of this world have the spirit and power of philosophy, and political greatness and wisdom meet in one, and those commoner natures who pursue either to the exclusion of the other are compelled to stand aside, cities will never have rest from their evils,—nor the human race, as I believe,—and then only will this our State have a possibility of life and behold the light of day. Such was the thought, my dear Glaucon, which I would fain have uttered if it had not seemed too extravagant; for to be convinced that in no other State can there be happiness private or public is indeed a hard thing.

Socrates, what do you mean? I would have you consider that the word which you have uttered is one at which numerous persons, and very respectable persons too, in a figure pulling off their coats all in a moment, and seizing any weapon that comes to hand, will run at you might and main, before you know where you are, intending to do heaven knows what; and if you don't prepare an answer, and put yourself in motion, you will be prepared by their fine wits,' and no mistake.

You got me into the scrape, I said.

And I was quite right; however, I will do all I can to get you out of it; but I can only give you good-will and good advice, and, perhaps, I may be able to fit answers to your questions better than another—that is all. And now, having such an auxiliary, you must do your best to show the unbelievers that you are right. I ought to try, I said, since you offer me such invaluable assistance. And I think that, if there is to be a chance of our escaping, we must explain to them whom we mean when we say that philosophers are to rule in the State; then we shall be able to defend ourselves: There will be discovered to be some natures who ought to study philosophy and to be leaders in the State; and others who are not born to be philosophers, and are meant to be followers rather than leaders.

Then now for a definition, he said.

Follow me, I said, and I hope that I may in some way or other be able to give you a satisfactory explanation.

Proceed.

I dare say that you remember, and therefore I need not remind you, that a lover, if he is worthy of the name, ought to show his love, not to some one part of that which he loves, but to the whole.

I really do not understand, and therefore beg of you to assist my memory.

Another person, I said, might fairly reply as you do; but a man of pleasure like yourself ought to know that all who are in the flower of youth do somehow or other raise a pang or emotion in a lover's breast, and are thought by him to be worthy of his affectionate regards. Is not this a way which you have with the fair: one has a snub nose, and you praise his charming face; the hook-nose of another has, you say, a royal look; while he who is neither snub nor hooked has the grace of regularity: the dark visage is manly, the fair are children of the gods; and as to the sweet 'honey pale,' as they are called, what is the very name but the invention of a lover who talks in diminutives, and is not adverse to paleness if appearing on the cheek of youth? In a word, there is no excuse which you will not make, and nothing which you will not say, in order not to lose a single flower that blooms in the spring-time of youth.

If you make me an authority in matters of love, for the sake of the argument, I assent.

And what do you say of lovers of wine? Do you not see them doing the same? They are glad of any pretext of drinking any wine.

Very good.

And the same is true of ambitious men; if they cannot command an army, they are willing to command a file; and if they cannot be honoured by really great and important persons, they are glad to be honoured by lesser and meaner people, but honour of some kind they must have.

Exactly.

Once more let me ask: Does he who desires any class of goods, desire the whole class or a part only? The whole.

And may we not say of the philosopher that he is a lover, not of a part of wisdom only, but of the whole?

Yes, of the whole.

And he who dislikes learnings, especially in youth, when he has no power of judging what is good and what is not, such an one we maintain not to be a philosopher or a lover of knowledge, just as he who refuses his food is not hungry, and may be said to have a bad appetite and not a good one?

Very true, he said.

Whereas he who has a taste for every sort of knowledge and who is curious to learn and is never satisfied, may be justly termed a philosopher? Am I not right?

Glaucon said: If curiosity makes a philosopher, you will find many a strange being will have a title to the name. All the lovers of sights have a delight in learning, and must therefore be included. Musical amateurs, too, are a folk strangely out of place among philosophers, for they are the last persons in the world who would come to anything like a philosophical discussion, if they could help, while they run about at the Dionysiac festivals as if they had let out their ears to hear every chorus; whether the performance is in town or country—that makes no difference—they are there. Now are we to maintain that all these and any who have similar tastes, as well as the professors of quite minor arts, are philosophers?

Certainly not, I replied; they are only an imitation.

He said: Who then are the true philosophers?

Those, I said, who are lovers of the vision of truth.

That is also good, he said; but I should like to know what you mean?

To another, I replied, I might have a difficulty in explaining; but I am sure that you will admit a proposition which I am about to make.

What is the proposition?

That since beauty is the opposite of ugliness, they are two?

Certainly.

And inasmuch as they are two, each of them is one?

True again.

And of just and unjust, good and evil, and of every other class, the same remark holds: taken singly, each of them one; but from the various combinations of them with actions and things and with one another, they are seen in all sorts of lights and appear many? Very true.

And this is the distinction which I draw between the sight-loving, art-loving, practical class and those of whom I am speaking, and who are alone worthy of the name of philosophers.

How do you distinguish them? he said.

The lovers of sounds and sights, I replied, are, as I conceive, fond of fine tones and colours and forms and all the artificial products that are made out of them, but their mind is incapable of seeing or loving absolute beauty.

True, he replied.

Few are they who are able to attain to the sight of this.

Very true.

And he who, having a sense of beautiful things has no sense of absolute beauty, or who, if another lead him to a knowledge of that beauty is unable to follow—of such an one I ask, Is he awake or in a dream only? Reflect: is not the dreamer, sleeping or waking, one who likens dissimilar things, who puts the copy in the place of the real object?

I should certainly say that such an one was dreaming.

But take the case of the other, who recognises the existence of absolute beauty and is able to distinguish the idea from the objects which participate in the idea, neither putting the objects in the place of the idea nor the idea in the place of the objects—is he a dreamer, or is he awake?

He is wide awake.

And may we not say that the mind of the one who knows has knowledge, and that the mind of the other, who opines only, has opinion.

Certainly.

But suppose that the latter should quarrel with us and dispute our statement, can we administer any soothing cordial or advice to him, without revealing to him that there is sad disorder in his wits?

We must certainly offer him some good advice, he replied.

Come, then, and let us think of something to say to him. Shall we begin by assuring him that he is welcome to any knowledge which he may have, and that we are rejoiced at his having it? But we should like to ask him a question: Does he who has knowledge know something or nothing? (You must answer for him.)

I answer that he knows something.

Something that is or is not?

Something that is; for how can that which is not ever be known?

And are we assured, after looking at the matter from many points of view, that absolute being is or may be absolutely known, but that the utterly non-existent is utterly unknown?

Nothing can be more certain.

Good. But if there be anything which is of such a nature as to be and not to be, that will have a place intermediate between pure being and the absolute negation of being?

Yes, between them.

And, as knowledge corresponded to being and ignorance of necessity to not-being, for that intermediate between being and not-being there has to be discovered a corresponding intermediate between ignorance and knowledge, if there be such?

Certainly.

Do we admit the existence of opinion?

Undoubtedly.

As being the same with knowledge, or another faculty?

Another faculty.

Then opinion and knowledge have to do with different kinds of matter corresponding to this difference of faculties?

Yes.

And knowledge is relative to being and knows being. But before I proceed further I will make a division.

What division?

I will begin by placing faculties in a class by themselves: they are powers in us, and in all other things, by which we do as we do. Sight and hearing, for example, I should call faculties. Have I clearly explained the class which I mean?

Yes, I quite understand.

Then let me tell you my view about them. I do not see them, and therefore the distinctions of fire, colour, and the like, which enable me to discern the differences of some things, do not apply to them. In speaking of a faculty I think only of its sphere and its result; and that which has the same sphere and the same result I call the same faculty, but that which has another sphere and another result I call different. Would that be your way of speaking?

Yes.

And will you be so very good as to answer one more question? Would you say that knowledge is a faculty, or in what class would you place it?

Certainly knowledge is a faculty, and the mightiest of all faculties.

And is opinion also a faculty?

Certainly, he said; for opinion is that with which we are able to form an opinion.

And yet you were acknowledging a little while ago that knowledge is not the same as opinion?

Why, yes, he said: how can any reasonable being ever identify that which is infallible with that which errs?

An excellent answer, proving, I said, that we are quite conscious of a distinction between them.

Yes.

Then knowledge and opinion having distinct powers have also distinct spheres or subject-matters?

That is certain.

Being is the sphere or subject-matter of knowledge, and knowledge is to know the nature of being?

Yes.

And opinion is to have an opinion?

Yes.

And do we know what we opine? or is the subject-matter of opinion the same as the subject-matter of knowledge?

Nay, he replied, that has been already disproven; if difference in faculty implies difference in the sphere or subject matter, and if, as we were saying, opinion and knowledge are distinct faculties, then the sphere of knowledge and of opinion cannot be the same.

Then if being is the subject-matter of knowledge, something else must be the subject-matter of opinion?

Yes, something else.

Well then, is not-being the subject-matter of opinion? or, rather, how can there be an opinion at all about not-being? Reflect: when a man has an opinion, has he not an opinion about something? Can he have an opinion which is an opinion about nothing?

Impossible.

He who has an opinion has an opinion about some one thing?

Yes.

And not-being is not one thing but, properly speaking, nothing?

True.

Of not-being, ignorance was assumed to be the necessary correlative; of being, knowledge?

True, he said.

Then opinion is not concerned either with being or with not-being?

Not with either.

And can therefore neither be ignorance nor knowledge?

That seems to be true.

But is opinion to be sought without and beyond either of them, in a greater clearness than knowledge, or in a greater darkness than ignorance?

In neither.

Then I suppose that opinion appears to you to be darker than knowledge, but lighter than ignorance?

Both; and in no small degree.

And also to be within and between them?

Yes.

Then you would infer that opinion is intermediate?

No question.

But were we not saying before, that if anything appeared to be of a sort which is and is not at the same time, that sort of thing would appear also to lie in the interval between pure being and absolute not-being; and that the corresponding faculty is neither knowledge nor ignorance, but will be found in the interval between them?

True.

And in that interval there has now been discovered something which we call opinion?

There has.

Then what remains to be discovered is the object which partakes equally of the nature of being and not-being, and cannot rightly be termed either, pure and simple; this unknown term, when discovered, we may truly call the subject of opinion, and assign each to its proper faculty,—the extremes to the faculties of the extremes and the mean to the faculty of the mean.

True.

This being premised, I would ask the gentleman who is of opinion that there is no absolute or unchangeable idea of beauty—in whose opinion the beautiful is the manifold—he, I say, your lover of beautiful sights, who cannot bear to be told that the beautiful is one, and the just is one, or that anything is one—to him I would appeal, saying, Will you be so very kind, sir, as to tell us whether, of all these beautiful things, there is one which will not be found ugly; or of the just, which will not be found unjust; or of the holy, which will not also be unholy?

No, he replied; the beautiful will in some point of view be found ugly; and the same is true of the rest.

And may not the many which are doubles be also halves?—doubles, that is, of one thing, and halves of another?

Quite true.

And things great and small, heavy and light, as they are termed, will not be denoted by these any more than by the opposite names?

True; both these and the opposite names will always attach to all of them.

And can any one of those many things which are called by particular names be said to be this rather than not to be this?

He replied: They are like the punning riddles which are asked at feasts or the children's puzzle about the eunuch aiming at the bat, with what he hit him, as they say in the puzzle, and upon what the bat was sitting. The individual objects of which I am speaking are also a riddle, and have a double sense: nor can you fix them in your mind, either as being or not-being, or both, or neither.

Then what will you do with them? I said. Can they have a better place than between being and not-being? For they are clearly not in greater darkness or negation than not-being, or more full of light and existence than being.

That is quite true, he said.

Thus then we seem to have discovered that the many ideas which the multitude entertain about the beautiful and about all other things are tossing about in some region which is halfway between pure being and pure not-being?

We have.

Yes; and we had before agreed that anything of this kind which we might find was to be described as matter of opinion, and not as matter of knowledge; being the intermediate flux which is caught and detained by the intermediate faculty.

Quite true.

Then those who see the many beautiful, and who yet neither see absolute beauty, nor can follow any guide who points the way thither; who see the many just, and not absolute justice, and the like,—such persons may be said to have opinion but not knowledge?

That is certain.

But those who see the absolute and eternal and immutable may be said to know, and not to have opinion only?

Neither can that be denied.

The one loves and embraces the subjects of knowledge, the other those of opinion? The latter are the same, as I dare say will remember, who listened to sweet sounds and gazed upon fair colours, but would not tolerate the existence of absolute beauty.

Yes, I remember.

Shall we then be guilty of any impropriety in calling them lovers of opinion rather than lovers of wisdom, and will they be very angry with us for thus describing them?

I shall tell them not to be angry; no man should be angry at what is true.

But those who love the truth in each thing are to be called lovers of wisdom and not lovers of opinion.

Assuredly.

5. Introduction to *Plato on Democracy*

In this chapter from my book *Plato on Democracy* I analyze the political and the moral psychology theories of the *Republic*. I conclude that Plato's overall argument does not work even on its own terms.

Plato posits three classes in the *Republic*: Guardians (philosopher-rulers), Auxiliaries (the armed forces of the city) and Producers. He asserts that there are four virtues and that our souls are tripartite. They have a rational, a spirited and a desiring, irrational part.

The Guardians and the Auxiliaries together are leisured classes who correspond to the aristocrats in the historical world of Classical Greece. The Producers correspond to the lower classes of laboring citizens.

Plato's moral psychology is anchored on the assertion that the rational part dominates the soul of the Guardians, the spirited part the soul of the Auxiliaries, and the desiring part the soul of the Producers. This psychological profile works very well in terms of justifying the political authority of the Guardians, who rule the city, and the political impotence of the Producers, whose irrationality means that they should not have an active political role.

The problem with this grand scheme, however, is that Plato expects the Producers to obey the Guardians willingly and unwaveringly. But, as I show through detailed discussion of the relevant passages, it is not possible to expect the Producers to behave in this way. If they are the irrational individuals that Plato's moral theory has suggested, how can they act rationally in politics and accept the philosophers' rule? On the other hand, if they are not completely dominated by their desires and have enough rationality to obey the Guardians willingly, why completely denude them of any vestige of political self-determination?

Either the Producers are absolutely irrational and thus cannot be trusted to follow the Guardians, or they are rational enough to obey, but, precisely because of their rationality, they ought to have some political role, however limited. Plato's failure to appreciate this point entails one of two things: either the Producers are to some extent rational, in which case they are wrongfully deprived of some degree of political participation, or they are not rational at all, in which case they cannot be trusted to obey the philosophers and the only way that the best possible constitution can be maintained is by force. But although Plato explicitly sanctions the use of force against the Producers, the dictatorial character of this rule would make his city as unacceptable to his contemporaries as it ought to be to liberals today.

Plato on Democracy

Thanassis Samaras

The challenge to which Socrates responds in the *Republic* is set in Book One by Thrasymachus, who argues that the unjust individual is happier than the just. In his endeavour to disprove this thesis, Socrates begins by proposing justice to be sought first in the city, because there it exists on a 'larger' scale (368e). He suggests that the first *polis* is created because everyone is 'not self-sufficient, but has many needs which he can't supply himself' (369b). Division of labour produces efficiency (369e–370a) and conforms to the fact that each individual is by nature suited to do a certain job (370a–b). As more production needs arise, more people are required for different jobs to be done and the city grows (370d ff.). Its people, in Socrates' description, have only the bare essentials for a simple life. This invites Glaucon to complain that Socrates is talking of a city of pigs (372d). Socrates responds that the city so far described is 'healthy' (372e7), whereas the 'luxurious' (372e3) one that Glaucon wants will be 'suffering from inflammation' (372e8).[1]

There are two points worth making about the 'city of pigs.' First, Plato realises with exceptional acuteness that a city starts as an economic association destined to provide for the needs of its members. In order for this to happen more efficiently, the philosopher claims, distribution of labour has to come into effect and this is actually a good thing not only in economic terms (because it produces more efficiency, 369e–370a), but also in terms of human self-fulfilment (because it is obviously best for every individual to do the job he or she was destined to do by nature, 370a–b). This economic insight, which demonstrates Plato's clear understanding of the significance of the division of labour, coupled with his assumption that an individual is by nature best suited to do one job, play a crucial part in the formation of the social structure of Callipolis.

Second, as some commentators have pointed out, it is this germinal city which is Plato's 'ideal' city and not Callipolis which is often so described.[2] The primitive community is indeed 'ideal' in that it does not include, in its initial stages, the features of Plato's contemporary societies which lead to divisions between individuals, factions and cities. But Plato realises that such a situation without any conflict bears no resemblance to the political realities of his time. In a community which is *a priori* peaceful, politics does not apply, because politics is primarily concerned with the restriction or elimination of conflict.[3] So, Plato's proto-community might be 'ideal,' but, unlike the city of the *Republic*, it is ideal on a non-political plane.

The desire for luxury in this primitive city leads to a point where its own land is not sufficient to sustain its people and it ends up going to war with its neighbours (373d).[4] At this point the necessity of an army presents itself. This army, according to Socrates, must be professional.[5] It is with the discussion of the character required for the soldiers and the education which they receive that the description of the Platonic 'just city' eventually begins.

The city is divided into three classes: the Guardians (*phylakes*), who come out of the soldierly class as its oldest and most competent members and become the rulers of the city; the Auxiliaries, who constitute the rest of the soldierly class (the term *phylakes* is introduced in 374d8 and is used to designate the professional soldiers up to 414b5, where the distinction between rulers and soldiers, the latter now called *epikouroi*, is introduced. From then on the two terms are used in a specific technical sense); the third class is not ascribed a specific name by Plato. He refers to them by different names like 'workers' (421d1), 'the other citizens' [Guardians and Auxiliaries excluded] (423d3) or 'businessmen' (434c7). This Platonic failure to name this class consistently is indicative of Plato's lack of interest in them, which is further demonstrated by the fact that he devotes large parts of the *Republic* to the specification of the education of the Auxiliaries (376c–412b) and the Guardians (502e–541b), but never supplies a single word about the formal education of the Producers.

The city is wise, for Plato, not due to the wisdom of its craftsmen (428b–c), but due to the knowledge which is concerned with the benefit of the city as a whole; the latter belongs to the Guardians, a class by nature consisting of very few members (428e9–429a1).[6] The Guardians are, according to Plato, the only class that places the overall interest of the city above its individual class interest. The philosopher's insistence that very few individuals will achieve wisdom, the cardinal virtue which legitimises power, is not only one feature of his theory of virtue, but a key element of his political doctrine as well. If wisdom is rare, the political virtue which is grounded on it will also be a highly exclusive quality. In terms of the development of Plato's thought, this position springs directly from Socrates' emphasis on the importance of expertise in politics and is self-evidently anti-democratic.[7]

The city is brave by virtue of the courageous behaviour not of all its citizens, but only of those who have to perform military duty (429b), i.e. the Auxiliaries. This courageous behaviour consists in having an unshakeable right opinion (430b3) as to what is to be feared and what not, which is imparted into their souls by the education that was prescribed for them in 376c ff.

Temperance is a blend of 'concord' (430e3) and 'harmony' (430e4). This 'concord' and 'harmony' consist in an agreement that the best ought to rule over the worst (432a). Justice is declared to be 'in a certain sense' (433b3) for each 'to mind his own business' (433b4). It is also what 'makes it possible for them [the other virtues] to come into being . . . and preserves them' (433b) and what makes the city 'perfectly good'[8] (433d). Finally, one brief argument is added to demonstrate why 'to mind one's own business' is a good definition of justice. The role of the courts, which in the just city are to be manned by the rulers, is to give everybody what is due to him or her and this is just (433e–434a).

The definitions of the four virtues of the city hereby summarised have to be regarded as, in a sense, provisional. A full account of wisdom can be produced only after the introduction of the philosopher and the meaning of justice is not fully elaborated until the end of Book Nine. But they are of great importance in that they provide the first explicit formulation of Plato's theory of virtue and, from a political point of view, because they are specifically definitions of the virtues of the *polis*.

Nevertheless, Plato's definition of the city's virtues is not free of problems. One such problem is the philosopher's perplexing belief that the virtues cannot be more or less than four. When wisdom, bravery and temperance have been defined, Socrates asserts that 'what remains' is justice (432b). But Plato has nowhere given the slightest indication that the virtues must necessarily be four and a serious gap appears in his argument on this point. Cross and Woozley characterise this argument by elimination as a 'worthless procedure.'[9]

A more serious question arises with regard to Plato's judicial argument. In fact, an obvious fallacy is involved if the latter is taken in its literal form. The first premise is that the judges ought to make sure that everybody gets what is his or her own. Since the judges aim at justice, it follows that it is just that everybody should have his or her own. So far Plato's reasoning is faultless. But Plato claims that his premises prove not only that it is just that one should have one's own, but also that one should do one's own. However, the premises state nothing about one doing one's own and the argument cannot be accepted in this form.

Vlastos has argued that this fallacy is too gross to have gone unnoticed by Plato and that the argument is in fact elliptical. There is an unstated premise which is that 'each shall have one's own if each does one's own.'[10] According to Vlastos, this argument represents a Platonic attempt to connect the particular notion of justice proposed in the *Republic* (which might be called Platonic justice) with the common conception of justice (ordinary justice). Vlastos asserts that the argument includes a specific attempt to show that Platonic justice, exactly like ordinary justice, involves refraining from Πλεονεξηα (having more than one is due) and that Plato can expect agreement from common opinion on this point. Treated this way, Vlastos suggests, the argument is valid and does establish the correspondence between Platonic and ordinary morality that the philosopher aims at: Plato is counting on his readers 'to understand his definition to imply that in any community in which everyone lived up to the maxim "do your own" there would be no *pleonexia*.'[11] Vlastos's point about *pleonexia* is plausible: the statement that 'men should not take other people's belongings or be deprived of their own' (433e), to which he draws attention, does read as an expression of what an ordinary Greek would understand by *pleonexia*.

Read as elliptical in this manner, Plato's argument is in fact formally valid. There is, however, one question which remains to be asked: does the hidden premise that each shall have one's own if and only if one does one's own establish a connection between Platonic and ordinary justice? In other words, would such a correspondence be recognisable in any Greek society? If not, Plato cannot claim to have succeeded in connecting the *Republic's* morality to common morality, because even if there were general agreement that justice consists in refraining from *pleonexia*, there would be no similar agreement that to have one's own is equivalent to doing one's own.

The bi-conditional relation between 'having' and 'doing' one's own, which Vlastos asserts, means in socio-political terms that one's property should be related to one's social status and/or one's function in the state. In Plato's city, which is rigidly stratified, this condition is, indeed, satisfied (it is satisfied not in the sense that the highest classes have more possessions, but in the sense that, as we will see in chapter 3, they control economic power by commanding the labour of others). But in the real world, though this principle might partially apply to some strict oligarchies like Sparta, it hardly applies to societies where economic power is not exclusively concentrated in the hands of the classes traditionally regarded as the highest ones. In Athens, for example, a metic could be extremely rich, but still be excluded from participation in common affairs. But we have no evidence that the Greeks considered this asymmetry between one's property and one's social status as unjust. Therefore, Plato's equivalence of having and doing one's own cannot be accepted as a point on which he could justifiably expect general agreement and this invalidates the claim that by his judicial argument he establishes a full rapport between his own and the common conception of justice. It is fair enough to say that he uses a commonly accepted notion of justice (as entailing rejection of *pleonexia*), but it is far from certain that he can achieve universal agreement for his equivocation between having one's own and doing one's own. This fact does not entail that Vlastos's addition of a suppressed premise in order to save Plato's argument at the formal level is unsound: this move remains both tenable and plausible. It indicates, however, a serious unresolved problem in Plato's account of justice in the city.[12]

One cardinal characteristic of Plato's theory of virtue, and a vital one from a political point of view, is that no specific virtue is attributed to the Producers and that the potentiality to achieve virtue, rather than any fully developed particular virtue, is attributed to the Auxiliaries. The city derives its wisdom from the wisdom of its Guardians and Plato leaves no doubt that wisdom is the 'property' of individual Guardians (428d and e). The latter are also brave, and brave on a higher plane than the Auxiliaries, because they start their careers as Auxiliaries and are accepted into the highest class by virtue of being distinguished in their soldierly duties as well as by coming eventually to possess full knowledge as opposed to the Auxiliaries' right opinion. The Auxiliaries do demonstrate bravery, but, as will soon be explained, they do not 'possess' this virtue in the strict sense of the word. As for temperance and justice, Plato defines them not as properties of particular classes, in which case they would be attributed to all the individuals of these classes, but as relations between classes. In this way he is able to include the Producers in the political framework of the *Republic* without being obliged to allow them any claim to virtue.

The case of temperance is particurlarly interesting in this respect, because Plato's presentation of it involves a deep-seated ambiguity. If temperance, whose essence is that rulers and ruled agree about who must govern, is a kind of 'concord' (430e), then by implication the Producers should have at least some degree of freedom and rationality. They should have freedom because their consent would become a substantial part of the justification of the Guardians' rule, and they should have rationality because this is essential for their recognition of the 'natural' (431c, 432a) superiority of the Guardians. Plato also writes that temperance 'exists among [both] the rulers and the ruled' (431e). *Eneinai*, the verb used in this sentence, literally means 'to exist in' them; it appears then that Plato comes close here to attributing temperance to the Producers as individuals.[13]

Nevertheless, as Irwin remarks, Plato's language here can be misleading:

> [i]n a temperate state (a) the same belief about who should rule *enestin* in rulers and ruled, 431a9; (b) this concord about who should rule is temperance, 432a4; (c) the state's temperance, unlike its wisdom and courage is not *en merei tini* of the state, 431e10, but is spread through the whole city, 432a2. These uses of *en* might mislead us into thinking all the individuals are temperate . . . But Plato says only that all the classes in the state contribute to the state's temperance, which implies nothing about the temperance of individuals.[14]

This interpretation is supported by the fact that there is a decisively darker side to Plato's psychological treatment of the Producers: 'the greatest number and variety of desires and pleasures and pains is generally to be found in children and women and slaves, and in the less respectable majority of free men',[15] the philosopher writes in 431b–c. In the psychological and sociological typology of the *Republic*, the 'majority of free men' corresponds of course to the Producers. The passage quoted occurs in the context of the examination of temperance in the city and thus its significance is not merely psychological, but political as well. What it underlines is the difficulty of making the Producers recognise the superiority of the Guardians. In order to achieve this, they have to overcome their deeply-rooted tendency to be dominated by their desires and pleasures. But this tendency, as we discover with the unfolding of Plato's psychology, is neither an accidental nor a peripheral element of their moral character; it is built into it as its most fundamental characteristic. This being the case, the rationality which they can demonstrate by their temperance can only be severely limited; and the freedom which is allowed them is not the substantial freedom of checking the Guardians' power, with the latter depending on their continuous consent, but rather the nominal freedom of accepting the Guardians' authority in an acquiescent way which, as Cross and Woozley explain, does not necessarily involve real freedom:

> [i]t is fairly clear that [Plato] regarded it as [the Producers'] business to stay in their place and get on with their jobs, leaving the job of government to better and wiser men. There is no suggestion that the Guardians rule because the Economic Class allow them to rule. It is not over-cynical to conclude that Plato thought it was more important that the most competent men should rule than that less competent men should have any say in deciding who should rule; and that the freedom accorded to the Economic Class was an exceedingly limited or even spurious freedom, the freedom which they would be allowed

only for so long as they used it in the way which Plato wanted. There is very little doubt what would become of their freedom, if they showed any signs of getting out of line.[16]

The expression *ton eleutheron legomenon* (431c2) strongly supports this interpretation: literally, it means that common people are free in name only.

Leaving political freedom aside for a moment, one has to remark that psychological freedom is not attributed to the third class either. As Muller has shown, in the *Republic* Plato operates with a notion of freedom which involves the acceptance of the authority of reason and the absence of subordination to an external principle.[17] But this type of freedom can only be achieved by those who conceive and comprehend reason, the philosopher-rulers. This is why Plato remarks in 590c that manual workers 'must be "enslaved" to the best man who has a divine ruler within himself.'[18] As this passage demonstrates, all the attractive talk about concord notwithstanding, the third class remains ethically heteronomous and in constant need of moral control. The choice of 'slave,' despite the very strong negative connotations of the word which would be immediately striking to the Greek reader, is indicative of Plato's refusal to take seriously the possibility of a moral autonomy—however limited—of the Producers. Significantly, this passage, to which we shall return soon, culminates with a reference to a rule and a concord (590d6) preserved by external force. It thus vindicates the interpretation that the Producers are invested neither with the virtue of temperance nor with political freedom, and, in consequence, that their freedom cannot be regarded as going beyond a passive acceptance—at the very best—of their betters' rule.

As for the rationality of the third class, it is in fact an open question whether in the framework of Plato's psychological scheme the Producers, who are by definition ruled by their desires, can display any rationality at all. Given the city-soul analogy (435b), appetite is the dominant element in their souls (see also 590c). In his definition of temperance in the soul, Plato claims that the latter will be temperate if the appetitive part is willingly subjected to the rule of reason (442c–d). But this presupposes the existence of a reasoning part within the appetitive part itself. Cross and Woozley argue that this is an untenable position, for attributing a reasoning part to the appetitive part can only be defended if one assigns 'to *each* of the elements of the soul three sub-elements of reason, spirit and appetite' and this 'would make nonsense of Plato's whole psychology, and it would lead to a vicious regress.'[19] Strictly speaking, their claim is not true. Plato's argument does not lead necessarily to an infinite regress, because the argument does not require a multiplication of all of the three elements in each part of the soul. It only demands that the appetitive part is assigned a reasoning capacity and this could be considered a peculiar case.[20] But the authors are right in essence, because even if that much is conceded to Plato, his position remains untenable. In 436a ff., it is *exactly* the antithesis of desire and reason that Plato uses to posit different parts of the soul. This entails that the assumption of a rationally behaving appetitive part is absolutely incompatible with the way Plato's psychological model is set up, and can only lead to the collapse of this model. Given the distinction between reason and appetite in Book Four,[21] an appetitive part ruled by a reasoning sub-part within it cannot be regarded as an appetitive part anymore. It is quite simply a contradiction in terms.[22]

The core of Plato's problem is that, if the third class is irrational, there can be no possibility of harmony in his state, whereas if it is rational, even to a limited extent, its absolute exclusion from any form of political participation cannot be justified. The picture of an irrational third class is incompatible with the possibility of a harmonious state ruled by amicable agreement, because harmony depends on concord between the citizens and consent on the issue of who is to rule. But without at least some rationality on the part of the labouring class neither of those can come into being. If, on the other hand, too much faith is placed in the rationality and the moral qualities of the Producers, Plato's political argument is seriously undermined. Since rationality and virtue—the two being inextricably linked[23]—constitute the fundamental attributes which legitimise political authority in the *Republic*, the greater the extent to which the Producers 'possess' those attributes, the greater the potentiality of their laying a claim to power becomes.[24] Plato's presentation of justice is a good example of this. Like temperance, justice is a relationship between classes, but not a property of all three classes. If the latter was the case, and, given that justice is the central virtue which brings into being and preserves the other virtues (433b), the Producers would be put on an ethical stance high enough to enable them to make a claim to power. They would have no technical claim, since politics demands expertise and they lack wisdom; but they would have a strong moral claim in that they would 'own' the principal virtue, justice. So, on the one hand, Plato blocks this moral claim by refusing to call them just. But, on the other, if the state is to be based on consent and not on sheer force, the Producers have to be somehow part of the justice of the state. By putting forward justice and temperance as relations between classes, Plato attempts to achieve both objectives.

The assertion that Plato does not attribute any sort of virtue to the Producers is decisively supported by two subsequent passages in the *Republic*. The first is 495b–e. Here Plato declares that when philosophy is abandoned by 'its true lovers,' it is taken over by 'a whole crowd of squatters [who] sally out from the meaner trades,' because philosophy 'still retains a far higher reputation than other occupations, a reputation that these stunted natures being as cramped and crushed by their mechanical lives as their bodies are deformed by manual trades.' What the philosopher declares here, and in the most unmistakable language, is that philosophy (i.e. the intellectual activity on which the full virtue of the Guardians is absolutely dependent) is not appropriate for anybody involved in manual labour, because such people have by nature a fundamental moral deficiency. This passage not only denies manual workers the full virtue of the Guardians, but goes further in refusing to allow them even the partial virtue that a superficial reading of 431a ff. might suggest. The definition of temperance in both the state (432a) and the individual (442c–d) involves a harmonious agreement between their respective three elements. It is evident that a deformed and amputated soul cannot be expected to achieve this type of agreement. Given that the typical social property of the Producers is that they engage in manual activities, it becomes clear that the deformity of their souls precludes the possibility that they could ever achieve even a single virtue like temperance.[25] Moreover, if one accepted that Plato attributes temperance to all the Producers individually, one would in all probability have to allow for the Producers to 'possess' justice as well, since this virtue is defined in terms remarkably similar to temperance and it is the second virtue which depends on the relationship between the classes. But it is absurd to suggest that a deformed soul can achieve justice, the highest virtue of the *Republic* and the one which brings about and preserves all the others (433b). Consequently, 495b–e has to be accepted as indubitably ruling out the possibility of the Producers individually possessing either justice or temperance.

The second passage which fortifies the conclusion that the Producers are credited with no virtue in the *Republic* is 590c, where Socrates asks '[a]nd why do we despise manual work as vulgar?' and goes on to answer his own question: '[i]sn't it because it indicates a certain weakness in our higher nature, which is unable to control the animal part of us, and can only serve and learn how to pander it?' This passage has striking similarities with 495b–e: it connects virtue (or rather the lack of it) with manual labour and it asserts that the incompatibility of the two is founded on nature. The difference between them is that in 590c Plato makes a reference to the rational and the desiring parts of the soul and, therefore, this passage explicitly falls within the framework of his psychological scheme. The typical psychological characteristic of the Producers, Plato asserts, is that they are dominated by the lowest part of their soul, that they are incapable of controlling their appetite. But in a philosophical work where virtue is defined as the domination of the better elements of oneself over the worse,[26] domination by one's animal desires and virtue can only be mutually exclusive. It is therefore obvious that the characterisation of the Producers by the domination of the irrational part in their souls irrevocably rules out any suggestion that they might possess any individual virtue.

Furthermore, it is the Producers' lack of virtue which sanctions the possible use of repressive measures against them. Plato's definition of temperance in the city represents his attempt to achieve rule by consent. Despite the incompatibility of coercion and the ideal character of his state, however, Plato is explicit on the question of force. When he discusses the relationship between appetite (the dominant element in the souls of the Producers), spirit (which characterises the Auxiliaries) and reason (which typifies the Guardians) Plato's language leaves little doubt about what means will be employed to control the desiring part of the soul: it is full of military analogies suggesting force: *polemein* (440a5), *stasiazontoin* (440b3), *symmachon* (440b3), *stasei* (440e5), *tithesthai ta opla* (440e5), *symmacho* (441e6), *katadoulosasthai* (442b1), *polemious* (442b5), *propolemoun* (442b7), *stasiazontin* (442d1).[27] The accumulation of such an extraordinary number of military analogies in the space of less than three Stephanus pages leaves little doubt about Plato's recommendations. Provided that the Producers accept their social role voluntarily, the use of force is unnecessary. If they do not, however (and Plato's insistence on force in the passages just mentioned demonstrates how seriously he takes this possibility), it is unreservedly sanctioned by Plato. And any remaining doubts on the issue are finally dissolved by what the philosopher states in three other passages.

The first is 414b, where he writes that part of the Auxiliaries' duties will be 'to see that friends at home shall not wish . . . to harm our state' (one should notice the euphemistic use of 'friends').

The second is 415d–e, where he declares that the Guardians should camp on a spot enabling them to 'control those within'.[28] The use of the verb *katechoien* here plainly reveals Plato's intentions: in this context, the verb designates the type of military occupation usually imposed on an external enemy.[29]

Third, there is the already noted passage in 590d: 'wisdom and control should, if possible, come from within; failing that it must be imposed from without, in order that, being under the same guidance, we may all be friends and equals.' This phrase is indeed exceptional in that it refers to a friendship created by force. Occurring towards the end of Book Nine, and given that the last Book is some kind of excursus, this final acceptance of force as a legitimate means of controlling the Producers[30] clearly demonstrates Plato's ultimate failure to reconcile his wish for social equality[31] and friendship with his low opinion of the moral qualities of the Producers.[32]

Unlike the Producers, who have no virtue, the Guardians possess all four virtues and therefore virtue in its entirety. The virtue which typifies them is wisdom. The whole city is wise because of the wisdom of its Guardians (428d). The Guardians also possess bravery, and, despite the fact that it is the Auxiliaries' military dexterity which makes the city brave (429b ff.), the bravery of the Guardians is superior to that of the Auxiliaries because it is grounded on reason, not merely on right opinion. The Guardians are temperate *par excellence*, because they are the class in whose souls reason is dominant over the other two elements. Exactly because this part, which is concerned with 'the whole [soul]' (441e), is in command in their souls, the Guardians are also just and have the right to rule the city.

The underlying assumptions of the *Republic's* theory of virtue (though not its metaphysical justification) can be identified as Socratic. The idea that the Guardians have perfect virtue and the Producers no virtue at all squares with the Socratic belief in the unity of virtue which is forcefully expressed in the *Protagoras*. In this dialogue, the unity of virtue centres upon the idea of wisdom or knowledge. Socrates argues that knowledge is necessary and sufficient for virtue and therefore no one can willingly act wrongly, because that would be equivalent to acting against one's better judgement. It follows that one either has knowledge and thus virtue as a whole, or has no virtue at all. In the *Republic*, although the possibility of someone acting against reason's commands is now acknowledged,[33] the cardinal position of wisdom is guaranteed by the fact that Plato presents knowledge as the quality which is indispensable to the achievement of virtue. Since justice is the highest virtue which brings into existence and preserves all the others (433b) and since one cannot be truly just without knowledge of the Form of Justice, and, even further, knowledge of the Form of the Good, knowledge remains absolutely essential for full virtue. (In grounding ethical knowledge on a transcendent basis, Plato goes of course beyond Socrates, since the latter did not introduce Forms in his ethical argument. Nevertheless, Plato's metaphysical theory is designed in such a way as to support the Socratic assertion that virtue presupposes knowledge).[34] The suggestion that there is one class which possesses knowledge and hence has all individual virtues and virtue as a whole and another which has no real knowledge and thus no virtue at all stems exactly from this assertion. It means that virtue is not compartmentalised so that someone might have one virtue without having all the others.[35]

But what about the Auxiliaries? Though they definitely lack wisdom, which is the exclusive property of the Guardians, as can be safely extracted from 428c–429a, they might still 'possess' bravery. Plato states in 429b that the city will be brave 'with sole reference to the part which defends it and campaigns for it' and that the bravery or cowardice of the other classes except for the Auxiliaries are irrelevant to the city's bravery. Given the principle that a city has a virtue when the part in it for which it is appropriate to have this virtue has it, and, moreover, given that a brave army can consist only of—at least a majority of—brave soldiers, it seems to follow that the Auxiliaries are individually brave. In this case the reciprocity and thus the unity of the virtues appears to be abandoned: the Auxiliaries have at least one virtue, bravery, while lacking at least one other, wisdom.

A detailed examination of Plato's presentation of the Auxiliaries, however, does not confirm this picture. In fact, as the argument proceeds, Plato seems to suggest not that individual Auxiliaries are positively brave, but rather that they can be relied upon to demonstrate, even in the most adverse circumstances, courageous behaviour. This result is achieved through their education, whose

> whole object was to steep them in the spirit of our laws like a dye, so that nature and nurture might combine to fix in them indelibly their convictions about what is dangerous, and about all other topics, and prevent them being washed out by those most powerful detergents, pleasure . . . and pain and fear and desire, the most effective of all. This kind of ability to retain safely in all circumstances a judgement about what is to be feared, which is correct and in accord with law, is what I propose to call courage (430a–b).

But is this correct judgement by itself sufficient for the acquisition of bravery, as this part of the text might be taken to imply? The answer is no. '[W]on't those two elements [the reasoning and the *thymoeidic* parts of the soul] be the defence that mind and body have against external enemies? One of them will do the thinking, the other will fight *under the orders of its superiors* and provide the courage to carry its decisions into effect,' Plato writes in 442b. What this passage makes clear is that the Auxiliaries' bravery, which originates in the *thymoeidic* element in their souls, will count as a virtue only if activated under proper authority. Otherwise, it is conceivable that the Auxiliaries may use their courage in the service of an evil cause, in which case it would not, of course, count as a virtue. Left to their own intellectual resources, Callipolis' soldiers cannot be trusted to demonstrate virtuous behaviour under all circumstances. To put it another way, they are not morally autonomous. Even if they can, through their [ορθ`η δόξα, correctly assess danger and stand up to it, they still need the political elucidation of the knowledgeable Guardians to tell them in what situations they ought to use their bravery. So, even if the Auxiliaries can be safely expected to show courage under any conditions, no confidence can be placed in them as far as deciding how to employ their courage is concerned.[36] To give a simple example, the city will need the Auxiliaries' brave behaviour in war, but it will be the Rulers who decide whether it should wage war in the first place.

Furthermore, in the framework of Plato's epistemology, correct opinion, unlike knowledge, can never be absolutely reliable (see chapter 6). This entails that, despite Plato's definition of bravery in terms of correct opinion in 430b, consistently virtuous behaviour cannot be grounded on opinion. As the philosopher writes in 442b–c, 'we call an individual brave because of this part of him [which] has a spirit which holds fast *to the orders of reason* about what he ought or ought not to fear, in spite of pleasure and pain.'[37] This new definition of bravery, this time in the individual, effectively effaces the impression, which might have been created in 430b, that correct opinion may be sufficient for bravery.[38] It now becomes plain that it is reason—and thus knowledge, which corresponds to it in Plato's epistemology—which defines what is fearful and what not. Spirit and reason are also clearly distinguished in this passage, with Plato stating that spirit, the typical psychological attribute of the Auxiliaries, is impotent to bring about bravery without the contribution of reason. But reason belongs exclusively to the Guardians and this means that only the latter are brave in the full sense.[39] The Auxiliaries, on their part, do not unconditionally 'possess' bravery, because all the conditions necessary for really brave behaviour are not concentrated in their *thymoeidic* souls.

Unlike the Producers, however, the Auxiliaries are recognised by Plato as having a strong potentiality for virtue. Their brave behaviour, founded on correct opinion, constitutes a first stage in the moral development of the individual, which eventually leads the most talented of them to acquire full virtue. This is demonstrated by the fact that the Guardians start their careers as Auxiliaries and are initially given an education which is based on opinion (376c ff.). In spite of the vast difference between the latter and knowledge, however, the two are continuous in the epistemology of the *Republic* (see chapter 6). This entails that the Guardians start from correct opinion and proceed to acquire knowledge. The brave behaviour of the Auxiliaries, then, though it cannot be formally considered a virtue, is not completely unrelated to virtue either. It can be regarded as a first step in the process of acquiring full virtue.

The fact that the correct opinion of the Auxiliaries is connected with knowledge and reason has one crucial consequence for the political argument of the *Republic*. Though the military class lacks the perfect knowledge of the Guardians, its members are characterised by 'love of knowledge' (376b), and thus by a philosophical disposition, and their education involves the ability to recognise reason (ëüãïí, 402a2). This is of major political significance, because given the fact that the rationality of the Producers cannot be trusted and given that the Guardians have no other physical means at their disposal for controlling the Producers except for the armed force of the Auxiliaries, this force is vital for the implementation of the Guardians' political will. Therefore, the rationality of the Auxiliaries, though substantially inferior to that of the Guardians and insufficient for the achievement of virtue in itself, is still essential for the political stability of Callipolis. It is necessary for making sure that the Auxiliaries will not disobey the Guardians or ally with the Producers against them. It is for this reason that, in his psychological scheme, Plato presents the spirited part as the 'natural ally' of reason (441a).

So far, I have argued that in the *Republic* Plato adheres to the reciprocity of the virtues, a weak form of the thesis of the unity of virtue that is. But a stronger form of this thesis is also defended in the work. In 441d–e, the philosopher states that 'each of us will be just and perform his proper function only if each part of him is performing its proper function.' This function consists in the rational part of the soul governing, the spirited part assisting it (441e) and neither the spirited nor the appetitive parts revolting against the rational part (442c–d).

Justice, then, is identified with the proper function of each part of the soul. In other words, it is identified with the right psychic order. But justice had earlier been defined as what 'makes it possible for [the other three virtues] to come into being . . . and preserves them by its continuous presence' (433b). If wisdom, bravery and temperance can only be generated and sustained by the continuous presence of justice and if justice is equated with harmonious psychic order, it follows that this psychic order becomes the common denominator of all the particular virtues and that the latter are identical in that they are features or manifestations of this harmony.[40] From this point of view, it can be asserted that the *Republic* endorses the unity of the virtues in a way which involves more than the mere reciprocity of the virtues.

In conclusion: the *Republic's* moral psychology upholds the unity of virtue. It attributes full virtue to the Guardians, a strong potentiality for virtue to the Auxiliaries and no actual virtue, not even the possibility of ever achieving virtue, to the Producers. The political consequences of this distribution are self-evident. They are discussed in more detail in chapter 4.

We are now in a position to assess some arguments that have been advanced in order to defend Plato from the charge of unhesitatingly prescribing the psychological and political suppression of the Producers. Such arguments can be roughly divided into two categories: those which use primarily psychological premises and those which use political ones. Here we shall evaluate some of the former, postponing examination of the latter until Plato's conception of democracy is explored more fully.

One scholar who attempted a defence of Plato on moral and psychological grounds was Demos. He argued that the cardinal virtues can be divided into two, one part involving virtues relating to institutions (one could say political virtues) and one involving virtues concerning the inner life of the individual (one could say private virtues).[41] On the basis of this distinction, Demos argued that, whereas as citizens the people of Callipolis will perform one specific function, in their private life they will 'remain whole and self-ordering.'[42] Wisdom is not only a prerogative of the philosopher-kings, because in the private realm everybody is a 'completely developed [person].'[43]

There are substantial objections which can be raised to this type of interpretation. To start with, the suggestion that somebody might have an orderly, well-balanced personality in one's private life, but be dominated by one's irrational desires in public activities is obviously a psychological implausibility. On a more formal level, the fundamental problem with Demos's thesis is that in the *Republic*, as Mulgan succinctly puts it '[t]here is no evidence for two sets of virtues; indeed, Plato clearly thinks there is only one.'[44] This objection induced Skemp to modify Demos's position. Skemp accepted that all classes share justice and temperance and conceded that 'there is one set of virtues, but their civic effect varies as between the classes.'[45] However, this is only a thinly disguised repetition of Demos's argument and amounts essentially to the same thing. Skemp does not explain how one set of virtues can produce different civic effects in different classes, and without this explanation his argument is open to the same major objections as Demos'.

A more recent attempt to show how Plato makes moral 'salvation' possible for all classes was made by Kraut.[46] Kraut draws attention to 590c, where Plato claims that manual workers are characterised by the domination of the desiring part in their souls. This is a surprising choice of text for someone who wants to defend Plato from the charge of sanctioning the oppression of the lower class, since this passage brings out most clearly the philosopher's contempt for manual work and his conception of working people as fundamentally morally deficient beings. Kraut challenges this interpretation by arguing that 'craftsmen can be trained to prefer the goals of reason to those of appetite,'[47] obviously forgetting that there is not in the whole *Republic* one word about the education of the third class.[48] He points out that the citizens of Callipolis 'are tied to each other by feelings of affection,'[49] ignoring that this affection might be imposed from without (590d, which is cited by Kraut),[50] in which case it is a self-defeating notion. He also claims that the Producers will benefit from the rule of the philosophers and explains this as follows: because the Producers are not 'intellectually gifted' and are therefore likely to 'develop appetitive values,' 'it is . . . better for the artisan if the ruler of an ideal state interferes with his natural moral growth and inculcates values other than the ones the artisan would adopt on his own.'[51] Kraut finds this intervention beneficial for the Producers, ignoring the fact that it is imposed from without and it involves a very strong element of psychological suppression. His final argument is that since an artisan can demonstrate some intelligence in learning his craft, he is not completely devoid of reason. The philosopher-ruler takes advantage of this fact and installs in the artisan's soul a rule similar (though on a lower plane) to his own.[52] This thesis is no more tenable than the previous ones. First of all, it depends on the obvious paradox of the idea that the Producers benefit from giving away any claim to self-determination. Second, it is completely incompatible with Plato's thesis that manual work inadvertently deforms the soul (495d–e). But the main inadequacy of Kraut's position lies in the fact that he fails to realise that the need for the Producers to be morally 'saved' from without would not arise in the first place, if Plato did not hold such a low opinion of them. If the Producers were not the morally and intellectually depleted beings that Plato takes them to be, there would be no need for them to be assisted, or rather controlled, by the philosophers in their moral development. From the moment such a need exists, they cannot be as rational as Kraut presents them to be.

Klosko has tried to meet this objection by offering a milder defence of a Producers' virtue.[53] He draws a distinction between instrumental and normative reason and argues that all men are rational because they all have the former.[54] Given the right education, even those people in whose souls appetite is dominant can come under what he terms a 'holistic' (i.e., caring for the whole soul, not just for a part of it) rule of reason. This leads to a more harmonious and happier life.[55]

But Klosko's interpretation is as unsuccessful as Kraut's, because a number of his premises are demonstrably wrong. First of all, like Kraut, he is wrong in asserting that the Producers are given any kind of formal education. Secondly, having set up the distinction between instrumental and normative reason and having made the claim that the Producers are to some extent rational and therefore virtuous because they 'possess' the former, Klosko disregards the essential difference between the two. Instrumental reason, like Hume's 'reason,' is concerned only with means. It is the sort of reason that a robber uses in planning his next attack. Therefore, in attributing this type of calculating ability to all people, Plato does not clear the ground for crediting them with any virtue.[56] He simply acknowledges an empirical psychological fact. Platonic reason proper, what Klosko terms normative reason, involves this type of reasoning, but is not typified by it. It is characterised by reason's self-motivation in setting its own aims. Only when controlled by the aims of normative reason does instrumental reason lead to virtue. So, the presence of instrumental reason in the Producers' souls does not by any means guarantee that the Guardians can inculcate in their souls a rational order. This would entail that the Producers abandon their own preferences and cease to be dominated by their instinctive desires. But it is precisely this domination which constitutes the essence of what it is to be a Producer in the *Republic's* psychological scheme.

The idea that the Producers' possession of instrumental reason can furnish the basis for a psychological transformation in them which would lead them to care for the whole soul more than they care for the gratification of their desires ought to be rejected for one more reason. To the extent that the Producers undergo this transformation, they become rational, even if only on a limited scale. Why, then, does Plato unequivocally deny them even the most elementary forms of political participation, instead of permitting them a limited political role corresponding to their limited rationality? The discrepancy between Plato's psychology and his politics becomes in this case inexplicable.

Since both the unity of virtue and the assertion that knowledge is necessary for virtue are endorsed in the *Republic*, the possibility of conquering virtue without normative reason does not exist. Given that Plato categorically denies the possibility that the Producers can ever achieve this highest type of reason, a fact acknowledged by Klosko himself,[57] it becomes plain that the ordinary citizens of Callipolis cannot achieve any type of virtue at all.[58]

Endnotes

1   Translation after Cornford.

2   See Crombie, *Plato's Doctrines*, vol. 1, p. 90; Clay, 'Reading the *Republic*,' p. 25; Pradeau, *Platon et la Cité*, p. 34.

3   The fact that in the *Republic* Plato views politics as being concerned with the elimination of conflict is demonstrated both by his repeated affirmation of the importance of political unity (e.g. 422e–423b, 465b, 545c–d, 551d) and by his definition of temperance—which has to do with the relationship between citizen classes and is therefore a political virtue *par excellence*—as agreement on the issue of who is to rule.

4   The fact that Callipolis emerges out of the inevitability of war is another strong indication that in the *Republic* Plato tries to address real-life politics and not an idealised version of it, which would be irrelevant to the reality of the fourth-century BC.

5   Craig, *The War Lover*, p. 7, rightly points out that 'in meeting this need [for guardians], there are obvious alternatives to a professional standing army. None, however, is considered.' Although in the framework of the *Republic* Plato's choice of a professional army can be justified on the basis of the specialisation principle, introduced earlier by Socrates, the fact remains that this choice is indicative of the philosopher's aristocratic inclinations. Even if exceptions to the rule were possible, in general professional armies were typical of aristocratic cities following the Spartan model, whereas democracies relied on their citizens taking up arms in case of war. Plato actually endorses the latter model for his second-best city of the *Laws*.

6   See also 431c–d, 491a–b and 503d. Annas, *Introduction*, p. 113, suggests that Plato 'commits himself without argument to the anti-democratic thesis that the citizens with the wisdom that will make it well-governed will be the smallest class in the city.' Plato would have substantiated his position, in her opinion, only if he had proved that most people—and the people who work for a living in particular—are incapable of looking beyond their private interests, towards the interest of society as a whole. Annas is certainly right in that Plato nowhere presents a specific argument in support of the claim that wisdom will belong only to a few individuals. But, on the other hand, it has to be noted that his insistence on the exclusiveness of knowledge is not an incidental characteristic of the *Republic*, briefly discussed in Book Four. It is an intrinsic part of his overall argument. It is repeated a number of times in the dialogue and it is absolutely vital for the shaping of its political theory. As for the fact that Plato does not feel the need to argue specifically for it in 428e–429a, two things can be said in his defence. First, as Annas herself points out, the thesis under discussion is pertinent to the *Republic's* psychological scheme. In 495e and in 590c Plato emphasises that manual work irrevocably and irreversibly deforms and destroys the soul. It follows that people involved in this type of labour—i.e. the majority of people—can never achieve an important form of virtue like wisdom (or, indeed, any other kind of virtue). Second, Plato has a better understanding of economic matters than he is usually credited for. Given the economic structure of the *Republic*, where the Guardians and the Auxiliaries are sustained on the labour of the Producers, the higher classes must not consist of too many members, because otherwise the economic system of the *Republic* would become too obviously dysfunctional.

7   In the *Republic*, Plato abandons the Craft Analogy (i.e., the idea that virtue presupposes knowledge of a kind analogous to the expertise of the craftsman). He is obliged to do so by the fact that the craftsman's knowledge belongs to the sensible world and is therefore different from the metaphysical knowledge which in the *Republic* becomes the ultimate justification of political authority. Thus, the Craft Analogy is nowhere used after the end of Book One, with one exception (488a ff.) which can be explained (see chapter 4). Nevertheless, Plato retains the anti-democratic implications of the Socratic argument by insisting that metaphysical knowledge, like the artisan's expertise, is to be found only in a small minority of people.

8   My translation.

9   Cross and Woozley, *Plato's Republic*, p. 105. The authors concede, however, that Plato's 'conclusions as to the nature of justice, although invalidly reached, might still be correct.'

10   Vlastos, 'Justice and Happiness,' p. 76.

11   Ibid.

12   The question whether the Platonically just individual, whose justice depends on having the right psychic order, will also necessarily be just in the common sense of the word was asked by Sachs, 'A Fallacy in Plato's *Republic*.' Sachs argues that Socrates does not prove to his interlocutors that the commonly just individual is the happiest, but only that the Platonically just individual is. Given that the former proposition is what Socrates sets out to prove, this 'fallacy of irrelevance . . . wrecks the *Republic's* main argument' (p. 35). Sachs rightly asserts that in order to connect Platonic and common justice, Plato 'must prove that the conduct of his just man also conforms to the ordinary or vulgar canons of justice' and that 'his conception of the just man applies to—is exemplified by—every man who is just according to the vulgar conception'. But, in his opinion, 'Plato met neither requirement' (p. 46). He only asserted, without argument, that his just individual would abstain from deeds commonly held to be unjust.

Apart from Vlastos' argument discussed in the text, many attempts have been made to repudiate Sachs' argument, but none has been entirely successful. Demos, 'A Fallacy in Plato's *Republic*?', pp. 52–56, suggests that Plato is not guilty, strictly speaking, of a fallacy, but he admits that there is a gap in his argument (p. 54). Even if he is technically correct, though, the essence of Sachs' position is not affected, since the question is whether there is a connection between Platonic and common justice or not, and the gap in the argument means, of course, that this connection is not established beyond doubt. Demos readily concedes this point (p. 55). Irwin, *Plato's Ethics*, p. 259, argues that the moral argument of the *Republic* invites the picture of a Platonically just individual who is concerned with the benefit of others. This provides a link between Platonic justice, which is essentially a state of the soul, and ordinary justice, which is concerned with the relationships between individuals. But Irwin agrees that Plato does not answer all the relevant questions (p. 261) and, thus, even if his argument is correct, the connection between the two types of justice is not proved beyond dispute. Smith, 'Plato's Cave,' pp. 189–92, argues that Plato takes pains to establish a close relationship between the 'vulgar' and the Platonic conceptions of justice, but that he could never satisfy Sachs' demand of equivalence between the two: the conception of 'vulgar' justice is incoherent and, thus, equivalence would make the Platonic conception of justice incoherent, too. Nevertheless, if what Plato shows is that the Platonically just individual achieves happiness, and if there is no equivalence between the two conceptions of justice, then Socrates has not proven that common justice brings happiness. In this case, Sachs' position holds.

Schipper, *Forms in Plato's Later Dialogues*, p. 113, argues that 'Thrasymachus and Socrates both refer their conception to the same kind of acts which are commonly (if only provisionally) reputed to be just' and that 'those acts not only can be, but in some cases are, shown to be those of a "Platonically just" man.' But even if both points are conceded, Sachs is not refuted, because to say that Plato expects his just individual to be just in the common sense of the term—as he evidently does—is one thing; to prove it quite another. Annas, 'Plato and Common Morality', p. 451, finds the difficulty lying not 'in any simple fallacy,' but in the ambivalence of Plato's theory of justice as a whole. She agrees, however, that Sachs' assumption is not implausible (p. 450). Finally, Kraut's attempt to repudiate Sachs' argument ('Reason and Justice') is unsuccessful, because it depends on an interpretation of the *Republic's* moral psychology which, as I argue in this chapter, is untenable.

13   The assumption that Plato attributes temperance—and probably also justice—to the Producers is shared by Vlastos, 'The Evidence of Aristotle and Xenophon,' pp. 88–89 and n. 30; Pradeau, *Platon et la Cité*, p. 71; Rice, *Guide*, p. 58; Mulgan, 'Individual and Collective Virtues', pp. 84–85; Kahn, 'Unity of the Virtues', p. 32; Rosen, 'Σωφροσύνη', p. 627; Boger, 'Plato and Protagoras', p. 34; Ostenfeld, 'Eudaimonia', p. 78; and Lane, 'Plato, Popper, Strauss', p. 131.

14   Irwin, *Plato's Moral Theory*, p. 329, n. 26. See also Irwin, *Plato's Ethics*, pp. 230–31.

[15] The use of *phauloi* here is interesting, because the word designates the low-born, as opposed to the *chrestoi*, the well-born who enjoyed social prestige (see Connor, *The New Politicians*, pp. 88–89).

[16] Cross and Woozley, *Plato's Republic*, pp. 108–109.

[17] Muller, *La Doctrine Platonicienne*, p. 132.

[18] Grube's translation.

[19] Cross and Woozley, *Plato's Republic*, p. 124.

[20] On this point I am in agreement with Moline, 'The Complexity of the Psyche,' p. 24. Moline also notes Plato's use of the term *eide* when he refers to parts of the soul and suggests that the affinity between the Forms, which are also called *eide*, and the parts of the soul is that both are 'pure.' The former are pure in that they do not accept anything incompatible with themselves (for example the Form of equality can never accept inequality), the latter in that they are 'constant in their priorities' (p. 25). What Moline does not sufficiently explain, however, is how that purity is to be conceived in the case of the appetitive part, which, by his own admission, is subject to internal conflict (p. 24).

[21] The beastly and irrational character of the desires of the appetitive part is repeatedly underlined throughout the *Republic* (439b–d, 442a, 590c; cf. 586a–b). In 588c, the appetitive part is likened to a 'many-headed sort of beast' and in 589b it is treated as a vegetable (the rational man acts towards it 'like a farmer, nursing and cultivating its tamer elements and preventing the wilder ones growing'). It is true that in his exposition of temperance Plato presents the desires as susceptible to rational exhortation (e.g. 432a). What he does not explain, however, is how a part which is typified by irrationality could ever come to behave rationally by itself.

[22] Williams, 'City and Soul,' p. 199, calls the assumption that the desiring part has a rational part of its own an 'absurdity.' For the substantial problems involved in this assumption, see also Bobonich, 'Akrasia and Agency,' pp. 14–17.

[23] Although Plato goes beyond Socrates in recognising non-cognitive components in virtue, he does not in essence repudiate the unity of virtue in the *Republic*. This entails that wisdom remains a *sine qua non* for virtue as a whole. See below in this chapter.

[24] The incompatibility of the idea that the Producers are morally autonomous with the prescription that the Guardians should exercise absolute political control in the city is pointed out by Taylor, 'Plato's Totalitarianism,' p. 295:

> [e]ither [the Producers] have a coherent scheme of values, and are capable of organizing their lives in the light of it, or left to themselves they are merely a prey to their unco-ordinated, short-term bodily desires. In the latter case they can provide no direction to their lives, and must therefore be externally directed for their own good; but since they can make no autonomous choices at all, *a fortiori* they cannot autonomously choose to be directed by the guardians. If, on the other hand, they can direct their own lives in the light of their values, why do they need to be subject in every detail of their lives to the control of the guardians?

[25] One might object here that farming was not always included in the *banausic* activities (see for example Xenophon, *Oeconomicus* 4.3–4 and 5.1–17) and that given that a substantial number of the Producers would have to be farmers in order to provide food for the other classes, Plato's argument about βαναυσK2α does not refer to them. However, not only is there not in the *Republic* the slightest hint that Plato wants to differentiate between farmers and the rest of the Producers, but in 415a he explicitly groups them together (415a6–7). Moreover, in the *Timaeus*, Socrates starts the recapitulation of the *Republic's* political arrangements by emphasising the separation of 'the farmers and the other craftsmen from the defence forces' (17c). Therefore, the argument about the deformed souls of the manual workers covers the whole of the Producers, farmers and artisans alike.

[26] See 430e–431d.

[27] The word *polemein* and its cognates mean to fight at war; *stasis*, a politically important word, means civil war; a *symmachos* is an ally at war; *Tithesthai ta hopla* means to take up arms; finally, *katadoulosasthai*, 'to be enslaved,' designates either metaphorically the loss of a city-state's political independence, or literally the selling of a defeated population. In the Greek world, either misfortune could only be the outcome of war.

[28] Grube's translation.

[29] Interestingly enough, in the *Politics* 1264a24–27 Aristotle writes that if the Guardians have common family and goods and the Producers do not, '[t]here will inevitably be two states in one, and those states will be opposed to one another—the guardians being made into something of the nature of an army of occupation and the farmers, artisans, and others being given the position of ordinary civilians.' The use of the term 'army of occupation' clearly demonstrates that Aristotle takes for granted the possibility of force being used against the Producers.

[30] Further evidence that Plato does not rule out the possibility of the Auxiliaries using force against the Producers is furnished by the summary of the main points of the *Republic* which occurs in the opening pages of the *Timaeus*: in 17d, Socrates explicitly states that 'those whose duty it was to defend the community would be its sole guardians against threats of injury, whether external or internal.'

[31] Social equality does not mean for Plato that all are equal. It means that everyone gets his due. More on this issue in chapter 3.

[32] The same conclusion is reached, on a different basis, by Williams, 'City and Soul,' p. 199. Rice, 'Plato on Force,' examines some of the interpretations of Plato's two definitions of temperance that have been proposed by commentators and concludes that there is a major inconsistency between Plato's psychology and his political sociology, which entails that the use of force cannot be ruled out.

[33] See Leontius' and Odysseus' cases (439e ff.).

[34] However, the assertion that knowledge is sufficient for virtue is now dropped, since the possibility of *akrasia* is accepted. Thus, in the *Republic's* ethical theory, temperance and, along with it, justice are also required to secure that reason will not be impeded by the other two psychic elements and that the individual will act on the basis of his or her knowledge.

[35] For an analysis of the reasons why Plato's recognition of non-cognitive components of virtue, and the consequent rejection of Socrates' denial of *akrasia*, does not lead to a rejection of the reciprocity of the virtues, see Irwin, *Plato's Ethics*, pp. 224–29; cf. also Reeve, *Philosopher-Kings*, p. 243.

[36] It is for this reason that Plato likens Callipolis' soldiers to 'well-bred watch-dog[s]' in 375a. Like watch-dogs, they are effective in their guarding duties, but they must always act on the orders of their masters.

[37] My emphasis.

[38] Kahn, who accepts that the Auxiliaries are individually brave ('Unity of the Virtues', p. 32), is perplexed by the fact that opinion is not mentioned in 442c (p. 38, n. 5). But this omission is quite deliberate on Plato's part. The philosopher wants to deny the possibility that real bravery might be grounded on opinion.

[39] Although the Auxiliaries are not completely devoid of reason (see below in this chapter), their rationality is limited. According to Gill, 'Education of Character,' p. 9, their education 'involves the use of reason, but reason only in a passive and unanalytic sense.' '[A]ctive, analytic reason' remains an attribute of the Guardians.

[40] In this paragraph, I take the 'unity of virtue' to entail identity of reference and not identity of meaning. In other words, Socrates' position is that the different names of individual virtues refer to the same thing—the psychological state which produces virtuous actions; it is not that they mean exactly the same thing. I think that the former is the most plausible way to understand the unity of virtue in both the *Protagoras* and the *Republic*. To suggest that when claiming that all virtues are one, Socrates claims that the terms referring to them are synonymous would create two serious, if not insurmountable, difficulties: first, this assumption is too obviously counter-

intuitive; second, and more significantly, Socrates would then have to explain why we use many different terms to designate the same thing. But no such attempt is made in either dialogue. The case for this interpretation is convincingly argued by Penner, 'Unity of Virtue.'

41 Demos, 'Paradoxes in Plato's Doctrine,' pp. 167 ff.

42 Ibid., p. 170.

43 Ibid., p. 172.

44 Mulgan, 'Individual and Collective Virtues,' p. 85.

45 Skemp, 'Communal and Individual Justice,' p. 37.

46 Kraut, 'Reason and Justice.'

47 Ibid., p. 217.

48 The same criticism applies to Irwin, *Plato's Ethics,* p. 221, who claims that by conditioning itself to following the orders of the rational part, the appetitive part is given 'a place in moral education.' Klosko, 'Demotike Arete,' p. 375 and n. 25, argues that the Producers are given an education in the *Republic* on the basis of 415b–c, where the ascent of talented children from the third class to the other two classes is discussed and of 590c–591b, where Plato says that children are in need of moral control until they become rational themselves through education. But why is education necessary for the Guardians to identify gifted Producers' children? Surely, they can do it merely by observing their behaviour. And there is nothing in 590c–591b which obliges us to take the remarks there as covering the Producers' offspring.

The position that the Producers are not to receive any formal education going beyond training in their craft is argued for, in my opinion conclusively, by Reeve, *Philosopher-Kings,* pp. 186–90, who follows Hourani, 'Education,' pp. 58–60 and Guthrie, *History,* vol. 4, p. 455 and n. 2. Reeve points out, among other things, that primary education is part of a 'unified package . . . designed to turn into guardians children who already possess the natural assets requisite in good soldier-police' (p. 186); that this education involves imitation of *kaloi kagathoi* men; but the Producers' role-model cannot be such people; it should rather be obedient hard-working labourers, of whom we hear nothing (p. 187); that, in the Phoenician myth, there would be no point in the relegated guardians' children being sent away to producers and farmers if all children received the same education (p. 187); and that not only is there not a single word in the *Republic* about the Producers' children receiving education, but that no tests are devised for children to be separated in Guardians and Producers in the same way that tests exist for Guardians to be separated from those who are to remain Auxiliaries.

But the strongest evidence for the assumption that the Producers are not to receive formal education comes from three parts of the text. In 376c, at the point of introducing his educational proposals, Socrates asks: '[b]ut how are [our Guardians] to be brought up and educated?' In 456d he asks another question: '[t]hen in our imaginary state which will produce the better men—the education which we have prescribed for the Guardians or the training [in their craft] our shoemakers get?' Finally, in 496a Plato unequivocally states that manually working people are 'unfit for education' (496a5). The distinction between Guardians and Producers made in all three of those passages is so explicit that it would suffice to settle the issue even without the rest of the substantial evidence provided by Hourani (who points out the first two passages, p. 59) and Reeve (who points out the second, pp. 187–88).

49 Kraut, 'Reason and Jusice,' p. 217.

50 Ibid., p. 218.

51 Ibid.

52 Ibid., p. 221.

53 Klosko, 'Demotike Arete.'

54   Ibid., p. 372.

55   Ibid., p. 376.

56   Irwin, *Plato's Ethics,* pp. 220–21, argues that appetite might succumb to reason for reasons of prudence, i.e. because in this way it achieves greater security for the satisfaction of its desires over time. If this happens often enough, Irwin suggests, the appetitive part might reach a point where it 'may . . . form a second-order desire to do what the rational part tells it to do' (p. 221). But if the appetitive part obeys the rational part only in order to achieve long-term efficiency in the gratification of its desires, no stable psychic—and by analogy political—order can be achieved: as Irwin admits, every time one of the appetite's immediate desires is too strong, it will be inclined to disobey. As for the suggestion of a second-order desire to follow the rational part's lead, it does not lead to a vicious regress, that is a multiplication *ad infinitum* of the parts of the soul, because Irwin takes those parts basically as agents and this means that it is the whole part that has this desire rather than a sub-part within it. The problem with this specific interpretation, however, is that a desiring part that has been conditioned to behave rationally becomes *de facto* rational itself and this position is untenable in view of Plato's overall psychological model (see n. 21).

57   Klosko, 'Demotike Arete,' pp. 374 and 379. Klosko accepts that the Producers' virtue will be substantially inferior to that of the Rulers.

58   Klosko, 'Demotike Arete,' p. 363, n. 2, in addition believes that the demotic virtue of 500d is attributed to the Producers as individuals, but this assumption receives no support from the text. The Greek reads: '[t]hen if the philosopher is compelled to try to introduce the standards which he has seen there, and weave them not into himself only, but into the habits of men both in their private and public lives, will he lack the skill to produce self-discipline and justice and all the other ordinary virtues?' All that Plato claims here is that the philosopher will be the moulder of people's habits and the 'creator' (*demiourgon*, 500d6) of temperance and justice and demotic virtue. But to shape the people's habits is not equivalent to imparting virtue in them. As we know from the *Phaedo* 82c, people can be in the habit of doing the right thing without having either philosophical knowledge or intelligence—in other words they can act virtuously without being virtuous in the proper, philosophical sense of the word. And the individual virtues that Plato mentions in 500d can—and on this occasion I believe should—be understood as virtues of the city. Nothing in this passage necessitates that this statement should be read as posing a virtue individually possessed by the Producers and the careful phrasing of the last sentence, which avoids any statement made in terms of the virtue of the individual, is consistent with the way Plato talks about temperance in 431e ff. From this point of view, it supports rather than undermines the interpretation of the Republic's theory of virtue offered in this chapter.

6. Introduction to Aristotle's *Politics* Book I

Plato's model science was mathematics. Aristotle's is biology. Aristotle believes that all knowledge begins with experience and that one can arrive at universal concepts, forms, only after observing things in the material world. In other words, it is only by experiencing individual trees that one can arrive at the concept (or the form) of the tree. The form of the tree does not exist before and independently of particular trees in the sensible world.

Aristotle's interest in biology also influences his political thinking. Human beings are, in his famous phrase, 'political animals,' and therefore human communities are formed according to nature and not by convention. Aristotle thinks of the Greek city-state as the highest form of community and he believes that the city has a function in the same way that an organism does. In claiming that the city is not a conventional association between individuals willingly entering into some kind of agreement, Aristotle decisively rejects social contract theories. Moreover, his analogy of the city to an organism is clearly anti-liberal.

In the first two chapters of the First Book of the *Politics*, Aristotle establishes the biological foundation of human communities and argues that the city is created from smaller political units, the household (*oikos*) and the village. But the aim of any association is human flourishing (*eudaimonia*), and this flourishing can be achieved only in the city. From this point of view, the city is logically prior to the village and the household.

As for human flourishing, Aristotle thinks that the best life is the life of the free citizen who contributes to the well-being of his city (the political life) and has the leisure to devote himself to theoretical studies (the theoretical life). Whether Aristotle thinks of the best life as comprising both the political and the theoretical life, or if he thinks of the political life as a second-best to the absolutely best theoretical life, is a difficult question of interpretation. Nevertheless, given that the *eudaimon* citizen would probably not refuse his services to his city just to enjoy the privilege of engaging in philosophy, it is my view that the political life and the theoretical life are both components of the best life. In any case, this is a life that is possible only for a small segment of the citizen population, the leisured and well-educated aristocrats, and Aristotle, like Plato, is unapologetically antiegalitarian. Unlike Plato, however, Aristotle recognizes that there are lower forms of *eudaimonia* that are achievable by women, poorer citizens and even slaves. But, for Aristotle, none of the members of these groups could ever reach the highest form of human flourishing, the absolutely best life.

Politics

Aristotle
Translated by William Ellis, A.M.

Book I
Chapter I

As we see that every city is a society, and every society is established for some good purpose; for an apparent [Bekker 1252a] good is the spring of all human actions; it is evident that this is the principle upon which they are every one founded, and this is more especially true of that which has for its object the best possible, and is itself the most excellent, and comprehends all the rest. Now this is called a city, and the society thereof a political society; for those who think that the principles of a political, a regal, a family, and a herile government are the same are mistaken, while they suppose that each of these differ in the numbers to whom their power extends, but not in their constitution: so that with them a herile government is one composed of a very few, a domestic of more, a civil and a regal of still more, as if there was no difference between a large family and a small city, or that a regal government and a political one are the same, only that in the one a single person is continually at the head of public affairs; in the other, that each member of the state has in his turn a share in the government, and is at one time a magistrate, at another a private person, according to the rules of political science. But now this is not true, as will be evident to any one who will consider this question in the most approved method. As, in an inquiry into every other subject, it is necessary to separate the different parts of which it is compounded, till we arrive at their first elements, which are the most minute parts thereof; so by the same proceeding we shall acquire a knowledge of the primary parts of a city and see wherein they differ from each other, and whether the rules of art will give us any assistance in examining into each of these things which are mentioned.

Chapter II

Now if in this particular science any one would attend to its original seeds, and their first shoot, he would then as in others have the subject perfectly before him; and perceive, in the first place, that it is requisite that those should be joined together whose species cannot exist without each other, as the male and the female, for the business of propagation; and this not through choice, but by that natural impulse which acts both upon plants and animals also, for the purpose of their leaving behind them others like themselves. It is also from natural causes that some beings command and others obey, that each may obtain their mutual safety; for a being who is endowed with a mind capable of reflection and forethought is by nature the superior and governor, whereas he whose excellence is merely corporeal is formed to be a slave; whence it follows that the different state of master [1252b] and slave is equally advantageous to both. But there is a natural difference between a female and a slave: for nature is not like the artists who make the Delphic swords for the use of the poor, but for every particular purpose she has her separate instruments, and thus her ends are most complete, for whatsoever is employed on one subject only, brings that one to much greater perfection than when employed on many; and yet among the barbarians, a female and a slave are upon a level in the community, the reason for which is, that amongst them there are none qualified by nature to govern, therefore their society can be nothing but between slaves of different sexes. For which reason the poets say, it is proper for the Greeks to govern the barbarians, as if a barbarian and a slave were by nature one. Now of these two societies the domestic is the first, and Hesiod is right when he says, "First a house, then a wife, then an ox for the plough," for the poor man has always an ox before a household slave. That society then which nature has established for daily support is the domestic, and those who compose it are called by Charondas homosipuoi, and by Epimenides the Cretan homokapnoi; but the society of many families, which was first instituted for their lasting, mutual advantage, is called a village, and a village is most naturally composed of the descendants of one family, whom some persons call homogalaktes, the children and the children's children thereof: for which reason cities were originally governed by kings, as the barbarian states now are, which are composed of those who had before submitted to kingly government; for every family is governed by the elder, as are the branches thereof, on account of their relationship thereunto, which is what Homer says, "Each one ruled his wife and child;" and in this scattered manner they formerly lived. And the opinion which universally prevails, that the gods themselves are subject to kingly government, arises from hence, that all men formerly were, and many are so now; and as they imagined themselves to be made in the likeness of the gods, so they supposed their manner of life must needs be the same. And when many villages so entirely join themselves together as in every respect to form but one society, that society is a city, and contains in itself, if I may so speak, the end and perfection of government: first founded that we might live, but continued that we may live happily. For which reason every city must be allowed to be the work of nature, if we admit that the original society between male and female is; for to this as their end all subordinate societies tend, and the end of everything is the nature of it. For what every being is in its most perfect state, that certainly is the nature of that being, whether it be a man, a horse, or a house: besides, whatsoever produces the final cause and the end which we [1253a] desire, must be best; but a government complete in itself is that final cause and what is best. Hence it is evident that a city is a natural production, and that man is naturally a political animal, and that whosoever is naturally and not accidentally unfit for society, must be either inferior or superior to man: thus the man in Homer, who is reviled for being "without society, without law, without family." Such a one must naturally be of a quarrelsome disposition, and as solitary as the birds. The gift of speech also evidently proves that man is a more social animal than the bees, or any of the herding cattle: for nature, as we say, does nothing in vain, and man is the only animal who enjoys it. Voice indeed, as being the token of pleasure and pain, is imparted to others also, and thus much their nature is capable of, to perceive pleasure and pain, and to impart these sensations to others; but it is by speech that we are enabled to express what is useful for us, and what is hurtful, and of course what is just and what is unjust: for in this particular man differs from other animals, that he alone has a perception of good and evil, of just and unjust, and it is a participation of these common sentiments which forms a family and a city. Besides, the notion of a city naturally precedes that of a family or an individual, for the whole must necessarily be prior to the parts, for if you take away the whole man, you cannot say a foot or a hand remains, unless by equivocation, as supposing a hand of stone to be made, but that would only be a dead one; but everything is understood to be this or that by its energic qualities and powers, so that when these no longer remain, neither can that be said to be the same, but something of the same name. That a city then precedes an individual is plain, for if an individual is not in himself sufficient to compose a perfect government, he is to a city as other parts are to a whole; but he that is incapable of society, or so complete in himself as not to want it, makes no part of a city, as a beast or a god. There is then in all persons a natural impetus to associate with each other in this manner, and he who first founded civil society was the cause of the greatest good; for as by the completion of it man is the most excellent of all living beings, so without law and justice he would be the worst of all, for nothing is so difficult to subdue as injustice in arms: but these arms man is born with, namely, prudence and valour, which he may apply to the most opposite purposes, for he who abuses them will be the most wicked, the most cruel, the most lustful, and most gluttonous being imaginable; for justice is a political virtue, by the rules of it the state is regulated, and these rules are the criterion of what is right.

7. Introduction to Aristotle's *Politics* Book III

The fifth chapter of the Third Book of the *Politics* is crucial in that it settles the much debated question of Aristotle's attitude towards democracy. Aristotle recognizes that there is a distinct social group, the manually working potential citizens called *banausics*, who are accepted as citizens in some constitutions (the democracies), but not in others (the aristocracies). In a crucial statement, he writes that 'the best city will not make a *banausic* a citizen.' Given that, according to his own analysis, it is the inclusion or non-inclusion of this particular group into the citizen-body that defines the character of the constitution, it follows that Aristotle is not a pro-democratic thinker, as it is sometimes assumed.

In the eleventh chapter of the same book, Aristotle gives his famous 'summation argument':

> it seems proper to prove, that the supreme power ought to be lodged with the many, rather than with those of the better sort, who are few; and also to explain what doubts (and probably just ones) may arise: now, though not one individual of the many may himself be fit for the supreme power, yet when these many are joined together . . . they may be better qualified for it than those; and this not separately, but as a collective body;

Prima facie, this looks like an endorsement of majority rule and, ultimately, of democracy, and it has actually been interpreted this way. Robinson, one of the experts on Aristotle's *Politics*, thinks that it 'expounds an important consideration in favor of democracy, including our kind of democracy as well as Aristotle's.' But does it?

There are a few remarks which are relevant at this point:

1. Aristotle says only that 'the many' 'may' be wiser than the few. But only the assertion that any large group is *always* wiser than a small one would signify unconditional espousal of democracy, and Aristotle never says this.
2. The 'summation argument' does not legitimize the opening of administrative positions to all citizens, as required by the ancient democracy (this crucial point is made by Keyt).

3. In the remainder of this chapter Aristotle claims that it is unsafe to give major officialdoms to 'the many,' because of their axiomatic *injustice* and *folly*. But the assumption that 'the many' are by definition unjust and lack practical wisdom is completely incompatible with democratic ideology, ancient or modern.

4. Aristotle claims that the 'summation argument' remains true only if the multitude does not happen to be 'brutal' (literally, 'slavish'). By the term 'brutal' Aristotle designates the *banausics*, whose inclusion in the citizen-body was used as the criterion for distinguishing democracy from aristocracy in chapter 5. This means that when he talks about the multitude in chapter 11, Aristotle does not have in mind the wide citizenship conferred by democracy, but the much narrower citizenship which is typical of oligarchic constitutions.

For all these reasons, it can be proven, by premises that Aristotle himself postulates, that the 'summation argument' does not entail support for democracy.

Politics

Aristotle
Translated by William Ellis, A.M.

Book III
Chapter V

But with respect to citizens there is a doubt remaining, whether those only are truly so who are allowed to share in the government, or whether the mechanics also are to be considered as such? for if those who are not permitted to rule are to be reckoned among them, it is impossible that the virtue of all the citizens should be the same, for these also are citizens; and if none of them are admitted to be citizens, where shall they be ranked? for they are neither [1278a] sojourners nor foreigners? or shall we say that there will no inconvenience arise from their not being citizens, as they are neither slaves nor freedmen: for this is certainly true, that all those are not citizens who are necessary to the existence of a city, as boys are not citizens in the same manner that men are, for those are perfectly so, the others under some conditions; for they are citizens, though imperfect ones: for in former times among some people the mechanics were either slaves or foreigners, for which reason many of them are so now: and indeed the best regulated states will not permit a mechanic to be a citizen; but if it be allowed them, we cannot then attribute the virtue we have described to every citizen or freeman, but to those only who are disengaged from servile offices. Now those who are employed by one person in them are slaves; those who do them for money are mechanics and hired servants: hence it is evident on the least reflection what is their situation, for what I have said is fully explained by appearances. Since the number of communities is very great, it follows necessarily that there will be many different sorts of citizens, particularly of those who are governed by others, so that in one state it may be necessary to admit mechanics and hired servants to be citizens, but in others it may be impossible; as particularly in an aristocracy, where honours are bestowed on virtue and dignity: for it is impossible for one who lives the life of a mechanic or hired servant to acquire the practice of virtue. In an oligarchy also hired servants are not admitted to be citizens; because there a man's right to bear any office is regulated by his fortune; but mechanics are, for many citizens are very rich.

There was a law at Thebes that no one could have a share in the government till he had been ten years out of trade. In many states the law invites strangers to accept the freedom of the city; and in some democracies the son of a free-woman is himself free. The same is also observed in many others with respect to natural children; but it is through want of citizens regularly born that they admit such: for these laws are always made in consequence of a scarcity of inhabitants; so, as their numbers increase, they first deprive the children of a male or female slave of this privilege, next the child of a free-woman, and last of all they will admit none but those whose fathers and mothers were both free.

That there are many sorts of citizens, and that he may be said to be as completely who shares the honours of the state, is evident from what has been already said. Thus Achilles, in Homer, complains of Agamemnon's treating him like an unhonoured stranger; for a stranger or sojourner is one who does not partake of the honours of the state: and whenever the right to the freedom of the city is kept obscure, it is for the sake of the inhabitants. [1278b] From what has been said it is plain whether the virtue of a good man and an excellent citizen is the same or different: and we find that in some states it is the same, in others not; and also that this is not true of each citizen, but of those only who take the lead, or are capable of taking the lead, in public affairs, either alone or in conjunction with others.

Book III
Chapter XI

Other particulars we will consider separately; but it seems proper to prove, that the supreme power ought to be lodged with the many, rather than with those of the better sort, who are few; and also to explain what doubts (and probably just ones) may arise: now, though not one individual of the many may himself be fit for the supreme power, yet when these many are joined together, it does not follow but they may be better qualified for it than those; and this not separately, but as a collective body; as the public suppers exceed those which are given at one person's private expense: for, as they are many, each person brings in his share of virtue and wisdom; and thus, coming together, they are like one man made up of a multitude, with many feet, many hands, and many intelligences: thus is it with respect to the manners and understandings of the multitude taken together; for which reason the public are the best judges of music and poetry; for some understand one part, some another, and all collectively the whole; and in this particular men of consequence differ from each of the many; as they say those who are beautiful do from those who are not so, and as fine pictures excel any natural objects, by collecting the several beautiful parts which were dispersed among different originals into one, although the separate parts, as the eye or any other, might be handsomer than in the picture.

But if this distinction is to be made between every people and every general assembly, and some few men of consequence, it may be doubtful whether it is true; nay, it is clear enough that, with respect to a few, it is not; since the same conclusion might be applied even to brutes: and indeed wherein do some men differ from brutes? Not but that nothing prevents what I have said being true of the people in some states. The doubt then which we have lately proposed, with all its consequences, may be settled in this manner; it is necessary that the freemen who compose the bulk of the people should have absolute power in some things; but as they are neither men of property, nor act uniformly upon principles of virtue, it is not safe to trust them with the first offices in the state, both on account of their iniquity and their ignorance; from the one of which they will do what is wrong, from the other they will mistake: and yet it is dangerous to allow them no power or share in the government; for when there are many poor people who are incapable of acquiring the honours of their country, the state must necessarily have many enemies in it; let them then be permitted to vote in the public assemblies and to determine causes; for which reason Socrates, and some other legislators, gave them the power of electing the officers of the state, and also of inquiring into their conduct when they came out of office, and only prevented their being magistrates by themselves; for the multitude when they are collected together have all of them sufficient understanding for these purposes, and, mixing among those of higher rank, are serviceable to the city, as some things, which alone are improper for food, when mixed with others make the whole more wholesome than a few of them would be.

But there is a difficulty attending this form of government, for it seems, that the person who himself was capable of curing any one who was then sick, must be the best judge whom to employ as a physician; but such a one must be himself a physician; and the same holds true in every other practice and art: and as a physician ought [1282a] to give an account of his practice to a physician, so ought it to be in other arts: those whose business is physic may be divided into three sorts, the first of these is he who makes up the medicines; the second prescribes, and is to the other as the architect is to the mason; the third is he who understands the science, but never practises it: now these three distinctions may be found in those who understand all other arts; nor have we less opinion of their judgment who are only instructed in the principles of the art than of those who practise it: and with respect to elections the same method of proceeding seems right; for to elect a proper person in any science is the business of those who are skilful therein; as in geometry, of geometricians; in steering, of steersmen: but if some individuals should know something of particular arts and works, they do not know more than the professors of them: so that even upon this principle neither the election of magistrates, nor the censure of their conduct, should be entrusted to the many.

But probably all that has been here said may not be right; for, to resume the argument I lately used, if the people are not very brutal indeed, although we allow that each individual knows less of these affairs than those who have given particular attention to them, yet when they come together they will know them better, or at least not worse; besides, in some particular arts it is not the workman only who is the best judge; namely, in those the works of which are understood by those who do not profess them: thus he who builds a house is not the only judge of it, for the master of the family who inhabits it is a better; thus also a steersman is a better judge of a tiller than he who made it; and he who gives an entertainment than the cook. What has been said seems a sufficient solution of this difficulty; but there is another that follows: for it seems absurd that the power of the state should be lodged with those who are but of indifferent morals, instead of those who are of excellent characters. Now the power of election and censure are of the utmost consequence, and this, as has been said, in some states they entrust to the people; for the general assembly is the supreme court of all, and they have a voice in this, and deliberate in all public affairs, and try all causes, without any objection to the meanness of their circumstances, and at any age: but their treasurers, generals, and other great officers of state are taken from men of great fortune and worth. This difficulty also may be solved upon the same principle; and here too they may be right, for the power is not in the man who is member of the assembly, or council, but the assembly itself, and the council, and the people, of which each individual of the whole community are the parts, I mean as senator, adviser, or judge; for which reason it is very right, that the many should have the greatest powers in their own hands; for the people, the council, and the judges are composed of them, and the property of all these collectively is more than the property of any person or a few who fill the great offices of the state: and thus I determine these points.

The first question that we stated shows plainly, that the supreme power should be lodged in laws duly made and that the magistrate or magistrates, either one or more, should be authorised to determine those cases which the laws cannot particularly speak to, as it is impossible for them, in general language, to explain themselves upon everything that may arise: but what these laws are which are established upon the best foundations has not been yet explained, but still remains a matter of some question: but the laws of every state will necessarily be like every state, either trifling or excellent, just or unjust; for it is evident, that the laws must be framed correspondent to the constitution of the government; and, if so, it is plain, that a well-formed government will have good laws, a bad one, bad ones.

8.   Introduction to Saint Augustine

Saint Augustine is a Catholic theologian who played a crucial part in the formation of the doctrines of the Catholic Church. He is also an important figure in the history of Western philosophy, because of his substantial contribution to the marriage of the Judeo-Christian religious and the Greek philosophical traditions. By his death, in the mid-fifth century AD, Catholic theology and philosophy had been to a very large extent unified, and they would be hardly distinguishable for the next thousand years.

Augustine often expresses his views in polemics, and the non-systematic character of his work, as well as the diverse influences on his thought, make his interpretation an arduous task. One of the reasons that there is no text from Augustine in this book is that it is difficult to isolate one reasonably brief text that may be treated as typical of his thinking on any particular issue.

Augustine's views are shaped by his reading of the Scripture and the Greek philosophical and rationalistic tradition, in particular Neo-Platonism. He attacks, with exceptional zeal, two religious doctrines. The first is Donatism, a grass roots movement which connects the sanctity of mysteries with the moral quality of the priests who administer them and expresses a tendency to question the authority of the Church hierarchy. The second is Pelagianism. Pelagianism maintains that original sin does not absolutely condemn humans, who may still be saved, if they follow a very strict moral code. Although Divine Grace is a useful ally in leading such a life, it is not absolutely necessary for salvation. Pelagianism, at least as understood by Augustine, implies that human beings may be saved by their own efforts. This position expresses a trust in human reason and an optimism about the human condition—ultimately stemming from Greek philosophy—which Augustine finds impossible to accept. Moreover, it tends to diminish the role of he Church in the quest for salvation, since the individual can achieve exceptional moral rectitude even without the help of the Church. Donatism is a movement of the lowest classes in North Africa, Pelagianism a current of thought popular with the Roman aristocracy. Augustine fights against both with equal tenacity.

Augustine is also famous, and rightly so, for his discussion of the problems of the human free will and the existence of evil. Both issues are closely connected with the ultimate question of salvation. The first issue, in its simplest possible form, can be formulated as follows: if God is omniscient, then he knows that I am going to be in class tomorrow morning. In what sense am I then free to go or not to go to this class? In other words, either Divine Foreknowledge is true, in which case I am not free to decide whether to go to tomorrow's class or not, or I am free to choose, but then there can be no foreknowledge of my actions. Augustine argues that foreknowledge essentially includes knowledge of the exercise of human free will: this means that God may know what I am about to do, but he does not cause me to do it. In addition, to know something in advance is not the same as to cause it. Imagine that you watch your favorite movie for the fifteenth time. You know what the protagonist will do next, but you are not the cause of his or her actions.

The question of evil is a particularly pressing one for early Christian theology. Everybody agrees that evil exists all around us. But if God created everything that exists in the world, does not this mean that he has created evil, too? But how is this possible if God is omnibenevolent? And even if he has not created it, why does he not eradicate it, since he is omnipotent? Augustine addresses the first leg of this question by using the resources of Platonic philosophy and in particular Neo-Platonism. Evil does not exist in itself, but is rather the absence of goodness. Think of Plato's famous analogy of the *Republic* Book Six. When one moves away from the sun, one encounters coldness and darkness. But it is not the sun itself which is cold and dark, it is one's distance from it which leads to these conditions. In the same way, God remains always good, but when one distances himself or herself from Him, one encounters evil. Using this Neo-Platonic notion, Augustine can explain evil without substantiating it. From a strictly philosophical point of view, evil does not exist. It is the negation of Being (which is identified with God) and therefore it is in itself not-Being, it does not exist.

On this foundation, Augustine argues that evil does not really exist in the world. Natural evils like the tsunami or an epidemic are evil only when viewed through the lens of the limited human understanding. In the wider order of things, which is known only to God, they are actually good, because they contribute to the realization of God's ultimate aims (in his late dialogues Plato maintained that absolute goodness in the world presupposes the existence of patches of evil in it, rather than the complete absence of evil). As for human evil, individual wrongful actions, they are the manifestation of the deficiency of the human will. Attracted by material goods, the will turns away from God. But unjust actions must be understood not as an evil in themselves, but rather as a failure of the will to follow the path of God and produce goodness.

Along with this solution to the problem of evil, Augustine holds a pessimistic theory of salvation. Against the Pelagians, he claims that no salvation is possible without Divine Grace. Because of the weakness of the human will, the majority of mankind are condemned to a just damnation. In the afterlife, the majority of the damned will take back their resurrected bodies, which will be eternally tortured by flames inflicting pain to the body without destroying it. This torment is eternal, but the extent of the pain is proportional to the extent of the sins committed. The small number of people undeservedly saved by God's Grace, on the other hand, live in the constant presence of God and enjoy an incredible happiness which can hardly be imagined on the basis of our earthly experience.

9. Introduction to Descartes

From late antiquity until the seventeenth century AD Western philosophy is practically identified with theology. Although secular thinking clearly re-emerges as early as the thirteenth century, it will take a long time for philosophy to become again secular and distinct from theology.

Descartes is instrumental in this change. He sets out to devise a comprehensive plan for applying mathematical methods in order to achieve perfect certainty in human knowledge. This move is the philosophical equivalent of Newton's replacement of Aristotle's qualitative physics with a new, mathematized one. Descartes' philosophy can be fully understood only in the framework of the developments of seventeenth century science. Descartes, who is one of the greatest mathematicians of his time, accepts a Copernican astronomy, although he does not make his beliefs public.

In his *Meditations on First Philosophy*, Descartes begins by questioning all previous authority, which means the scholastic interpretation of Aristotle which dominates Western thought, and attempts to ground human knowledge on the self-consciousness of the individual. This movement expresses a new spirit, secular and individualistic. After beginning with the most radical doubt, Descartes argues that there is at least one certainty, one's own existence as a thinking thing. From this basis, and using our clear and distinct ideas, it is possible to prove the existence of God, to demonstrate the reliability of reason and to prove the existence of the material world. Descartes believes that all our knowledge is *a priori*, that is intuitive, and that there is a strict dualism between mind and body. Descartes, however, ultimately fails to account for the relationship of mind and body, coming up with the unsatisfactory idea that it is through the pineal gland that the immaterial mind communicates with the body.

Meditations

René Descartes

Meditation I
Of the Things of Which We May Doubt

1. Several years have now elapsed since I first became aware that I had accepted, even from my youth, many false opinions for true, and that consequently what I afterward based on such principles was highly doubtful; and from that time I was convinced of the necessity of undertaking once in my life to rid myself of all the opinions I had adopted, and of commencing anew the work of building from the foundation, if I desired to establish a firm and abiding superstructure in the sciences. But as this enterprise appeared to me to be one of great magnitude, I waited until I had attained an age so mature as to leave me no hope that at any stage of life more advanced I should be better able to execute my design. On this account, I have delayed so long that I should henceforth consider I was doing wrong were I still to consume in deliberation any of the time that now remains for action. To-day, then, since I have opportunely freed my mind from all cares [and am happily disturbed by no passions], and since I am in the secure possession of leisure in a peaceable retirement, I will at length apply myself earnestly and freely to the general overthrow of all my former opinions.

2. But, to this end, it will not be necessary for me to show that the whole of these are false—a point, perhaps, which I shall never reach; but as even now my reason convinces me that I ought not the less carefully to withhold belief from what is not entirely certain and indubitable, than from what is manifestly false, it will be sufficient to justify the rejection of the whole if I shall find in each some ground for doubt. Nor for this purpose will it be necessary even to deal with each belief individually, which would be truly an endless labor; but, as the removal from below of the foundation necessarily involves the downfall of the whole edifice, I will at once approach the criticism of the principles on which all my former beliefs rested.

3. All that I have, up to this moment, accepted as possessed of the highest truth and certainty, I received either from or through the senses. I observed, however, that these sometimes misled us; and it is the part of prudence not to place absolute confidence in that by which we have even once been deceived.

4. But it may be said, perhaps, that, although the senses occasionally mislead us respecting minute objects, and such as are so far removed from us as to be beyond the reach of close observation, there are yet many other of their informations (presentations), of the truth of which it is manifestly impossible to doubt; as for example, that I am in this place, seated by the fire, clothed in a winter dressing gown, that I hold in my hands this piece of paper, with other intimations of the same nature. But how could I deny that I possess these hands and this body, and withal escape being classed with persons in a state of insanity, whose brains are so disordered and clouded by dark bilious vapors as to cause them pertinaciously to assert that they are monarchs when they are in the greatest poverty; or clothed [in gold] and purple when destitute of any covering; or that their head is made of clay, their body of

glass, or that they are gourds? I should certainly be not less insane than they, were I to regulate my procedure according to examples so extravagant.

5. Though this be true, I must nevertheless here consider that I am a man, and that, consequently, I am in the habit of sleeping, and representing to myself in dreams those same things, or even sometimes others less probable, which the insane think are presented to them in their waking moments. How often have I dreamt that I was in these familiar circumstances, that I was dressed, and occupied this place by the fire, when I was lying undressed in bed? At the present moment, however, I certainly look upon this paper with eyes wide awake; the head which I now move is not asleep; I extend this hand consciously and with express purpose, and I perceive it; the occurrences in sleep are not so distinct as all this. But I cannot forget that, at other times I have been deceived in sleep by similar illusions; and, attentively considering those cases, I perceive so clearly that there exist no certain marks by which the state of waking can ever be distinguished from sleep, that I feel greatly astonished; and in amazement I almost persuade myself that I am now dreaming.

6. Let us suppose, then, that we are dreaming, and that all these particulars—namely, the opening of the eyes, the motion of the head, the forth-putting of the hands—are merely illusions; and even that we really possess neither an entire body nor hands such as we see. Nevertheless it must be admitted at least that the objects which appear to us in sleep are, as it were, painted representations which could not have been formed unless in the likeness of realities; and, therefore, that those general objects, at all events, namely, eyes, a head, hands, and an entire body, are not simply imaginary, but really existent. For, in truth, painters themselves, even when they study to represent sirens and satyrs by forms the most fantastic and extraordinary, cannot bestow upon them natures absolutely new, but can only make a certain medley of the members of different animals; or if they chance to imagine something so novel that nothing at all similar has ever been seen before, and such as is, therefore, purely fictitious and absolutely false, it is at least certain that the colors of which this is composed are real. And on the same principle, although these general objects, viz., [a body], eyes, a head, hands, and the like, be imaginary, we are nevertheless absolutely necessitated to admit the reality at least of some other objects still more simple and universal than these, of which, just as of certain real colors, all those images of things, whether true and real, or false and fantastic, that are found in our consciousness (*cogitatio*), are formed.

7. To this class of objects seem to belong corporeal nature in general and its extension; the figure of extended things, their quantity or magnitude, and their number, as also the place in, and the time during, which they exist, and other things of the same sort.

8. We will not, therefore, perhaps reason illegitimately if we conclude from this that Physics, Astronomy, Medicine, and all the other sciences that have for their end the consideration of composite objects, are indeed of a doubtful character; but that Arithmetic, Geometry, and the other sciences of the same class, which regard merely the simplest and most general objects, and scarcely inquire whether or not these are really existent, contain somewhat that is certain and indubitable: for whether I am awake or dreaming, it remains true that two and three make five, and that a square has but four sides; nor does it seem possible that truths so apparent can ever fall under a suspicion of falsity [or incertitude].

9. Nevertheless, the belief that there is a God who is all powerful, and who created me, such as I am, has, for a long time, obtained steady possession of my mind. How, then, do I know that he has not arranged that there should be neither earth, nor sky, nor any extended thing, nor figure, nor magnitude, nor place, providing at the same time, however, for [the rise in me of the perceptions of all these objects, and] the persuasion that these do not exist otherwise than as I perceive them? And further, as I sometimes think that others are in error respecting matters of which they believe themselves to

possess a perfect knowledge, how do I know that I am not also deceived each time I add together two and three, or number the sides of a square, or form some judgment still more simple, if more simple indeed can be imagined? But perhaps Deity has not been willing that I should be thus deceived, for he is said to be supremely good. If, however, it were repugnant to the goodness of Deity to have created me subject to constant deception, it would seem likewise to be contrary to his goodness to allow me to be occasionally deceived; and yet it is clear that this is permitted.

10. Some, indeed, might perhaps be found who would be disposed rather to deny the existence of a Being so powerful than to believe that there is nothing certain. But let us for the present refrain from opposing this opinion, and grant that all which is here said of a Deity is fabulous: nevertheless, in whatever way it be supposed that I reach the state in which I exist, whether by fate, or chance, or by an endless series of antecedents and consequents, or by any other means, it is clear (since to be deceived and to err is a certain defect) that the probability of my being so imperfect as to be the constant victim of deception, will be increased exactly in proportion as the power possessed by the cause, to which they assign my origin, is lessened. To these reasonings I have assuredly nothing to reply, but am constrained at last to avow that there is nothing of all that I formerly believed to be true of which it is impossible to doubt, and that not through thoughtlessness or levity, but from cogent and maturely considered reasons; so that henceforward, if I desire to discover anything certain, I ought not the less carefully to refrain from assenting to those same opinions than to what might be shown to be manifestly false.

11. But it is not sufficient to have made these observations; care must be taken likewise to keep them in remembrance. For those old and customary opinions perpetually recur—long and familiar usage giving them the right of occupying my mind, even almost against my will, and subduing my belief; nor will I lose the habit of deferring to them and confiding in them so long as I shall consider them to be what in truth they are, viz., opinions to some extent doubtful, as I have already shown, but still highly probable, and such as it is much more reasonable to believe than deny. It is for this reason I am persuaded that I shall not be doing wrong, if, taking an opposite judgment of deliberate design, I become my own deceiver, by supposing, for a time, that all those opinions are entirely false and imaginary, until at length, having thus balanced my old by my new prejudices, my judgment shall no longer be turned aside by perverted usage from the path that may conduct to the perception of truth. For I am assured that, meanwhile, there will arise neither peril nor error from this course, and that I cannot for the present yield too much to distrust, since the end I now seek is not action but knowledge.

12. I will suppose, then, not that Deity, who is sovereignly good and the fountain of truth, but that some malignant demon, who is at once exceedingly potent and deceitful, has employed all his artifice to deceive me; I will suppose that the sky, the air, the earth, colors, figures, sounds, and all external things, are nothing better than the illusions of dreams, by means of which this being has laid snares for my credulity; I will consider myself as without hands, eyes, flesh, blood, or any of the senses, and as falsely believing that I am possessed of these; I will continue resolutely fixed in this belief, and if indeed by this means it be not in my power to arrive at the knowledge of truth, I shall at least do what is in my power, viz., [suspend my judgment], and guard with settled purpose against giving my assent to what is false, and being imposed upon by this deceiver, whatever be his power and artifice. But this undertaking is arduous, and a certain indolence insensibly leads me back to my ordinary course of life; and just as the captive, who, perchance, was enjoying in his dreams an imaginary liberty, when he begins to suspect that it is but a vision, dreads awakening, and conspires with the agreeable illusions that the deception may be prolonged; so I, of my own accord, fall back into the train of my former beliefs, and fear to arouse myself from my slumber, lest the time of laborious wakefulness that would

succeed this quiet rest, in place of bringing any light of day, should prove inadequate to dispel the darkness that will arise from the difficulties that have now been raised.

Meditation II
Of the Nature of the Human Mind; and that
it is More Easily Known than the Body

1. The Meditation of yesterday has filled my mind with so many doubts, that it is no longer in my power to forget them. Nor do I see, meanwhile, any principle on which they can be resolved; and, just as if I had fallen all of a sudden into very deep water, I am so greatly disconcerted as to be unable either to plant my feet firmly on the bottom or sustain myself by swimming on the surface. I will, nevertheless, make an effort, and try anew the same path on which I had entered yesterday, that is, proceed by casting aside all that admits of the slightest doubt, not less than if I had discovered it to be absolutely false; and I will continue always in this track until I shall find something that is certain, or at least, if I can do nothing more, until I shall know with certainty that there is nothing certain. Archimedes, that he might transport the entire globe from the place it occupied to another, demanded only a point that was firm and immovable; so, also, I shall be entitled to entertain the highest expectations, if I am fortunate enough to discover only one thing that is certain and indubitable.

2. I suppose, accordingly, that all the things which I see are false (fictitious); I believe that none of those objects which my fallacious memory represents ever existed; I suppose that I possess no senses; I believe that body, figure, extension, motion, and place are merely fictions of my mind. What is there, then, that can be esteemed true? Perhaps this only, that there is absolutely nothing certain.

3. But how do I know that there is not something different altogether from the objects I have now enumerated, of which it is impossible to entertain the slightest doubt? Is there not a God, or some being, by whatever name I may designate him, who causes these thoughts to arise in my mind? But why suppose such a being, for it may be I myself am capable of producing them? Am I, then, at least not something? But I before denied that I possessed senses or a body; I hesitate, however, for what follows from that? Am I so dependent on the body and the senses that without these I cannot exist? But I had the persuasion that there was absolutely nothing in the world, that there was no sky and no earth, neither minds nor bodies; was I not, therefore, at the same time, persuaded that I did not exist? Far from it; I assuredly existed, since I was persuaded. But there is I know not what being, who is possessed at once of the highest power and the deepest cunning, who is constantly employing all his ingenuity in deceiving me. Doubtless, then, I exist, since I am deceived; and, let him deceive me as he may, he can never bring it about that I am nothing, so long as I shall be conscious that I am something. So that it must, in fine, be maintained, all things being maturely and carefully considered, that this proposition (pronunciatum) *I am, I exist*, is necessarily true each time it is expressed by me, or conceived in my mind.

4. But I do not yet know with sufficient clearness what I am, though assured that I am; and hence, in the next place, I must take care, lest perchance I inconsiderately substitute some other object in room of what is properly myself, and thus wander from truth, even in that knowledge (cognition) which I hold to be of all others the most certain and evident. For this reason, I will now consider anew what I formerly believed myself to be, before I entered on the present train of thought; and of my previous opinion I will retrench all that can in the least be invalidated by the grounds of doubt I have adduced, in order that there may at length remain nothing but what is certain and indubitable.

5. What then did I formerly think I was? Undoubtedly I judged that I was a man. But what is a man? Shall I say a rational animal? Assuredly not; for it would be necessary forthwith to inquire into

what is meant by animal, and what by rational, and thus, from a single question, I should insensibly glide into others, and these more difficult than the first; nor do I now possess enough of leisure to warrant me in wasting my time amid subtleties of this sort. I prefer here to attend to the thoughts that sprung up of themselves in my mind, and were inspired by my own nature alone, when I applied myself to the consideration of what I was. In the first place, then, I thought that I possessed a countenance, hands, arms, and all the fabric of members that appears in a corpse, and which I called by the name of body. It further occurred to me that I was nourished, that I walked, perceived, and thought, and all those actions I referred to the soul; but what the soul itself was I either did not stay to consider, or, if I did, I imagined that it was something extremely rare and subtile, like wind, or flame, or ether, spread through my grosser parts. As regarded the body, I did not even doubt of its nature, but thought I distinctly knew it, and if I had wished to describe it according to the notions I then entertained, I should have explained myself in this manner: By body I understand all that can be terminated by a certain figure; that can be comprised in a certain place, and so fill a certain space as therefrom to exclude every other body; that can be perceived either by touch, sight, hearing, taste, or smell; that can be moved in different ways, not indeed of itself, but by something foreign to it by which it is touched [and from which it receives the impression]; for the power of self-motion, as likewise that of perceiving and thinking, I held as by no means pertaining to the nature of body; on the contrary, I was somewhat astonished to find such faculties existing in some bodies.

6. But [as to myself, what can I now say that I am], since I suppose there exists an extremely powerful, and, if I may so speak, malignant being, whose whole endeavors are directed toward deceiving me? Can I affirm that I possess any one of all those attributes of which I have lately spoken as belonging to the nature of body? After attentively considering them in my own mind, I find none of them that can properly be said to belong to myself. To recount them were idle and tedious. Let us pass, then, to the attributes of the soul. The first mentioned were the powers of nutrition and walking; but, if it be true that I have no body, it is true likewise that I am capable neither of walking nor of being nourished. Perception is another attribute of the soul; but perception too is impossible without the body; besides, I have frequently, during sleep, believed that I perceived objects which I afterward observed I did not in reality perceive. Thinking is another attribute of the soul; and here I discover what properly belongs to myself. This alone is inseparable from me. I am—I exist: this is certain; but how often? As often as I think; for perhaps it would even happen, if I should wholly cease to think, that I should at the same time altogether cease to be. I now admit nothing that is not necessarily true. I am therefore, precisely speaking, only a thinking thing, that is, a mind (*mens sive animus*), understanding, or reason, terms whose signification was before unknown to me. I am, however, a real thing, and really existent; but what thing? The answer was, a thinking thing.

7. The question now arises, am I aught besides? I will stimulate my imagination with a view to discover whether I am not still something more than a thinking being. Now it is plain I am not the assemblage of members called the human body; I am not a thin and penetrating air diffused through all these members, or wind, or flame, or vapor, or breath, or any of all the things I can imagine; for I supposed that all these were not, and, without changing the supposition, I find that I still feel assured of my existence. But it is true, perhaps, that those very things which I suppose to be non-existent, because they are unknown to me, are not in truth different from myself whom I know. This is a point I cannot determine, and do not now enter into any dispute regarding it. I can only judge of things that are known to me: I am conscious that I exist, and I who know that I exist inquire into what I am. It is, however, perfectly certain that the knowledge of my existence, thus precisely taken, is not dependent on things, the existence of which is as yet unknown to me: and consequently it is not dependent on any of the things I can feign in imagination. Moreover, the phrase itself, I frame an image (*efffingo*),

reminds me of my error; for I should in truth frame one if I were to imagine myself to be anything, since to imagine is nothing more than to contemplate the figure or image of a corporeal thing; but I already know that I exist, and that it is possible at the same time that all those images, and in general all that relates to the nature of body, are merely dreams [or chimeras]. From this I discover that it is not more reasonable to say, I will excite my imagination that I may know more distinctly what I am, than to express myself as follows: I am now awake, and perceive something real; but because my perception is not sufficiently clear, I will of express purpose go to sleep that my dreams may represent to me the object of my perception with more truth and clearness. And, therefore, I know that nothing of all that I can embrace in imagination belongs to the knowledge which I have of myself, and that there is need to recall with the utmost care the mind from this mode of thinking, that it may be able to know its own nature with perfect distinctness.

8. But what, then, am I? A thinking thing, it has been said. But what is a thinking thing? It is a thing that doubts, understands, [conceives], affirms, denies, wills, refuses; that imagines also, and perceives.

9. Assuredly it is not little, if all these properties belong to my nature. But why should they not belong to it? Am I not that very being who now doubts of almost everything; who, for all that, understands and conceives certain things; who affirms one alone as true, and denies the others; who desires to know more of them, and does not wish to be deceived; who imagines many things, sometimes even despite his will; and is likewise percipient of many, as if through the medium of the senses. Is there nothing of all this as true as that I am, even although I should be always dreaming, and although he who gave me being employed all his ingenuity to deceive me? Is there also any one of these attributes that can be properly distinguished from my thought, or that can be said to be separate from myself? For it is of itself so evident that it is I who doubt, I who understand, and I who desire, that it is here unnecessary to add anything by way of rendering it more clear. And I am as certainly the same being who imagines; for although it may be (as I before supposed) that nothing I imagine is true, still the power of imagination does not cease really to exist in me and to form part of my thought. In fine, I am the same being who perceives, that is, who apprehends certain objects as by the organs of sense, since, in truth, I see light, hear a noise, and feel heat. But it will be said that these presentations are false, and that I am dreaming. Let it be so. At all events it is certain that I seem to see light, hear a noise, and feel heat; this cannot be false, and this is what in me is properly called perceiving (*sentire*), which is nothing else than thinking.

10. From this I begin to know what I am with somewhat greater clearness and distinctness than heretofore. But, nevertheless, it still seems to me, and I cannot help believing, that corporeal things, whose images are formed by thought [which fall under the senses], and are examined by the same, are known with much greater distinctness than that I know not what part of myself which is not imaginable; although, in truth, it may seem strange to say that I know and comprehend with greater distinctness things whose existence appears to me doubtful, that are unknown, and do not belong to me, than others of whose reality I am persuaded, that are known to me, and appertain to my proper nature; in a word, than myself. But I see clearly what is the state of the case. My mind is apt to wander, and will not yet submit to be restrained within the limits of truth. Let us therefore leave the mind to itself once more, and, according to it every kind of liberty [permit it to consider the objects that appear to it from without], in order that, having afterward withdrawn it from these gently and opportunely [and fixed it on the consideration of its being and the properties it finds in itself], it may then be the more easily controlled.

11. Let us now accordingly consider the objects that are commonly thought to be [the most easily, and likewise] the most distinctly known, viz., the bodies we touch and see; not, indeed, bodies in general, for these general notions are usually somewhat more confused, but one body in particular. Take, for

example, this piece of wax; it is quite fresh, having been but recently taken from the beehive; it has not yet lost the sweetness of the honey it contained; it still retains somewhat of the odor of the flowers from which it was gathered; its color, figure, size, are apparent (to the sight); it is hard, cold, easily handled; and sounds when struck upon with the finger. In fine, all that contributes to make a body as distinctly known as possible, is found in the one before us. But, while I am speaking, let it be placed near the fire—what remained of the taste exhales, the smell evaporates, the color changes, its figure is destroyed, its size increases, it becomes liquid, it grows hot, it can hardly be handled, and, although struck upon, it emits no sound. Does the same wax still remain after this change? It must be admitted that it does remain; no one doubts it, or judges otherwise. What, then, was it I knew with so much distinctness in the piece of wax? Assuredly, it could be nothing of all that I observed by means of the senses, since all the things that fell under taste, smell, sight, touch, and hearing are changed, and yet the same wax remains.

12. It was perhaps what I now think, viz., that this wax was neither the sweetness of honey, the pleasant odor of flowers, the whiteness, the figure, nor the sound, but only a body that a little before appeared to me conspicuous under these forms, and which is now perceived under others. But, to speak precisely, what is it that I imagine when I think of it in this way? Let it be attentively considered, and, retrenching all that does not belong to the wax, let us see what remains. There certainly remains nothing, except something extended, flexible, and movable. But what is meant by flexible and movable? Is it not that I imagine that the piece of wax, being round, is capable of becoming square, or of passing from a square into a triangular figure? Assuredly such is not the case, because I conceive that it admits of an infinity of similar changes; and I am, moreover, unable to compass this infinity by imagination, and consequently this conception which I have of the wax is not the product of the faculty of imagination. But what now is this extension? Is it not also unknown? For it becomes greater when the wax is melted, greater when it is boiled, and greater still when the heat increases; and I should not conceive [clearly and] according to truth, the wax as it is, if I did not suppose that the piece we are considering admitted even of a wider variety of extension than I ever imagined, I must, therefore, admit that I cannot even comprehend by imagination what the piece of wax is, and that it is the mind alone (*mens*, Lat., *entendement*, F.) which perceives it. I speak of one piece in particular; for as to wax in general, this is still more evident. But what is the piece of wax that can be perceived only by the [understanding or] mind? It is certainly the same which I see, touch, imagine; and, in fine, it is the same which, from the beginning, I believed it to be. But (and this it is of moment to observe) the perception of it is neither an act of sight, of touch, nor of imagination, and never was either of these, though it might formerly seem so, but is simply an intuition (*inspectio*) of the mind, which may be imperfect and confused, as it formerly was, or very clear and distinct, as it is at present, according as the attention is more or less directed to the elements which it contains, and of which it is composed.

13. But, meanwhile, I feel greatly astonished when I observe [the weakness of my mind, and] its proneness to error. For although, without at all giving expression to what I think, I consider all this in my own mind, words yet occasionally impede my progress, and I am almost led into error by the terms of ordinary language. We say, for example, that we see the same wax when it is before us, and not that we judge it to be the same from its retaining the same color and figure: whence I should forthwith be disposed to conclude that the wax is known by the act of sight, and not by the intuition of the mind alone, were it not for the analogous instance of human beings passing on in the street below, as observed from a window. In this case I do not fail to say that I see the men themselves, just as I say that I see the wax; and yet what do I see from the window beyond hats and cloaks that might cover artificial machines, whose motions might be determined by springs? But I judge that there are human beings from these appearances, and thus I comprehend, by the faculty of judgment alone which is in the mind, what I believed I saw with my eyes.

14. The man who makes it his aim to rise to knowledge superior to the common, ought to be ashamed to seek occasions of doubting from the vulgar forms of speech: instead, therefore, of doing this, I shall proceed with the matter in hand, and inquire whether I had a clearer and more perfect perception of the piece of wax when I first saw it, and when I thought I knew it by means of the external sense itself, or, at all events, by the common sense (*sensus communis*), as it is called, that is, by the imaginative faculty; or whether I rather apprehend it more clearly at present, after having examined with greater care, both what it is, and in what way it can be known. It would certainly be ridiculous to entertain any doubt on this point. For what, in that first perception, was there distinct? What did I perceive which any animal might not have perceived? But when I distinguish the wax from its exterior forms, and when, as if I had stripped it of its vestments, I consider it quite naked, it is certain, although some error may still be found in my judgment, that I cannot, nevertheless, thus apprehend it without possessing a human mind.

15. But finally, what shall I say of the mind itself, that is, of myself? For as yet I do not admit that I am anything but mind. What, then! I who seem to possess so distinct an apprehension of the piece of wax, do I not know myself, both with greater truth and certitude, and also much more distinctly and clearly? For if I judge that the wax exists because I see it, it assuredly follows, much more evidently, that I myself am or exist, for the same reason: for it is possible that what I see may not in truth be wax, and that I do not even possess eyes with which to see anything; but it cannot be that when I see, or, which comes to the same thing, when I think I see, I myself who think am nothing. So likewise, if I judge that the wax exists because I touch it, it will still also follow that I am; and if I determine that my imagination, or any other cause, whatever it be, persuades me of the existence of the wax, I will still draw the same conclusion. And what is here remarked of the piece of wax, is applicable to all the other things that are external to me. And further, if the [notion or] perception of wax appeared to me more precise and distinct, after that not only sight and touch, but many other causes besides, rendered it manifest to my apprehension, with how much greater distinctness must I now know myself, since all the reasons that contribute to the knowledge of the nature of wax, or of any body whatever, manifest still better the nature of my mind? And there are besides so many other things in the mind itself that contribute to the illustration of its nature, that those dependent on the body, to which I have here referred, scarcely merit to be taken into account.

16. But, in conclusion, I find I have insensibly reverted to the point I desired; for, since it is now manifest to me that bodies themselves are not properly perceived by the senses nor by the faculty of imagination, but by the intellect alone; and since they are not perceived because they are seen and touched, but only because they are understood [or rightly comprehended by thought], I readily discover that there is nothing more easily or clearly apprehended than my own mind. But because it is difficult to rid one's self so promptly of an opinion to which one has been long accustomed, it will be desirable to tarry for some time at this stage, that, by long continued meditation, I may more deeply impress upon my memory this new knowledge.

Meditation III
Of God: That He Exists

1. I will now close my eyes, I will stop my ears, I will turn away my senses from their objects, I will even efface from my consciousness all the images of corporeal things; or at least, because this can hardly be accomplished, I will consider them as empty and false; and thus, holding converse only with myself, and closely examining my nature, I will endeavor to obtain by degrees a more intimate and familiar knowledge of myself. I am a thinking (conscious) thing, that is, a being who doubts, affirms, denies, knows

a few objects, and is ignorant of many,—[who loves, hates], wills, refuses, who imagines likewise, and perceives; for, as I before remarked, although the things which I perceive or imagine are perhaps nothing at all apart from me [and in themselves], I am nevertheless assured that those modes of consciousness which I call perceptions and imaginations, in as far only as they are modes of consciousness, exist in me.

2. And in the little I have said I think I have summed up all that I really know, or at least all that up to this time I was aware I knew. Now, as I am endeavoring to extend my knowledge more widely, I will use circumspection, and consider with care whether I can still discover in myself anything further which I have not yet hitherto observed. I am certain that I am a thinking thing; but do I not therefore likewise know what is required to render me certain of a truth? In this first knowledge, doubtless, there is nothing that gives me assurance of its truth except the clear and distinct perception of what I affirm, which would not indeed be sufficient to give me the assurance that what I say is true, if it could ever happen that anything I thus clearly and distinctly perceived should prove false; and accordingly it seems to me that I may now take as a general rule, that all that is very clearly and distinctly apprehended (conceived) is true.

3. Nevertheless I before received and admitted many things as wholly certain and manifest, which yet I afterward found to be doubtful. What, then, were those? They were the earth, the sky, the stars, and all the other objects which I was in the habit of perceiving by the senses. But what was it that I clearly [and distinctly] perceived in them? Nothing more than that the ideas and the thoughts of those objects were presented to my mind. And even now I do not deny that these ideas are found in my mind. But there was yet another thing which I affirmed, and which, from having been accustomed to believe it, I thought I clearly perceived, although, in truth, I did not perceive it at all; I mean the existence of objects external to me, from which those ideas proceeded, and to which they had a perfect resemblance; and it was here I was mistaken, or if I judged correctly, this assuredly was not to be traced to any knowledge I possessed (the force of my perception, Lat.).

4. But when I considered any matter in arithmetic and geometry, that was very simple and easy, as, for example, that two and three added together make five, and things of this sort, did I not view them with at least sufficient clearness to warrant me in affirming their truth? Indeed, if I afterward judged that we ought to doubt of these things, it was for no other reason than because it occurred to me that a God might perhaps have given me such a nature as that I should be deceived, even respecting the matters that appeared to me the most evidently true. But as often as this preconceived opinion of the sovereign power of a God presents itself to my mind, I am constrained to admit that it is easy for him, if he wishes it, to cause me to err, even in matters where I think I possess the highest evidence; and, on the other hand, as often as I direct my attention to things which I think I apprehend with great clearness, I am so persuaded of their truth that I naturally break out into expressions such as these: Deceive me who may, no one will yet ever be able to bring it about that I am not, so long as I shall be conscious that I am, or at any future time cause it to be true that I have never been, it being now true that I am, or make two and three more or less than five, in supposing which, and other like absurdities, I discover a manifest contradiction. And in truth, as I have no ground for believing that Deity is deceitful, and as, indeed, I have not even considered the reasons by which the existence of a Deity of any kind is established, the ground of doubt that rests only on this supposition is very slight, and, so to speak, metaphysical. But, that I may be able wholly to remove it, I must inquire whether there is a God, as soon as an opportunity of doing so shall present itself; and if I find that there is a God, I must examine likewise whether he can be a deceiver; for, without the knowledge of these two truths, I do not see that I can ever be certain of anything. And that I may be enabled to examine this without interrupting the order of meditation I have proposed to myself [which is, to pass by degrees

from the notions that I shall find first in my mind to those I shall afterward discover in it], it is necessary at this stage to divide all my thoughts into certain classes, and to consider in which of these classes truth and error are, strictly speaking, to be found.

5. Of my thoughts some are, as it were, images of things, and to these alone properly belongs the name IDEA; as when I think [represent to my mind] a man, a chimera, the sky, an angel or God. Others, again, have certain other forms; as when I will, fear, affirm, or deny, I always, indeed, apprehend something as the object of my thought, but I also embrace in thought something more than the representation of the object; and of this class of thoughts some are called volitions or affections, and others judgments.

6. Now, with respect to ideas, if these are considered only in themselves, and are not referred to any object beyond them, they cannot, properly speaking, be false; for, whether I imagine a goat or chimera, it is not less true that I imagine the one than the other. Nor need we fear that falsity may exist in the will or affections; for, although I may desire objects that are wrong, and even that never existed, it is still true that I desire them. There thus only remain our judgments, in which we must take diligent heed that we be not deceived. But the chief and most ordinary error that arises in them consists in judging that the ideas which are in us are like or conformed to the things that are external to us; for assuredly, if we but considered the ideas themselves as certain modes of our thought (consciousness), without referring them to anything beyond, they would hardly afford any occasion of error.

7. But among these ideas, some appear to me to be innate, others adventitious, and others to be made by myself (factitious); for, as I have the power of conceiving what is called a thing, or a truth, or a thought, it seems to me that I hold this power from no other source than my own nature; but if I now hear a noise, if I see the sun, or if I feel heat, I have all along judged that these sensations proceeded from certain objects existing out of myself; and, in fine, it appears to me that sirens, hippogryphs, and the like, are inventions of my own mind. But I may even perhaps come to be of opinion that all my ideas are of the class which I call adventitious, or that they are all innate, or that they are all factitious; for I have not yet clearly discovered their true origin.

8. What I have here principally to do is to consider, with reference to those that appear to come from certain objects without me, what grounds there are for thinking them like these objects. The first of these grounds is that it seems to me I am so taught by nature; and the second that I am conscious that those ideas are not dependent on my will, and therefore not on myself, for they are frequently presented to me against my will, as at present, whether I will or not, I feel heat; and I am thus persuaded that this sensation or idea (*sensum vel ideam*) of heat is produced in me by something different from myself, viz., by the heat of the fire by which I sit. And it is very reasonable to suppose that this object impresses me with its own likeness rather than any other thing.

9. But I must consider whether these reasons are sufficiently strong and convincing. When I speak of being taught by nature in this matter, I understand by the word nature only a certain spontaneous impetus that impels me to believe in a resemblance between ideas and their objects, and not a natural light that affords a knowledge of its truth. But these two things are widely different; for what the natural light shows to be true can be in no degree doubtful, as, for example, that I am because I doubt, and other truths of the like kind; inasmuch as I possess no other faculty whereby to distinguish truth from error, which can teach me the falsity of what the natural light declares to be true, and which is equally trustworthy; but with respect to [seemingly] natural impulses, I have observed, when the question related to the choice of right or wrong in action, that they frequently led me to take the worse part; nor do I see that I have any better ground for following them in what relates to truth and error.

10. Then, with respect to the other reason, which is that because these ideas do not depend on my will, they must arise from objects existing without me, I do not find it more convincing than the

former, for just as those natural impulses, of which I have lately spoken, are found in me, notwith-standing that they are not always in harmony with my will, so likewise it may be that I possess some power not sufficiently known to myself capable of producing ideas without the aid of external objects, and, indeed, it has always hitherto appeared to me that they are formed during sleep, by some power of this nature, without the aid of aught external.

11. And, in fine, although I should grant that they proceeded from those objects, it is not a nec-essary consequence that they must be like them. On the contrary, I have observed, in a number of instances, that there was a great difference between the object and its idea. Thus, for example, I find in my mind two wholly diverse ideas of the sun; the one, by which it appears to me extremely small draws its origin from the senses, and should be placed in the class of adventitious ideas; the other, by which it seems to be many times larger than the whole earth, is taken up on astronomical grounds, that is, elicited from certain notions born with me, or is framed by myself in some other manner. These two ideas cannot certainly both resemble the same sun; and reason teaches me that the one which seems to have immediately emanated from it is the most unlike.

12. And these things sufficiently prove that hitherto it has not been from a certain and deliberate judgment, but only from a sort of blind impulse, that I believed existence of certain things different from myself, which, by the organs of sense, or by whatever other means it might be, conveyed their ideas or images into my mind [and impressed it with their likenesses].

13. But there is still another way of inquiring whether, of the objects whose ideas are in my mind, there are any that exist out of me. If ideas are taken in so far only as they are certain modes of consciousness, I do not remark any difference or inequality among them, and all seem, in the same manner, to proceed from myself; but, considering them as images, of which one represents one thing and another a different, it is evident that a great diversity obtains among them. For, without doubt, those that represent substances are something more, and contain in themselves, so to speak, more objective reality [that is, participate by representation in higher degrees of being or perfection], than those that represent only modes or accidents; and again, the idea by which I conceive a God [sovereign], eternal, infinite, [immutable], all-knowing, all-powerful, and the creator of all things that are out of himself, this, I say, has certainly in it more objective reality than those ideas by which finite substances are represented.

14. Now, it is manifest by the natural light that there must at least be as much reality in the ef-ficient and total cause as in its effect; for whence can the effect draw its reality if not from its cause? And how could the cause communicate to it this reality unless it possessed it in itself? And hence it follows, not only that what is cannot be produced by what is not, but likewise that the more perfect, in other words, that which contains in itself more reality, cannot be the effect of the less perfect; and this is not only evidently true of those effects, whose reality is actual or formal, but likewise of ideas, whose reality is only considered as objective. Thus, for example, the stone that is not yet in existence, not only cannot now commence to be, unless it be produced by that which possesses in itself, formal-ly or eminently, all that enters into its composition, [in other words, by that which contains in itself the same properties that are in the stone, or others superior to them]; and heat can only be produced in a subject that was before devoid of it, by a cause that is of an order, [degree or kind], at least as perfect as heat; and so of the others. But further, even the idea of the heat, or of the stone, cannot exist in me unless it be put there by a cause that contains, at least, as much reality as I conceive ex-istent in the heat or in the stone for although that cause may not transmit into my idea anything of its actual or formal reality, we ought not on this account to imagine that it is less real; but we ought to consider that, [as every idea is a work of the mind], its nature is such as of itself to demand no other formal reality than that which it borrows from our consciousness, of which it is but a mode [that is, a

manner or way of thinking]. But in order that an idea may contain this objective reality rather than that, it must doubtless derive it from some cause in which is found at least as much formal reality as the idea contains of objective; for, if we suppose that there is found in an idea anything which was not in its cause, it must of course derive this from nothing. But, however imperfect may be the mode of existence by which a thing is objectively [or by representation] in the understanding by its idea, we certainly cannot, for all that, allege that this mode of existence is nothing, nor, consequently, that the idea owes its origin to nothing.

15. Nor must it be imagined that, since the reality which considered in these ideas is only objective, the same reality need not be formally (actually) in the causes of these ideas, but only objectively: for, just as the mode of existing objectively belongs to ideas by their peculiar nature, so likewise the mode of existing formally appertains to the causes of these ideas (at least to the first and principal), by their peculiar nature. And although an idea may give rise to another idea, this regress cannot, nevertheless, be infinite; we must in the end reach a first idea, the cause of which is, as it were, the archetype in which all the reality [or perfection] that is found objectively [or by representation] in these ideas is contained formally [and in act]. I am thus clearly taught by the natural light that ideas exist in me as pictures or images, which may, in truth, readily fall short of the perfection of the objects from which they are taken, but can never contain anything greater or more perfect.

16. And in proportion to the time and care with which I examine all those matters, the conviction of their truth brightens and becomes distinct. But, to sum up, what conclusion shall I draw from it all? It is this: if the objective reality [or perfection] of any one of my ideas be such as clearly to convince me, that this same reality exists in me neither formally nor eminently, and if, as follows from this, I myself cannot be the cause of it, it is a necessary consequence that I am not alone in the world, but that there is besides myself some other being who exists as the cause of that idea; while, on the contrary, if no such idea be found in my mind, I shall have no sufficient ground of assurance of the existence of any other being besides myself, for, after a most careful search, I have, up to this moment, been unable to discover any other ground.

17. But, among these my ideas, besides that which represents myself, respecting which there can be here no difficulty, there is one that represents a God; others that represent corporeal and inanimate things; others angels; others animals; and, finally, there are some that represent men like myself.

18. But with respect to the ideas that represent other men, or animals, or angels, I can easily suppose that they were formed by the mingling and composition of the other ideas which I have of myself, of corporeal things, and of God, although they were, apart from myself, neither men, animals, nor angels.

19. And with regard to the ideas of corporeal objects, I never discovered in them anything so great or excellent which I myself did not appear capable of originating; for, by considering these ideas closely and scrutinizing them individually, in the same way that I yesterday examined the idea of wax, I find that there is but little in them that is clearly and distinctly perceived. As belonging to the class of things that are clearly apprehended, I recognize the following, viz., magnitude or extension in length, breadth, and depth; figure, which results from the termination of extension; situation, which bodies of diverse figures preserve with reference to each other; and motion or the change of situation; to which may be added substance, duration, and number. But with regard to light, colors, sounds, odors, tastes, heat, cold, and the other tactile qualities, they are thought with so much obscurity and confusion, that I cannot determine even whether they are true or false; in other words, whether or not the ideas I have of these qualities are in truth the ideas of real objects. For although I before remarked that it is only in judgments that formal falsity, or falsity properly so called, can be met with, there may nevertheless be found in ideas a certain material falsity, which arises when they represent what is nothing as if it were something. Thus, for example, the ideas I have of cold and heat are so far from being clear and

distinct, that I am unable from them to discover whether cold is only the privation of heat, or heat the privation of cold; or whether they are or are not real qualities: and since, ideas being as it were images there can be none that does not seem to us to represent some object, the idea which represents cold as something real and positive will not improperly be called false, if it be correct to say that cold is nothing but a privation of heat; and so in other cases.

20. To ideas of this kind, indeed, it is not necessary that I should assign any author besides myself: for if they are false, that is, represent objects that are unreal, the natural light teaches me that they proceed from nothing; in other words, that they are in me only because something is wanting to the perfection of my nature; but if these ideas are true, yet because they exhibit to me so little reality that I cannot even distinguish the object represented from nonbeing, I do not see why I should not be the author of them.

21. With reference to those ideas of corporeal things that are clear and distinct, there are some which, as appears to me, might have been taken from the idea I have of myself, as those of substance, duration, number, and the like. For when I think that a stone is a substance, or a thing capable of existing of itself, and that I am likewise a substance, although I conceive that I am a thinking and non-extended thing, and that the stone, on the contrary, is extended and unconscious, there being thus the greatest diversity between the two concepts, yet these two ideas seem to have this in common that they both represent substances. In the same way, when I think of myself as now existing, and recollect besides that I existed some time ago, and when I am conscious of various thoughts whose number I know, I then acquire the ideas of duration and number, which I can afterward transfer to as many objects as I please. With respect to the other qualities that go to make up the ideas of corporeal objects, viz., extension, figure, situation, and motion, it is true that they are not formally in me, since I am merely a thinking being; but because they are only certain modes of substance, and because I myself am a substance, it seems possible that they may be contained in me eminently.

22. There only remains, therefore, the idea of God, in which I must consider whether there is anything that cannot be supposed to originate with myself. By the name God, I understand a substance infinite, [eternal, immutable], independent, all-knowing, all-powerful, and by which I myself, and every other thing that exists, if any such there be, were created. But these properties are so great and excellent, that the more attentively I consider them the less I feel persuaded that the idea I have of them owes its origin to myself alone. And thus it is absolutely necessary to conclude, from all that I have before said, that God exists.

23. For though the idea of substance be in my mind owing to this, that I myself am a substance, I should not, however, have the idea of an infinite substance, seeing I am a finite being, unless it were given me by some substance in reality infinite.

24. And I must not imagine that I do not apprehend the infinite by a true idea, but only by the negation of the finite, in the same way that I comprehend repose and darkness by the negation of motion and light: since, on the contrary, I clearly perceive that there is more reality in the infinite substance than in the finite, and therefore that in some way I possess the perception (notion) of the infinite before that of the finite, that is, the perception of God before that of myself, for how could I know that I doubt, desire, or that something is wanting to me, and that I am not wholly perfect, if I possessed no idea of a being more perfect than myself, by comparison of which I knew the deficiencies of my nature?

25. And it cannot be said that this idea of God is perhaps materially false, and consequently that it may have arisen from nothing [in other words, that it may exist in me from my imperfections as I before said of the ideas of heat and cold, and the like: for, on the contrary, as this idea is very clear and distinct, and contains in itself more objective reality than any other, there can be no one of itself more true, or less open to the suspicion of falsity. The idea, I say, of a being supremely perfect, and

infinite, is in the highest degree true; for although, perhaps, we may imagine that such a being does not exist, we cannot, nevertheless, suppose that his idea represents nothing real, as I have already said of the idea of cold. It is likewise clear and distinct in the highest degree, since whatever the mind clearly and distinctly conceives as real or true, and as implying any perfection, is contained entire in this idea. And this is true, nevertheless, although I do not comprehend the infinite, and although there may be in God an infinity of things that I cannot comprehend, nor perhaps even compass by thought in any way; for it is of the nature of the infinite that it should not be comprehended by the finite; and it is enough that I rightly understand this, and judge that all which I clearly perceive, and in which I know there is some perfection, and perhaps also an infinity of properties of which I am ignorant, are formally or eminently in God, in order that the idea I have of him may be come the most true, clear, and distinct of all the ideas in my mind.

26. But perhaps I am something more than I suppose myself to be, and it may be that all those perfections which I attribute to God, in some way exist potentially in me, although they do not yet show themselves, and are not reduced to act. Indeed, I am already conscious that my knowledge is being increased [and perfected] by degrees; and I see nothing to prevent it from thus gradually increasing to infinity, nor any reason why, after such increase and perfection, I should not be able thereby to acquire all the other perfections of the Divine nature; nor, in fine, why the power I possess of acquiring those perfections, if it really now exist in me, should not be sufficient to produce the ideas of them.

27. Yet, on looking more closely into the matter, I discover that this cannot be; for, in the first place, although it were true that my knowledge daily acquired new degrees of perfection, and although there were potentially in my nature much that was not as yet actually in it, still all these excellences make not the slightest approach to the idea I have of the Deity, in whom there is no perfection merely potentially [but all actually] existent; for it is even an unmistakable token of imperfection in my knowledge, that it is augmented by degrees. Further, although my knowledge increases more and more, nevertheless I am not, therefore, induced to think that it will ever be actually infinite, since it can never reach that point beyond which it shall be incapable of further increase. But I conceive God as actually infinite, so that nothing can be added to his perfection. And, in fine, I readily perceive that the objective being of an idea cannot be produced by a being that is merely potentially existent, which, properly speaking, is nothing, but only by a being existing formally or actually.

28. And, truly, I see nothing in all that I have now said which it is not easy for any one, who shall carefully consider it, to discern by the natural light; but when I allow my attention in some degree to relax, the vision of my mind being obscured, and, as it were, blinded by the images of sensible objects, I do not readily remember the reason why the idea of a being more perfect than myself, must of necessity have proceeded from a being in reality more perfect. On this account I am here desirous to inquire further, whether I, who possess this idea of God, could exist supposing there were no God.

29. And I ask, from whom could I, in that case, derive my existence? Perhaps from myself, or from my parents, or from some other causes less perfect than God; for anything more perfect, or even equal to God, cannot be thought or imagined.

30. But if I [were independent of every other existence, and] were myself the author of my being, I should doubt of nothing, I should desire nothing, and, in fine, no perfection would be awanting to me; for I should have bestowed upon myself every perfection of which I possess the idea, and I should thus be God. And it must not be imagined that what is now wanting to me is perhaps of more difficult acquisition than that of which I am already possessed; for, on the contrary, it is quite manifest that it was a matter of much higher difficulty that I, a thinking being, should arise from nothing, than it would be for me to acquire the knowledge of many things of which I am ignorant, and which are merely the accidents of a thinking substance; and certainly, if I possessed of myself the greater perfection of which

I have now spoken [in other words, if I were the author of my own existence], I would not at least have denied to myself things that may be more easily obtained [as that infinite variety of knowledge of which I am at present destitute]. I could not, indeed, have denied to myself any property which I perceive is contained in the idea of God, because there is none of these that seems to me to be more difficult to make or acquire; and if there were any that should happen to be more difficult to acquire, they would certainly appear so to me (supposing that I myself were the source of the other things I possess), because I should discover in them a limit to my power.

31. And though I were to suppose that I always was as I now am, I should not, on this ground, escape the force of these reasonings, since it would not follow, even on this supposition, that no author of my existence needed to be sought after. For the whole time of my life may be divided into an infinity of parts, each of which is in no way dependent on any other; and, accordingly, because I was in existence a short time ago, it does not follow that I must now exist, unless in this moment some cause create me anew as it were, that is, conserve me. In truth, it is perfectly clear and evident to all who will attentively consider the nature of duration, that the conservation of a substance, in each moment of its duration, requires the same power and act that would be necessary to create it, supposing it were not yet in existence; so that it is manifestly a dictate of the natural light that conservation and creation differ merely in respect of our mode of thinking [and not in reality].

32. All that is here required, therefore, is that I interrogate myself to discover whether I possess any power by means of which I can bring it about that I, who now am, shall exist a moment afterward: for, since I am merely a thinking thing (or since, at least, the precise question, in the meantime, is only of that part of myself), if such a power resided in me, I should, without doubt, be conscious of it; but I am conscious of no such power, and thereby I manifestly know that I am dependent upon some being different from myself.

33. But perhaps the being upon whom I am dependent is not God, and I have been produced either by my parents, or by some causes less perfect than Deity. This cannot be: for, as I before said, it is perfectly evident that there must at least be as much reality in the cause as in its effect; and accordingly, since I am a thinking thing and possess in myself an idea of God, whatever in the end be the cause of my existence, it must of necessity be admitted that it is likewise a thinking being, and that it possesses in itself the idea and all the perfections I attribute to Deity. Then it may again be inquired whether this cause owes its origin and existence to itself, or to some other cause. For if it be self-existent, it follows, from what I have before laid down, that this cause is God; for, since it possesses the perfection of self-existence, it must likewise, without doubt, have the power of actually possessing every perfection of which it has the idea—in other words, all the perfections I conceive to belong to God. But if it owe its existence to another cause than itself, we demand again, for a similar reason, whether this second cause exists of itself or through some other, until, from stage to stage, we at length arrive at an ultimate cause, which will be God.

34. And it is quite manifest that in this matter there can be no infinite regress of causes, seeing that the question raised respects not so much the cause which once produced me, as that by which I am at this present moment conserved.

35. Nor can it be supposed that several causes concurred in my production, and that from one I received the idea of one of the perfections I attribute to Deity, and from another the idea of some other, and thus that all those perfections are indeed found somewhere in the universe, but do not all exist together in a single being who is God; for, on the contrary, the unity, the simplicity, or inseparability of all the properties of Deity, is one of the chief perfections I conceive him to possess; and the idea of this unity of all the perfections of Deity could certainly not be put into my mind by any cause from which I did not likewise receive the ideas of all the other perfections; for no power could enable me

to embrace them in an inseparable unity, without at the same time giving me the knowledge of what they were [and of their existence in a particular mode].

36. Finally, with regard to my parents [from whom it appears I sprung], although all that I believed respecting them be true, it does not, nevertheless, follow that I am conserved by them, or even that I was produced by them, in so far as I am a thinking being. All that, at the most, they contributed to my origin was the giving of certain dispositions (modifications) to the matter in which I have hitherto judged that I or my mind, which is what alone I now consider to be myself, is inclosed; and thus there can here be no difficulty with respect to them, and it is absolutely necessary to conclude from this alone that I am, and possess the idea of a being absolutely perfect, that is, of God, that his existence is most clearly demonstrated.

37. There remains only the inquiry as to the way in which I received this idea from God; for I have not drawn it from the senses, nor is it even presented to me unexpectedly, as is usual with the ideas of sensible objects, when these are presented or appear to be presented to the external organs of the senses; it is not even a pure production or fiction of my mind, for it is not in my power to take from or add to it; and consequently there but remains the alternative that it is innate, in the same way as is the idea of myself.

38. And, in truth, it is not to be wondered at that God, at my creation, implanted this idea in me, that it might serve, as it were, for the mark of the workman impressed on his work; and it is not also necessary that the mark should be something different from the work itself; but considering only that God is my creator, it is highly probable that he in some way fashioned me after his own image and likeness, and that I perceive this likeness, in which is contained the idea of God, by the same faculty by which I apprehend myself, in other words, when I make myself the object of reflection, I not only find that I am an incomplete, [imperfect] and dependent being, and one who unceasingly aspires after something better and greater than he is; but, at the same time, I am assured likewise that he upon whom I am dependent possesses in himself all the goods after which I aspire [and the ideas of which I find in my mind], and that not merely indefinitely and potentially, but infinitely and actually, and that he is thus God. And the whole force of the argument of which I have here availed myself to establish the existence of God, consists in this, that I perceive I could not possibly be of such a nature as I am, and yet have in my mind the idea of a God, if God did not in reality exist—this same God, I say, whose idea is in my mind—that is, a being who possesses all those lofty perfections, of which the mind may have some slight conception, without, however, being able fully to comprehend them, and who is wholly superior to all defect [and has nothing that marks imperfection]: whence it is sufficiently manifest that he cannot be a deceiver, since it is a dictate of the natural light that all fraud and deception spring from some defect.

39. But before I examine this with more attention, and pass on to the consideration of other truths that may be evolved out of it, I think it proper to remain here for some time in the contemplation of God himself—that I may ponder at leisure his marvelous attributes—and behold, admire, and adore the beauty of this light so unspeakably great, as far, at least, as the strength of my mind, which is to some degree dazzled by the sight, will permit. For just as we learn by faith that the supreme felicity of another life consists in the contemplation of the Divine majesty alone, so even now we learn from experience that a like meditation, though incomparably less perfect, is the source of the highest satisfaction of which we are susceptible in this life.

Meditation IV
Of Truth and Error

1. I have been habituated these bygone days to detach my mind from the senses, and I have accurately observed that there is exceedingly little which is known with certainty respecting corporeal objects, that we know much more of the human mind, and still more of God himself. I am thus able now without difficulty to abstract my mind from the contemplation of [sensible or] imaginable objects, and apply it to those which, as disengaged from all matter, are purely intelligible. And certainly the idea I have of the human mind in so far as it is a thinking thing, and not extended in length, breadth, and depth, and participating in none of the properties of body, is incomparably more distinct than the idea of any corporeal object; and when I consider that I doubt, in other words, that I am an incomplete and dependent being, the idea of a complete and independent being, that is to say of God, occurs to my mind with so much clearness and distinctness, and from the fact alone that this idea is found in me, or that I who possess it exist, the conclusions that God exists, and that my own existence, each moment of its continuance, is absolutely dependent upon him, are so manifest, as to lead me to believe it impossible that the human mind can know anything with more clearness and certitude. And now I seem to discover a path that will conduct us from the contemplation of the true God, in whom are contained all the treasures of science and wisdom, to the knowledge of the other things in the universe.

2. For, in the first place, I discover that it is impossible for him ever to deceive me, for in all fraud and deceit there is a certain imperfection: and although it may seem that the ability to deceive is a mark of subtlety or power, yet the will testifies without doubt of malice and weakness; and such, accordingly, cannot be found in God.

3. In the next place, I am conscious that I possess a certain faculty of judging [or discerning truth from error], which I doubtless received from God, along with whatever else is mine; and since it is impossible that he should will to deceive me, it is likewise certain that he has not given me a faculty that will ever lead me into error, provided I use it aright.

4. And there would remain no doubt on this head, did it not seem to follow from this, that I can never therefore be deceived; for if all I possess be from God, and if he planted in me no faculty that is deceitful, it seems to follow that I can never fall into error. Accordingly, it is true that when I think only of God (when I look upon myself as coming from God, Fr.), and turn wholly to him, I discover [in myself] no cause of error or falsity: but immediately thereafter, recurring to myself, experience assures me that I am nevertheless subject to innumerable errors. When I come to inquire into the cause of these, I observe that there is not only present to my consciousness a real and positive idea of God, or of a being supremely perfect, but also, so to speak, a certain negative idea of nothing, in other words, of that which is at an infinite distance from every sort of perfection, and that I am, as it were, a mean between God and nothing, or placed in such a way between absolute existence and non-existence, that there is in truth nothing in me to lead me into error, in so far as an absolute being is my creator; but that, on the other hand, as I thus likewise participate in some degree of nothing or of nonbeing, in other words, as I am not myself the supreme Being, and as I am wanting in many perfections, it is not surprising I should fall into error. And I hence discern that error, so far as error is not something real, which depends for its existence on God, but is simply defect; and therefore that, in order to fall into it, it is not necessary God should have given me a faculty expressly for this end, but that my being deceived arises from the circumstance that the power which God has given me of discerning truth from error is not infinite.

5. Nevertheless this is not yet quite satisfactory; for error is not a pure negation, [in other words, it is not the simple deficiency or want of some knowledge which is not due], but the privation or want of some knowledge which it would seem I ought to possess. But, on considering the nature of God,

it seems impossible that he should have planted in his creature any faculty not perfect in its kind, that is, wanting in some perfection due to it: for if it be true, that in proportion to the skill of the maker the perfection of his work is greater, what thing can have been produced by the supreme Creator of the universe that is not absolutely perfect in all its parts? And assuredly there is no doubt that God could have created me such as that I should never be deceived; it is certain, likewise, that he always wills what is best: is it better, then, that I should be capable of being deceived than that I should not?

6. Considering this more attentively the first thing that occurs to me is the reflection that I must not be surprised if I am not always capable of comprehending the reasons why God acts as he does; nor must I doubt of his existence because I find, perhaps, that there are several other things besides the present respecting which I understand neither why nor how they were created by him; for, knowing already that my nature is extremely weak and limited, and that the nature of God, on the other hand, is immense, incomprehensible, and infinite, I have no longer any difficulty in discerning that there is an infinity of things in his power whose causes transcend the grasp of my mind: and this consideration alone is sufficient to convince me, that the whole class of final causes is of no avail in physical [or natural] things; for it appears to me that I cannot, without exposing myself to the charge of temerity, seek to discover the [impenetrable] ends of Deity.

7. It further occurs to me that we must not consider only one creature apart from the others, if we wish to determine the perfection of the works of Deity, but generally all his creatures together; for the same object that might perhaps, with some show of reason, be deemed highly imperfect if it were alone in the world, may for all that be the most perfect possible, considered as forming part of the whole universe: and although, as it was my purpose to doubt of everything, I only as yet know with certainty my own existence and that of God, nevertheless, after having remarked the infinite power of Deity, I cannot deny that we may have produced many other objects, or at least that he is able to produce them, so that I may occupy a place in the relation of a part to the great whole of his creatures.

8. Whereupon, regarding myself more closely, and considering what my errors are (which alone testify to the existence of imperfection in me), I observe that these depend on the concurrence of two causes, viz., the faculty of cognition, which I possess, and that of election or the power of free choice,—in other words, the understanding and the will. For by the understanding alone, I [neither affirm nor deny anything but] merely apprehend (*percipio*) the ideas regarding which I may form a judgment; nor is any error, properly so called, found in it thus accurately taken. And although there are perhaps innumerable objects in the world of which I have no idea in my understanding, it cannot, on that account be said that I am deprived of those ideas [as of something that is due to my nature], but simply that I do not possess them, because, in truth, there is no ground to prove that Deity ought to have endowed me with a larger faculty of cognition than he has actually bestowed upon me; and however skillful a workman I suppose him to be, I have no reason, on that account, to think that it was obligatory on him to give to each of his works all the perfections he is able to bestow upon some. Nor, moreover, can I complain that God has not given me freedom of choice, or a will sufficiently ample and perfect, since, in truth, I am conscious of will so ample and extended as to be superior to all limits. And what appears to me here to be highly remarkable is that, of all the other properties I possess, there is none so great and perfect as that I do not clearly discern it could be still greater and more perfect. For, to take an example, if I consider the faculty of understanding which I possess, I find that it is of very small extent, and greatly limited, and at the same time I form the idea of another faculty of the same nature, much more ample and even infinite, and seeing that I can frame the idea of it, I discover, from this circumstance alone, that it pertains to the nature of God. In the same way, if I examine the faculty of memory or imagination, or any other faculty I possess, I find none that is not small and circumscribed, and in God immense [and infinite]. It is the faculty of will only, or freedom

of choice, which I experience to be so great that I am unable to conceive the idea of another that shall be more ample and extended; so that it is chiefly my will which leads me to discern that I bear a certain image and similitude of Deity. For although the faculty of will is incomparably greater in God than in myself, as well in respect of the knowledge and power that are conjoined with it, and that render it stronger and more efficacious, as in respect of the object, since in him it extends to a greater number of things, it does not, nevertheless, appear to me greater, considered in itself formally and precisely: for the power of will consists only in this, that we are able to do or not to do the same thing (that is, to affirm or deny, to pursue or shun it), or rather in this alone, that in affirming or denying, pursuing or shunning, what is proposed to us by the understanding, we so act that we are not conscious of being determined to a particular action by any external force. For, to the possession of freedom, it is not necessary that I be alike indifferent toward each of two contraries; but, on the contrary, the more I am inclined toward the one, whether because I clearly know that in it there is the reason of truth and goodness, or because God thus internally disposes my thought, the more freely do I choose and embrace it; and assuredly divine grace and natural knowledge, very far from diminishing liberty, rather augment and fortify it. But the indifference of which I am conscious when I am not impelled to one side rather than to another for want of a reason, is the lowest grade of liberty, and manifests defect or negation of knowledge rather than perfection of will; for if I always clearly knew what was true and good, I should never have any difficulty in determining what judgment I ought to come to, and what choice I ought to make, and I should thus be entirely free without ever being indifferent.

9. From all this I discover, however, that neither the power of willing, which I have received from God, is of itself the source of my errors, for it is exceedingly ample and perfect in its kind; nor even the power of understanding, for as I conceive no object unless by means of the faculty that God bestowed upon me, all that I conceive is doubtless rightly conceived by me, and it is impossible for me to be deceived in it. Whence, then, spring my errors? They arise from this cause alone, that I do not restrain the will, which is of much wider range than the understanding, within the same limits, but extend it even to things I do not understand, and as the will is of itself indifferent to such, it readily falls into error and sin by choosing the false in room of the true, and evil instead of good.

10. For example, when I lately considered whether aught really existed in the world, and found that because I considered this question, it very manifestly followed that I myself existed, I could not but judge that what I so clearly conceived was true, not that I was forced to this judgment by any external cause, but simply because great clearness of the understanding was succeeded by strong inclination in the will; and I believed this the more freely and spontaneously in proportion as I was less indifferent with respect to it. But now I not only know that I exist, in so far as I am a thinking being, but there is likewise presented to my mind a certain idea of corporeal nature; hence I am in doubt as to whether the thinking nature which is in me, or rather which I myself am, is different from that corporeal nature, or whether both are merely one and the same thing, and I here suppose that I am as yet ignorant of any reason that would determine me to adopt the one belief in preference to the other; whence it happens that it is a matter of perfect indifference to me which of the two suppositions I affirm or deny, or whether I form any judgment at all in the matter.

11. This indifference, moreover, extends not only to things of which the understanding has no knowledge at all, but in general also to all those which it does not discover with perfect clearness at the moment the will is deliberating upon them; for, however probable the conjectures may be that dispose me to form a judgment in a particular matter, the simple knowledge that these are merely conjectures, and not certain and indubitable reasons, is sufficient to lead me to form one that is directly the opposite. Of this I lately had abundant experience, when I laid aside as false all that I had before held for true, on the single ground that I could in some degree doubt of it.

12. But if I abstain from judging of a thing when I do not conceive it with sufficient clearness and distinctness, it is plain that I act rightly, and am not deceived; but if I resolve to deny or affirm, I then do not make a right use of my free will; and if I affirm what is false, it is evident that I am deceived; moreover, even although I judge according to truth, I stumble upon it by chance, and do not therefore escape the imputation of a wrong use of my freedom; for it is a dictate of the natural light, that the knowledge of the understanding ought always to precede the determination of the will. And it is this wrong use of the freedom of the will in which is found the privation that constitutes the form of error. Privation, I say, is found in the act, in so far as it proceeds from myself, but it does not exist in the faculty which I received from God, nor even in the act, in so far as it depends on him.

13. For I have assuredly no reason to complain that God has not given me a greater power of intelligence or more perfect natural light than he has actually bestowed, since it is of the nature of a finite understanding not to comprehend many things, and of the nature of a created understanding to be finite; on the contrary, I have every reason to render thanks to God, who owed me nothing, for having given me all the perfections I possess, and I should be far from thinking that he has unjustly deprived me of, or kept back, the other perfections which he has not bestowed upon me.

14. I have no reason, moreover, to complain because he has given me a will more ample than my understanding, since, as the will consists only of a single element, and that indivisible, it would appear that this faculty is of such a nature that nothing could be taken from it [without destroying it]; and certainly, the more extensive it is, the more cause I have to thank the goodness of him who bestowed it upon me.

15. And, finally, I ought not also to complain that God concurs with me in forming the acts of this will, or the judgments in which I am deceived, because those acts are wholly true and good, in so far as they depend on God; and the ability to form them is a higher degree of perfection in my nature than the want of it would be. With regard to privation, in which alone consists the formal reason of error and sin, this does not require the concurrence of Deity, because it is not a thing [or existence], and if it be referred to God as to its cause, it ought not to be called privation, but negation [according to the signification of these words in the schools]. For in truth it is no imperfection in Deity that he has accorded to me the power of giving or withholding my assent from certain things of which he has not put a clear and distinct knowledge in my understanding; but it is doubtless an imperfection in me that I do not use my freedom aright, and readily give my judgment on matters which I only obscurely and confusedly conceive. I perceive, nevertheless, that it was easy for Deity so to have constituted me as that I should never be deceived, although I still remained free and possessed of a limited knowledge, viz., by implanting in my understanding a clear and distinct knowledge of all the objects respecting which I should ever have to deliberate; or simply by so deeply engraving on my memory the resolution to judge of nothing without previously possessing a clear and distinct conception of it, that I should never forget it. And I easily understand that, in so far as I consider myself as a single whole, without reference to any other being in the universe, I should have been much more perfect than I now am, had Deity created me superior to error; but I cannot therefore deny that it is not somehow a greater perfection in the universe, that certain of its parts are not exempt from defect, as others are, than if they were all perfectly alike. And I have no right to complain because God, who placed me in the world, was not willing that I should sustain that character which of all others is the chief and most perfect.

16. I have even good reason to remain satisfied on the ground that, if he has not given me the perfection of being superior to error by the first means I have pointed out above, which depends on a clear and evident knowledge of all the matters regarding which I can deliberate, he has at least left in my power the other means, which is, firmly to retain the resolution never to judge where the truth is not clearly known to me: for, although I am conscious of the weakness of not being able to keep my

mind continually fixed on the same thought, I can nevertheless, by attentive and oft-repeated meditation, impress it so strongly on my memory that I shall never fail to recollect it as often as I require it, and I can acquire in this way the habitude of not erring.

17. And since it is in being superior to error that the highest and chief perfection of man consists, I deem that I have not gained little by this day's meditation, in having discovered the source of error and falsity. And certainly this can be no other than what I have now explained: for as often as I so restrain my will within the limits of my knowledge, that it forms no judgment except regarding objects which are clearly and distinctly represented to it by the understanding, I can never be deceived; because every clear and distinct conception is doubtless something, and as such cannot owe its origin to nothing, but must of necessity have God for its author—God, I say, who, as supremely perfect, cannot, without a contradiction, be the cause of any error; and consequently it is necessary to conclude that every such conception [or judgment] is true. Nor have I merely learned to-day what I must avoid to escape error, but also what I must do to arrive at the knowledge of truth; for I will assuredly reach truth if I only fix my attention sufficiently on all the things I conceive perfectly, and separate these from others which I conceive more confusedly and obscurely; to which for the future I shall give diligent heed.

Meditation V
Of the Essence of Material Things; and, Again, of God; That He Exists.

1. Several other questions remain for consideration respecting the attributes of God and my own nature or mind. I will, however, on some other occasion perhaps resume the investigation of these. Meanwhile, as I have discovered what must be done and what avoided to arrive at the knowledge of truth, what I have chiefly to do is to essay to emerge from the state of doubt in which I have for some time been, and to discover whether anything can be known with certainty regarding material objects.

2. But before considering whether such objects as I conceive exist without me, I must examine their ideas in so far as these are to be found in my consciousness, and discover which of them are distinct and which confused.

3. In the first place, I distinctly imagine that quantity which the philosophers commonly call continuous, or the extension in length, breadth, and depth that is in this quantity, or rather in the object to which it is attributed. Further, I can enumerate in it many diverse parts, and attribute to each of these all sorts of sizes, figures, situations, and local motions; and, in fine, I can assign to each of these motions all degrees of duration.

4. And I not only distinctly know these things when I thus consider them in general; but besides, by a little attention, I discover innumerable particulars respecting figures, numbers, motion, and the like, which are so evidently true, and so accordant with my nature, that when I now discover them I do not so much appear to learn anything new, as to call to remembrance what I before knew, or for the first time to remark what was before in my mind, but to which I had not hitherto directed my attention.

5. And what I here find of most importance is, that I discover in my mind innumerable ideas of certain objects, which cannot be esteemed pure negations, although perhaps they possess no reality beyond my thought, and which are not framed by me though it may be in my power to think, or not to think them, but possess true and immutable natures of their own. As, for example, when I imagine a triangle, although there is not perhaps and never was in any place in the universe apart from my thought one such figure, it remains true nevertheless that this figure possesses a certain determinate nature, form, or essence, which is immutable and eternal, and not framed by me, nor in any degree dependent on my thought; as appears from the circumstance, that diverse properties of the triangle may be demonstrated, viz., that its three angles are equal to two right, that its greatest side is subtended by its greatest angle,

and the like, which, whether I will or not, I now clearly discern to belong to it, although before I did not at all think of them, when, for the first time, I imagined a triangle, and which accordingly cannot be said to have been invented by me.

6. Nor is it a valid objection to allege, that perhaps this idea of a triangle came into my mind by the medium of the senses, through my having seen bodies of a triangular figure; for I am able to form in thought an innumerable variety of figures with regard to which it cannot be supposed that they were ever objects of sense, and I can nevertheless demonstrate diverse properties of their nature no less than of the triangle, all of which are assuredly true since I clearly conceive them: and they are therefore something, and not mere negations; for it is highly evident that all that is true is something, [truth being identical with existence]; and I have already fully shown the truth of the principle, that whatever is clearly and distinctly known is true. And although this had not been demonstrated, yet the nature of my mind is such as to compel me to assert to what I clearly conceive while I so conceive it; and I recollect that even when I still strongly adhered to the objects of sense, I reckoned among the number of the most certain truths those I clearly conceived relating to figures, numbers, and other matters that pertain to arithmetic and geometry, and in general to the pure mathematics.

7. But now if because I can draw from my thought the idea of an object, it follows that all I clearly and distinctly apprehend to pertain to this object, does in truth belong to it, may I not from this derive an argument for the existence of God? It is certain that I no less find the idea of a God in my consciousness, that is the idea of a being supremely perfect, than that of any figure or number whatever: and I know with not less clearness and distinctness that an [actual and] eternal existence pertains to his nature than that all which is demonstrable of any figure or number really belongs to the nature of that figure or number; and, therefore, although all the conclusions of the preceding Meditations were false, the existence of God would pass with me for a truth at least as certain as I ever judged any truth of mathematics to be.

8. Indeed such a doctrine may at first sight appear to contain more sophistry than truth. For, as I have been accustomed in every other matter to distinguish between existence and essence, I easily believe that the existence can be separated from the essence of God, and that thus God may be conceived as not actually existing. But, nevertheless, when I think of it more attentively, it appears that the existence can no more be separated from the essence of God, than the idea of a mountain from that of a valley, or the equality of its three angles to two right angles, from the essence of a [rectilinear] triangle; so that it is not less impossible to conceive a God, that is, a being supremely perfect, to whom existence is awanting, or who is devoid of a certain perfection, than to conceive a mountain without a valley.

9. But though, in truth, I cannot conceive a God unless as existing, any more than I can a mountain without a valley, yet, just as it does not follow that there is any mountain in the world merely because I conceive a mountain with a valley, so likewise, though I conceive God as existing, it does not seem to follow on that account that God exists; for my thought imposes no necessity on things; and as I may imagine a winged horse, though there be none such, so I could perhaps attribute existence to God, though no God existed.

10. But the cases are not analogous, and a fallacy lurks under the semblance of this objection: for because I cannot conceive a mountain without a valley, it does not follow that there is any mountain or valley in existence, but simply that the mountain or valley, whether they do or do not exist, are inseparable from each other; whereas, on the other hand, because I cannot conceive God unless as existing, it follows that existence is inseparable from him, and therefore that he really exists: not that this is brought about by my thought, or that it imposes any necessity on things, but, on the contrary, the necessity which lies in the thing itself, that is, the necessity of the existence of God, determines me to think in this way: for it is not in my power to conceive a God without existence, that is, a being supremely perfect, and yet devoid of an absolute perfection, as I am free to imagine a horse with or without wings.

11. Nor must it be alleged here as an objection, that it is in truth necessary to admit that God exists, after having supposed him to possess all perfections, since existence is one of them, but that my original supposition was not necessary; just as it is not necessary to think that all quadrilateral figures can be inscribed in the circle, since, if I supposed this, I should be constrained to admit that the rhombus, being a figure of four sides, can be therein inscribed, which, however, is manifestly false. This objection is, I say, incompetent; for although it may not be necessary that I shall at any time entertain the notion of Deity, yet each time I happen to think of a first and sovereign being, and to draw, so to speak, the idea of him from the storehouse of the mind, I am necessitated to attribute to him all kinds of perfections, though I may not then enumerate them all, nor think of each of them in particular. And this necessity is sufficient, as soon as I discover that existence is a perfection, to cause me to infer the existence of this first and sovereign being; just as it is not necessary that I should ever imagine any triangle, but whenever I am desirous of considering a rectilinear figure composed of only three angles, it is absolutely necessary to attribute those properties to it from which it is correctly inferred that its three angles are not greater than two right angles, although perhaps I may not then advert to this relation in particular. But when I consider what figures are capable of being inscribed in the circle, it is by no means necessary to hold that all quadrilateral figures are of this number; on the contrary, I cannot even imagine such to be the case, so long as I shall be unwilling to accept in thought aught that I do not clearly and distinctly conceive; and consequently there is a vast difference between false suppositions, as is the one in question, and the true ideas that were born with me, the first and chief of which is the idea of God. For indeed I discern on many grounds that this idea is not factitious depending simply on my thought, but that it is the representation of a true and immutable nature: in the first place because I can conceive no other being, except God, to whose essence existence [necessarily] pertains; in the second, because it is impossible to conceive two or more gods of this kind; and it being supposed that one such God exists, I clearly see that he must have existed from all eternity, and will exist to all eternity; and finally, because I apprehend many other properties in God, none of which I can either diminish or change.

12. But, indeed, whatever mode of probation I in the end adopt, it always returns to this, that it is only the things I clearly and distinctly conceive which have the power of completely persuading me. And although, of the objects I conceive in this manner, some, indeed, are obvious to every one, while others are only discovered after close and careful investigation; nevertheless after they are once discovered, the latter are not esteemed less certain than the former. Thus, for example, to take the case of a right-angled triangle, although it is not so manifest at first that the square of the base is equal to the squares of the other two sides, as that the base is opposite to the greatest angle; nevertheless, after it is once apprehended, we are as firmly persuaded of the truth of the former as of the latter. And, with respect to God if I were not pre-occupied by prejudices, and my thought beset on all sides by the continual presence of the images of sensible objects, I should know nothing sooner or more easily than the fact of his being. For is there any truth more clear than the existence of a Supreme Being, or of God, seeing it is to his essence alone that [necessary and eternal] existence pertains?

13. And although the right conception of this truth has cost me much close thinking, nevertheless at present I feel not only as assured of it as of what I deem most certain, but I remark further that the certitude of all other truths is so absolutely dependent on it that without this knowledge it is impossible ever to know anything perfectly.

14. For although I am of such a nature as to be unable, while I possess a very clear and distinct apprehension of a matter, to resist the conviction of its truth, yet because my constitution is also such as to incapacitate me from keeping my mind continually fixed on the same object, and as I frequently recollect a past judgment without at the same time being able to recall the grounds of it, it may happen meanwhile that other reasons are presented to me which would readily cause me to change my opinion,

if I did not know that God existed; and thus I should possess no true and certain knowledge, but merely vague and vacillating opinions. Thus, for example, when I consider the nature of the [rectilinear] triangle, it most clearly appears to me, who have been instructed in the principles of geometry, that its three angles are equal to two right angles, and I find it impossible to believe otherwise, while I apply my mind to the demonstration; but as soon as I cease from attending to the process of proof, although I still remember that I had a clear comprehension of it, yet I may readily come to doubt of the truth demonstrated, if I do not know that there is a God: for I may persuade myself that I have been so constituted by nature as to be sometimes deceived, even in matters which I think I apprehend with the greatest evidence and certitude, especially when I recollect that I frequently considered many things to be true and certain which other reasons afterward constrained me to reckon as wholly false.

15. But after I have discovered that God exists, seeing I also at the same time observed that all things depend on him, and that he is no deceiver, and thence inferred that all which I clearly and distinctly perceive is of necessity true: although I no longer attend to the grounds of a judgment, no opposite reason can be alleged sufficient to lead me to doubt of its truth, provided only I remember that I once possessed a clear and distinct comprehension of it. My knowledge of it thus becomes true and certain. And this same knowledge extends likewise to whatever I remember to have formerly demonstrated, as the truths of geometry and the like: for what can be alleged against them to lead me to doubt of them? Will it be that my nature is such that I may be frequently deceived? But I already know that I cannot be deceived in judgments of the grounds of which I possess a clear knowledge. Will it be that I formerly deemed things to be true and certain which I afterward discovered to be false? But I had no clear and distinct knowledge of any of those things, and, being as yet ignorant of the rule by which I am assured of the truth of a judgment, I was led to give my assent to them on grounds which I afterward discovered were less strong than at the time I imagined them to be. What further objection, then, is there? Will it be said that perhaps I am dreaming (an objection I lately myself raised), or that all the thoughts of which I am now conscious have no more truth than the reveries of my dreams? But although, in truth, I should be dreaming, the rule still holds that all which is clearly presented to my intellect is indisputably true.

16. And thus I very clearly see that the certitude and truth of all science depends on the knowledge alone of the true God, insomuch that, before I knew him, I could have no perfect knowledge of any other thing. And now that I know him, I possess the means of acquiring a perfect knowledge respecting innumerable matters, as well relative to God himself and other intellectual objects as to corporeal nature, in so far as it is the object of pure mathematics [which do not consider whether it exists or not].

10. Introduction to Spinoza

Baruch de Spinoza was born to Jewish parents in Holland in 1632. In his philosophical work, he draws from both Descartes and the Christian and Jewish tradition. His main project is to demonstrate that the universe is a unified whole governed by inescapable laws and absolute logical necessity. Spinoza essentially drives to its logical conclusion the new world image which came out from seventeenth century physics, especially Newton. What mainly differentiates Spinoza from other thinkers of the period, including Descartes, is his preparedness to trust reason and what can be proven scientifically over religious explanation. So, whereas Descartes begins by radical doubt but quickly moves to reestablish the existence of (the Christian) God, Spinoza rejects altogether the notion of a personal god and identifies God with the physical universe and with the idea of the universe. His views were treated as heretical by Jews and Christians alike. By the age of 24, he was excommunicated by his Jewish community and his philosophical masterpiece, the *Ethics*, was published only after his death.

In his *Ethics*, Spinoza replaces Aristotle's numerous substances with one and only substance—'God or Nature.' This impersonal god, who is in the world, does not create it, and acts out of necessity, has indefinite attributes which account for all the things which exist and happen in the universe. Causal necessity absolutely governs the universe: everything that happens has a cause and, going all the way back, the first cause is God, who is the cause of itself. This means, in other words, that nature is self-caused.

The two attributes of the universe which are better known to us are thought and extension. This is why we comprehend 'ideas' and conceive of the physical things which exist in the universe as the 'ideas' and the 'things' with which we become acquainted in the course of our lives. Although there is no direct relationship between ideas and physical things, they are part of the same divine pattern and so they correspond. Spinoza thus offers a better solution of the mind-body problem than Descartes. Understanding the—strictly deterministic—pattern of the universe means fully understanding the world. Spinoza therefore establishes the possibility of certain human knowledge.

Understanding and accepting our position as humans in the world is for Spinoza the key to knowledge, happiness and freedom. Spinoza denounces free will as an illusion, and argues that only the knowledge of the laws of the universe, including psychological laws, will give to one peace of mind and real freedom, whereas free will theories only provide an illusion of freedom. The idea that it is knowledge which liberates us will have a long history in Western thought. In different forms it will be endorsed by Hegel, Marx and Freud. For Spinoza, the knowledge of the laws of the universe, our recognition of our place in it and our control over our desires and our negative passions lead to the best possible life.

Spinoza applied similar principles to human desires and agency in Books III–V of the *Ethics*. He recommended a way of life that acknowledges the fundamental consequences of our position in the world as mere modes of the one true being. It would be moral bondage if we were motivated only by causes of which we remain unaware, Spinoza held, so genuine freedom comes only with knowledge of what it is that necessitates our actions. Recognizing the invariable influence of desire over our passionate natures, we then strive for the peace of mind that comes through an impartial attachment to reason. Although such an attitude is not easy to maintain, Spinoza concluded that "All noble things are as difficult as they are rare."

The Ethics
(Ethica Ordine Geometrico Demonstrata)

Benedict de Spinoza
Translated by R. H. M. Elwes

Part I: Concerning God
Definitions

I. By that which is 'self-caused' I mean that of which the essence involves existence, or that of which the nature is only conceivable as existent.

II. A thing is called 'finite after its kind' when it can be limited by another thing of the same nature; for instance, a body is called finite because we always conceive another greater body. So, also, a thought is limited by another thought, but a body is not limited by thought, nor a thought by body.

III. By 'substance' I mean that which is in itself, and is conceived through itself: in other words, that of which a conception can be formed independently of any other conception.

IV. By 'attribute' I mean that which the intellect perceives as constituting the essence of substance.

V. By 'mode' I mean the modifications ("affectiones") of substance, or that which exists in, and is conceived through, something other than itself.

VI. By 'God' I mean a being absolutely infinite—that is, a substance consisting in infinite attributes, of which each expresses eternal and infinite essentiality.

Explanation—I say absolutely infinite, not infinite after its kind: for, of a thing infinite only after its kind, infinite attributes may be denied; but that which is absolutely infinite, contains in its essence whatever expresses reality, and involves no negation.

VII. That thing is called 'free,' which exists solely by the necessity of its own nature, and of which the action is determined by itself alone. On the other hand, that thing is necessary, or rather constrained, which is determined by something external to itself to a fixed and definite method of existence or action.

VIII. By 'eternity' I mean existence itself, in so far as it is conceived necessarily to follow solely from the definition of that which is eternal.

Explanation—Existence of this kind is conceived as an eternal truth, like the essence of a thing and, therefore, cannot be explained by means of continuance or time, though continuance may be conceived without a beginning or end.

AXIOMS

I. Everything which exists, exists either in itself or in something else.

II. That which cannot be conceived through anything else must be conceived through itself.

III. From a given definite cause an effect necessarily follows; and, on the other hand, if no definite cause be granted, it is impossible that an effect can follow.

IV. The knowledge of an effect depends on and involves the knowledge of a cause.

V. Things which have nothing in common cannot be understood, the one by means of the other; the conception of one does not involve the conception of the other.

VI. A true idea must correspond with its ideate or object.

VII. If a thing can be conceived as non-existing, its essence does not involve existence.

PROPOSITIONS

I. Substance is by nature prior to its modifications.

Proof—This is clear from Deff. iii. and v.

II. Two substances, whose attributes are different, have nothing in common.

Proof—Also evident from Def. iii. For each must exist in itself, and be conceived through itself; in other words, the conception of one does not imply the conception of the other.

III. Things which have nothing in common cannot be one the cause of the other.

Proof—If they have nothing in common, it follows that one cannot be apprehended by means of the other (Ax. v.), and, therefore, one cannot be the cause of the other (Ax. iv.). Q.E.D.

IV. Two or more distinct things are distinguished one from the other, either by the difference of the attributes of the substances, or by the difference of their modifications.

Proof—Everything which exists, exists either in itself or in something else (Ax. i.),—that is (by Deff. iii. and v.), nothing is granted in addition to the understanding, except substance and its modifications. Nothing is, therefore, given besides the understanding, by which several things may be distinguished one from the other, except the substances, or, in other words (see Ax. iv.), their attributes and modifications. Q.E.D.

V. There cannot exist in the universe two or more substances having the same nature or attribute.

Proof—If several distinct substances be granted, they must be distinguished one from the other, either by the difference of their attributes, or by the difference of their modifications (Prop. iv.). If only by the difference of their attributes, it will be granted that there cannot be more than one with an identical attribute. If by the difference of their modifications—as substance is naturally prior to its modifications (Prop. i.)—it follows that setting the modifications aside, and considering substance in itself, that is truly, (Deff. iii and vi.), there cannot be conceived one substance different from another—that is (by Prop. iv.), there cannot be granted several substances, but one substance only. Q.E.D.

VI. One substance cannot be produced by another substance.

Proof—It is impossible that there should be in the universe two substances with an identical attribute, i.e. which have anything common to them both (Prop ii.), and, therefore (Prop. iii.), one cannot be the cause of the other, neither can one be produced by the other. Q.E.D.

VI. Corollary—Hence it follows that a substance cannot be produced by anything external to itself. For in the universe nothing is granted, save substances and their modifications (as appears from Ax. i. and Deff. iii. and v.). Now (by the last Prop.) substance cannot be produced by another substance, therefore it cannot be produced by anything external to itself. Q.E.D. This is shown still more readily by the absurdity of the contradictory. For, if substance be produced by an external cause, the knowledge of it would depend on the knowledge of its cause (Ax. iv.), and (by Deff. iii.) it would itself not be substance.

VII. Existence belongs to the nature of substances.

Proof—Substance cannot be produced by anything external (Cor., Prop vi.), it must, therefore, be its own cause—that is, its essence necessarily involves existence, or existence belongs to its nature.

VIII. Every substance is necessarily infinite.

Proof—There can only be one substance with an identical attribute, and existence follows from its nature (Prop. vii.); its nature, therefore, involves existence, either as finite or infinite. It does not exist as finite, for (by Deff. ii.) it would then be limited by something else of the same kind, which would also necessarily exist (Prop. vii.); and there would b) e two substances with an identical attribute, which is absurd (Prop. v.). It therefore exists as infinite. Q.E.D.

Note I.—As finite existence involves a partial negation, and infinite existence is the absolute affirmation of the given nature, it follows (solely from Prop. vii.) that every substance is necessarily infinite.

Note II.—No doubt it will be difficult for those who think about things loosely, and have not been accustomed to know them by their primary causes, to comprehend the demonstration of Prop. vii.: for such persons make no distinction between the modifications of substances and the substances themselves, and are ignorant of the manner in which things are produced; hence they may attribute to substances the beginning which they observe in natural objects. Those who are ignorant of true causes make complete confusion—think that trees might talk just as well as men—that men might be formed from stones as well as from seed; and imagine that any form might be changed into any other. So, also, those who confuse the two natures, divine and human, readily attribute human passions to the deity, especially so long as they do not know how passions originate in the mind. But, if people would consider the nature of substance, they would have no doubt about the truth of Prop. vii. In fact, this proposition would be a universal axiom, and accounted a truism. For, by substance, would be understood that which is in itself, and is conceived through itself—that is, something of which the conception requires not the conception of anything else; whereas modifications exist in something external to themselves, and a conception of them is formed by means of a conception of the things in which they exist. Therefore, we may have true ideas of non-existent modifications; for, although they may have no actual existence apart from the conceiving intellect, yet their essence is so involved in something external to themselves that they may through it be conceived. Whereas the only truth substances can have, external to the intellect, must consist in their existence, because they are conceived through themselves. Therefore, for a person to say that he has a clear and distinct—that is, a true—idea of a substance, but that he is not sure whether such substance exists, would be the same as if he said that he had a true idea, but was not sure whether or no it was false (a little consideration will make this plain); or if anyone affirmed that substance is created, it would be the same as saying that a false idea was true—in short, the height of absurdity. It must, then, necessarily be admitted that the existence of substance as its essence is an eternal truth. And we can hence conclude by another process of reasoning—that there is but one such substance. I think that this may profitably be done at once; and, in order to proceed regularly with the demonstration, we must premise:—

1. The true definition of a thing neither involves nor expresses anything beyond the nature of the thing defined. From this it follows that—

2. No definition implies or expresses a certain number of individuals, inasmuch as it expresses nothing beyond the nature of the thing defined. For instance, the definition of a triangle expresses nothing beyond the actual nature of a triangle: it does not imply any fixed number of triangles.

3. There is necessarily for each individual existent thing a cause why it should exist.

4. This cause of existence must either be contained in the nature and definition of the thing defined, or must be postulated apart from such definition.

It therefore follows that, if a given number of individual things exist in nature, there must be some cause for the existence of exactly that number, neither more nor less. For example, if twenty men exist in the universe (for simplicity's sake, I will suppose them existing simultaneously, and to have had no predecessors), and we want to account for the existence of these twenty men, it will not be enough to show the cause of human existence in general; we must also show why there are exactly twenty men, neither more nor less: for a cause must be assigned for the existence of each individual. Now this cause cannot be contained in the actual nature of man, for the true definition of man does not involve any consideration of the number twenty. Consequently, the cause for the existence of these twenty men, and, consequently, of each of them, must necessarily be sought externally to each individual. Hence we may lay down the absolute rule, that everything which may consist of several individuals must have an external cause. And, as it has been shown already that existence appertains to the nature of substance, existence must necessarily be included in its definition; and from its definition alone existence must be deducible. But from its definition (as we have shown, Notes ii., iii.), we cannot infer the existence of several substances; therefore it follows that there is only one substance of the same nature. Q.E.D.

IX. The more reality or being a thing has, the greater the number of its attributes (Def. iv.).

X. Each particular attribute of the one substance must be conceived through itself.

Proof—An attribute is that which the intellect perceives of substance, as constituting its essence (Def. iv.), and, therefore, must be conceived through itself (Def. iii.). Q.E.D.

Note—It is thus evident that, though two attributes are, in fact, conceived as distinct—that is, one without the help of the other—yet we cannot, therefore, conclude that they constitute two entities, or two different substances. For it is the nature of substance that each of its attributes is conceived through itself, inasmuch as all the attributes it has have always existed simultaneously in it, and none could be produced by any other; but each expresses the reality or being of substance. It is, then, far from an absurdity to ascribe several attributes to one substance: for nothing in nature is more clear than that each and every entity must be conceived under some attribute, and that its reality or being is in proportion to the number of its attributes expressing necessity or eternity and infinity. Consequently it is abundantly clear, that an absolutely infinite being must necessarily be defined as consisting in infinite attributes, each of which expresses a certain eternal and infinite essence.

If anyone now ask, by what sign shall he be able to distinguish different substances, let him read the following propositions, which show that there is but one substance in the universe, and that it is absolutely infinite, wherefore such a sign would be sought in vain.

XI. God, or substance, consisting of infinite attributes, of which each expresses eternal and infinite essentiality, necessarily exists.

Proof—If this be denied, conceive, if possible, that God does not exist: then his essence does not involve existence. But this (Prop. vii.) is absurd. Therefore God necessarily exists.

Another proof—Of everything whatsoever a cause or reason must be assigned, either for its existence, or for its non-existence—e.g. if a triangle exist, a reason or cause must be granted for its existence; if, on the contrary, it does not exist, a cause must also be granted, which prevents it from existing, or annuls its existence. This reason or cause must either be contained in the nature of the thing in question, or be external to it. For instance, the reason for the non-existence of a square circle is indicated in its nature, namely, because it would involve a contradiction. On the other hand, the existence of substance follows also solely from its nature, inasmuch as its nature involves existence. (See Prop. vii.)

But the reason for the existence of a triangle or a circle does not follow from the nature of those figures, but from the order of universal nature in extension. From the latter it must follow, either that a triangle necessarily exists, or that it is impossible that it should exist. So much is self-evident. It follows therefrom that a thing necessarily exists, if no cause or reason be granted which prevents its existence.

If, then, no cause or reason can be given, which prevents the existence of God, or which destroys his existence, we must certainly conclude that he necessarily does exist. If such a reason or cause should be given, it must either be drawn from the very nature of God, or be external to him—that is, drawn from another substance of another nature. For if it were of the same nature, God, by that very fact, would be admitted to exist. But substance of another nature could have nothing in common with God (by Prop. ii.), and therefore would be unable either to cause or to destroy his existence.

As, then, a reason or cause which would annul the divine existence cannot be drawn from anything external to the divine nature, such cause must perforce, if God does not exist, be drawn from God's own nature, which would involve a contradiction. To make such an affirmation about a being absolutely infinite and supremely perfect is absurd; therefore, neither in the nature of God, nor externally to his nature, can a cause or reason be assigned which would annul his existence. Therefore, God necessarily exists. Q.E.D.

Another proof—The potentiality of non-existence is a negation of power, and contrariwise the potentiality of existence is a power, as is obvious. If, then, that which necessarily exists is nothing but finite beings, such finite beings are more powerful than a being absolutely infinite, which is obviously absurd; therefore, either nothing exists, or else a being absolutely infinite necessarily exists also. Now we exist either in ourselves, or in something else which necessarily exists (see Ax. i. and Prop. vii.). Therefore a being absolutely infinite—in other words, God (Def. vi.)—necessarily exists. Q.E.D.

Note—In this last proof, I have purposely shown God's existence 'a posteriori,' so that the proof might be more easily followed, not because, from the same premises, God's existence does not follow 'a priori.' For, as the potentiality of existence is a power, it follows that, in proportion as reality increases in the nature of a thing, so also will it increase its strength for existence. Therefore a being absolutely infinite, such as God, has from himself an absolutely infinite power of existence, and hence he does absolutely exist. Perhaps there will be many who will be unable to see the force of this proof, inasmuch as they are accustomed only to consider those things which flow from external causes. Of such things, they see that those which quickly come to pass—that is, quickly come into existence—quickly also disappear; whereas they regard as more difficult of accomplishment—that is, not so easily brought into existence—those things which they conceive as more complicated.

However, to do away with this misconception, I need not here show the measure of truth in the proverb, "What comes quickly, goes quickly," nor discuss whether, from the point of view of universal nature, all things are equally easy, or otherwise: I need only remark that I am not here speaking of things, which come to pass through causes external to themselves, but only of substances which (by Prop. vi.) cannot be produced by any external cause. Things which are produced by external causes, whether they consist of many parts or few, owe whatsoever perfection or reality they possess solely to the efficacy of their external cause; wherefore the existence of substance must arise solely from its own nature, which is nothing else but its essence. Thus, the perfection of a thing does not annul its existence, but, on the contrary, asserts it. Imperfection, on the other hand, does annul it; therefore we cannot be more certain of the existence of anything, than of the existence of a being absolutely infinite or perfect—that is, of God. For inasmuch as his essence excludes all imperfection, and involves absolute perfection, all cause for doubt concerning his existence is done away, and the utmost certainty on the question is given. This, I think, will be evident to every moderately attentive reader.

XII. No attribute of substance can be conceived from which it would follow that substance can be divided.

Proof—The parts into which substance as thus conceived would be divided either will retain the nature of substance, or they will not. If the former, then (by Prop. viii.) each part will necessarily be infinite, and (by Prop vi.) self-caused, and (by Prop. v.) will perforce consist of a different attribute, so that, in that case, several substances could be formed out of one substance, which (by Prop. vi.) is absurd. Moreover, the parts (by Prop. ii.) would have nothing in common with their whole, and the whole (by Def. iv. and Prop. X) could both exist and be conceived without its parts, which everyone will admit to be absurd. If we adopt the second alternative—namely, that the parts will not retain the nature of substance—then, if the whole substance were divided into equal parts, it would lose the nature of substance, and would cease to exist, which (by Prop. vii.) is absurd.

XIII. Substance absolutely infinite is indivisible.

Proof—If it could be divided, the parts into which it was divided would either retain the nature of absolutely infinite substance, or they would not. If the former, we should have several substances of the same nature, which (by Prop. v.) is absurd. If the latter, then (by Prop. vii.) substance absolutely infinite could cease to exist, which (by Prop. xi.) is also absurd.

Corollary—It follows that no substance, and consequently no extended substance, in so far as it is substance, is divisible.

Note—The indivisibility of substance may be more easily understood as follows. The nature of substance can only be conceived as infinite, and by a part of substance, nothing else can be understood than finite substance, which (by Prop. viii.) involves a manifest contradiction.

XIV. Besides God no substance can be granted or conceived.

Proof—As God is a being absolutely infinite, of whom no attribute that expresses the essence of substance can be denied (by Def. vi.), and he necessarily exists (by Prop. xi.); if any substance besides God were granted, it would have to be explained by some attribute of God, and thus two substances with the same attribute would exist, which (by Prop. v.) is absurd; therefore, besides God no substance can be granted, or consequently be conceived. If it could be conceived, it would necessarily have to be conceived as existent; but this (by the first part of this proof) is absurd. Therefore, besides God no substance can be granted or conceived. Q.E.D.

Corollary I.—Clearly, therefore: 1. God is one, that is (by Def. vi.) only one substance can be granted in the universe, and that substance is absolutely infinite, as we have already indicated (in the note to Prop. x.).

Corollary II.—It follows: 2. That extension and thought are either attributes of God or (by Ax. i.) accidents ("affectiones") of the attributes of God.

XV. Whatsoever is, is in God, and without God nothing can be, or be conceived.

Proof—Besides God, no substance is granted or can be conceived (by Prop. xiv.), that is (by Def. iii.) nothing which is in itself and is conceived through itself. But modes (by Def. v.) can neither be, nor be conceived without substance; wherefore they can only be in the divine nature, and can only through it be conceived. But substances and modes form the sum total of existence (by Ax. i.), therefore, without God nothing can be, or be conceived. Q.E.D.

Note—Some assert that God, like a man, consists of body and mind, and is susceptible of passions. How far such persons have strayed from the truth is sufficiently evident from what has been said. But these I pass over. For all who have in anywise reflected on the divine nature deny that God has a body. Of this they find excellent proof in the fact that we understand by body a definite quantity, so long, so broad, so deep, bounded by a certain shape, and it is the height of absurdity to predicate such a thing of God, a being absolutely infinite. But meanwhile by other reasons with which they try to prove their point, they show that they think corporeal or extended substance wholly apart from the divine nature, and say it was created by God. Wherefrom the divine nature can have been created, they are wholly ignorant; thus they clearly show that they do not know the meaning of their own words. I myself have proved sufficiently clearly, at any rate in my own judgment (Cor. Prop. vi., and Note 2, Prop. viii.), that no substance can be produced or created by anything other than itself. Further, I showed (in Prop. xiv.) that besides God no substance can be granted or conceived. Hence we drew the conclusion that extended substance is one of the infinite attributes of God. However, in order to explain more fully, I will refute the arguments of my adversaries, which all start from the following points:—

Extended substance, in so far as it is substance, consists, as they think, in parts, wherefore they deny that it can be infinite, or consequently, that it can appertain to God. This they illustrate with many examples, of which I will take one or two. If extended substance, they say, is infinite, let it be conceived to be divided into two parts; each part will then be either finite or infinite. If the former, then infinite substance is composed of two finite parts, which is absurd. If the latter, then one infinite will be twice as large as another infinite, which is also absurd.

Further, if an infinite line be measured out in foot lengths, it will consist of an infinite number of such parts; it would equally consist of an infinite number of parts, if each part measured only an inch: therefore, one infinity would be twelve times as great as the other.

Lastly, if from a single point there be conceived to be drawn two diverging lines which at first are at a definite distance apart, but are produced to infinity, it is certain that the distance between the two lines will be continually increased, until at length it changes from definite to indefinable. As these absurdities follow, it is said, from considering quantity as infinite, the conclusion is drawn that extended substance must necessarily be finite, and, consequently, cannot appertain to the nature of God.

The second argument is also drawn from God's supreme perfection. God, it is said, inasmuch as he is a supremely perfect being, cannot be passive; but extended substance, insofar as it is divisible, is passive. It follows, therefore, that extended substance does not appertain to the essence of God.

Such are the arguments I find on the subject in writers, who by them try to prove that extended substance is unworthy of the divine nature, and cannot possibly appertain thereto. However, I think an attentive reader will see that I have already answered their propositions; for all their arguments are founded on the hypothesis that extended substance is composed of parts, and such a hypothesis I have shown (Prop. xii., and Cor. Prop. xiii.) to be absurd. Moreover, anyone who reflects will see that all these absurdities (if absurdities they be, which I am not now discussing), from which it is sought to extract the conclusion that extended substance is finite, do not at all follow from the notion of an infinite quantity, but merely from the notion that an infinite quantity is measurable, and composed of finite parts: therefore, the only fair conclusion to be drawn is that infinite quantity is not measurable, and cannot be composed of finite parts. This is exactly what we have already proved (in Prop. xii.). Wherefore the weapon which they aimed at us has in reality recoiled upon themselves. If, from this absurdity of theirs, they persist in drawing the conclusion that extended substance must be finite, they will in good sooth be acting like a man who asserts that circles have the properties of squares, and, finding himself thereby landed in absurdities, proceeds to deny that circles have any center, from which all lines drawn to the circumference are equal. For, taking extended substance, which can only be conceived as infinite, one, and indivisible (Props. viii., v., xii.) they assert, in order to prove that it is finite, that it is composed of finite parts, and that it can be multiplied and divided.

So, also, others, after asserting that a line is composed of points, can produce many arguments to prove that a line cannot be infinitely divided. Assuredly it is not less absurd to assert that extended substance is made up of bodies or parts, than it would be to assert that a solid is made up of surfaces, a surface of lines, and a line of points. This must be admitted by all who know clear reason to be infallible, and most of all by those who deny the possibility of a vacuum. For if extended substance could be so divided that its parts were really separate, why should not one part admit of being destroyed, the others remaining joined together as before? And why should all be so fitted into one another as to leave no vacuum? Surely in the case of things, which are really distinct one from the other, one can exist without the other, and can remain in its original condition. As, then, there does not exist a vacuum in nature (of which anon), but all parts are bound to come together to prevent it, it follows from this that the parts cannot really be distinguished, and that extended substance in so far as it is substance cannot be divided.

If anyone asks me the further question, Why are we naturally so prone to divide quantity? I answer, that quantity is conceived by us in two ways; in the abstract and superficially, as we imagine it; or as substance, as we conceive it solely by the intellect. If, then, we regard quantity as it is represented in our imagination, which we often and more easily do, we shall find that it is finite, divisible, and compounded of parts; but if we regard it as it is represented in our intellect, and conceive it as substance, which it is very difficult to do, we shall then, as I have sufficiently proved, find that it is infinite, one, and indivisible. This will be plain enough to all who make a distinction between the intellect and the imagination, especially if it be remembered that matter is everywhere the same, that its parts are not distinguishable, except in so far as we conceive matter as diversely modified, whence its parts are distinguished, not really, but modally. For instance, water, in so far as it is water, we conceive to be divided, and its parts to be separated one from the other; but not in so far as it is extended substance; from this point of view it is neither separated nor divisible. Further, water, in so far as it is water, is produced and corrupted; but, in so far as it is substance, it is neither produced nor corrupted.

I think I have now answered the second argument; it is, in fact, founded on the same assumption as the first—namely, that matter, in so far as it is substance, is divisible, and composed of parts. Even if it were so, I do not know why it should be considered unworthy of the divine nature, inasmuch as besides God (by Prop. xiv.) no substance can be granted, wherefrom it could receive its modifications. All things, I repeat, are in God, and all things which come to pass, come to pass solely through the laws of the infinite nature of God, and follow (as I will shortly show) from the necessity of his essence. Wherefore it can in nowise be said that God is passive in respect to anything other than himself, or that extended substance is unworthy of the divine nature, even if it be supposed divisible, so long as it is granted to be infinite and eternal. But enough of this for the present.

* * * * * * * *

Part II
Propositions

XLVIII. In the mind there is no absolute or free will; but the mind is determined to wish this or that by a cause, which has also been determined by another cause, and this last by another cause, and so on to infinity.

Proof—The mind is a fixed and definite mode of thought (II. xi.), therefore it cannot be the free cause of its actions (I. xvii. Cor. ii.); in other words, it cannot have an absolute faculty of positive or negative volition; but (by I. xxviii.) it must be determined by a cause, which has also been determined by another cause, and this last by another, &c. Q.E.D.

Note—In the same way it is proved, that there is in the mind no absolute faculty of understanding, desiring, loving, &c. Whence it follows, that these and similar faculties are either entirely fictitious, or are merely abstract and general terms, such as we are accustomed to put together from particular things. Thus the intellect and the will stand in the same relation to this or that idea, or this or that volition, as "lapidity" to this or that stone, or as "man" to Peter and Paul. The cause which leads men to consider themselves free has been set forth in the Appendix to Part I. But, before I proceed further, I would here remark that, by the will to affirm and decide, I mean the faculty, not the desire. I mean, I repeat, the faculty, whereby the mind affirms or denies what is true or false, not the desire, wherewith the mind wishes for or turns away from any given thing. After we have proved, that these faculties of ours are general notions, which cannot be distinguished from the particular instances on which they are based, we must inquire whether volitions themselves are anything besides the ideas of things. We must inquire, I say, whether there is in the mind any affirmation or negation beyond that, which the idea, in so far as it is an idea, involves. On which subject see the following proposition, and II. Def. iii., lest the idea of pictures should suggest itself. For by ideas I do not mean images such as are formed at the back of the eye, or in the midst of the brain, but the conceptions of thought.

XLIX. There is in the mind no volition or affirmation and negation, save that which an idea, inasmuch as it is an idea, involves.

Proof—There is in the mind no absolute faculty of positive or negative volition, but only particular volitions, namely, this or that affirmation, and this or that negation. Now let us conceive a particular volition, namely, the mode of thinking whereby the mind affirms, that the three interior angles of a triangle are equal to two right angles. This affirmation involves the conception or idea of a triangle, that is, without the idea of a triangle it cannot be conceived. It is the same thing to say, that the concept A must involve the concept B, as it is to say, that A cannot be conceived without B. Further, this affirmation cannot be made (II. Ax. iii.) without the idea of a triangle. Therefore, this affirmation can neither be nor be conceived, without the idea of a triangle. Again, this idea of a triangle must involve this same affirmation, namely, that its three interior angles are equal to two right angles. Wherefore, and vice versa, this idea of a triangle can neither be nor be conceived without this affirmation, therefore, this affirmation belongs to the essence of the idea of a triangle, and is nothing besides. What we have said of this volition (inasmuch as we have selected it at random) may be said of any other volition, namely, that it is nothing but an idea. Q.E.D.

Corollary—Will and understanding are one and the same.

Proof—Will and understanding are nothing beyond the individual volitions and ideas (II. xlviii. and note). But a particular volition and a particular idea are one and the same (by the foregoing Prop.); therefore, will and understanding are one and the same. Q.E.D.

Note—We have thus removed the cause which is commonly assigned for error. For we have shown above, that falsity consists solely in the privation of knowledge involved in ideas which are fragmentary and confused. Wherefore, a false idea, inasmuch as it is false, does not involve certainty. When we say, then, that a man acquiesces in what is false, and that he has no doubts on the subject, we do not say that he is certain, but only that he does not doubt, or that he acquiesces in what is false, inasmuch as there are no reasons, which should cause his imagination to waver (see II. xliv. note). Thus, although the man be assumed to acquiesce in what is false, we shall never say that he is certain. For by certainty we mean something positive (II. xliii. and note), not merely the absence of doubt.

However, in order that the foregoing proposition may be fully explained, I will draw attention to a few additional points, and I will furthermore answer the objections which may be advanced against our doctrine. Lastly, in order to remove every scruple, I have thought it worth while to point out some of the advantages, which follow therefrom. I say "some," for they will be better appreciated from what we shall set forth in the fifth part.

I begin, then, with the first point, and warn my readers to make an accurate distinction between an idea, or conception of the mind, and the images of things which we imagine. It is further necessary that they should distinguish between idea and words, whereby we signify things. These three—namely, images, words, and ideas—are by many persons either entirely confused together, or not distinguished with sufficient accuracy or care, and hence people are generally in ignorance, how absolutely necessary is a knowledge of this doctrine of the will, both for philosophic purposes and for the wise ordering of life. Those who think that ideas consist in images which are formed in us by contact with external bodies, persuade themselves that the ideas of those things, whereof we can form no mental picture, are not ideas, but only figments, which we invent by the free decree of our will; they thus regard ideas as though they were inanimate pictures on a panel, and, filled with this misconception, do not see that an idea, inasmuch as it is an idea, involves an affirmation or negation. Again, those who confuse words with ideas, or with the affirmation which an idea involves, think that they can wish something contrary to what they feel, affirm, or deny. This misconception will easily be laid aside by one, who reflects on the nature of knowledge, and seeing that it in no wise involves the conception of extension, will therefore clearly understand, that an idea (being a mode of thinking) does not consist in the image of anything, nor in words. The essence of words and images is put together by bodily motions, which in no wise involve the conception of thought.

These few words on this subject will suffice: I will therefore pass on to consider the objections, which may be raised against our doctrine. Of these, the first is advanced by those, who think that the will has a wider scope than the understanding, and that therefore it is different therefrom. The reason for their holding the belief, that the will has wider scope than the understanding, is that they assert, that they have no need of an increase in their faculty of assent, that is of affirmation or negation, in order to assent to an infinity of things which we do not perceive, but that they have need of an increase in their faculty of understanding. The will is thus distinguished from the intellect, the latter being finite and the former infinite. Secondly, it may be objected that experience seems to teach us especially clearly, that we are able to suspend our judgment before assenting to things which we perceive; this is confirmed by the fact that no one is said to be deceived, in so far as he perceives anything, but only in so far as he assents or dissents.

For instance, he who feigns a winged horse, does not therefore admit that a winged horse exists; that is, he is not deceived, unless he admits in addition that a winged horse does exist. Nothing therefore seems to be taught more clearly by experience, than that the will or faculty of assent is free and different from the faculty of understanding. Thirdly, it may be objected that one affirmation does not apparently contain more reality than another; in other words, that we do not seem to need for affirming, that what is true is true, any greater power than for affirming, that what is false is true. We have, however, seen that one idea has more reality or perfection than another, for as objects are some more excellent than others, so also are the ideas of them some more excellent than others; this also seems to point to a difference between the understanding and the will. Fourthly, it may be objected, if man does not act from free will, what will happen if the incentives to action are equally balanced, as in the case of Buridan's ass? Will he perish of hunger and thirst? If I say that he would not, he would then determine his own action, and would consequently possess the faculty of going and doing whatever he liked. Other objections might also be raised, but, as I am not bound to put in evidence everything that anyone may dream, I will only set myself to the task of refuting those I have mentioned, and that as briefly as possible.

To the first objection I answer, that I admit that the will has a wider scope than the understanding, if by the understanding be meant only clear and distinct ideas; but I deny that the will has a wider scope than the perceptions, and the faculty of forming conceptions; nor do I see why the faculty of volition should be called infinite, any more than the faculty of feeling: for, as we are able by the same faculty of volition to affirm an infinite number of things (one after the other, for we cannot affirm an infinite number simultaneously), so also can we, by the same faculty of feeling, feel or perceive (in succession) an infinite number of bodies. If it be said that there is an infinite number of things which we cannot perceive, I answer, that we cannot attain to such things by any thinking, nor, consequently, by any faculty of volition. But, it may still be urged, if God wished to bring it about that we should perceive them, he would be obliged to endow us with a greater faculty of perception, but not a greater faculty of volition than we have already. This is the same as to say that, if God wished to bring it about that we should understand an infinite number of other entities, it would be necessary for him to give us a greater understanding, but not a more universal idea of entity than that which we have already, in order to grasp such infinite entities. We have shown that will is a universal entity or idea, whereby we explain all particular volitions—in other words, that which is common to all such volitions.

As, then, our opponents maintain that this idea, common or universal to all volitions, is a faculty, it is little to be wondered at that they assert, that such a faculty extends itself into the infinite, beyond the limits of the understanding: for what is universal is predicated alike of one, of many, and of an infinite number of individuals.

To the second objection I reply by denying, that we have a free power of suspending our judgment: for, when we say that anyone suspends his judgment, we merely mean that he sees, that he does not perceive the matter in question adequately. Suspension of judgment is, therefore, strictly speaking, a perception, and not free will. In order to illustrate the point, let us suppose a boy imagining a horse, and perceive nothing else. Inasmuch as this imagination involves the existence of the horse (II. xvii. Cor.), and the boy does not perceive anything which would exclude the existence of the horse, he will necessarily regard the horse as present: he will not be able to doubt of its existence, although he be not certain thereof. We have daily experience of such a state of things in dreams; and I do not suppose that there is anyone, who would maintain that, while he is dreaming, he has the free power of suspending his judgment concerning the things in his dream, and bringing it about that he should not dream those things, which he dreams that he sees; yet it happens, notwithstanding, that even in dreams we suspend our judgment, namely, when we dream that we are dreaming.

Further, I grant that no one can be deceived, so far as actual perception extends—that is, I grant that the mind's imaginations, regarded in themselves, do not involve error (II. xvii. note); but I deny, that a man does not, in the act of perception, make any affirmation. For what is the perception of a winged horse, save affirming that a horse has wings? If the mind could perceive nothing else but the winged horse, it would regard the same as present to itself: it would have no reasons for doubting its existence, nor any faculty of dissent, unless the imagination of a winged horse be joined to an idea which precludes the existence of the said horse, or unless the mind perceives that the idea which it possess of a winged horse is inadequate, in which case it will either necessarily deny the existence of such a horse, or will necessarily be in doubt on the subject.

I think that I have anticipated my answer to the third objection, namely, that the will is something universal which is predicated of all ideas, and that it only signifies that which is common to all ideas, namely, an affirmation, whose adequate essence must, therefore, in so far as it is thus conceived in the abstract, be in every idea, and be, in this respect alone, the same in all, not in so far as it is considered as constituting the idea's essence: for, in this respect, particular affirmations differ one from the other, as much as do ideas. For instance, the affirmation which involves the idea of a circle, differs from that which involves the idea of a triangle, as much as the idea of a circle differs from the idea of a triangle.

Further, I absolutely deny, that we are in need of an equal power of thinking, to affirm that that which is true is true, and to affirm that that which is false is true. These two affirmations, if we regard the mind, are in the same relation to one another as being and not-being; for there is nothing positive in ideas, which constitutes the actual reality of falsehood (II. xxxv. note, and xlvii. note).

We must therefore conclude, that we are easily deceived, when we confuse universals with singulars, and the entities of reason and abstractions with realities. As for the fourth objection, I am quite ready to admit, that a man placed in the equilibrium described (namely, as perceiving nothing but hunger and thirst, a certain food and a certain drink, each equally distant from him) would die of hunger and thirst. If I am asked, whether such an one should not rather be considered an ass than a man; I answer, that I do not know, neither do I know how a man should be considered, who hangs himself, or how we should consider children, fools, madmen, &c.

It remains to point out the advantages of a knowledge of this doctrine as bearing on conduct, and this may be easily gathered from what has been said. The doctrine is good,

1. Inasmuch as it teaches us to act solely according to the decree of God, and to be partakers in the Divine nature, and so much the more, as we perform more perfect actions and more and more understand God. Such a doctrine not only completely tranquilizes our spirit, but also shows us where our highest happiness or blessedness is, namely, solely in the knowledge of God, whereby we are led to act only as love and piety shall bid us. We may thus clearly understand, how far astray from a true estimate of virtue are those who expect to be decorated by God with high rewards for their virtue, and their best actions, as for having endured the direst slavery; as if virtue and the service of God were not in itself happiness and perfect freedom.

2. Inasmuch as it teaches us, how we ought to conduct ourselves with respect to the gifts of fortune, or matters which are not in our power, and do not follow from our nature. For it shows us, that we should await and endure fortune's smiles

or frowns with an equal mind, seeing that all things follow from the eternal decree of God by the same necessity, as it follows from the essence of a triangle, that the three angles are equal to two right angles.

3. This doctrine raises social life, inasmuch as it teaches us to hate no man, neither to despise, to deride, to envy, or to be angry with any. Further, as it tells us that each should be content with his own, and helpful to his neighbour, not from any womanish pity, favour, or superstition, but solely by the guidance of reason, according as the time and occasion demand, as I will show in Part III.

4. Lastly, this doctrine confers no small advantage on the commonwealth; for it teaches how citizens should be governed and led, not so as to become slaves, but so that they may freely do whatsoever things are best.

I have thus fulfilled the promise made at the beginning of this note, and I thus bring the second part of my treatise to a close. I think I have therein explained the nature and properties of the human mind at sufficient length, and, considering the difficulty of the subject, with sufficient clearness. I have laid a foundation, whereon may be raised many excellent conclusions of the highest utility and most necessary to be known, as will, in what follows, be partly made plain.

11. Introduction to Kant's
The Critique of Pure Reason

Throughout most of the seventeenth and eighteenth centuries, the major metaphysical issue in Western philosophy is whether human knowledge is intuitional and *a priori,* as asserted by the rationalists like Descartes, Spinoza and Leibniz, or based on experience and *a posteriori*, as claimed by the British empiricists like John Locke. In his *Critique of Pure Reason*, Kant provides a solution to this problem, by arguing that both experience and intuition contribute to knowledge.

Kant's problem, in a nutshell, is the following: How can we have determinism, i.e. causal necessity, in nature and free will in humans? If everything in the world, including human actions, is predetermined, ethics becomes impossible. If, on the other hand one denies determinism, like the great Scottish philosopher David Hume, there is no problem with the notion of free will and ethics becomes possible, but both physics and metaphysics become impossible as sciences. In a non-deterministic universe, no safe prediction about what is going to happen in the physical world is possible. Although engineers can still go on and build bridges, they will know only from experience that these bridges will not collapse. They can never be absolutely certain about it.

Given that Newtonian determinism was universally accepted in physics in the eighteenth century, Kant is justified in viewing Hume's solution as unsatisfactory. Kant argues that the world exists as a possible object of experience. Because human beings have a certain type of sense apparatus, they can only get to know the world as it *appears* to them, and never as it really *is*. Kant asserts that there are things-in-themselves, which we can never possibly get to know, and things as they appear to us, appearances. We can only have knowledge of these appearances, and the limits of our experience are the limits of our world, which is only a fraction of the world as it is. (Hypothetically, only God would know all things-in-themselves, i.e. the world as it really is.)

So, Kant agrees with the Empiricists that all knowledge begins with experience. But he then proceeds to claim that this experience means nothing, and does not lead to knowledge, unless it is 'processed' by our mind, more or less in the same way that a computer program organizes data.

According to Kant, space and time are not things-in-themselves, but are two such 'programs' that our mind uses to organize the data of experience. They are, as he calls them, Forms of Sensibility. Geometry is the specification of the Form of Sensibility which is space and arithmetic is the specification of the Form of Sensibility which is time: we count moments, 1, 2, 3, 4 . . .

Except for the Forms of Sensibility, there are also Forms of Understanding. The first of them is universal causal determinism, because any perceptible world must be in some ways orderly and predictable. The second Form of Understanding is Newton's law of the conservation of matter.

Time, space and causality are therefore in our minds. They are categories that our mind uses to organize the data we get from experience. This means that, contrary to the claims of the rationalists, individual perceptions are valid.

One consequence of this is that anything falling outside the range of our sense perception and the Forms of Sensibility and Understanding, we cannot possibly know. Philosophy cannot answer questions such as whether God exists, or whether there is an afterlife. Although Kant himself is a devout Christian, he concedes that subjects of this kind fall outside the scope of philosophy, in that they are to be decided by belief and not by reason. This view also provides a strong argument for religious tolerance, which in Kant's time is still an important political issue.

The Critique of Pure Reason

Immanuel Kant
Translated by J. M. D. Meiklejohn

Introduction

I. Of the difference between Pure and Empirical Knowledge

That all our knowledge begins with experience there can be no doubt. For how is it possible that the faculty of cognition should be awakened into exercise otherwise than by means of objects which affect our senses, and partly of themselves produce representations, partly rouse our powers of understanding into activity, to compare to connect, or to separate these, and so to convert the raw material of our sensuous impressions into a knowledge of objects, which is called experience? In respect of time, therefore, no knowledge of ours is antecedent to experience, but begins with it.

But, though all our knowledge begins with experience, it by no means follows that all arises out of experience. For, on the contrary, it is quite possible that our empirical knowledge is a compound of that which we receive through impressions, and that which the faculty of cognition supplies from itself (sensuous impressions giving merely the occasion), an addition which we cannot distinguish from the original element given by sense, till long practice has made us attentive to, and skilful in separating it. It is, therefore, a question which requires close investigation, and not to be answered at first sight, whether there exists a knowledge altogether independent of experience, and even of all sensuous impressions? Knowledge of this kind is called a priori, in contradistinction to empirical knowledge, which has its sources a posteriori, that is, in experience.

But the expression, "a priori," is not as yet definite enough adequately to indicate the whole meaning of the question above started. For, in speaking of knowledge which has its sources in experience, we are wont to say, that this or that may be known a priori, because we do not derive this knowledge immediately from experience, but from a general rule, which, however, we have itself borrowed from experience. Thus, if a man undermined his house, we say, "he might know a priori that it would have fallen;" that is, he needed not to have waited for the experience that it did actually fall. But still, a priori, he could not know even this much. For, that bodies are heavy, and, consequently, that they fall when their supports are taken away, must have been known to him previously, by means of experience.

By the term "knowledge a priori," therefore, we shall in the sequel understand, not such as is independent of this or that kind of experience, but such as is absolutely so of all experience. Opposed to this is empirical knowledge, or that which is possible only a posteriori, that is, through experience. Knowledge a priori is either pure or impure. Pure knowledge a priori is that with which no empirical element is mixed up. For example, the proposition, "Every change has a cause," is a proposition a priori, but impure, because change is a conception which can only be derived from experience.

II. The Human Intellect, even in an Unphilosophical State, is in Possession of Certain Cognitions "a priori"

The question now is as to a criterion, by which we may securely distinguish a pure from an empirical cognition. Experience no doubt teaches us that this or that object is constituted in such and such a manner, but not that it could not possibly exist otherwise. Now, in the first place, if we have a proposition which contains the idea of necessity in its very conception, it is a if, moreover, it is not derived from any other proposition, unless from one equally involving the idea of necessity, it is absolutely priori. Secondly, an empirical judgement never exhibits strict and absolute, but only assumed and comparative universality (by induction); therefore, the most we can say is—so far as we have hitherto observed, there is no exception to this or that rule. If, on the other hand, a judgement carries with it strict and absolute universality, that is, admits of no possible exception, it is not derived from experience, but is valid absolutely a priori.

Empirical universality is, therefore, only an arbitrary extension of validity, from that which may be predicated of a proposition valid in most cases, to that which is asserted of a proposition which holds good in all; as, for example, in the affirmation, "All bodies are heavy." When, on the contrary, strict universality characterizes a judgement, it necessarily indicates another peculiar source of knowledge, namely, a faculty of cognition a priori. Necessity and strict universality, therefore, are infallible tests for distinguishing pure from empirical knowledge, and are inseparably connected with each other. But as in the use of these criteria the empirical limitation is sometimes more easily detected than the contingency of the judgement, or the unlimited universality which we attach to a judgement is often a more convincing proof than its necessity, it may be advisable to use the criteria separately, each being by itself infallible.

Now, that in the sphere of human cognition we have judgements which are necessary, and in the strictest sense universal, consequently pure a priori, it will be an easy matter to show. If we desire an example from the sciences, we need only take any proposition in mathematics. If we cast our eyes upon the commonest operations of the understanding, the proposition, "Every change must have a cause," will amply serve our purpose. In the latter case, indeed, the conception of a cause so plainly involves the conception of a necessity of connection with an effect, and of a strict universality of the law, that the very notion of a cause would entirely disappear, were we to derive it, like Hume, from a frequent association of what happens with that which precedes; and the habit thence originating of connecting representations—the necessity inherent in the judgement being therefore merely subjective. Besides, without seeking for such examples of principles existing a priori in cognition, we might easily show that such principles are the indispensable basis of the possibility of experience itself, and consequently prove their existence a priori. For whence could our experience itself acquire certainty, if all the rules on which it depends were themselves empirical, and consequently fortuitous? No one, therefore, can admit the validity of the use of such rules as first principles. But, for the present, we may content ourselves with having established the fact, that we do possess and exercise a faculty of pure a priori cognition; and, secondly, with having pointed out the proper tests of such cognition, namely, universality and necessity.

Not only in judgements, however, but even in conceptions, is an a priori origin manifest. For example, if we take away by degrees from our conceptions of a body all that can be referred to mere sensuous experience—colour, hardness or softness, weight, even impenetrability—the body will then vanish; but the space which it occupied still remains, and this it is utterly impossible to annihilate in thought. Again, if we take away, in like manner, from our empirical conception of any object, corporeal or incorporeal, all properties which mere experience has taught us to connect with it, still we cannot think away those through which we cogitate it as substance, or adhering to substance, although our conception of substance is more determined than that of an object. Compelled, therefore, by that necessity with which the conception of substance forces itself upon us, we must confess that it has its seat in our faculty of cognition a priori.

III. Philosophy stands in need of a Science which shall Determine the Possibility, Principles, and Extent of Human Knowledge "a priori"

Of far more importance than all that has been above said, is the consideration that certain of our cognitions rise completely above the sphere of all possible experience, and by means of conceptions, to which there exists in the whole extent of experience no corresponding object, seem to extend the range of our judgements beyond its bounds. And just in this transcendental or supersensible sphere, where experience affords us neither instruction nor guidance, lie the investigations of reason, which, on account of their importance, we consider far preferable to, and as having a far more elevated aim than, all that the understanding can achieve within the sphere of sensuous phenomena. So high a value do we set upon these investigations, that even at the risk of error, we persist in following them out, and permit neither doubt nor disregard nor indifference to restrain us from the pursuit. These unavoidable problems of mere pure reason are God, freedom (of will), and immortality. The science which, with all its preliminaries, has for its especial object the solution of these problems is named metaphysics—a science which is at the very outset dogmatical, that is, it confidently takes upon itself the execution of this task without any previous investigation of the ability or inability of reason for such an undertaking.

Now the safe ground of experience being thus abandoned, it seems nevertheless natural that we should hesitate to erect a building with the cognitions we possess, without knowing whence they come, and on the strength of principles, the origin of which is undiscovered. Instead of thus trying to build without a foundation, it is rather to be expected that we should long ago have put the question, how the understanding can arrive at these a priori cognitions, and what is the extent, validity, and worth which they may possess? We say, "This is natural enough," meaning by the word natural, that which is consistent with a just and reasonable way of thinking; but if we understand by the term, that which usually happens, nothing indeed could be more natural and more comprehensible than that this investigation should be left long unattempted. For one part of our pure knowledge, the science of mathematics, has been long firmly established, and thus leads us to form flattering expectations with regard to others, though these may be of quite a different nature. Besides, when we get beyond the bounds of experience, we are of course safe from opposition in that quarter; and the charm of widening the range of our knowledge is so great that, unless we are brought to a standstill by some evident contradiction, we hurry on undoubtingly in our course. This, however, may be avoided, if we are sufficiently cautious in the construction of our fictions, which are not the less fictions on that account.

Mathematical science affords us a brilliant example, how far, independently of all experience, we may carry our a priori knowledge. It is true that the mathematician occupies himself with objects and cognitions only in so far as they can be represented by means of intuition. But this circumstance is easily overlooked, because the said intuition can itself be given a priori, and therefore is hardly to be distinguished from a mere pure conception. Deceived by such a proof of the power of reason, we can perceive no limits to the extension of our knowledge. The light dove cleaving in free flight the thin air, whose resistance it feels, might imagine that her movements would be far more free and rapid in airless space. Just in the same way did Plato, abandoning the world of sense because of the narrow limits it sets to the understanding, venture upon the wings of ideas beyond it, into the void space of pure intellect. He did not reflect that he made no real progress by all his efforts; for he met with no resistance which might serve him for a support, as it were, whereon to rest, and on which he might apply his powers, in order to let the intellect acquire momentum for its progress. It is, indeed, the common fate of human reason in speculation, to finish the imposing edifice of thought as rapidly as possible, and then for the first time to begin to examine whether the foundation is a solid one or no. Arrived at this point, all sorts of excuses are sought after, in order to console us for its want of stability, or rather, indeed, to enable us to dispense altogether with so late and dangerous an investigation. But what frees us during the process of building from all apprehension or suspicion, and flatters us into the belief of its solidity, is this. A great part, perhaps the greatest part, of the business of our reason consists in the analysation of the conceptions which we already possess of objects. By this means we gain a multitude of cognitions, which although really nothing more than elucidations or explanations of that which (though in a confused manner) was already thought in our conceptions, are, at least in respect of their form, prized as new introspections; whilst, so far as regards their matter or content, we have really made no addition to our conceptions, but only disinvolved them. But as this process does furnish a real priori knowledge, which has a sure progress and useful results, reason, deceived by this, slips in, without being itself aware of it, assertions of a quite different kind; in which, to given conceptions it adds others, a priori indeed, but entirely foreign to them, without our knowing how it arrives at these, and, indeed, without such a question ever suggesting itself. I shall therefore at once proceed to examine the difference between these two modes of knowledge.

IV. Of the Difference Between Analytical and Synthetical Judgements

In all judgements wherein the relation of a subject to the predicate is cogitated (I mention affirmative judgements only here; the application to negative will be very easy), this relation is possible in two different ways. Either the predicate B belongs to the subject A, as somewhat which is contained (though covertly) in the conception A; or the predicate B lies completely out of the conception A, although it stands in connection with it. In the first instance, I term the judgement analytical, in the second, synthetical. Analytical judgements (affirmative) are therefore those in which the connection of the predicate with the subject is cogitated through identity; those in which this connection is cogitated without identity, are called synthetical judgements. The former may be called explicative, the latter augmentative judgements; because the former add in the predicate nothing to the conception of the subject, but only analyse it into its constituent conceptions, which were thought already in the subject, although in a confused manner; the latter add to our conceptions of the subject a predicate which was not contained in it, and which no analysis could ever have discovered therein. For example, when I say, "All bodies are extended," this is an analytical judgement. For I need not go beyond the conception of body in order to find extension connected with it, but merely analyse the conception, that is, become conscious of the manifold properties which I think in that conception, in order to discover this predicate in it: it is therefore an analytical judgement. On the other hand, when I say, "All bodies are heavy," the predicate is something totally different from that which I think in the mere conception of a body. By the addition of such a predicate, therefore, it becomes a synthetical judgement.

Judgements of experience, as such, are always synthetical. For it would be absurd to think of grounding an analytical judgement on experience, because in forming such a judgement I need not go out of the sphere of my conceptions, and therefore recourse to the testimony of experience is quite unnecessary. That "bodies are extended" is not an empirical judgement, but a proposition which stands firm a priori. For before addressing myself to experience, I already have in my conception all the requisite conditions for the judgement, and I have only to extract the predicate from the conception, according to the principle of contradiction, and thereby at the same time become conscious of the necessity of the judgement, a necessity which I could never learn from experience. On the other hand, though at first I do not at all include the predicate of weight in my conception of body in general, that conception still indicates an object of experience, a part of the totality of experience, to which I can still add other parts; and this I do when I recognize by observation that bodies are heavy. I can cognize beforehand by analysis the conception of body through the characteristics of extension, impenetrability, shape, etc., all which are cogitated in this conception. But now I extend my knowledge, and looking back on experience from which I had derived this conception of body, I find weight at all times connected with the above characteristics, and therefore I synthetically add to my conceptions this as a predicate, and say, "All bodies are heavy." Thus it is experience upon which rests the possibility of the synthesis of the predicate of weight with the conception of body, because both conceptions, although the one is not contained in the other, still belong to one another (only contingently, however), as parts of a whole, namely, of experience, which is itself a synthesis of intuitions.

But to synthetical judgements a priori, such aid is entirely wanting. If I go out of and beyond the conception A, in order to recognize another B as connected with it, what foundation have I to rest on, whereby to render the synthesis possible? I have here no longer the advantage of looking out in the sphere of experience for what I want. Let us take, for example, the proposition, "Everything that happens has a cause." In the conception of "something that happens," I indeed think an existence which a certain time antecedes, and from this I can derive analytical judgements. But the conception of a cause lies quite out of the above conception, and indicates something entirely different from "that which happens," and is consequently not contained in that conception. How then am I able to assert concerning the general conception—"that which happens"—something entirely different from that conception, and to recognize the conception of cause although not contained in it, yet as belonging to it, and even necessarily? What is here the unknown = X, upon which the understanding rests when it believes it has found, out of the conception A a foreign predicate B, which it nevertheless considers to be connected with it? It cannot be experience, because the principle adduced annexes the two representations, cause and effect, to the representation existence, not only with universality, which experience cannot give, but also with the expression of necessity, therefore completely a priori and from pure conceptions. Upon such synthetical, that is augmentative propositions, depends the whole aim of our speculative knowledge a priori; for although analytical judgements are indeed highly important and necessary, they are so, only to arrive at that clearness of conceptions which is requisite for a sure and extended synthesis, and this alone is a real acquisition.

V. In all Theoretical Sciences of Reason, Synthetical Judgements "a priori" are Contained as Principles

1. Mathematical judgements are always synthetical. Hitherto this fact, though incontestably true and very important in its consequences, seems to have escaped the analysts of the human mind, nay, to be in complete opposition to all their conjectures. For as it was found that mathematical conclusions all proceed according to the principle of contradiction (which the nature of every apodeictic certainty requires), people became persuaded that the fundamental principles of the science also were recognized and admitted in the same way. But the notion is fallacious; for although a synthetical proposition can certainly be discerned by means of the principle of contradiction, this is possible only when another synthetical proposition precedes, from which the latter is deduced, but never of itself.

Before all, be it observed, that proper mathematical propositions are always judgements a priori, and not empirical, because they carry along with them the conception of necessity, which cannot be given by experience. If this be demurred to, it matters not; I will then limit my assertion to pure mathematics, the very conception of which implies that it consists of knowledge altogether non-empirical and a priori.

We might, indeed at first suppose that the proposition $7 + 5 = 12$ is a merely analytical proposition, following (according to the principle of contradiction) from the conception of a sum of seven and five. But if we regard it more narrowly, we find that our conception of the sum of seven and five contains nothing more than the uniting of both sums into one, whereby it cannot at all be cogitated what this single number is which embraces both. The conception of twelve is by no means obtained by merely cogitating the union of seven and five; and we may analyse our conception of such a possible sum as long as we will, still we shall never discover in it the notion of twelve. We must go beyond these conceptions, and have recourse to an intuition which corresponds to one of the two—our five fingers, for example, or like Segner in his Arithmetic five points, and so by degrees, add the units contained in the five given in the intuition, to the conception of seven. For I first take the number 7, and, for the conception of 5 calling in the aid of the fingers of my hand as objects of intuition, I add the units, which I before took together to make up the number 5, gradually now by means of the material image my hand, to the number 7, and by this process, I at length see the number 12 arise. That 7 should be added to 5, I have certainly cogitated in my conception of a sum = 7 + 5, but not that this sum was equal to 12. Arithmetical propositions are therefore always synthetical, of which we may become more clearly convinced by trying large numbers. For it will thus become quite evident that, turn and twist our conceptions as we may, it is impossible, without having recourse to intuition, to arrive at the sum total or product by means of the mere analysis of our conceptions. Just as little is any principle of pure geometry analytical. "A straight line between two points is the shortest," is a synthetical proposition. For my conception of straight contains no notion of quantity, but is merely qualitative. The conception of the shortest is therefore fore wholly an addition, and by no analysis can it be extracted from our conception of a straight line. Intuition must therefore here lend its aid, by means of which, and thus only, our synthesis is possible.

Some few principles preposited by geometricians are, indeed, really analytical, and depend on the principle of contradiction. They serve, however, like identical propositions, as links in the chain of method, not as principles—for example, a = a, the whole is equal to itself, or (a + b) > a, the whole is greater than its part. And yet even these principles themselves, though they derive their validity from pure conceptions, are only admitted in mathematics because they can be presented in intuition. What causes us here commonly to believe that the predicate of such apodeictic judgements is already contained in our conception, and that the judgement is therefore analytical, is merely the equivocal nature of the expression. We must join in thought a certain predicate to a given conception, and this necessity cleaves already to the conception. But the question is, not what we must join in thought to the given conception, but what we really think therein, though only obscurely, and then it becomes manifest that the predicate pertains to these conceptions, necessarily indeed, yet not as thought in the conception itself, but by virtue of an intuition, which must be added to the conception.

2. The science of natural philosophy (physics) contains in itself synthetical judgements a priori, as principles. I shall adduce two propositions. For instance, the proposition, "In all changes of the material world, the quantity of matter remains unchanged"; or, that, "In all communication of motion, action and reaction must always be equal." In both of these, not only is the necessity, and therefore their origin a priori clear, but also that they are synthetical propositions. For in the conception of matter, I do not cogitate its permanency, but merely its presence in space, which it fills. I therefore really go out of and beyond the conception of matter, in order to think on to it something a priori, which I did not think in it. The proposition is therefore not analytical, but synthetical, and nevertheless conceived a priori; and so it is with regard to the other propositions of the pure part of natural philosophy.

3. As to metaphysics, even if we look upon it merely as an attempted science, yet, from the nature of human reason, an indispensable one, we find that it must contain synthetical propositions a priori. It is not merely the duty of metaphysics to dissect, and thereby analytically to illustrate the conceptions which we form a priori of things; but we seek to widen the range of our a priori knowledge. For this purpose, we must avail ourselves of such principles as add something to the original conception—something not identical with, nor contained in it, and by means of synthetical judgements a priori, leave far behind us the limits of experience; for example, in the proposition, "the world must have a

beginning," and such like. Thus metaphysics, according to the proper aim of the science, consists merely of synthetical propositions a priori.

VI. The Universal Problem of Pure Reason

It is extremely advantageous to be able to bring a number of investigations under the formula of a single problem. For in this manner, we not only facilitate our own labour, inasmuch as we define it clearly to ourselves, but also render it more easy for others to decide whether we have done justice to our undertaking. The proper problem of pure reason, then, is contained in the question: "How are synthetical judgements a priori possible?"

That metaphysical science has hitherto remained in so vacillating a state of uncertainty and contradiction, is only to be attributed to the fact that this great problem, and perhaps even the difference between analytical and synthetical judgements, did not sooner suggest itself to philosophers. Upon the solution of this problem, or upon sufficient proof of the impossibility of synthetical knowledge a priori, depends the existence or downfall of the science of metaphysics. Among philosophers, David Hume came the nearest of all to this problem; yet it never acquired in his mind sufficient precision, nor did he regard the question in its universality. On the contrary, he stopped short at the synthetical proposition of the connection of an effect with its cause (principium causalitatis), insisting that such proposition a priori was impossible. According to his conclusions, then, all that we term metaphysical science is a mere delusion, arising from the fancied insight of reason into that which is in truth borrowed from experience, and to which habit has given the appearance of necessity. Against this assertion, destructive to all pure philosophy, he would have been guarded, had he had our problem before his eyes in its universality. For he would then have perceived that, according to his own argument, there likewise could not be any pure mathematical science, which assuredly cannot exist without synthetical propositions a priori—an absurdity from which his good understanding must have saved him.

In the solution of the above problem is at the same time comprehended the possibility of the use of pure reason in the foundation and construction of all sciences which contain theoretical knowledge a priori of objects, that is to say, the answer to the following questions:

How is pure mathematical science possible?
How is pure natural science possible?

Respecting these sciences, as they do certainly exist, it may with propriety be asked, how they are possible?—for that they must be possible is shown by the fact of their really existing.* But as to metaphysics, the miserable progress it has hitherto made, and the fact that of no one system yet brought forward, far as regards its true aim, can it be said that this science really exists, leaves any one at liberty to doubt with reason the very possibility of its existence.

Yet, in a certain sense, this kind of knowledge must unquestionably be looked upon as given; in other words, metaphysics must be considered as really existing, if not as a science, nevertheless as a natural disposition of the human mind (metaphysica naturalis). For human reason, without any instigations imputable to the mere vanity of great knowledge, unceasingly progresses, urged on by

---

*As to the existence of pure natural science, or physics, perhaps many may still express doubts. But we have only to look at the different propositions which are commonly treated of at the commencement of proper (empirical) physical science—those, for example, relating to the permanence of the same quantity of matter, the vis inertiae, the equality of action and reaction, etc.—to be soon convinced that they form a science of pure physics (physica pura, or rationalis), which well deserves to be separately exposed as a special science, in its whole extent, whether that be great or confined.

its own feeling of need, towards such questions as cannot be answered by any empirical application of reason, or principles derived therefrom; and so there has ever really existed in every man some system of metaphysics. It will always exist, so soon as reason awakes to the exercise of its power of speculation. And now the question arises: "How is metaphysics, as a natural disposition, possible?" In other words, how, from the nature of universal human reason, do those questions arise which pure reason proposes to itself, and which it is impelled by its own feeling of need to answer as well as it can?

But as in all the attempts hitherto made to answer the questions which reason is prompted by its very nature to propose to itself, for example, whether the world had a beginning, or has existed from eternity, it has always met with unavoidable contradictions, we must not rest satisfied with the mere natural disposition of the mind to metaphysics, that is, with the existence of the faculty of pure reason, whence, indeed, some sort of metaphysical system always arises; but it must be possible to arrive at certainty in regard to the question whether we know or do not know the things of which metaphysics treats. We must be able to arrive at a decision on the subjects of its questions, or on the ability or inability of reason to form any judgement respecting them; and therefore either to extend with confidence the bounds of our pure reason, or to set strictly defined and safe limits to its action. This last question, which arises out of the above universal problem, would properly run thus: "How is metaphysics possible as a science?"

Thus, the critique of reason leads at last, naturally and necessarily, to science; and, on the other hand, the dogmatical use of reason without criticism leads to groundless assertions, against which others equally specious can always be set, thus ending unavoidably in scepticism.

Besides, this science cannot be of great and formidable prolixity, because it has not to do with objects of reason, the variety of which is inexhaustible, but merely with Reason herself and her problems; problems which arise out of her own bosom, and are not proposed to her by the nature of outward things, but by her own nature. And when once Reason has previously become able completely to understand her own power in regard to objects which she meets with in experience, it will be easy to determine securely the extent and limits of her attempted application to objects beyond the confines of experience.

We may and must, therefore, regard the attempts hitherto made to establish metaphysical science dogmatically as non-existent. For what of analysis, that is, mere dissection of conceptions, is contained in one or other, is not the aim of, but only a preparation for metaphysics proper, which has for its object the extension, by means of synthesis, of our a priori knowledge. And for this purpose, mere analysis is of course useless, because it only shows what is contained in these conceptions, but not how we arrive, a priori, at them; and this it is her duty to show, in order to be able afterwards to determine their valid use in regard to all objects of experience, to all knowledge in general. But little self-denial, indeed, is needed to give up these pretensions, seeing the undeniable, and in the dogmatic mode of procedure, inevitable contradictions of Reason with herself, have long since ruined the reputation of every system of metaphysics that has appeared up to this time. It will require more firmness to remain undeterred by difficulty from within, and opposition from without, from endeavouring, by a method quite opposed to all those hitherto followed, to further the growth and fruitfulness of a science indispensable to human reason—a science from which every branch it has borne may be cut away, but whose roots remain indestructible.

VII. Idea and Division of a Particular Science, under the Name of a Critique of Pure Reason

From all that has been said, there results the idea of a particular science, which may be called the Critique of Pure Reason. For reason is the faculty which furnishes us with the principles of knowledge a priori. Hence, pure reason is the faculty which contains the principles of cognizing anything absolutely a priori. An organon of pure reason would be a compendium of those principles according to which alone all pure cognitions a priori can be obtained. The completely extended application of such an organon would afford us a system of pure reason. As this, however, is demanding a great deal, and it is yet doubtful whether any extension of our knowledge be here possible, or, if so, in what cases; we can regard a science of the mere criticism of pure reason, its sources and limits, as the propaedeutic to a system of pure reason. Such a science must not be called a doctrine, but only a critique of pure reason; and its use, in regard to speculation, would be only negative, not to enlarge the bounds of, but to purify, our reason, and to shield it against error—which alone is no little gain. I apply the term transcendental to all knowledge which is not so much occupied with objects as with the mode of our cognition of these objects, so far as this mode of cognition is possible a priori. A system of such conceptions would be called transcendental philosophy. But this, again, is still beyond the bounds of our present essay. For as such a science must contain a complete exposition not only of our synthetical a priori, but of our analytical a priori knowledge, it is of too wide a range for our present purpose, because we do not require to carry our analysis any farther than is necessary to understand, in their full extent, the principles of synthesis a priori, with which alone we have to do. This investigation, which we cannot properly call a doctrine, but only a transcendental critique, because it aims not at the enlargement, but at the correction and guidance, of our knowledge, and is to serve as a touchstone of the worth or worthlessness of all knowledge a priori, is the sole object of our present essay. Such a critique is consequently, as far as possible, a preparation for an organon; and if this new organon should be found to fail, at least for a canon of pure reason, according to which the complete system of the philosophy of pure reason, whether it extend or limit the bounds of that reason, might one day be set forth both analytically and synthetically. For that this is possible, nay, that such a system is not of so great extent as to preclude the hope of its ever being completed, is evident. For we have not here to do with the nature of outward objects, which is infinite, but solely with the mind, which judges of the nature of objects, and, again, with the mind only in respect of its cognition a priori. And the object of our investigations, as it is not to be sought without, but, altogether within, ourselves, cannot remain concealed, and in all probability is limited enough to be completely surveyed and fairly estimated, according to its worth or worthlessness. Still less let the reader here expect a critique of books and systems of pure reason; our present object is exclusively a critique of the faculty of pure reason itself. Only when we make this critique our foundation, do we possess a pure touchstone for estimating the philosophical value of ancient and modern writings on this subject; and without this criterion, the incompetent historian or judge decides upon and corrects the groundless assertions of others with his own, which have themselves just as little foundation.

Transcendental philosophy is the idea of a science, for which the Critique of Pure Reason must sketch the whole plan architectonically, that is, from principles, with a full guarantee for the validity and stability of all the parts which enter into the building. It is the system of all the principles of pure reason. If this Critique itself does not assume the title of transcendental philosophy, it is only because, to be a complete system, it ought to contain a full analysis of all human knowledge a priori. Our critique must, indeed, lay before us a complete enumeration of all the radical conceptions which constitute the said pure knowledge. But from the complete analysis of these conceptions themselves, as also from a complete investigation of those derived from them, it abstains with reason; partly because it would be deviating from the end in view to occupy itself with this analysis, since this process is not attended with the difficulty and insecurity to be found in the synthesis, to which our critique is entirely devoted, and partly because it would be inconsistent with the unity of our plan to burden this essay with the vindication of the completeness of such an analysis and deduction, with which, after all, we have at present nothing to do. This completeness of the analysis of these radical conceptions, as well as of the deduction from the conceptions a priori which may be given by the analysis, we can, however, easily attain, provided only that we are in possession of all these radical conceptions, which are to serve as principles of the synthesis, and that in respect of this main purpose nothing is wanting.

To the Critique of Pure Reason, therefore, belongs all that constitutes transcendental philosophy; and it is the complete idea of transcendental philosophy, but still not the science itself; because it only proceeds so far with the analysis as is necessary to the power of judging completely of our synthetical knowledge a priori.

The principal thing we must attend to, in the division of the parts of a science like this, is that no conceptions must enter it which contain aught empirical; in other words, that the knowledge a priori must be completely pure. Hence, although the highest principles and fundamental conceptions of morality are certainly cognitions a priori, yet they do not belong to transcendental philosophy; because, though they certainly do not lay the conceptions of pain, pleasure, desires, inclinations, etc. (which are all of empirical origin), at the foundation of its precepts, yet still into the conception of duty—as an obstacle to be overcome, or as an incitement which should not be made into a motive—these empirical conceptions must necessarily enter, in the construction of a system of pure morality. Transcendental philosophy is consequently a philosophy of the pure and merely speculative reason. For all that is practical, so far as it contains motives, relates to feelings, and these belong to empirical sources of cognition.

If we wish to divide this science from the universal point of view of a science in general, it ought to comprehend, first, a Doctrine of the Elements, and, secondly, a Doctrine of the Method of pure reason. Each of these main divisions will have its subdivisions, the separate reasons for which we cannot here particularize. Only so much seems necessary, by way of introduction of premonition, that there are two sources of human knowledge (which probably spring from a common, but to us unknown root), namely, sense and understanding. By the former, objects are given to us; by the latter, thought. So far as the faculty of sense may contain representations a priori, which form the conditions under which objects are given, in so far it belongs to transcendental philosophy. The transcendental doctrine of sense must form the first part of our science of elements, because the conditions under which alone the objects of human knowledge are given must precede those under which they are thought.

12. Introduction to Kant's *Fundamental Principles of the Metaphysic of Morals*

As already noted, the question of how is ethics possible in a universe governed by causal necessity is a fundamental problem for Kant. He solves this problem by posing two separate realms:

1. A realm of necessity, in which the deterministic natural laws prevail
2. A realm of freedom

To be free, for Kant, is not to be subject to the laws of nature. Our bodies are subject to these laws, but our minds/souls are not.

Because natural laws do not apply in the realm of things-in-themselves, it becomes possible to talk about free will and good and evil. Nevertheless, two serious problems arise at this point:

1. If this is true, how can our ethical decisions, coming from a world outside the world of experience, have any bearing on this world? How does acting morally make any difference in the physical world? Kant never addresses this issue.
2. How are people to decide what is right and what wrong? Kant answers this question, by asserting that all people share the same fundamental moral intuitions. Every human being knows what is right and wrong. Everybody knows, for example, that it is wrong to kill. Kant does not allow for cultural, religious or other differences to play a part in one's moral intuitions. His approach is non-historical and, to the extent that he takes the European values of his time to be the values of all mankind, Eurocentric.

The idea that makes ethics possible is freedom. Freedom is an idea of Reason. Reason conceives of freedom, and then there can be ethical theory. Because it comes from Reason, our will is always rational, at least *in abstractio*. Nevertheless, in real life our will is restricted by our instincts and desires. Moreover, having the right intention may not produce the right result. We do not always get things right. Kant's reaction to this is to argue that it is one's intention which counts morally, not the outcome of one's actions. Provided I do everything in my power in order to do the right thing, my behavior is ethical even if I do not achieve the desired result. Ultimately, the only absolutely good thing in the world is a good will, because all other goods (like wealth, health, power) can be used for sinister ends.

The will is the faculty of acting according to some law. The right law to follow is the moral law. An action is moral if and only if it is done out of respect for the moral law ('duty ethics'). There is no material reward for virtue in this or any other life.

Reason gives two types of law. The first is the Hypothetical Imperative (I do a, in order to achieve b). But this is conditional (a is good on condition b is achieved) and will not do as moral law. Moral law must be absolute, irrespective of any kind of end. The second type of law is the Categorical Imperative. This is the kind of law produced by moral law. There are several formulations of the Categorical Imperative in the *Fundamental Principles of the Metaphysic of Morals*, but the most well-known one is the first one: *Act as if the maxim of thy action were to become by thy will a universal law of nature*.

Another formulation, which is crucial for Kant's argument is the following: *Act as to treat humanity, whether in thine own person or in that of any other, in every case as an end withal, never as a means only.*

Kant's ethical theory demands that all human beings are always treated as ends-in-themselves, are not exploited, and have their freedom respected. In this respect, it epitomizes the fundamental ideas of the Enlightenment. It also provides a smashing argument against slavery, since it makes freedom an intrinsic part of humanity.

Fundamental Principles of the Metaphysic of Morals

Immanuel Kant
Translated by Thomas Kingsmill Abbott

Second Section

Transition from Popular Moral Philosophy to the Metaphysic of Morals

If we have hitherto drawn our notion of duty from the common use of our practical reason, it is by no means to be inferred that we have treated it as an empirical notion. On the contrary, if we attend to the experience of men's conduct, we meet frequent and, as we ourselves allow, just complaints that one cannot find a single certain example of the disposition to act from pure duty. Although many things are done in conformity with what duty prescribes, it is nevertheless always doubtful whether they are done strictly from duty, so as to have a moral worth. Hence there have at all times been philosophers who have altogether denied that this disposition actually exists at all in human actions, and have ascribed everything to a more or less refined self-love. Not that they have on that account questioned the soundness of the conception of morality; on the contrary, they spoke with sincere regret of the frailty and corruption of human nature, which, though noble enough to take its rule an idea so worthy of respect, is yet weak to follow it and employs reason which ought to give it the law only for the purpose of providing for the interest of the inclinations, whether singly or at the best in the greatest possible harmony with one another.

In fact, it is absolutely impossible to make out by experience with complete certainty a single case in which the maxim of an action, however right in itself, rested simply on moral grounds and on the conception of duty. Sometimes it happens that with the sharpest self-examination we can find nothing beside the moral principle of duty which could have been powerful enough to move us to this or that action and to so great a sacrifice; yet we cannot from this infer with certainty that it was not really some secret impulse of self-love, under the false appearance of duty, that was the actual determining cause of the will. We like them to flatter ourselves by falsely taking credit for a more noble motive; whereas in fact we can never, even by the strictest examination, get completely behind the secret springs of action; since, when the question is of moral worth, it is not with the actions which we see that we are concerned, but with those inward principles of them which we do not see.

Moreover, we cannot better serve the wishes of those who ridicule all morality as a mere chimera of human imagination over stepping itself from vanity, than by conceding to them that notions of duty must be drawn only from experience (as from indolence, people are ready to think is also the case with all other notions); for or is to prepare for them a certain triumph. I am willing to admit out of love of humanity that even most of our actions are correct, but if we look closer at them we everywhere come upon the dear self which is always prominent, and it is this they have in view and not the strict command of duty which would often require self-denial. Without being an enemy of virtue, a cool observer, one that does not mistake the wish for good, however lively, for its reality, may sometimes doubt whether true virtue is actually found anywhere in the world, and this especially as years increase and the judgement is partly made wiser by experience and partly, also, more acute in observation. This being so, nothing can secure us from falling away altogether from our ideas of duty, or maintain in the soul a well-grounded respect for its law, but the clear conviction that although there should never have been actions which really sprang from such pure sources, yet whether this or that takes place is not at all the question; but that reason of itself, independent on all experience, ordains what ought to take place, that accordingly actions of which perhaps the world has hitherto never given an example, the feasibility even of which might be very much doubted by one who founds everything on experience, are nevertheless inflexibly commanded by reason; that, e.g., even though there might never yet have been a sincere friend, yet not a whit the less is pure sincerity in friendship required of every man, because, prior to all experience, this duty is involved as duty in the idea of a reason determining the will by a priori principles.

When we add further that, unless we deny that the notion of morality has any truth or reference to any possible object, we must admit that its law must be valid, not merely for men but for all rational creatures generally, not merely under certain contingent conditions or with exceptions but with absolute necessity, then it is clear that no experience could enable us to infer even the possibility of such apodeictic laws. For with what right could we bring into unbounded respect as a universal precept for every rational nature that which perhaps holds only under the contingent conditions of humanity? Or how could laws of the determination of our will be regarded as laws of the determination of the will of rational beings generally, and for us only as such, if they were merely empirical and did not take their origin wholly a priori from pure but practical reason?

Nor could anything be more fatal to morality than that we should wish to derive it from examples. For every example of it that is set before me must be first itself tested by principles of morality, whether it is worthy to serve as an original example, i.e., as a pattern; but by no means can it authoritatively furnish the conception of morality. Even the Holy One of the Gospels must first be compared with our ideal of moral perfection before we can recognise Him as such; and so He says of Himself, "Why call ye Me (whom you see) good; none is good (the model of good) but God only (whom ye do not see)?" But whence have we the conception of God as the supreme good? Simply from the idea of moral perfection, which reason frames a priori and connects inseparably with the notion of a free will. Imitation finds no place at all in morality, and examples serve only for encouragement, i.e., they put beyond doubt the feasibility of what the law commands, they make visible that which the practical rule expresses more generally, but they can never authorize us to set aside the true original which lies in reason and to guide ourselves by examples.

If then there is no genuine supreme principle of morality but what must rest simply on pure reason, independent of all experience, I think it is not necessary even to put the question whether it is good to exhibit these concepts in their generality (in abstracto) as they are established a priori along with the principles belonging to them, if our knowledge is to be distinguished from the vulgar and to be called philosophical.

In our times indeed this might perhaps be necessary; for if we collected votes whether pure rational knowledge separated from everything empirical, that is to say, metaphysic of morals, or whether popular practical philosophy is to be preferred, it is easy to guess which side would preponderate. This descending to popular notions is certainly very commendable, if the ascent to the principles of pure reason has first taken place and been satisfactorily accomplished. This implies that we first found ethics on metaphysics, and then, when it is firmly established, procure a hearing for it by giving it a popular character. But it is quite absurd to try to be popular in the first inquiry, on which the soundness of the principles depends. It is not only that this proceeding can never lay claim to the very rare merit of a true philosophical popularity, since there is no art in being intelligible if one renounces all thoroughness of insight; but also it produces a disgusting medley of compiled observations and half-reasoned principles. Shallow pates enjoy this because it can be used for every-day chat, but the sagacious find in it only confusion, and being unsatisfied and unable to help themselves, they turn away their eyes, while philosophers, who see quite well through this delusion, are little listened to when they call men off for a time from this pretended popularity, in order that they might be rightfully popular after they have attained a definite insight.

We need only look at the attempts of moralists in that favourite fashion, and we shall find at one time the special constitution of human nature (including, however, the idea of a rational nature generally), at one time perfection, at another happiness, here moral sense, there fear of God. A little of this, and a little of that, in marvellous mixture, without its occurring to them to ask whether the principles of morality are to be sought in the knowledge of human nature at all (which we can have only from experience); or, if this is not so, if these principles are to be found altogether a priori, free from everything empirical, in pure rational concepts only and nowhere else, not even in the smallest degree; then rather to adopt the method of making this a separate inquiry, as pure practical philosophy, or (if one may use a name so decried) as metaphysic of morals,[1] to bring it by itself to completeness, and to require the public, which wishes for popular treatment, to await the issue of this undertaking.

Such a metaphysic of morals, completely isolated, not mixed with any anthropology, theology, physics, or hyperphysics, and still less with occult qualities (which we might call hypophysical), is not only an indispensable substratum of all sound theoretical knowledge of duties, but is at the same time a desideratum of the highest importance to the actual fulfilment of their precepts. For the pure conception of duty, unmixed with any foreign addition of empirical attractions, and, in a word, the conception of the moral law, exercises on the human heart, by way of reason alone (which first becomes aware with this that it can of itself be practical), an influence so much more powerful than all other springs[2] which may be derived from the field of experience, that, in the consciousness of its worth, it despises the latter, and can by degrees become their master; whereas a mixed ethics, compounded partly of motives drawn from feelings and inclinations, and partly also of conceptions of reason, must make the mind waver between motives which cannot be brought under any principle, which lead to good only by mere accident and very often also to evil.

From what has been said, it is clear that all moral conceptions have their seat and origin completely a priori in the reason, and that, moreover, in the commonest reason just as truly as in that which is in the highest degree speculative; that they cannot be obtained by abstraction from any empirical, and therefore merely contingent, knowledge; that it is just this purity of their origin that makes them worthy to serve as our supreme practical principle, and that just in proportion as we add anything

---

[1] Just as pure mathematics are distinguished from applied, pure logic from applied, so if we choose we may also distinguish pure philosophy of morals (metaphysic) from applied (viz., applied to human nature). By this designation we are also at once reminded that moral principles are not based on properties of human nature, but must subsist a priori of themselves, while from such principles practical rules must be capable of being deduced for every rational nature, and accordingly for that of man.

[2] I have a letter from the late excellent Sulzer, in which he asks me what can be the reason that moral instruction, although containing much that is convincing for the reason, yet accomplishes so little? My answer was postponed in order that I might make it complete. But it is simply this: that the teachers themselves have not got their own notions clear, and when they endeavour to make up for this by raking up motives of moral goodness from every quarter, trying to make their physic right strong, they spoil it. For the commonest understanding shows that if we imagine, on the one hand, an act of honesty done with steadfast mind, apart from every view to advantage of any kind in this world or another, and even under the greatest temptations of necessity or allurement, and, on the other hand, a similar act which was affected, in however low a degree, by a foreign motive, the former leaves far behind and eclipses the second; it elevates the soul and inspires the wish to be able to act in like manner oneself. Even moderately young children feel this impression, and one should never represent duties to them in any other light.

empirical, we detract from their genuine influence and from the absolute value of actions; that it is not only of the greatest necessity, in a purely speculative point of view, but is also of the greatest practical importance, to derive these notions and laws from pure reason, to present them pure and unmixed, and even to determine the compass of this practical or pure rational knowledge, i.e., to determine the whole faculty of pure practical reason; and, in doing so, we must not make its principles dependent on the particular nature of human reason, though in speculative philosophy this may be permitted, or may even at times be necessary; but since moral laws ought to hold good for every rational creature, we must derive them from the general concept of a rational being. In this way, although for its application to man morality has need of anthropology, yet, in the first instance, we must treat it independently as pure philosophy, i.e., as metaphysic, complete in itself (a thing which in such distinct branches of science is easily done); knowing well that unless we are in possession of this, it would not only be vain to determine the moral element of duty in right actions for purposes of speculative criticism, but it would be impossible to base morals on their genuine principles, even for common practical purposes, especially of moral instruction, so as to produce pure moral dispositions, and to engraft them on men's minds to the promotion of the greatest possible good in the world.

But in order that in this study we may not merely advance by the natural steps from the common moral judgement (in this case very worthy of respect) to the philosophical, as has been already done, but also from a popular philosophy, which goes no further than it can reach by groping with the help of examples, to metaphysic (which does allow itself to be checked by anything empirical and, as it must measure the whole extent of this kind of rational knowledge, goes as far as ideal conceptions, where even examples fail us), we must follow and clearly describe the practical faculty of reason, from the general rules of its determination to the point where the notion of duty springs from it.

Everything in nature works according to laws. Rational beings alone have the faculty of acting according to the conception of laws, that is according to principles, i.e., have a will. Since the deduction of actions from principles requires reason, the will is nothing but practical reason. If reason infallibly determines the will, then the actions of such a being which are recognised as objectively necessary are subjectively necessary also, i.e., the will is a faculty to choose that only which reason independent of inclination recognises as practically necessary, i.e., as good. But if reason of itself does not sufficiently determine the will, if the latter is subject also to subjective conditions (particular impulses) which do not always coincide with the objective conditions; in a word, if the will does not in itself completely accord with reason (which is actually the case with men), then the actions which objectively are recognised as necessary are subjectively contingent, and the determination of such a will according to objective laws is obligation, that is to say, the relation of the objective laws to a will that is not thoroughly good is conceived as the determination of the will of a rational being by principles of reason, but which the will from its nature does not of necessity follow.

The conception of an objective principle, in so far as it is obligatory for a will, is called a command (of reason), and the formula of the command is called an imperative.

All imperatives are expressed by the word ought [or shall], and thereby indicate the relation of an objective law of reason to a will, which from its subjective constitution is not necessarily determined by it (an obligation). They say that something would be good to do or to forbear, but they say it to a will which does not always do a thing because it is conceived to be good to do it. That is practically good, however, which determines the will by means of the conceptions of reason, and consequently not from subjective causes, but objectively, that is on principles which are valid for every rational being as such. It is distinguished from the pleasant, as that which influences the will only by means of sensation from merely subjective causes, valid only for the sense of this or that one, and not as a principle of reason, which holds for every one.[3]

A perfectly good will would therefore be equally subject to objective laws (viz., laws of good), but could not be conceived as obliged thereby to act lawfully, because of itself from its subjective constitution it can only be determined by the conception of good. Therefore no imperatives hold for the Divine will, or in general for a holy will; ought is here out of place, because the volition is already of itself necessarily in unison with the law. Therefore imperatives are only formulae to express the relation of objective laws of all volition to the subjective imperfection of the will of this or that rational being, e.g., the human will.

Now all imperatives command either hypothetically or categorically. The former represent the practical necessity of a possible action as means to something else that is willed (or at least which one might possibly will). The categorical imperative would be that which represented an action as necessary of itself without reference to another end, i.e., as objectively necessary.

Since every practical law represents a possible action as good and, on this account, for a subject who is practically determinable by reason, necessary, all imperatives are formulae determining an action which is necessary according to the principle of a will good in some respects. If now the action is good only as a means to something else, then the imperative is hypothetical; if it is conceived as good in itself and consequently as being necessarily the principle of a will which of itself conforms to reason, then it is categorical.

Thus the imperative declares what action possible by me would be good and presents the practical rule in relation to a will which does not forthwith perform an action simply because it is good, whether because the subject does not always know that it is good, or because, even if it know this, yet its maxims might be opposed to the objective principles of practical reason.

Accordingly the hypothetical imperative only says that the action is good for some purpose, possible or actual. In the first case it is a problematical, in the second an assertorial practical principle. The categorical imperative which declares an action to be objectively necessary in itself without reference to any purpose, i.e., without any other end, is valid as an apodeictic (practical) principle.

Whatever is possible only by the power of some rational being may also be conceived as a possible purpose of some will; and therefore the principles of action as regards the means necessary to attain some possible purpose are in fact infinitely numerous. All sciences have a practical part, consisting of problems expressing that some end is possible for us and of imperatives directing how it may be attained. These may, therefore, be called in general imperatives of skill. Here there is no question whether the end is rational and good, but only what one must do in order to attain it. The precepts for the physician to make his patient thoroughly healthy, and for a poisoner to ensure certain death, are of equal value in this respect, that each serves to effect its purpose perfectly. Since in early youth it cannot be known what ends are likely to occur to us in the course of life, parents seek to have their children taught a great many things, and provide for their skill in the use of means for all sorts of arbitrary ends, of

---

[3] The dependence of the desires on sensations is called inclination, and this accordingly always indicates a want. The dependence of a contingently determinable will on principles of reason is called an interest. This therefore, is found only in the case of a dependent will which does not always of itself conform to reason; in the Divine will we cannot conceive any interest. But the human will can also take an interest in a thing without therefore acting from interest. The former signifies the practical interest in the action, the latter the pathological in the object of the action. The former indicates only dependence of the will on principles of reason in themselves; the second, dependence on principles of reason for the sake of inclination, reason supplying only the practical rules how the requirement of the inclination may be satisfied. In the first case the action interests me; in the second the object of the action (because it is pleasant to me). We have seen in the first section that in an action done from duty we must look not to the interest in the object, but only to that in the action itself, and in its rational principle (viz., the law).

none of which can they determine whether it may not perhaps hereafter be an object to their pupil, but which it is at all events possible that he might aim at; and this anxiety is so great that they commonly neglect to form and correct their judgement on the value of the things which may be chosen as ends.

There is one end, however, which may be assumed to be actually such to all rational beings (so far as imperatives apply to them, viz., as dependent beings), and, therefore, one purpose which they not merely may have, but which we may with certainty assume that they all actually have by a natural necessity, and this is happiness. The hypothetical imperative which expresses the practical necessity of an action as means to the advancement of happiness is assertorial. We are not to present it as necessary for an uncertain and merely possible purpose, but for a purpose which we may presuppose with certainty and a priori in every man, because it belongs to his being. Now skill in the choice of means to his own greatest well-being may be called prudence,[4] in the narrowest sense. And thus the imperative which refers to the choice of means to one's own happiness, i.e., the precept of prudence, is still always hypothetical; the action is not commanded absolutely, but only as means to another purpose.

Finally, there is an imperative which commands a certain conduct immediately, without having as its condition any other purpose to be attained by it. This imperative is categorical. It concerns not the matter of the action, or its intended result, but its form and the principle of which it is itself a result; and what is essentially good in it consists in the mental disposition, let the consequence be what it may. This imperative may be called that of morality.

There is a marked distinction also between the volitions on these three sorts of principles in the dissimilarity of the obligation of the will. In order to mark this difference more clearly, I think they would be most suitably named in their order if we said they are either rules of skill, or counsels of prudence, or commands (laws) of morality. For it is law only that involves the conception of an unconditional and objective necessity, which is consequently universally valid; and commands are laws which must be obeyed, that is, must be followed, even in opposition to inclination. Counsels, indeed, involve necessity, but one which can only hold under a contingent subjective condition, viz., they depend on whether this or that man reckons this or that as part of his happiness; the categorical imperative, on the contrary, is not limited by any condition, and as being absolutely, although practically, necessary, may be quite properly called a command. We might also call the first kind of imperatives technical (belonging to art), the second pragmatic[5] (to welfare), the third moral (belonging to free conduct generally, that is, to morals).

Now arises the question, how are all these imperatives possible? This question does not seek to know how we can conceive the accomplishment of the action which the imperative ordains, but merely how we can conceive the obligation of the will which the imperative expresses. No special explanation is needed to show how an imperative of skill is possible. Whoever wills the end, wills also (so far as reason decides his conduct) the means in his power which are indispensably necessary thereto. This proposition is, as regards the volition, analytical; for, in willing an object as my effect, there is

---

[4]The word prudence is taken in two senses: in the one it may bear the name of knowledge of the world, in the other that of private prudence. The former is a man's ability to influence others so as to use them for his own purposes. The latter is the sagacity to combine all these purposes for his own lasting benefit. This latter is properly that to which the value even of the former is reduced, and when a man is prudent in the former sense, but not in the latter, we might better say of him that he is clever and cunning, but, on the whole, imprudent.

[5]It seems to me that the proper signification of the word pragmatic may be most accurately defined in this way. For sanctions are called pragmatic which flow properly not from the law of the states as necessary enactments, but from precaution for the general welfare. A history is composed pragmatically when it teaches prudence, i.e., instructs the world how it can provide for its interests better, or at least as well as, the men of former time.

already thought the causality of myself as an acting cause, that is to say, the use of the means; and the imperative educes from the conception of volition of an end the conception of actions necessary to this end. Synthetical propositions must no doubt be employed in defining the means to a proposed end; but they do not concern the principle, the act of the will, but the object and its realization. E.g., that in order to bisect a line on an unerring principle I must draw from its extremities two intersecting arcs; this no doubt is taught by mathematics only in synthetical propositions; but if I know that it is only by this process that the intended operation can be performed, then to say that, if I fully will the operation, I also will the action required for it, is an analytical proposition; for it is one and the same thing to conceive something as an effect which I can produce in a certain way, and to conceive myself as acting in this way.

If it were only equally easy to give a definite conception of happiness, the imperatives of prudence would correspond exactly with those of skill, and would likewise be analytical. For in this case as in that, it could be said: "Whoever wills the end, wills also (according to the dictate of reason necessarily) the indispensable means thereto which are in his power." But, unfortunately, the notion of happiness is so indefinite that although every man wishes to attain it, yet he never can say definitely and consistently what it is that he really wishes and wills. The reason of this is that all the elements which belong to the notion of happiness are altogether empirical, i.e., they must be borrowed from experience, and nevertheless the idea of happiness requires an absolute whole, a maximum of welfare in my present and all future circumstances. Now it is impossible that the most clear-sighted and at the same time most powerful being (supposed finite) should frame to himself a definite conception of what he really wills in this. Does he will riches, how much anxiety, envy, and snares might he not thereby draw upon his shoulders? Does he will knowledge and discernment, perhaps it might prove to be only an eye so much the sharper to show him so much the more fearfully the evils that are now concealed from him, and that cannot be avoided, or to impose more wants on his desires, which already give him concern enough. Would he have long life? who guarantees to him that it would not be a long misery? would he at least have health? how often has uneasiness of the body restrained from excesses into which perfect health would have allowed one to fall? and so on. In short, he is unable, on any principle, to determine with certainty what would make him truly happy; because to do so he would need to be omniscient. We cannot therefore act on any definite principles to secure happiness, but only on empirical counsels, e.g., of regimen, frugality, courtesy, reserve, etc., which experience teaches do, on the average, most promote well-being. Hence it follows that the imperatives of prudence do not, strictly speaking, command at all, that is, they cannot present actions objectively as practically necessary; that they are rather to be regarded as counsels (*consilia*) than precepts of reason, that the problem to determine certainly and universally what action would promote the happiness of a rational being is completely insoluble, and consequently no imperative respecting it is possible which should, in the strict sense, command to do what makes happy; because happiness is not an ideal of reason but of imagination, resting solely on empirical grounds, and it is vain to expect that these should define an action by which one could attain the totality of a series of consequences which is really endless. This imperative of prudence would however be an analytical proposition if we assume that the means to happiness could be certainly assigned; for it is distinguished from the imperative of skill only by this, that in the latter the end is merely possible, in the former it is given; as however both only ordain the means to that which we suppose to be willed as an end, it follows that the imperative which ordains the willing of the means to him who wills the end is in both cases analytical. Thus there is no difficulty in regard to the possibility of an imperative of this kind either.

On the other hand, the question how the imperative of morality is possible, is undoubtedly one, the only one, demanding a solution, as this is not at all hypothetical, and the objective necessity which it presents cannot rest on any hypothesis, as is the case with the hypothetical imperatives. Only here we must never leave out of consideration that we cannot make out by any example, in other words empirically, whether there is such an imperative at all, but it is rather to be feared that all those which seem to be categorical may yet be at bottom hypothetical. For instance, when the precept is: "Thou shalt not promise deceitfully"; and it is assumed that the necessity of this is not a mere counsel to avoid some other evil, so that it should mean: "Thou shalt not make a lying promise, lest if it become known thou shouldst destroy thy credit," but that an action of this kind must be regarded as evil in itself, so that the imperative of the prohibition is categorical; then we cannot show with certainty in any example that the will was determined merely by the law, without any other spring of action, although it may appear to be so. For it is always possible that fear of disgrace, perhaps also obscure dread of other dangers, may have a secret influence on the will. Who can prove by experience the non-existence of a cause when all that experience tells us is that we do not perceive it? But in such a case the so-called moral imperative, which as such appears to be categorical and unconditional, would in reality be only a pragmatic precept, drawing our attention to our own interests and merely teaching us to take these into consideration.

We shall therefore have to investigate a priori the possibility of a categorical imperative, as we have not in this case the advantage of its reality being given in experience, so that [the elucidation of] its possibility should be requisite only for its explanation, not for its establishment. In the meantime it may be discerned beforehand that the categorical imperative alone has the purport of a practical law; all the rest may indeed be called principles of the will but not laws, since whatever is only necessary for the attainment of some arbitrary purpose may be considered as in itself contingent, and we can at any time be free from the precept if we give up the purpose; on the contrary, the unconditional command leaves the will no liberty to choose the opposite; consequently it alone carries with it that necessity which we require in a law.

Secondly, in the case of this categorical imperative or law of morality, the difficulty (of discerning its possibility) is a very profound one. It is an a priori synthetical practical proposition;[6] and as there is so much difficulty in discerning the possibility of speculative propositions of this kind, it may readily be supposed that the difficulty will be no less with the practical.

In this problem we will first inquire whether the mere conception of a categorical imperative may not perhaps supply us also with the formula of it, containing the proposition which alone can be a categorical imperative; for even if we know the tenor of such an absolute command, yet how it is possible will require further special and laborious study, which we postpone to the last section.

When I conceive a hypothetical imperative, in general I do not know beforehand what it will contain until I am given the condition. But when I conceive a categorical imperative, I know at once what it contains. For as the imperative contains besides the law only the necessity that the maxims[7]

---

[6] I connect the act with the will without presupposing any condition resulting from any inclination, but a priori, and therefore necessarily (though only objectively, i.e., assuming the idea of a reason possessing full power over all subjective motives). This is accordingly a practical proposition which does not deduce the willing of an action by mere analysis from another already presupposed (for we have not such a perfect will), but connects it immediately with the conception of the will of a rational being, as something not contained in it.

[7] A maxim is a subjective principle of action, and must be distinguished from the objective principle, namely, practical law. The former contains the practical rule set by reason according to the conditions of the subject (often its ignorance or its inclinations), so that it is the principle on which the subject acts; but the law is the objective principle valid for every rational being, and is the principle on which it ought to act that is an imperative.

shall conform to this law, while the law contains no conditions restricting it, there remains nothing but the general statement that the maxim of the action should conform to a universal law, and it is this conformity alone that the imperative properly represents as necessary.

There is therefore but one categorical imperative, namely, this: Act only on that maxim whereby thou canst at the same time will that it should become a universal law.

Now if all imperatives of duty can be deduced from this one imperative as from their principle, then, although it should remain undecided what is called duty is not merely a vain notion, yet at least we shall be able to show what we understand by it and what this notion means.

Since the universality of the law according to which effects are produced constitutes what is properly called nature in the most general sense (as to form), that is the existence of things so far as it is determined by general laws, the imperative of duty may be expressed thus: Act as if the maxim of thy action were to become by thy will a universal law of nature.

We will now enumerate a few duties, adopting the usual division of them into duties to ourselves and ourselves and to others, and into perfect and imperfect duties.[8]

1. A man reduced to despair by a series of misfortunes feels wearied of life, but is still so far in possession of his reason that he can ask himself whether it would not be contrary to his duty to himself to take his own life. Now he inquires whether the maxim of his action could become a universal law of nature. His maxim is: "From self-love I adopt it as a principle to shorten my life when its longer duration is likely to bring more evil than satisfaction." It is asked then simply whether this principle founded on self-love can become a universal law of nature. Now we see at once that a system of nature of which it should be a law to destroy life by means of the very feeling whose special nature it is to impel to the improvement of life would contradict itself and, therefore, could not exist as a system of nature; hence that maxim cannot possibly exist as a universal law of nature and, consequently, would be wholly inconsistent with the supreme principle of all duty.

2. Another finds himself forced by necessity to borrow money. He knows that he will not be able to repay it, but sees also that nothing will be lent to him unless he promises stoutly to repay it in a definite time. He desires to make this promise, but he has still so much conscience as to ask himself: "Is it not unlawful and inconsistent with duty to get out of a difficulty in this way?" Suppose however that he resolves to do so: then the maxim of his action would be expressed thus: "When I think myself in want of money, I will borrow money and promise to repay it, although I know that I never can do so." Now this principle of self-love or of one's own advantage may perhaps be consistent with my whole future welfare; but the question now is, "Is it right?" I change then the suggestion of self-love into a universal law, and state the question thus: "How would it be if my maxim were a universal law?" Then I see at once that it could never hold as a universal law of nature, but would necessarily contradict itself. For supposing it to be a universal law that everyone when he thinks himself in a difficulty should be able to promise whatever he pleases, with the purpose of not keeping his promise, the promise itself would become impossible, as well as the end that one might have in view in it, since no one would consider that anything was promised to him, but would ridicule all such statements as vain pretences.

3. A third finds in himself a talent which with the help of some culture might make him a useful man in many respects. But he finds himself in comfortable circumstances and prefers to indulge in pleasure rather than to take pains in enlarging and improving his happy natural capacities. He asks,

---

[8] It must be noted here that I reserve the division of duties for a future metaphysic of morals; so that I give it here only as an arbitrary one (in order to arrange my examples). For the rest, I understand by a perfect duty one that admits no exception in favour of inclination and then I have not merely external but also internal perfect duties. This is contrary to the use of the word adopted in the schools; but I do not intend to justify there, as it is all one for my purpose whether it is admitted or not.

however, whether his maxim of neglect of his natural gifts, besides agreeing with his inclination to indulgence, agrees also with what is called duty. He sees then that a system of nature could indeed subsist with such a universal law although men (like the South Sea islanders) should let their talents rest and resolve to devote their lives merely to idleness, amusement, and propagation of their species—in a word, to enjoyment; but he cannot possibly will that this should be a universal law of nature, or be implanted in us as such by a natural instinct. For, as a rational being, he necessarily wills that his faculties be developed, since they serve him and have been given him, for all sorts of possible purposes.

4. A fourth, who is in prosperity, while he sees that others have to contend with great wretchedness and that he could help them, thinks: "What concern is it of mine? Let everyone be as happy as Heaven pleases, or as he can make himself; I will take nothing from him nor even envy him, only I do not wish to contribute anything to his welfare or to his assistance in distress!" Now no doubt if such a mode of thinking were a universal law, the human race might very well subsist and doubtless even better than in a state in which everyone talks of sympathy and good-will, or even takes care occasionally to put it into practice, but, on the other side, also cheats when he can, betrays the rights of men, or otherwise violates them. But although it is possible that a universal law of nature might exist in accordance with that maxim, it is impossible to will that such a principle should have the universal validity of a law of nature. For a will which resolved this would contradict itself, inasmuch as many cases might occur in which one would have need of the love and sympathy of others, and in which, by such a law of nature, sprung from his own will, he would deprive himself of all hope of the aid he desires.

These are a few of the many actual duties, or at least what we regard as such, which obviously fall into two classes on the one principle that we have laid down. We must be able to will that a maxim of our action should be a universal law. This is the canon of the moral appreciation of the action generally. Some actions are of such a character that their maxim cannot without contradiction be even conceived as a universal law of nature, far from it being possible that we should will that it should be so. In others this intrinsic impossibility is not found, but still it is impossible to will that their maxim should be raised to the universality of a law of nature, since such a will would contradict itself. It is easily seen that the former violate strict or rigorous (inflexible) duty; the latter only laxer (meritorious) duty. Thus it has been completely shown how all duties depend as regards the nature of the obligation (not the object of the action) on the same principle.

If now we attend to ourselves on occasion of any transgression of duty, we shall find that we in fact do not will that our maxim should be a universal law, for that is impossible for us; on the contrary, we will that the opposite should remain a universal law, only we assume the liberty of making an exception in our own favour or (just for this time only) in favour of our inclination. Consequently if we considered all cases from one and the same point of view, namely, that of reason, we should find a contradiction in our own will, namely, that a certain principle should be objectively necessary as a universal law, and yet subjectively should not be universal, but admit of exceptions. As however we at one moment regard our action from the point of view of a will wholly conformed to reason, and then again look at the same action from the point of view of a will affected by inclination, there is not really any contradiction, but an antagonism of inclination to the precept of reason, whereby the universality of the principle is changed into a mere generality, so that the practical principle of reason shall meet the maxim half way. Now, although this cannot be justified in our own impartial judgement, yet it proves that we do really recognise the validity of the categorical imperative and (with all respect for it) only allow ourselves a few exceptions, which we think unimportant and forced from us.

We have thus established at least this much, that if duty is a conception which is to have any import and real legislative authority for our actions, it can only be expressed in categorical and not at all in hypothetical imperatives. We have also, which is of great importance, exhibited clearly and definitely for every practical application the content of the categorical imperative, which must contain the principle of all duty if there is such a thing at all. We have not yet, however, advanced so far as to prove a priori that there actually is such an imperative, that there is a practical law which commands absolutely of itself and without any other impulse, and that the following of this law is duty.

With the view of attaining to this, it is of extreme importance to remember that we must not allow ourselves to think of deducing the reality of this principle from the particular attributes of human nature. For duty is to be a practical, unconditional necessity of action; it must therefore hold for all rational beings (to whom an imperative can apply at all), and for this reason only be also a law for all human wills. On the contrary, whatever is deduced from the particular natural characteristics of humanity, from certain feelings and propensions, nay, even, if possible, from any particular tendency proper to human reason, and which need not necessarily hold for the will of every rational being; this may indeed supply us with a maxim, but not with a law; with a subjective principle on which we may have a propension and inclination to act, but not with an objective principle on which we should be enjoined to act, even though all our propensions, inclinations, and natural dispositions were opposed to it. In fact, the sublimity and intrinsic dignity of the command in duty are so much the more evident, the less the subjective impulses favour it and the more they oppose it, without being able in the slightest degree to weaken the obligation of the law or to diminish its validity.

Here then we see philosophy brought to a critical position, since it has to be firmly fixed, notwithstanding that it has nothing to support it in heaven or earth. Here it must show its purity as absolute director of its own laws, not the herald of those which are whispered to it by an implanted sense or who knows what tutelary nature. Although these may be better than nothing, yet they can never afford principles dictated by reason, which must have their source wholly a priori and thence their commanding authority, expecting everything from the supremacy of the law and the due respect for it, nothing from inclination, or else condemning the man to self-contempt and inward abhorrence.

Thus every empirical element is not only quite incapable of being an aid to the principle of morality, but is even highly prejudicial to the purity of morals, for the proper and inestimable worth of an absolutely good will consists just in this, that the principle of action is free from all influence of contingent grounds, which alone experience can furnish. We cannot too much or too often repeat our warning against this lax and even mean habit of thought which seeks for its principle amongst empirical motives and laws; for human reason in its weariness is glad to rest on this pillow, and in a dream of sweet illusions (in which, instead of Juno, it embraces a cloud) it substitutes for morality a bastard patched up from limbs of various derivation, which looks like anything one chooses to see in it, only not like virtue to one who has once beheld her in her true form.[9]

The question then is this: "Is it a necessary law for all rational beings that they should always judge of their actions by maxims of which they can themselves will that they should serve as universal laws?" If it is so, then it must be connected (altogether a priori) with the very conception of the will of a rational being generally. But in order to discover this connexion we must, however reluctantly, take a step into metaphysic, although into a domain of it which is distinct from speculative philosophy, namely, the metaphysic of morals. In a practical philosophy, where it is not the reasons of what happens that we have to ascertain, but the laws of what ought to happen, even

[9] To behold virtue in her proper form is nothing else but to contemplate morality stripped of all admixture of sensible things and of every spurious ornament of reward or self-love. How much she then eclipses everything else that appears charming to the affections, every one may readily perceive with the least exertion of his reason, if it be not wholly spoiled for abstraction.

although it never does, i.e., objective practical laws, there it is not necessary to inquire into the reasons why anything pleases or displeases, how the pleasure of mere sensation differs from taste, and whether the latter is distinct from a general satisfaction of reason; on what the feeling of pleasure or pain rests, and how from it desires and inclinations arise, and from these again maxims by the co-operation of reason: for all this belongs to an empirical psychology, which would constitute the second part of physics, if we regard physics as the philosophy of nature, so far as it is based on empirical laws. But here we are concerned with objective practical laws and, consequently, with the relation of the will to itself so far as it is determined by reason alone, in which case whatever has reference to anything empirical is necessarily excluded; since if reason of itself alone determines the conduct (and it is the possibility of this that we are now investigating), it must necessarily do so a priori.

The will is conceived as a faculty of determining oneself to action in accordance with the conception of certain laws. And such a faculty can be found only in rational beings. Now that which serves the will as the objective ground of its self-determination is the end, and, if this is assigned by reason alone, it must hold for all rational beings. On the other hand, that which merely contains the ground of possibility of the action of which the effect is the end, this is called the means. The subjective ground of the desire is the spring, the objective ground of the volition is the motive; hence the distinction between subjective ends which rest on springs, and objective ends which depend on motives valid for every rational being. Practical principles are formal when they abstract from all subjective ends; they are material when they assume these, and therefore particular springs of action. The ends which a rational being proposes to himself at pleasure as effects of his actions (material ends) are all only relative, for it is only their relation to the particular desires of the subject that gives them their worth, which therefore cannot furnish principles universal and necessary for all rational beings and for every volition, that is to say practical laws. Hence all these relative ends can give rise only to hypothetical imperatives.

Supposing, however, that there were something whose existence has in itself an absolute worth, something which, being an end in itself, could be a source of definite laws; then in this and this alone would lie the source of a possible categorical imperative, i.e., a practical law.

Now I say: man and generally any rational being exists as an end in himself, not merely as a means to be arbitrarily used by this or that will, but in all his actions, whether they concern himself or other rational beings, must be always regarded at the same time as an end. All objects of the inclinations have only a conditional worth, for if the inclinations and the wants founded on them did not exist, then their object would be without value. But the inclinations, themselves being sources of want, are so far from having an absolute worth for which they should be desired that on the contrary it must be the universal wish of every rational being to be wholly free from them. Thus the worth of any object which is to be acquired by our action is always conditional. Beings whose existence depends not on our will but on nature's, have nevertheless, if they are irrational beings, only a relative value as means, and are therefore called things; rational beings, on the contrary, are called persons, because their very nature points them out as ends in themselves, that is as something which must not be used merely as means, and so far therefore restricts freedom of action (and is an object of respect). These, therefore, are not merely subjective ends whose existence has a worth for us as an effect of our action, but objective ends, that is, things whose existence is an end in itself; an end moreover for which no other can be substituted, which they should subserve merely as means, for otherwise nothing whatever would possess absolute worth; but if all worth were conditioned and therefore contingent, then there would be no supreme practical principle of reason whatever.

If then there is a supreme practical principle or, in respect of the human will, a categorical imperative, it must be one which, being drawn from the conception of that which is necessarily an end for everyone because it is an end in itself, constitutes an objective principle of will, and can therefore serve as a universal practical law. The foundation of this principle is: rational nature exists as an end in itself. Man necessarily conceives his own existence as being so; so far then this is a subjective principle of human actions. But every other rational being regards its existence similarly, just on the same rational principle that holds for me:[10] so that it is at the same time an objective principle, from which as a supreme practical law all laws of the will must be capable of being deduced. Accordingly the practical imperative will be as follows: So act as to treat humanity, whether in thine own person or in that of any other, in every case as an end withal, never as means only. We will now inquire whether this can be practically carried out.

To abide by the previous examples:

Firstly, under the head of necessary duty to oneself: He who contemplates suicide should ask himself whether his action can be consistent with the idea of humanity as an end in itself. If he destroys himself in order to escape from painful circumstances, he uses a person merely as a mean to maintain a tolerable condition up to the end of life. But a man is not a thing, that is to say, something which can be used merely as means, but must in all his actions be always considered as an end in himself. I cannot, therefore, dispose in any way of a man in my own person so as to mutilate him, to damage or kill him. (It belongs to ethics proper to define this principle more precisely, so as to avoid all misunderstanding, e.g., as to the amputation of the limbs in order to preserve myself, as to exposing my life to danger with a view to preserve it, etc. This question is therefore omitted here.)

Secondly, as regards necessary duties, or those of strict obligation, towards others: He who is thinking of making a lying promise to others will see at once that he would be using another man merely as a mean, without the latter containing at the same time the end in himself. For he whom I propose by such a promise to use for my own purposes cannot possibly assent to my mode of acting towards him and, therefore, cannot himself contain the end of this action. This violation of the principle of humanity in other men is more obvious if we take in examples of attacks on the freedom and property of others. For then it is clear that he who transgresses the rights of men intends to use the person of others merely as a means, without considering that as rational beings they ought always to be esteemed also as ends, that is, as beings who must be capable of containing in themselves the end of the very same action.[11]

Thirdly, as regards contingent (meritorious) duties to oneself: It is not enough that the action does not violate humanity in our own person as an end in itself, it must also harmonize with it. Now there are in humanity capacities of greater perfection, which belong to the end that nature has in view in regard to humanity in ourselves as the subject: to neglect these might perhaps be consistent with the maintenance of humanity as an end in itself, but not with the advancement of this end.

Fourthly, as regards meritorious duties towards others: The natural end which all men have is their own happiness. Now humanity might indeed subsist, although no one should contribute anything to the happiness of others, provided he did not intentionally withdraw anything from it; but after all this would only harmonize negatively not positively with humanity as an end in itself, if every one does not also endeavour, as far as in him lies, to forward the ends of others. For the ends of any subject

---

[10] This proposition is here stated as a postulate. The ground of it will be found in the concluding section.

[11] Let it not be thought that the common "quod tibi non vis fieri, etc." could serve here as the rule or principle. For it is only a deduction from the former, though with several limitations; it cannot be a universal law, for it does not contain the principle of duties to oneself, nor of the duties of benevolence to others (for many a one would gladly consent that others should not benefit him, provided only that he might be excused from showing benevolence to them), nor finally that of duties of strict obligation to one another, for on this principle the criminal might argue against the judge who punishes him, and so on.

which is an end in himself ought as far as possible to be my ends also, if that conception is to have its full effect with me.

This principle, that humanity and generally every rational nature is an end in itself (which is the supreme limiting condition of every man's freedom of action), is not borrowed from experience, firstly, because it is universal, applying as it does to all rational beings whatever, and experience is not capable of determining anything about them; secondly, because it does not present humanity as an end to men (subjectively), that is as an object which men do of themselves actually adopt as an end; but as an objective end, which must as a law constitute the supreme limiting condition of all our subjective ends, let them be what we will; it must therefore spring from pure reason. In fact the objective principle of all practical legislation lies (according to the first principle) in the rule and its form of universality which makes it capable of being a law (say, e.g., a law of nature); but the subjective principle is in the end; now by the second principle the subject of all ends is each rational being, inasmuch as it is an end in itself. Hence follows the third practical principle of the will, which is the ultimate condition of its harmony with universal practical reason, viz.: the idea of the will of every rational being as a universally legislative will.

On this principle all maxims are rejected which are inconsistent with the will being itself universal legislator. Thus the will is not subject simply to the law, but so subject that it must be regarded as itself giving the law and, on this ground only, subject to the law (of which it can regard itself as the author).

In the previous imperatives, namely, that based on the conception of the conformity of actions to general laws, as in a physical system of nature, and that based on the universal prerogative of rational beings as ends in themselves—these imperatives, just because they were conceived as categorical, excluded from any share in their authority all admixture of any interest as a spring of action; they were, however, only assumed to be categorical, because such an assumption was necessary to explain the conception of duty. But we could not prove independently that there are practical propositions which command categorically, nor can it be proved in this section; one thing, however, could be done, namely, to indicate in the imperative itself, by some determinate expression, that in the case of volition from duty all interest is renounced, which is the specific criterion of categorical as distinguished from hypothetical imperatives. This is done in the present (third) formula of the principle, namely, in the idea of the will of every rational being as a universally legislating will.

For although a will which is subject to laws may be attached to this law by means of an interest, yet a will which is itself a supreme lawgiver so far as it is such cannot possibly depend on any interest, since a will so dependent would itself still need another law restricting the interest of its self-love by the condition that it should be valid as universal law.

Thus the principle that every human will is a will which in all its maxims gives universal laws,[12] provided it be otherwise justified, would be very well adapted to be the categorical imperative, in this respect, namely, that just because of the idea of universal legislation it is not based on interest, and therefore it alone among all possible imperatives can be unconditional. Or still better, converting the proposition, if there is a categorical imperative (i.e., a law for the will of every rational being), it can only command that everything be done from maxims of one's will regarded as a will which could at the same time will that it should itself give universal laws, for in that case only the practical principle and the imperative which it obeys are unconditional, since they cannot be based on any interest.

---

[12] I may be excused from adducing examples to elucidate this principle, as those which have already been used to elucidate the categorical imperative and its formula would all serve for the like purpose here.

Looking back now on all previous attempts to discover the principle of morality, we need not wonder why they all failed. It was seen that man was bound to laws by duty, but it was not observed that the laws to which he is subject are only those of his own giving, though at the same time they are universal, and that he is only bound to act in conformity with his own will; a will, however, which is designed by nature to give universal laws. For when one has conceived man only as subject to a law (no matter what), then this law required some interest, either by way of attraction or constraint, since it did not originate as a law from his own will, but this will was according to a law obliged by something else to act in a certain manner. Now by this necessary consequence all the labour spent in finding a supreme principle of duty was irrevocably lost. For men never elicited duty, but only a necessity of acting from a certain interest. Whether this interest was private or otherwise, in any case the imperative must be conditional and could not by any means be capable of being a moral command. I will therefore call this the principle of autonomy of the will, in contrast with every other which I accordingly reckon as heteronomy.

The conception of the will of every rational being as one which must consider itself as giving in all the maxims of its will universal laws, so as to judge itself and its actions from this point of view—this conception leads to another which depends on it and is very fruitful, namely that of a kingdom of ends.

By a kingdom I understand the union of different rational beings in a system by common laws. Now since it is by laws that ends are determined as regards their universal validity, hence, if we abstract from the personal differences of rational beings and likewise from all the content of their private ends, we shall be able to conceive all ends combined in a systematic whole (including both rational beings as ends in themselves, and also the special ends which each may propose to himself), that is to say, we can conceive a kingdom of ends, which on the preceding principles is possible.

For all rational beings come under the law that each of them must treat itself and all others never merely as means, but in every case at the same time as ends in themselves. Hence results a systematic union of rational being by common objective laws, i.e., a kingdom which may be called a kingdom of ends, since what these laws have in view is just the relation of these beings to one another as ends and means. It is certainly only an ideal.

A rational being belongs as a member to the kingdom of ends when, although giving universal laws in it, he is also himself subject to these laws. He belongs to it as sovereign when, while giving laws, he is not subject to the will of any other.

A rational being must always regard himself as giving laws either as member or as sovereign in a kingdom of ends which is rendered possible by the freedom of will. He cannot, however, maintain the latter position merely by the maxims of his will, but only in case he is a completely independent being without wants and with unrestricted power adequate to his will.

Morality consists then in the reference of all action to the legislation which alone can render a kingdom of ends possible. This legislation must be capable of existing in every rational being and of emanating from his will, so that the principle of this will is never to act on any maxim which could not without contradiction be also a universal law and, accordingly, always so to act that the will could at the same time regard itself as giving in its maxims universal laws. If now the maxims of rational beings are not by their own nature coincident with this objective principle, then the necessity of acting on it is called practical necessitation, i.e., duty. Duty does not apply to the sovereign in the kingdom of ends, but it does to every member of it and to all in the same degree.

The practical necessity of acting on this principle, i.e., duty, does not rest at all on feelings, impulses, or inclinations, but solely on the relation of rational beings to one another, a relation in which the will of a rational being must always be regarded as legislative, since otherwise it could not be conceived as an end in itself. Reason then refers every maxim of the will, regarding it as legislating universally, to every other will and also to every action towards oneself; and this not on account of any other practical motive or any future advantage, but from the idea of the dignity of a rational being, obeying no law but that which he himself also gives.

In the kingdom of ends everything has either value or dignity. Whatever has a value can be replaced by something else which is equivalent; whatever, on the other hand, is above all value, and therefore admits of no equivalent, has a dignity.

Whatever has reference to the general inclinations and wants of mankind has a market value; whatever, without presupposing a want, corresponds to a certain taste, that is to a satisfaction in the mere purposeless play of our faculties, has a fancy value; but that which constitutes the condition under which alone anything can be an end in itself, this has not merely a relative worth, i.e., value, but an intrinsic worth, that is, dignity.

Now morality is the condition under which alone a rational being can be an end in himself, since by this alone is it possible that he should be a legislating member in the kingdom of ends. Thus morality, and humanity as capable of it, is that which alone has dignity. Skill and diligence in labour have a market value; wit, lively imagination, and humour, have fancy value; on the other hand, fidelity to promises, benevolence from principle (not from instinct), have an intrinsic worth. Neither nature nor art contains anything which in default of these it could put in their place, for their worth consists not in the effects which spring from them, not in the use and advantage which they secure, but in the disposition of mind, that is, the maxims of the will which are ready to manifest themselves in such actions, even though they should not have the desired effect. These actions also need no recommendation from any subjective taste or sentiment, that they may be looked on with immediate favour and satisfaction: they need no immediate propension or feeling for them; they exhibit the will that performs them as an object of an immediate respect, and nothing but reason is required to impose them on the will; not to flatter it into them, which, in the case of duties, would be a contradiction. This estimation therefore shows that the worth of such a disposition is dignity, and places it infinitely above all value, with which it cannot for a moment be brought into comparison or competition without as it were violating its sanctity.

What then is it which justifies virtue or the morally good disposition, in making such lofty claims? It is nothing less than the privilege it secures to the rational being of participating in the giving of universal laws, by which it qualifies him to be a member of a possible kingdom of ends, a privilege to which he was already destined by his own nature as being an end in himself and, on that account, legislating in the kingdom of ends; free as regards all laws of physical nature, and obeying those only which he himself gives, and by which his maxims can belong to a system of universal law, to which at the same time he submits himself. For nothing has any worth except what the law assigns it. Now the legislation itself which assigns the worth of everything must for that very reason possess dignity, that is an unconditional incomparable worth; and the word respect alone supplies a becoming expression for the esteem which a rational being must have for it. Autonomy then is the basis of the dignity of human and of every rational nature.

The three modes of presenting the principle of morality that have been adduced are at bottom only so many formulae of the very same law, and each of itself involves the other two. There is, however, a difference in them, but it is rather subjectively than objectively practical, intended namely to bring an idea of the reason nearer to intuition (by means of a certain analogy) and thereby nearer to feeling. All maxims, in fact, have:

1. A form, consisting in universality; and in this view the formula of the moral imperative is expressed thus, that the maxims must be so chosen as if they were to serve as universal laws of nature.

2. A matter, namely, an end, and here the formula says that the rational being, as it is an end by its own nature and therefore an end in itself, must in every maxim serve as the condition limiting all merely relative and arbitrary ends.

3. A complete characterization of all maxims by means of that formula, namely, that all maxims ought by their own legislation to harmonize with a possible kingdom of ends as with a kingdom of nature.[13] There is a progress here in the order of the categories of unity of the form of the will (its universality), plurality of the matter (the objects, i.e., the ends), and totality of the system of these. In forming our moral judgement of actions, it is better to proceed always on the strict method and start from the general formula of the categorical imperative: Act according to a maxim which can at the same time make itself a universal law. If, however, we wish to gain an entrance for the moral law, it is very useful to bring one and the same action under the three specified conceptions, and thereby as far as possible to bring it nearer to intuition.

We can now end where we started at the beginning, namely, with the conception of a will unconditionally good. That will is absolutely good which cannot be evil—in other words, whose maxim, if made a universal law, could never contradict itself. This principle, then, is its supreme law: "Act always on such a maxim as thou canst at the same time will to be a universal law"; this is the sole condition under which a will can never contradict itself; and such an imperative is categorical. Since the validity of the will as a universal law for possible actions is analogous to the universal connexion of the existence of things by general laws, which is the formal notion of nature in general, the categorical imperative can also be expressed thus: Act on maxims which can at the same time have for their object themselves as universal laws of nature. Such then is the formula of an absolutely good will.

Rational nature is distinguished from the rest of nature by this, that it sets before itself an end. This end would be the matter of every good will. But since in the idea of a will that is absolutely good without being limited by any condition (of attaining this or that end) we must abstract wholly from every end to be effected (since this would make every will only relatively good), it follows that in this case the end must be conceived, not as an end to be effected, but as an independently existing end. Consequently it is conceived only negatively, i.e., as that which we must never act against and which, therefore, must never be regarded merely as means, but must in every volition be esteemed as an end likewise. Now this end can be nothing but the subject of all possible ends, since this is also the subject of a possible absolutely good will; for such a will cannot without contradiction be postponed to any other object. The principle: "So act in regard to every rational being (thyself and others), that he may always have place in thy maxim as an end in himself," is accordingly essentially identical with this other: "Act upon a maxim which, at the same time, involves its own universal validity for every rational being." For that in using means for every end I should limit my maxim by the condition of its holding good as a law for every subject, this comes to the same thing as that the fundamental principle of all maxims of action must be that the subject of all ends, i.e., the rational being himself, be never employed merely as means, but as the supreme condition restricting the use of all means, that is in every case as an end likewise.

It follows incontestably that, to whatever laws any rational being may be subject, he being an end in himself must be able to regard himself as also legislating universally in respect of these same laws, since it is just this fitness of his maxims for universal legislation that distinguishes him as an end in

---

[13] Teleology considers nature as a kingdom of ends; ethics regards a possible kingdom of ends as a kingdom nature. In the first case, the kingdom of ends is a theoretical idea, adopted to explain what actually is. In the latter it is a practical idea, adopted to bring about that which is not yet, but which can be realized by our conduct, namely, if it conforms to this idea.

himself; also it follows that this implies his dignity (prerogative) above all mere physical beings, that he must always take his maxims from the point of view which regards himself and, likewise, every other rational being as law-giving beings (on which account they are called persons). In this way a world of rational beings (mundus intelligibilis) is possible as a kingdom of ends, and this by virtue of the legislation proper to all persons as members. Therefore every rational being must so act as if he were by his maxims in every case a legislating member in the universal kingdom of ends. The formal principle of these maxims is: "So act as if thy maxim were to serve likewise as the universal law (of all rational beings)." A kingdom of ends is thus only possible on the analogy of a kingdom of nature, the former however only by maxims, that is self-imposed rules, the latter only by the laws of efficient causes acting under necessitation from without. Nevertheless, although the system of nature is looked upon as a machine, yet so far as it has reference to rational beings as its ends, it is given on this account the name of a kingdom of nature. Now such a kingdom of ends would be actually realized by means of maxims conforming to the canon which the categorical imperative prescribes to all rational beings, if they were universally followed. But although a rational being, even if he punctually follows this maxim himself, cannot reckon upon all others being therefore true to the same, nor expect that the kingdom of nature and its orderly arrangements shall be in harmony with him as a fitting member, so as to form a kingdom of ends to which he himself contributes, that is to say, that it shall favour his expectation of happiness, still that law: "Act according to the maxims of a member of a merely possible kingdom of ends legislating in it universally," remains in its full force, inasmuch as it commands categorically. And it is just in this that the paradox lies; that the mere dignity of man as a rational creature, without any other end or advantage to be attained thereby, in other words, respect for a mere idea, should yet serve as an inflexible precept of the will, and that it is precisely in this independence of the maxim on all such springs of action that its sublimity consists; and it is this that makes every rational subject worthy to be a legislative member in the kingdom of ends: for otherwise he would have to be conceived only as subject to the physical law of his wants. And although we should suppose the kingdom of nature and the kingdom of ends to be united under one sovereign, so that the latter kingdom thereby ceased to be a mere idea and acquired true reality, then it would no doubt gain the accession of a strong spring, but by no means any increase of its intrinsic worth. For this sole absolute lawgiver must, notwithstanding this, be always conceived as estimating the worth of rational beings only by their disinterested behaviour, as prescribed to themselves from that idea [the dignity of man] alone. The essence of things is not altered by their external relations, and that which, abstracting from these, alone constitutes the absolute worth of man, is also that by which he must be judged, whoever the judge may be, and even by the Supreme Being. Morality, then, is the relation of actions to the relation of actions will, that is, to the autonomy of potential universal legislation by its maxims. An action that is consistent with the autonomy of the will is permitted; one that does not agree therewith is forbidden. A will whose maxims necessarily coincide with the laws of autonomy is a holy will, good absolutely. The dependence of a will not absolutely good on the principle of autonomy (moral necessitation) is obligation. This, then, cannot be applied to a holy being. The objective necessity of actions from obligation is called duty.

From what has just been said, it is easy to see how it happens that, although the conception of duty implies subjection to the law, we yet ascribe a certain dignity and sublimity to the person who fulfils all his duties. There is not, indeed, any sublimity in him, so far as he is subject to the moral law; but inasmuch as in regard to that very law he is likewise a legislator, and on that account alone subject to it, he has sublimity. We have also shown above that neither fear nor inclination, but simply respect for the law, is the spring which can give actions a moral worth. Our own will, so far as we suppose it to act only under the condition that its maxims are potentially universal laws, this ideal will which is possible to us is the proper object of respect; and the dignity of humanity consists just in this capacity of being universally legislative, though with the condition that it is itself subject to this same legislation.

The Autonomy of the Will as the Supreme Principle of Morality

Autonomy of the will is that property of it by which it is a law to itself (independently of any property of the objects of volition). The principle of autonomy then is: "Always so to choose that the same volition shall comprehend the maxims of our choice as a universal law." We cannot prove that this practical rule is an imperative, i.e., that the will of every rational being is necessarily bound to it as a condition, by a mere analysis of the conceptions which occur in it, since it is a synthetical proposition; we must advance beyond the cognition of the objects to a critical examination of the subject, that is, of the pure practical reason, for this synthetic proposition which commands apodeictically must be capable of being cognized wholly a priori. This matter, however, does not belong to the present section. But that the principle of autonomy in question is the sole principle of morals can be readily shown by mere analysis of the conceptions of morality. For by this analysis we find that its principle must be a categorical imperative and that what this commands is neither more nor less than this very autonomy.

Heteronomy of the Will as the Source of all Spurious Principles of Morality

If the will seeks the law which is to determine it anywhere else than in the fitness of its maxims to be universal laws of its own dictation, consequently if it goes out of itself and seeks this law in the character of any of its objects, there always results heteronomy. The will in that case does not give itself the law, but it is given by the object through its relation to the will. This relation, whether it rests on inclination or on conceptions of reason, only admits of hypothetical imperatives: "I ought to do something because I wish for something else." On the contrary, the moral, and therefore categorical, imperative says: "I ought to do so and so, even though I should not wish for anything else." E.g., the former says: "I ought not to lie, if I would retain my reputation"; the latter says: "I ought not to lie, although it should not bring me the least discredit." The latter therefore must so far abstract from all objects that they shall have no influence on the will, in order that practical reason (will) may not be restricted to administering an interest not belonging to it, but may simply show its own commanding authority as the supreme legislation. Thus, e.g., I ought to endeavour to promote the happiness of others, not as if its realization involved any concern of mine (whether by immediate inclination or by any satisfaction indirectly gained through reason), but simply because a maxim which excludes it cannot be comprehended as a universal law in one and the same volition.

Classification of all Principles of Morality which can
be Founded on the Conception of Heteronomy

Here as elsewhere human reason in its pure use, so long as it was not critically examined, has first tried all possible wrong ways before it succeeded in finding the one true way.

All principles which can be taken from this point of view are either empirical or rational. The former, drawn from the principle of happiness, are built on physical or moral feelings; the latter, drawn from the principle of perfection, are built either on the rational conception of perfection as a possible effect, or on that of an independent perfection (the will of God) as the determining cause of our will. Empirical principles are wholly incapable of serving as a foundation for moral laws. For the universality with which these should hold for all rational beings without distinction, the unconditional practical necessity which is thereby imposed on them, is lost when their foundation is taken from the particular constitution of human nature, or the accidental circumstances in which it is placed. The principle of private happiness, however, is the most objectionable, not merely because it is false, and experience contradicts the supposition that prosperity is always proportioned to good conduct, nor yet merely because it contributes nothing to the establishment of morality—since it is quite a different thing to make a prosperous man and a good man, or to make one prudent and sharp-sighted for his own interests and to make him virtuous—but because the springs it provides for morality are such as rather undermine it and destroy its sublimity, since they put the motives to virtue and to vice in the same class and only teach us to make a better calculation, the specific difference between virtue and vice being entirely extinguished. On the other hand, as to moral feeling, this supposed special sense,[14] the appeal to it is indeed superficial when those who cannot think believe that feeling will help them out, even in what concerns general laws: and besides, feelings, which naturally differ infinitely in degree, cannot furnish a uniform standard of good and evil, nor has anyone a right to form judgements for others by his own feelings: nevertheless this moral feeling is nearer to morality and its dignity in this respect, that it pays virtue the honour of ascribing to her immediately the satisfaction and esteem we have for her and does not, as it were, tell her to her face that we are not attached to her by her beauty but by profit.

Amongst the rational principles of morality, the ontological conception of perfection, notwithstanding its defects, is better than the theological conception which derives morality from a Divine absolutely perfect will. The former is, no doubt, empty and indefinite and consequently useless for finding in the boundless field of possible reality the greatest amount suitable for us; moreover, in attempting to distinguish specifically the reality of which we are now speaking from every other, it inevitably tends to turn in a circle and cannot avoid tacitly presupposing the morality which it is to explain; it is nevertheless preferable to the theological view, first, because we have no intuition of the divine perfection and can only deduce it from our own conceptions, the most important of which is that of morality, and our explanation would thus be involved in a gross circle; and, in the next place, if we avoid this, the only notion of the Divine will remaining to us is a conception made up of the attributes of desire of glory and dominion, combined with the awful conceptions of might and vengeance, and any system of morals erected on this foundation would be directly opposed to morality.

However, if I had to choose between the notion of the moral sense and that of perfection in general (two systems which at least do not weaken morality, although they are totally incapable of serving as its foundation), then I should decide for the latter, because it at least withdraws the decision of the question from the sensibility and brings it to the court of pure reason; and although even here it decides nothing, it at all events preserves the indefinite idea (of a will good in itself free from corruption, until it shall be more precisely defined).

For the rest I think I may be excused here from a detailed refutation of all these doctrines; that would only be superfluous labour, since it is so easy, and is probably so well seen even by those whose office requires them to decide for one of these theories (because their hearers would not tolerate suspension of judgement). But what interests us more here is to know that the prime foundation of morality laid down by all these principles is nothing but heteronomy of the will, and for this reason they must necessarily miss their aim.

In every case where an object of the will has to be supposed, in order that the rule may be prescribed which is to determine the will, there the rule is simply heteronomy; the imperative is conditional, namely,

---

[14] I class the principle of moral feeling under that of happiness, because every empirical interest promises to contribute to our well-being by the agreeableness that a thing affords, whether it be immediately and without a view to profit, or whether profit be regarded. We must likewise, with Hutcheson, class the principle of sympathy with the happiness of others under his assumed moral sense.

if or because one wishes for this object, one should act so and so: hence it can never command morally, that is, categorically. Whether the object determines the will by means of inclination, as in the principle of private happiness, or by means of reason directed to objects of our possible volition generally, as in the principle of perfection, in either case the will never determines itself immediately by the conception of the action, but only by the influence which the foreseen effect of the action has on the will; I ought to do something, on this account, because I wish for something else; and here there must be yet another law assumed in me as its subject, by which I necessarily will this other thing, and this law again requires an imperative to restrict this maxim. For the influence which the conception of an object within the reach of our faculties can exercise on the will of the subject, in consequence of its natural properties, depends on the nature of the subject, either the sensibility (inclination and taste), or the understanding and reason, the employment of which is by the peculiar constitution of their nature attended with satisfaction. It follows that the law would be, properly speaking, given by nature, and, as such, it must be known and proved by experience and would consequently be contingent and therefore incapable of being an apodeictic practical rule, such as the moral rule must be. Not only so, but it is inevitably only heteronomy; the will does not give itself the law, but is given by a foreign impulse by means of a particular natural constitution of the subject adapted to receive it. An absolutely good will, then, the principle of which must be a categorical imperative, will be indeterminate as regards all objects and will contain merely the form of volition generally, and that as autonomy, that is to say, the capability of the maxims of every good will to make themselves a universal law, is itself the only law which the will of every rational being imposes on itself, without needing to assume any spring or interest as a foundation.

How such a synthetical practical a priori proposition is possible, and why it is necessary, is a problem whose solution does not lie within the bounds of the metaphysic of morals; and we have not here affirmed its truth, much less professed to have a proof of it in our power. We simply showed by the development of the universally received notion of morality that an autonomy of the will is inevitably connected with it, or rather is its foundation. Whoever then holds morality to be anything real, and not a chimerical idea without any truth, must likewise admit the principle of it that is here assigned. This section then, like the first, was merely analytical. Now to prove that morality is no creation of the brain, which it cannot be if the categorical imperative and with it the autonomy of the will is true, and as an a priori principle absolutely necessary, this supposes the possibility of a synthetic use of pure practical reason, which however we cannot venture on without first giving a critical examination of this faculty of reason. In the concluding section we shall give the principal outlines of this critical examination as far as is sufficient for our purpose.

13. Introduction to Hegel

Hegel's philosophy begins with the assumption that the ultimate structure of reality is reflected in the structure of human thought. Unlike Kant, Hegel asserts that reality, as a whole, is within the scope of human comprehension: in other words, there are no unknowable things-in-themselves. Reason is in a position to resolve apparent contradictions (a demand made urgent by the French Revolution, on the surface an incomprehensible event) and to produce a unified picture of reality. Reason can achieve this picture because reality itself is unified.

But in order for contradictions to be resolved in our thought, a new logical method is required. Hegel calls this method dialectic and it is a three step process. An initial position (a or thesis) is first negated by its opposite (b or antithesis), until, finally, a new position (c or synthesis) emerges. The synthesis includes elements of a and b, but transcends them both. Moreover, the synthesis is a new thesis, because in time it will be negated by its own antithesis, a new synthesis will be produced and so on. So, in the case of the French Revolution, the monarchy is the thesis, the Revolution and the social forces behind it are the antithesis, and the French state which eventually emerged out of the whole process is the synthesis. This state includes elements from both the *ancien régime* and the Revolution. We can see another example of how dialectic works in the case of fundamental metaphysical concepts. Being is a starting point for any ontology, but because it is such a logically wide notion it leads thought to conceive of its opposite, Nothing. The contradiction between the two is then resolved by their synthesis, Becoming.

Although Hegel expected dialectic to apply to both the natural and the human sciences, it was only in disciplines like history and sociology where it had a real impact. Some scholars actually believe that it was the experience of the French Revolution and the need to comprehend this momentous event that led Hegel to conceive of his dialectic.

But history is not simply one part of human knowledge among many for Hegel. It is the manifestation of God's appearance in the world. The highest metaphysical entity in Hegel's philosophy is Spirit (*Geist*). Spirit could be identified with the Christian God, but it may actually be closer to Spinoza's impersonal god. Spirit begins as an inactive abstraction (thesis), but then it negates itself, alienates itself from itself, and becomes what it was not, matter (antithesis). Matter means of course nature, and in this stage Spirit, like Spinoza's god, is identified with nature. But, in the process of its self-alienation Spirit does not become only nature; it also becomes history. History, then, understood as purposeful human activity, is also part of this transformation of Spirit. (One consequence of this is that, because Spirit is by definition rational, everything that happens in history is rational and can be rationally explained.) Finally, in the third and final stage, Spirit returns as Absolute Spirit (synthesis). It is now both spirit and matter, it has transcended itself by becoming the world and then returning to itself. The analogy with Christian apocalyptic doctrine is evident, but Hegel's thinking is primarily secular. Spirit is not a god to be religiously worshipped.

History is, therefore, the manifestation of Spirit in time. It is also the process by means of which World Spirit (*Weltgeist*) reaches its self-consciousness, gets to know itself fully. Because every stage in this process is, at least in principle, more developed than the previous one, it follows that Hegel's era must be the most advanced stage of all. In the context of Hegel's philosophy this entails that Romanticism is the ultimate artistic expression, Protestant Christianity the highest religion and Hegel's own philosophy the ultimate achievement of the human spirit. (At least, nobody can accuse Hegel of modesty!) One other consequence of the same reasoning is that Hegel treats the oppressive and absolute Prussian monarchy as the best possible constitution.

Although all these claims appear unjustified today, it must be emphasized that Hegel's philosophy as a whole is, like Kant's and Marx's, deeply rooted in the tradition of the Enlightenment, with its unconditional belief in Reason and its unlimited trust in the ability of Reason to resolve the problems of humanity. It was in this intellectual climate of extreme optimism that both Kant and Hegel claimed their writings to be the last word in philosophy.

The article by F. Beiser which follows gives a very reasonable, though by no means uncontroversial, account of Hegel's understanding of history. It was chosen in place of some text by Hegel, because of the notorious difficulty of Hegel's language, which makes his writings forbidden territory to those unfamiliar with his philosophical jargon.

In class we will also discuss Hegel's "Dialectic of Master and Slave" from his *Phenomenology of Spirit*. In this revolutionary text, Hegel argues that in any relationship of dependence, it is the 'slave' who has real power, because it is only by recognizing the 'master' that he turns him or her into a master. The argument does not apply only to slavery, but to any relationship involving division of labor. Marx will use it as a basis for his analysis of the relationship between the capitalist and the worker and will claim that as soon as the worker will realize his predicament he or she will withdraw his or her recognition of the capitalist to appropriate his or her labor, thus terminating capitalism. But it also applies to situations such as the division of labor within the household, and in the second half of the twentieth century it was often used by feminist authors.

Hegel's Historicism

Frederick C. Beiser

I. Hegel's Historical Revolution

History cannot be consigned to a corner in Hegel's system, relegated to a few paragraphs near the end of the *Encyclopedia* or confined to his *Lectures on the Philosophy of History*. For, as many scholars have long since recognized,[1] history is central to Hegel's conception of philosophy. One of the most striking and characteristic features of Hegel's thought is that it *historicizes* philosophy, explaining its purpose, principles, and problems in historical terms. Rather than seeing philosophy as a timeless *a priori* reflection upon eternal forms, Hegel regards it as the self-consciousness of a specific culture, the articulation, defense, and criticism of its essential values and beliefs. This historical conception of philosophy is epitomized clearly by Hegel himself in the famous lines from the preface to his *Philosophy of Right:* "Philosophy is its own age comprehended in thought" (VII, 26).

Hegel's historicism amounted to nothing less than a revolution in the history of philosophy. It implied that philosophy is possible only if it is historical, only if the philosopher is aware of the origins, context, and development of his doctrines. Hegel thus threw into question the revolution with which Descartes began modern philosophy. It is not possible to create a presuppositionless system of philosophy a la Descartes, Hegel believes, by abstracting from the past and by simply relying upon one's individual reason. For if Descartes were a completely self-sufficient, self-enclosed mind, transcending the realm of history, he would not have been able to produce his philosophy. The aims of his system, and the ideas he defended in it, were typical products of the culture of seventeenth-century France. So if philosophy is to be truly presuppositionless, Hegel maintains, then it must not abstract from, but incorporate history within itself.

Hegel's philosophical revolution consisted in not only subverting the Cartesian heritage, but also in historicizing the traditional objects of classical metaphysics, God, providence and immortality. Hegel argues that metaphysics is possible only if its central concepts are explicable in historical terms. He accepts Kant's critical teaching that metaphysics is not possible as speculation about a realm of transcendent entities, and that it is possible only if it does not transcend the limits of possible experience. He therefore attempts to provide a "schematism" of the central concepts of metaphysics, explaining them in empirical terms. To explain them in empirical terms means, however, defining them in historical terms, since for Hegel experience consists not only in present-sense perceptions but also in the totality of all forms of human experience, past, present and future.[2] Thus God is not an entity beyond the world, but the idea realized in history. Providence is not an "external end," a supernatural plan imposed by God upon nature, but an "internal end," the ultimate purpose of history itself. And immortality is not life in heaven, but the memory of someone's role in history. It is indeed noteworthy that, in Hegel, the philosophy of history usurps the traditional function of a theodicy: it explains the existence of evil by showing it to be necessary for the realization of the end of history.

If Hegel's historicism amounted to a revolution, it still was not a radical break with the past. For historicism, understood in a broad sense as the doctrine that emphasizes the importance of history for the understanding of human institutions and activities, must by definition also be the product of history. It was indeed anything but new in Hegel's day.[3] In his *Spirit of the Laws* (1749) Montesquieu saw the constitution of a nation as the product of its history, as the result of its changing economic, geographic, and climactic circumstances, and the evolving traditions, religion, and character of its people. In his *Inquiry Concerning the Principles of Political Economy* (1767), James Steuart developed an evolutionary theory of the development of society, explaining how mankind grew from primitive simplicity to complicated refinement through the pressure of economic factors. In his *Ideas for a Philosophy of History of Humanity* (1784–88), Herder explained how such human activities as philosophy, religion, and literature are the product of the history of a people, the characteristic form of their national culture. And in his *System of Transcendental Idealism* (1799), Schelling explained how the intellectual intuition of the "I am," the first principle of philosophy, was the product of the ego's history. Some forms of historicism had indeed become a commonplace by the middle of the eighteenth century. It had become a popular pastime among radicals and free-thinkers, for example, to explain away the supernatural claims of religion by exposing its all-too-human origins. Thus Spinoza, and the English free-thinkers John Toland and Matthew Tindal, attempted to debunk the supernatural status of the Bible by considering the circumstances and culture of the ancient Jews. It is clear, then, that historicism was not born with Hegel. Indeed, from his early life and writings we can see how much he learned from the works of Montesquieu, Ferguson, Herder, and Spinoza.[4]

If historicism does not begin with Hegel, what, if anything, is new and distinctive about his historicism? With Hegel, historicism becomes the self-conscious and general method of philosophy, the weapon to be wielded against its own pretenses and illusions. This self-reflective, self-critical element is not found in the historicism of Hegel's predecessors or contemporaries. Hegel made historicism the self-critical method of philosophy because he believed that philosophy stood in the same need of historical explanation as politics, religion, or literature. In adopting a timeless and a-historical view of their discipline, philosophers had made the same kind of mistake as theologians, jurists, and aestheticians. Just as the theologians believed the Bible to be the record of a supernatural revelation, just as the jurists saw their constitutions as the embodiment of a natural law, and just as the aestheticians claimed that their taste was the canon of a universal beauty, so the philosophers regarded their doctrines as the product of an eternal reason. They too had failed to learn the simple lesson of history: that what appears to be given, eternal, or natural is in fact the product of human activity, and indeed of that activity in a specific cultural context. To expose this illusion, Hegel believed that he had no choice but to historicize philosophy itself.

This self-critical dimension of Hegel's historicism was his completion of Kant's project for a critique of pure reason. Like Kant, Hegel believed that philosophy should become self-critical, aware of its own methods, presuppositions, and limits. He too saw the source of "transcendental illusion" in the self-hypostasis of reason, in its supposing that there are some eternal entities corresponding to its laws. But, unlike Kant, Hegel held that such self-critical reflection demands that philosophy be aware of the genesis, context, and development of its own doctrines. Rather than claiming that they were the product of pure reason, as Kant had done, the philosopher should see them as the result of history. The problem of transcendental illusion would become fully eradicated, Hegel thought, only when philosophy became fully historicized, for only then would the philosopher see how his belief in supernatural or eternal entities arose from his culture. The real source of transcendental illusion thus lay in amnesia, forgetting the origin, context, and development of our ideas.

To appreciate the point of Hegel's historical criticism, it is worthwhile to consider how deep-seated and widespread the illusion of a-historicity has been in the history of philosophy. There have been many forms of such a-historicity, and all of them became in one form or another the subject of Hegelian criticism. (a) The belief that certain laws, beliefs, or values are universal, eternal, or natural when they are in fact the product of, and only appropriate to, a specific culture. (b) The doctrine that certain ideas or principles are innate, the inherent elements of a pure *a priori* reason, although they are learned from experience, the product of a cultural tradition. (c) The claim that certain institutions and forms of activity have a supernatural origin (for example language, religion, and the state) when they in fact originate from all-too-human sources. (d) The reification of certain activities and values, as if they were entities existing independent of human consciousness, when they are in fact the product of its subconscious activity. (e) The belief that certain intuitions and feelings are the product of innate genius, although they are the result of education. (f) The attempt to create a presuppositionless philosophy by abstracting from all past philosophy and by relying upon individual reason alone.

However central to his philosophy, Hegel's historicism is never fully explained or defended in any single text. It is perhaps most explicit in his *Lectures on the History of Philosophy* when he argues that there is no distinction between philosophy and the history of philosophy.[5] But here he does not explain the critical dimension of his historicism. This is more the underlying message that we gain from some of his early writings, in particular *The Positivity of the Christian Religion* (1795), *The Spirit of Christianity* (1799), and especially *The Phenomenology of Spirit*.[6] Throughout these early writings we find Hegel criticizing a wide variety of philosophers for their a-historical beliefs. Thus he castigates the romantics for their claims to have eternal intellectual intuitions, which are in fact the product of their education. He attacks the Kantian theologians for ignoring the social and political factors behind the rise of early Christianity, and for assuming instead that it has its source in the eternal demands of practical reason. He scolds the Kantians for thinking that their categorical imperative is the demand of an eternal reason when it is only appropriate to the ethic of modern individualism. And he pours scorn upon those French *philosophes* who presume that they can recreate all of society *ab initio* in abstraction from all the historical traditions and institutions of France. What all these philosophers have in common, in Hegel's view, is a tendency to forget the past, to ignore the social, political, and historical origins and context of their own doctrines.

II. The Basis of Hegel's Historicism

What drove Hegel into his historical conception of philosophy? Why did he think that philosophy is only its own time comprehended in thought? One basic premise of Hegel's historicism is his doctrine that each society is a unique whole, all of whose parts are inseparable from one another.[7] The art, religion, constitution, traditions, manners, and language of a people form a systematic unity. We cannot separate one of these factors from the whole without changing its nature and that of the whole. This organic whole is what Hegel, following Montesquieu, calls "the spirit" of a nation, its characteristic manner of thinking and acting. Now philosophy, Hegel maintains, is simply one part of the social whole.[8] The philosopher cannot leap beyond his own age any more than he can jump outside his own skin. His task is simply to make each nation self-conscious of its underlying spirit, of its characteristic values and beliefs. The organic nature of the social whole, and the role of philosophy within it, then means that philosophy cannot be separated from its social context. If the factors composing the social whole were to change, then philosophy would be bound to change with them. It would simply have a new spirit to express.

Another central premise behind Hegel's historicism is his general Herderian view of the role of tradition in the development of the arts and sciences.[9] Citing Herder, Hegel refers to tradition as "the sacred chain" that links the present with the past. It is tradition that shows us that the past continues to live in the present. What we are now, Hegel says, is what we have become, and the process of our becoming is our history. The power of reason that mankind now possesses, he argues, is not given to it at birth, but has been acquired through centuries of effort. The arts and sciences have not been created immediately—shot from the pistol of absolute knowledge—but they are the product of all past achievements. Philosophy, Hegel reminds us, is no exception to this rule. The material or subject matter of philosophy is not given to the philosopher or created *a priori* by his individual reason. Rather, it is a legacy handed down to him from the past. Hegel does not mean, of course, that it is the role of the philosopher simply to transmit this tradition. He insists that it is his task to transform it, to assimilate it in his own individual and original manner. Only in this way, he says, does the tradition remain vital. Nevertheless, without a material handed down to him, the philosopher will have nothing to work upon or produce.

Hegel's historical conception of philosophy was not derived, however, simply from his general views about the nature of society and the arts and sciences. These considerations were important for his historicism, to be sure, but they do not account for the fundamental and characteristic conception that underlies it. There is a far more important argument at stake, one central to and distinctive of Hegel's philosophy as a whole. The arguments given so far show that philosophy is no more historical than other disciplines, such as art, science, and religion. But Hegel's central and characteristic argument for the historical nature of philosophy, which he expounds in his *Lectures on the History of Philosophy*,[10] maintains that there is something special about the very subject matter of philosophy that makes it more historical than other disciplines. Whereas the subject matter of other disciplines is fixed, given, and eternal, that of philosophy undergoes constant development and transformation. Why is this?

According to Hegel, the distinctive subject matter of philosophy is thought, the ideas or concepts by which we think about the world. This conception of the subject matter of philosophy is perhaps banal, but Hegel immediately adds to it a striking thesis central to his philosophy as a whole: that thought is by its very nature historical. Thought is not a fixed state of being, he maintains, but a restless activity, a process of development from the indeterminate to the determinate, from the vague to the clear, from the abstract to the concrete. The fundamental premise behind his historical conception of thought is that it is not possible to separate the object of thought from the activity of thinking about it, for it is only through our thinking about an idea that it becomes clear, determinate, and concrete. Like all activity, though, the activity of thought takes place not in an instant but throughout time. Hence thought itself must be historical.

In making this point, Hegel was taking issue with the Platonic tradition of philosophy, which had been responsible for so much of the a-historicism of the history of philosophy. According to the Platonic tradition, the object of thought is an eternal form, complete in all its meaning prior to our reflection upon it; and the reflection upon it is an eternal contemplation, a passive intuition or timeless perception of these forms. The main problem with this Platonic conception of thought, in Hegel's view, is that the meaning of ideas is never complete and given to us, as if it were only a question of our perceiving their transparent essence. Rather, they become clear and distinct and take on a determinate meaning only through our activity of thinking about them. Thus we must analyze the idea into its elements, contrast it with other ideas, find its context, and so on. Since the idea acquires its determinate meaning only through our activity of thinking about it, we cannot make a sharp distinction between the object and the activity of thought. The object of thought is not given to, but created by our thinking about it. It is posited by the very act of discovering its meaning. This is a point upon which Hegel laid some stress in his *Lectures on the History of Philosophy:* "The history [of philosophy] that we have before us is the history of the self-discovery of thought; and with thought it is the case that it discovers itself, indeed it exists and is actualized only through its discovery" (XVIII, 23).

Prima facie it would seem that the activity of thought takes place only within the mind of the individual philosopher, so that it is historical only in a trivial sense. But Hegel insists that the full development of the main idea underlying a system of philosophy is not the work of a single philosopher but of a whole generation. He stresses the enormous length of time, and the collective effort, required before the meaning of an idea becomes fully determinate. No single philosopher is able to develop alone all the implications of his system. As Hegel puts the point in his inimitable German: *"Der Weg des Geistes ist der Umweg."*[11] The path of the concept is not simple and easy, the day trip of a single individual, but involved and difficult, a detour negotiable only over many generations.

The epitome of Hegel's doctrine of the historicity of thought is his claim that we cannot separate philosophy from the history of philosophy. The discovery of the nature of thought in philosophy becomes the history of philosophy itself. Hegel's simplest and boldest formulation of this thesis is his statement that the temporal succession of ideas in the history of philosophy is the same as the logical succession of moments of the idea (cf. XVIII, 49 E XX 478). Each system of philosophy in the past stands for one stage or moment in the logical development of the idea, and the order in which these systems follow one another in time is the same as the order in which the moments of the idea follow one another in logic. In making such a bold equation, Hegel did not intend to equate temporal and logical succession *simpliciter.*[12] His point is only that the succession of these systems in time is primarily determined by the underlying logic of their main ideas. What compels system B to follow A in history, for example, is that B is more consistent or precise than A.

III. In Defense of Hegel's Historicism

It should not be surprising that the most revolutionary aspect of Hegel's thought has also been the most controversial. Hegel's historicism has been castigated as the chief source of his errors. Three kinds of objection have been hurled against it; each of them deserves careful consideration.

The first objection comes from the Marxist tradition, and in particular from Marx's attack upon Hegel in the *German Ideology.*[13] According to Marx, Hegel's historicism is vitiated by his metaphysics. Hegel did not go far enough in attempting to transform metaphysics; the point is to abolish it. Hegel's historicism involves a topsy-turvy picture of reality because it is infected with the metaphysics of absolute idealism. Rather than seeing the basic determining force of history as the concrete material needs of particular human beings, Hegel claims that they are found in the absolute idea. Allegedly, he holds that "the world is ruled by ideas, that ideas and concepts are its determining principles." To arrive at the true picture of reality, Marx argues, we should turn the Hegelian picture upside down: ideas and concepts are the product of human beings in a specific system of production. The Hegelian subject—the logic of the idea—has to be turned into the predicate of the real subject—the material needs of human beings. Thus Marx turned Hegel's historicism against itself: it too was simply the product of its age, the deification of the Prussian Restoration.

Yet Marx's critique is directed against a boogey-man. For there is nothing in Hegel's historicism that excludes in principle a naturalistic, indeed a materialistic, account of the origin of ideas.[14] Just as much as Marx, Hegel sees philosophy, religion, and literature as the product of social and political conditions; nor does he neglect the basic role of the economy in the formation of society.[15] Indeed, in his *Encyclopedia* Hegel explains human intelligence as the highest organization and development of all the powers in nature.[16] Of course Hegel, unlike Marx, assumes that social, political, and economic factors are ultimately manifestations of the absolute idea. But this still does not jeopardize any naturalistic or materialistic account of the origin of ideas. The point is that the idea realizes itself *only through* the workings of these social, political, and economic factors. It is important to avoid the vulgar error, sometimes suggested in Marx's critique, that Hegel thinks that ideas, as formulated in the minds of individual people, have a primary role in the development of history, a role prior to social and economic factors. Hegel not only holds that such ideas are the product of their social and political environment, but that it is naive for moral reformers to think that they can fashion all of society according to their moral ideals.[17] His scorn for the naivity of moral idealism is indeed equal to that of Marx. Ultimately, then, Hegel's historicism is much closer to Marx's historical materialism than Marx's tendentious caricature-filled polemic makes it appear. In tracing the genesis of ideas to their social, economic, and political context, in stressing the importance of economic factors in the formation of civil society, and in debunking the a-historical illusions of philosophers, Hegel anticipates much in Marx's own materialist historicism. Marx's materialism is indeed little more than Hegel's historicism without the metaphysics of the absolute idea.

The second objection to Hegel's historicism is that it leads to a complete relativism, the doctrine that all cultural values are incommensurable and not appraisable by any higher or absolute standard.[18] In attempting to show that apparently universal values are only those of a specific culture, and in stressing that philosophy is only the self-consciousness of its age, Hegel allegedly goes too far and undermines any basis for universal moral standards. Thus the only advice that he gives to someone who asks "What should I do?" is that he should follow the ethics of his own age. This is because Hegel has no basis to discriminate between different cultures.

Yet this objection fails to come to grips with the central thesis of Hegel's philosophy of history: that *the* end of history is the self-awareness of freedom. This goal is not purely formal and abstract, as if Hegel thinks that each culture achieves it in its own unique and incommensurable manner. For in his *Philosophy of Right* he outlines in very specific terms the necessary conditions for the realization of freedom. A state that is to achieve this end must fulfill very definite conditions, viz., it should provide for popular representation, it should have a written constitution limiting the powers of the central authority, it should permit liberty of press and freedom of conscience, and so on. Clearly, not any constitution or culture fulfills these conditions. In general, it is important to see that Hegel did not reject the tradition of natural law, which posited certain universal and necessary standards of right and wrong. Rather, he simply transformed and reinterpreted this tradition. Instead of seeing natural law as an eternal law above the process of history, Hegel historicizes it, so that it becomes the purpose of history itself. This then gives him an absolute standard by which he can appraise all the different cultures and constitutions of world history. They are good or bad according to whether they contribute toward the self-consciousness of freedom.

It might well be asked, then, how Hegel's absolute standpoint jibes with his theory that each constitution is appropriate for its age and circumstances.[19] Here it is necessary to recognize that Hegel's philosophy of history operates on two levels, one horizontal and the other vertical. The horizontal level comprises the specific circumstances of a nation, its economic, geographic, climactic, and demographic conditions. Since each nation must adapt to these circumstances, and since these circumstances are unique, each nation will have unique and incommensurable values. Its constitution and ethos will be appropriate to, and therefore justifiable in the light of its circumstances. The vertical level consists in world-history as a whole and the contribution each nation has made toward the realization of its end. It is clear that, from this perspective, different cultures will have different degrees of good and evil according to how they promote progress toward the self-consciousness of freedom.

The third and final objection against Hegel's historicism is that it is guilty of a simple logical mistake, "the genetic fallacy," the assumption that to determine the origin of an idea is also to determine its truth or falsity.[20] It is a simply fallacy to argue, for example, that the dogmas of Christianity are false simply because they serve the interests of a priestly caste, or that Smith's economics is mistaken since it supports the domination of the bourgeoisie. To assess the truth of a proposition according to the laws of logic and the evidence for it is one thing, but to determine its origins (the motivations behind it, the purposes it serves) is another. Now in attempting to debunk the a-historical pretensions of philosophers by making them aware of the genesis and context of their doctrines, this objection goes, Hegel is confusing the appraisal of the truth of a belief with the assessment of its origins.

Once we admit that the genetic fallacy is a fallacy, is Hegel guilty of committing it? The answer to this question must be a clear and simple "No." Hegel himself was perfectly aware of the pitfalls of the genetic fallacy and explicitly warned against it. In his polemic against the German historical school in the introduction to the *Philosophy of Right*, for example, he criticized the attempt to justify an institution or practice simply by revealing its historical origins (VII, 35–36, §3). To show the origins of an institution or practice is not *ipso facto* to justify it according to the principles of right, Hegel argued, for we can establish the historical origins and necessity of practices and institutions that are completely unjust and irrational. So, if Hegel is guilty of the genetic fallacy, it can be only by ignoring his own explicit warnings.

This objection rests upon two misunderstandings. First, it assumes a vulgar conception of Hegel's intentions. It is not his aim to discredit ideas by revealing their reprehensible origins. For it is central to his historicism that the philosopher accept the origin of ideas for what they are without passing judgment upon them. After all, the purpose of philosophy, as Hegel tells us in the preface to the *Philosophy of Right* (VII, 26), is not to prescribe how the world ought to be, but only to comprehend why it must be as it is. Second, this objection also fails to note the precise target of Hegel's criticism. This is not the truth of a philosopher's doctrine itself, but the a-historical claims he makes in its behalf. It is just a fact that philosophers attempt to give extra authority to their doctrines by making claims about their a-historical origins. They assume, for example, that their system is the product of pure reason alone, that their intellectual intuitions are the insights of pure genius, or that their principles are revolutionary and a complete break with the past. The truth of such assumptions can be properly appraised only by examining their genesis and origins.

In general, it is important to see that Hegel does not argue that because a philosophy has arisen from a specific social and political context that it is true only for that context. If this were the case, then he would indeed have to accept a complete relativism. But Hegel is no more a relativist in the sphere of epistemology than in ethics. Rather, he explicitly says the direct contrary: that the truth is eternal, universal, and permanent. This is a point upon which he lays much emphasis in the Berlin version of his *Lectures on the History of Philosophy*:

> The thought, the essential thought is, is in and for itself, is eternal. That which is true is contained in thought, is true not only today and tomorrow, but beyond all time; and insofar as it is in time it is always and at each time true. How is it then possible for the world of thought to have a history? (XII, 23–24)

The question Hegel raises here is indeed crucial. If the subject matter of philosophy is the eternal and universal truth, then how can philosophy have a history where everything undergoes change? In other words, how can philosophy be knowledge of the universal and eternal truth *and* the self-consciousness of its age?

To resolve this problem, it is again necessary to make a distinction (analogous to that above) between two standards of truth in Hegel's philosophy of history. The first standard of truth determines whether a philosophy adequately expresses the spirit of its age, whether it is true in describing its characteristic values and beliefs. According to this standard, different, and even incompatible, philosophies can be true as long as they succeed in expressing the spirits of their cultures, which have different and incompatible beliefs and values. The second standard is the universal goal of world history, the self-consciousness of freedom. It is this standard that allows Hegel to speak of a universal truth amid all the change of world history. Since each culture strives to attain this ideal, and since, as we have already seen, it can be achieved only under very specific conditions, it follows that some cultures will be more adequate and successful than others in attaining it. The philosophies that express these cultures will therefore have different degrees of truth according to the degree to which their culture achieves or approximates the goal of universal history.

IV. Hegel's Historical Method

Given the role of history in Hegel's thought, his ideas on historical method are obviously of the first importance. On this central issue, however, Hegel has surprisingly little to say. There is only one place where he does explain his views on historical method, and that is in the introduction to his *Lectures on World History*.[21] And even here Hegel's exposition is, as usual, very brief, dense, and obscure. Nevertheless, his introduction deserves close attention if only because so much has been written about Hegel's historical method without consulting his own views upon it. Philosophers of history have been more concerned to impose their own methodological paradigms and classifications upon Hegel than to interpret his own difficult texts. Thus Hegel has been seen as the paradigm of a "speculative historian," as someone whose main purpose is to explain the ultimate purpose of history according to his metaphysics rather than to examine facts for their own sake.[22] He has also been castigated as the chief practitioner of *a priori* history, as someone who imposes his own *a priori* schematism upon the facts, compelling them to conform to his own metaphysical preconceptions.[23] Yet it is significant that Hegel rejects both these approaches. He insists that the philosopher of history examine facts for their own sake, and that he lay aside all metaphysical presuppositions. Indeed, he states explicitly: "We must take history as it is; we must proceed historically, empirically" (XII, 22). He is painfully aware of the problems of applying *a priori* schemes to history, and he is even critical of other German historians for doing just this. So, given Hegel's explicit rejection of the methodologies that have been foisted upon him, there is all the more reason to examine his own ideas about historical method.

In his introduction Hegel distinguishes between three different kinds of history: original, reflective, and philosophical. In original history the writer narrates events in which he has participated. The spirit of the writer and that of the events he narrates is one and the same. The writer's account of the events is itself, then, an historical document. What the author has written about the events is constitutive of them. The classical examples of such original history, in Hegel's view, are Thucydides and Herodotus. Although Hegel praises the identity of the writer and his subject in original history, he also thinks that it suffers from a serious weakness: it considers only the events that the author witnesses. It lacks a universal perspective. This defect is surmounted by reflective history. Its perspective is broader, an entire epoch or all of world history. The reflective historian applies general ideas or conceptions to history and attempts to make sense of it; he does not limit himself to narrating events, as does the original historian. Like original history, though, reflective history is also subject to a fatal flaw. Although it has a more universal perspective, it imposes the view of the author upon the past. The identity between the writer and the event, the subject and object, in original history is destroyed; there is a dualism between the object (history) and the subject (the perspective of the historian).

Hegel's philosophical history is meant to cancel the weakness, and preserve the strengths, of original and reflective history. The philosophical historian has a universal perspective; but he does not impose his own ideas upon his subject matter. He achieves the identity of subject and object of original history, yet he does so on a "mediated," universal, or reflective level. How is this feat possible? What precise form must philosophical history take if it is to cancel the weaknesses and preserve the strengths of original and reflective history? It is just at this point that Hegel's explanation becomes very sketchy and obscure.

If Hegel is very vague about the method of philosophical history, he is at least very clear about the basic problem confronting it. In his introduction he explains that there is a "contradiction" between the methods of philosophy and history (XII, 20, 557–58). Philosophy has an *a priori* method where thought is active, producing its own content from itself. History, however, has an empirical method, demanding that we examine the given for its own sake and cast aside all *a priori* preconceptions. It would appear, then, as if the very idea of a philosophy of history is a contradiction in terms. How does it resolve this contradiction? Here again Hegel's text becomes very vague.

If we are to understand Hegel's method in the philosophy of history, then we have to reconstruct his meaning by considering his general ideas about philosophical method. It is necessary to consult other texts beside the *Lectures on World History*, and in particular the *Phenomenology of Spirit*, which also has an historical subject matter. The contradiction between the methods of philosophy and history that Hegel presents in his introduction has a striking resemblance to the conflict between the standpoints of orinary consciousness and philosophy in the introduction to the *Phenomenology*. Ordinary consciousness says that its object is given, something external to itself. Philosophy, however, stands by its principle of subject-object identity, according to which the object is not given but produced by pure thought. How, then, is it possible to resolve the conflict between them? Hegel's solution is his phenomenological method. This demands that the philosopher bracket his own principles and presuppositions and permit consciousness to examine itself according to its own standards. The philosopher will then find that, through its self-examination, ordinary consciousness will be compelled to admit the truth of subject-object identity. Ordinary consciousness will discover through its own experience that the object is not given to it but essential to its own self-consciousness.

Now the method of the philosophy of history is, I suggest, analogous to that of the *Phenomenology*. Like the phenomenologist, the philosopher of history suspends his own *a priori* metaphysical principles and examines his subject matter according to its own internal standards. In more historical terms, this means that the philosopher of history will examine the cultures of the past in terms of *their own* beliefs, values, and ideals. As in ordinary consciousness, each culture is subject to a dialectic where it discovers through its own *self*-examination that its ideals and goals are in conflict with its experience. The only means of resolving this conflict will be through the higher ideals of a more-advanced culture. The end of this dialectic will also be similar to the *Phenomenology*. What the philosopher knows *a priori* through reflection—that the end of history is the self-consciousness of freedom—becomes the result of the inner dialectic of history itself.

The advantage of this phenomenological reading of Hegel's method is that it explains (a) how the conflict between the methods of history and philosophy is resolved and (b) how the method of philosophical history maintains the strengths and avoids the weaknesses of original and reflective history. The phenomenological method avoids the conflict between the historical and philosophical methods by combining aspects of them both. It is empirical insofar as it surrenders all preconceptions and examines its subject matter for its own sake, according to its own ideals and goals; and it is *a priori* insofar as there is an inner dialectic, a logical necessity, in history where the contradictions of a culture are discovered and resolved. The phenomenological method also unites the strengths of original and reflective history. It has the subject-object identity of original history since the historical subject examines itself according to its own ideals; but it has the universal perspective of reflective history since the dialectic ascends from the narrow perspective of one culture to the higher perspective of another. This method also avoids the chief problem of reflective history, since the philosopher's standpoint is that of his subject matter itself, given that he examines it only in the light of its own ideals and aspirations.

If this account of Hegel's method is correct, then the subject matter of his philosophy of history should be not historical events *simpliciter*, which can be described by some reflective historian or external observer, but the agent's *consciousness* of these events. In other words, the subject matter of history should be the *self-consciousness of a nation* or, more precisely, *the dialectic* by which it arrives at its self-consciousness. This assumption finds more than ample confirmation from Hegel's introduction when he tells us that the subject matter of philosophical history is "the spirits of those nations which have become conscious of their inherent principles, and have become aware of what they are and of what their actions signify" (XII, 12, 545). Hegel makes the same point from another angle when he says that the subject matter of history is "spirit" (XII, 31). One of the "main characteristics" of spirit, he says, is "its consciousness of its own ends and interests and the principles which underlie them" (VG 7; 13). He then goes on to make self-consciousness into the defining characteristic of spirit; it is its very nature to have itself as an object. "I am not just this, that, or the other, but what I know myself to be" (VG 54; 47). This conception of spirit or the self as self-explaining or self-interpreting, which Hegel derives from Fichte, is crucial to the method of the *Phenomenology* and *Philosophy of History*. For it means that the philosopher does not have to import his own abstractions and principles to explain his subject matter. Rather, his subject matter will explain itself. This is what Hegel means when he says that the philosopher only has to describe "the thing itself" (*die Sache selbst*) or "the immanent movement of the concept."

It becomes all the more plausible to ascribe a phenomenological method to Hegel once we recognize that such a method had become current in his day. This is the very method that Herder had prescribed in his influential 1774 tract *Another Philosophy of the History of Mankind*. Before Hegel, Herder had castigated those historians who judged the past in the light of their own contemporary standards of right and wrong. He demanded that the historian should examine each age according to its own standards and values. The fundamental precept of the historian became "empathy" (*Einfühlung*) with the past, a sympathetic reconstruction of its guiding ideals. Herder preached to the new generation of historians: "go into the age, into the region, into the whole of history, feel yourself into everything—only now are you on the path of understanding."[24] In following a phenomenological approach, then, Hegel was simply following Herder's advice.

The obvious question that arises is how the historian is able to follow such a method. Is there not a danger that he will subconsciously apply the attitudes and values of his own age in his attempt to understand the past? Will not his sympathetic reconstruction be simply a projection of his own ethnocentric imagination? This problem certainly did not escape Hegel. In his introduction he warned that it is not possible to immerse ourselves fully in the past because we, as historians, belong to our own age. We cannot understand the ancient Greeks, he says, any more than "the perceptions of a dog" (VG, 13–14; 18). This difficulty seems to undermine the phenomenological method, however, which presupposes that we can understand an age as it would have understood itself. Yet the problem here, while it is a very real and serious one, should not be exaggerated. Although we cannot ever *fully* understand a past culture as it would have understood itself, we can still do this to some degree. We can approach, even if we cannot attain, this goal. There is indeed all the difference in the world between the historian who criticizes a past culture according to his contemporary prejudices and one who attempts to reconstruct it sympathetically on the basis of the most painstaking and detailed investigations. This difficulty, then, does not amount to an impossibility. The problems of Hegel's phenomenological method are simply part and parcel of the general problem of doing history in general.

Once we recognize that Hegel's method is phenomenological, we can quickly see what is wrong with those who accuse Hegel of following a "speculative" or *a priori* method. The very opposite is the case, given that it was precisely Hegel's aim to avoid the problems of such methods. His own phenomenological method is more akin to the empirical method of the historian, who immerses himself into his subject matter. Rather than beginning his philosophy of history with a metaphysics, Hegel intended metaphysics to be only its result.

Yet a nagging doubt still remains. If Hegel's method is *in principle* phenomenological, is it also *in practice*? Does Hegel abide by the guidelines that he sets for himself? It is in this respect that some of the objections of Hegel's critics have their point. However wrong they are about Hegel's principles and intentions, they are still correct about much of his practice. It is necessary for even the most-loyal Hegelian to admit that Hegel violates his own ideals. Rather than allowing his metaphysics to emerge from his analysis of the subject matter, he classifies and examines his subject matter according to his metaphysics. The dialectic proceeds from China to India, for example, because the idea of an organism means that a moment of diversity (the differentiated caste society of India) should follow that of unity (the uniformity of Chinese society) (XII, 180). The division of history into the Oriental, Classical, and Germanic worlds according to the principle of one, some, or all being free derives from Hegel's treatment of the forms of judgment in his *Logic*. In general, Hegel does not hesitate to pass harsh judgments upon foreign cultures (the American Indians, the Chinese, the Indians) according to the standpoint of modern Western individualism,[25] falling prey to the very ethnocentrism from which historicism should liberate us. When we consider factors like these it is difficult not to say of Hegel's historical method what Kierkegaard said of his philosophy as a whole: "Hegel is to be honored for having willed something great and having failed to accomplish it."[26]

V. The Metaphysics Hegel's Historicism

It seems obvious that Hegel employs metaphysics in his philosophy of history. His text literally teems with metaphysical terms, such as "spirit," "idea," "providence," and "God." It is this metaphysical dimension of Hegel's text that has given it such a bad name among historians, and that has provoked the criticism of Croce, Marx, and others. They can rightfully grumble that, however much Hegel preached against metaphysics, he certainly did practice it.

After we concede the metaphysical dimension of Hegel's philosophy of history, the next question to raise is whether its presence is necessarily fatal. We cannot provide here a general defense or criticism of Hegel's metaphysics. We can, however, answer a much more modest question: Does Hegel's metaphysics remain true to his own strictures about the limits of knowledge? Is it a strictly immanent metaphysics, remaining within the limits of experience? Or does it involve speculation about transcendent entities? Hegel's critics usually dismiss his metaphysics because it seems to them to be a transcendent metaphysics, describing obscure metaphysical entities not encountered in any possible experience. But is this attitude fair? I would like to argue here that it rests upon a misunderstanding.

The metaphysical dimension of Hegel's philosophy of history ultimately rests upon its teleology, its claim that world history is governed by a single dominating purpose. Rather than contenting himself with a piecemeal description of events, Hegel thinks that the philosophy of history should answer the question "What is the ultimate purpose of history?" No sooner has he raised this question, though, than he seems to plunge into the deeper end of metaphysics. He immediately refers to God's providence and the idea governing history (VG, 28–49; 27–44). Without any further explanation or justification, we seem to return to the old theology of the eighteenth century.

Read out of context, Hegel's language here can be extremely misleading. If, however, we consider Hegel's remarks in the light of his other works, it becomes clear that the kind of teleology in question is not that commonplace in the eighteenth century. In his *Logic* and *Encyclopedia*, Hegel rejects the idea that there is a supernatural design imposed upon history and nature by a transcendent God.[27] It is just such "external teleology," he argues, that has given metaphysics a bad name, because it involves illegitimate speculation about entities beyond experience. To avoid such speculation, Hegel insists that the end of history and nature must be *internal to* history and nature themselves. In other words, any explanation in teleological terms must not violate the principle that everything in nature is explicable in its own terms without reference to the supernatural. So rather than theologizing Hegel's account of history, as his initial remarks would seem to suggest, it is more appropriate to naturalize his theology. Providence will be determined by some end within history and nature.

What, then, is the ultimate purpose of history? Hegel's answer to this question involves no more metaphysics than his conception of natural law, his idea about the "essence" or characteristic nature of man. The nature or essence of man, Hegel tells us simply, is freedom (XII, 30). Just as the essence of matter is gravity, so the essence of the self is freedom. Freedom is not simply one quality of the self, he argues, but the basic quality that all others serve. To say that man is free "by nature" does not mean, Hegel explains (XII, 58), that he is *born* free or that he *exists* in some state of nature as a free being. Rather, it signifies only that the *purpose* or *end* of man is to realize his freedom. The essence or nature of man is of necessity, then, a goal that he must achieve, not a reality that is given to him. The realization of this goal therefore demands human activity. In other words, it can be achieved only in history.

This concept of the essence of man determines Hegel's view of the purpose of history itself. The end of history is nothing more nor less than the realization of human freedom. It is, as Hegel puts it, "the self-awareness of freedom," the knowledge that man as such is free (VG, 62–63; 54–55) Since Hegel thinks that the essence of freedom is realized only in the state, it follows that the purpose of history will be to achieve the perfect state, that in which human freedom is realized. It is for this reason, and not because of any Prussian authoritarianism, that Hegel believes that the state is the primary subject of history.

The dialectic of Hegel's philosophy of history is also structured by his account of the end or purpose of man. The dialectic consists in the conflict between the end of man and his actual political conditions, and the attempt by man to change these conditions so that they are more in accord with his nature. Since man is not from the beginning fully or clearly aware of his goal, and since he does not know the necessary conditions to realize it, the process of achieving his end will be a journey of self-discovery.

This non-metaphysical account of Hegel's philosophy of history is implausible, someone might say, because it assumes that the main agents of history are finite human beings. But such a reading seems to fly in the face of Hegel's texts. For he tells us time and again that the main subject of history is "spirit" (*Geist*):

the history of the world is a rational process, the rational and necessary evolution of the world spirit. This spirit is the substance of history; its nature is always one and the same; and it discloses this nature in the existence of the world. The world spirit is the absolute spirit. (VG, 30; 29)

If this absolute spirit is anything at all, this objection continues, then it is not this or that finite individual, nor even the mere sum of them. Rather, it is a suprapersonal substance of which all finite persons are only modes. This reading of spirit as a supernatural substance appears further strengthened by Hegel's famous concept of the "cunning of reason." According to this concept, all individual actions, though apparently directed by private ends, conform to a rational pattern or goal, the self-realization of spirit. Spirit, it would seem, is the super puppetmaster directing all individual actions.

This metaphysical reading of Hegel's concept of spirit is not, however, consistent with his general principles. Spirit by itself, apart from any of the finite individuals in which it appears, would be only a general term or universal. But Hegel insists that no universal can exist on its own apart from, and prior to, particular things. By itself it is simply an abstraction. Hegel's insistence on this point comes from his adherence to the Aristotelian dictum that universals exist only *in re*. Using a simple example, he clearly states this doctrine in his *Encyclopedia*:

> The animal is not to be found, but it is always something determinate. The animal does not exist, but it is always the universal nature of the individual animals; and every individual animal is something much more concretely determinate, a particular. (VIII, 82; §a4, Zusatz I)

It is this Aristotelian doctrine that Hegel applies to his concept of spirit in the *Philosophy of History* when he tells us most emphatically that spirit by itself is only an abstraction and comes into existence only through the activity of finite agents. In this passage Hegel explicitly warns us against any hypostasis of spirit:

> The first thing we have to notice is this: that what we have hitherto called the principle, or ultimate end, or destiny of the nature and concept of spirit in itself, is purely universal and abstract. A principle, fundamental rule, or law is something universal and implicit, and as such, it has not attained complete reality, however true it may be in itself. Aims, principles, and the like are present at first in our thoughts and inner intentions, or even in books, but not yet in reality itself. In other words, that which exists only in itself is a possibility or potentiality which has not yet emerged into existence. A second moment is necessary because it can attain reality—that of actualization or realization; and its principle is the will, the activity of mankind in the world at large. It is only by means of this activity that the original concepts or implicit determinations are realized and actualized. (VG, 81; 69–70)

Elsewhere in the *Philosophy of History*, Hegel further prohibits hypostasizing his concept of spirit by telling us that he does not mean by it some self-conscious being (VG, 37; 34).

It might be asked how the concept of spirit has any explanatory value at all if it exists only in finite agents. If spirit by itself is only an abstraction, how does it explain the rational plan behind the chaos of individual actions? If it exists only in individuals, it would seem to amount to nothing more than the sum of their disparate actions. The rational plan behind history, the cunning of reason, still seems to give some reason, then, for thinking of spirit as some suprapersonal substance acting behind the scenes. But such hypostasis is completely unwarrented, and indeed for good Hegelian reasons. Here it is important to invoke another Aristotelian doctrine, one that Hegel incorporates into his teleology. This is Aristotle's distinction between what is first in order of explanation and what is first in order of existence. A particular is first *in order of existence*, since to know *that* a thing exists we must know something about particular or determinate things. This is because a universal, if it exists, exists only in particulars. A universal, however, is first *in order of explanation* because to know *what* a thing is we must be able to specify some properties of it, some features that it shares in common with other things. We identify a thing, for example, by saying that it is red and round, or blue and square. Similarly, to know *why a* thing acts, for what purpose or end, we must also be able to state some universal. The final cause of a thing is, for Aristotle, some universal specifying its essence or characteristic nature. Now this Aristotelian distinction is crucial for Hegel's account of historical explanation. It means that the universal, in this case spirit, has an explanatory value even though it exists only in particular persons. It has an explanatory value because it is first in order of explanation, if not first in order of existence. Without the concept of spirit we cannot explain what all finite agents are trying to achieve throughout history (the realization of their freedom). Nevertheless, because it is first in order of explanation does not mean that it is first in order of existence; in other words, the concept of spirit still does not come into existence except through the activity of all finite agents. Hence, thanks to this Aristotelian distinction, the concept of spirit should have some explanatory value without the need to make some commitment to an abstract or transcendent entity.

If we further examine Hegel's concept of spirit, we find that it conforms perfectly to our non-metaphysical reading of the purpose of history. The concept of spirit is indeed simply a more-specific account of what Hegel means by the end of history, the self-awareness of freedom. If we closely consider those chapters of the *Phenomenology* where Hegel first deduces the concept of spirit, chapters IV and IV.A, then we find that it is indeed the self-awareness of freedom. It tells us precisely what form this self-awareness should take. More specifically, spirit is the mutual recognition between free and equal persons, their intersubjective self-awareness of their freedom. It is, as Hegel puts it, "the I that is a We and the We that is an I." In these chapters Hegel argues that my self-awareness as a free being must be social or intersubjective. It demands the recognition of others as equal and independent beings because only by this means do I achieve the recognition necessary to confirm to myself that I too am an independent being. The mutual self-awareness of spirit is of course not reducible to the self-awareness of particular persons. It is possible only through their abandoning their sense of themselves as separate individuals and by their identifying themselves with the social whole. But at the same time, neither is spirit a substance or entity that exists apart from the persons who become *mutually* self-aware. By itself it is simply mutual self-awareness, intersubjective self-consciousness, and hence an abstraction. It is the task of the *Philosophy of Right* to specify the political conditions necessary for the realization of spirit, for the development of the self-awareness of freedom. To say that the end of history is the realization of spirit *and* a state where there is a community between free and equal individuals is one and the same thing.

VI. The Politics of Hegel's Historicism

What were the political intentions and implications behind Hegel's historicism? This question has been the subject of a famous dispute, a controversy that has lasted more than a century. Some commentators have argued that Hegel's aims were fundamentally conservative, indeed reactionary.[28] They regard Hegel as the spokesman for the Restoration in Prussia, as the defender of the reactionary policies of the government of Friedrich Wilhelm III. Hegel's philosophy of history was, in their view, no less reactionary than his philosophy of the state. They argue that it was Hegel's purpose, in giving such importance to history, to defend the value of established institutions and traditions against those radicals who would model all of society according to abstract principles. Nowhere are Hegel's reactionary views more apparent, they contend, than in his making the present Prussian state into the apotheosis of world history. Other commentators, however, especially the left-wing Hegelian school, have acknowledged Hegel's philosophy of history as the inspiration for their own radical doctrines.[29] They stress the revolutionary implications, if not intentions, of his dialectic. In saying that history is a process of dialectical development, of ceaseless conflict, destruction, and regeneration, Hegel allegedly passed the death sentence upon any status quo.

If we carefully examine all the passages from Hegel's writings in which he draws some political point from history, we find that neither of these interpretations is correct. The truth lies somewhere in between. For Hegel appealed to history to justify the middle path of reform, to criticize both radicals and reactionaries alike. In his view, both the radicals and reactionaries had failed to understand history. The radicals could not see that their ideals have to be adapted to the history of a nation, while the reactionaries were blind to the fact that history undergoes ceaseless change. If history made it impossible to create a totally new society according to some abstract plan, it also prohibited attempts to return to the past.

In the spectrum of political belief in Germany after the French Revolution, Hegel reveals himself to be a progressive moderate. Unlike the reactionaries, he approved of the fundamental ideals of the French Revolution, such as equality of opportunity, constitutional government, individual liberty, and representative assemblies; and he insisted that it was impossible to return to the older institutions of the *ancien régime*. Unlike the radicals, however, Hegel did not believe that these ideals could be achieved through popular agitation, still less through sweeping away all the historical traditions and institutions of Germany. The ideals of the Revolution would have to be established through piecemeal reform from above, through gradually adapting them to the historical conditions prevalent in Germany.

There can be no doubt that there is a conservative side to Hegel's historicism. In many of his writings Hegel appealed to history to criticize the attempts by radicals to remodel all of society according to their abstract ideals.[30] The lesson to be drawn from the failure of the Revolution in France, in Hegel's view, was that it is not possible to change the constitution and institutions of a society in complete abstraction from its history, from such given circumstances as its religion, economy, traditions, and national character. When the French radicals discovered that their ideals could not be easily imposed upon these circumstances, Hegel maintains, they engaged in a "fury of destruction," destroying all the historical institutions and traditions of France. The result was that there was nothing for them to build upon, so that the country lapsed into anarchy and terror.

The conservative element of Hegel's historicism largely lay in his naturalism, his belief that the constitution and institutions of a nation are the product of its environment, and in particular its climate, geography, economy, religion, and traditions. Hegel acquired this doctrine from Montesquieu in his youth, and he adhered to it all his life. No less than his illustrious predecessor, he drew a conservative conclusion from it: that the constitution and institutions of a nation are adapted to its circumstances and are therefore appropriate to them. As Hegel put the point succinctly in his *Philosophy of Right*: "Every nation has the constitution appropriate to it and suitable for it" (VII, 440, §274). It was largely for this reason that Hegel sharply attacked utopian and radical reformers. In prescribing how the state ought to be, they failed to take into account its natural causes, the circumstances that make it of necessity as it is. The state cannot be created according to an arbitrary plan, but arises from historical causes, from the force of environment acting upon it.

It is no less clear, however, that there is a progressive side to Hegel's historicism. In seeing the end of history as the self-awareness of freedom, as the recognition that all are free, Hegel made the ideals of liberty and equality of the French Revolution into the very end of history itself. He thus bestowed the iron law of necessity upon these ideals. They were goals that people not only *ought to* strive for but *must* strive for through the inherent laws of history itself. Since these ideals were inherent in the natural development of history, Hegel argued that it was impossible in the post-revolutionary era to return to the old *status quo ante* of the *ancien régime*. This would be to fail to recognize the fate of the modern world, the fundamental spirit of modern life since the French Revolution. This was the principle of subjectivity, the idea that nothing could be accepted as valid until it accorded with the reason of the individual.

This progressive side of Hegel's historicism becomes especially plain from two of his political articles, his 1799 "On the German Constitution" and his 1814 "Proceedings of the Estates of Württemberg."[31] Although they were written on separate occasions and for different reasons, these articles shared a common critical orientation. Both attacked those jurists and aristocrats who were bent on returning to the political structure of the *ancien régime*. The jurists continued to write as if the Holy Roman Empire still existed and as if nothing had changed since Charlemagne, while the aristocrats insisted upon the return of all their old privileges and powers as if Napoleon had never revamped the entire structure of Germany. The trend of history since the revolution, Hegel argued, had been against restoring the old feudal constitution of the Holy Roman Empire, which had not been able to adapt to the new situation in Europe. If the princes' attempt to restore this constitution, ignoring all recent history, then they would revive only "empty forms without a substance." The spirit of the times demands, Hegel insisted, the creation of a completely new constitution for Germany, a constitution providing for a strong central government, representative institutions, the role of law, and popular influence on legislation.

The progressive and conservative sides of Hegel's historicism are succinctly captured by his famous dictum in the preface to the *Philosophy of Right*: "What is rational is actual, and what is actual is rational" (VII, 24). The first phrase expresses Hegel's progressive beliefs. To say that the rational is actual means that the ideals of liberty and equality, which have been sanctioned by reason, will become realized of necessity in history itself. The second phrase states Hegel's more-conservative convictions. Here he means that the present constitution and institutions of a nation are rational in the sense that they arise of necessity from their environment, and are therefore appropriate to it. These two phrases appear to conflict with one another, however, for what if the present constitution violates, or at least does not recognize, the principles of liberty and equality? Hegel's reply to this question is that each constitution is appropriate not only to its circumstances but also to its stage in the world-historical development of freedom and equality. The cunning of reason means that even if a nation does not recognize these ideals, it is still a necessary stage in their dialectical development.

What allows Hegel to unite the progressive and conservative sides of his historicism—to reconcile the ideals of the Revolution with the demand of historical continuity—is his belief that these ideals were already present within, and central to, the Middle Ages. They do not involve a complete break with feudalism, he believes, but they are simply the final coming to self-consciousness of its underlying spirit. In his essay on the German constitution, for example, Hegel ridicules those who think that the modern principle of representative government arose only with the French Revolution. This principle was in fact basic to government during the feudal period he contends. According to the medieval ideal of government, each vassal should have a direct personal share in the shaping of common policy. The representation of the individual in the government was direct and immediate, since each vassal personally stood for his own territory in the assemblies. The fundamental challenge to government in the modern age, Hegel maintains, is to unite the medieval ideal of participation in government with the need for a strong central authority. The modern state has simply grown too large and complex for direct participation. If, under these conditions, the principle of direct participation is not relinquished, as in the Holy Roman Empire, then the state will simply dissolve into anarchy, a jumble of separate territories.

Both the radicals and reactionaries, Hegel believed, had failed to see that there is reason in history, that the realization of freedom and equality is the inherent law of its development since the Middle Ages. The radicals recognized the authority of reason, to be sure, but they did not understand that it is the law of history itself. It was for this reason that they mistakenly believed that they had *to impose* reason upon history and to break with the past. On the other hand, the reactionaries fully recognized the value of historical continuity and development, but they did not comprehend that it has an underlying end or reason, the realization of freedom and equality.

In considering the politics of Hegel's historicism, it is illuminating to compare Hegel with Burke.[32] Both stressed the value of historical continuity and tradition. Both appealed to history to undermine the claims of French radicals to change all of society according to some abstract plan. Nevertheless Hegel, unlike Burke, saw history as an argument *for* rather than against a new constitution based upon reason. Burke argues against the attempt to create a new constitution on the grounds that it is *incompatible with* historical development. Hegel, however, argues in favor of such a constitution on the grounds that it is *necessary to* historical development. In general, Hegel affirmed the fundamental legal principle of the Revolution, that laws are legitimate only if they accord with a critical reason.[33] He criticized traditionalists like Burke on the grounds that historical precedent by itself could never be the source of law. Age, Hegel argued, has nothing to do with justice or rights. Even the abrogation of slavery, despotism, and human sacrifice was a violation of old rights and privileges. Turning the principle of positive law against the traditionalists, he argues that if the basis of law is history, then law must change with history.

Notes

All references in the text are to the *Werkausgabe* of Hegel's works edited by E. Moldenhauer and K. Michel, *Werke in Zwanzig Bänden* (Frankfurt, 1970). Roman numerals refer to volume numbers, Arabic numerals to page numbers. All translations of Hegel's works are my own (with the exception of the Nisbet translation of the *Philosophy of World History*). Page numbers cited after a semicolon are to the appropriate English translations cited below.

The following works and abbreviations have been used:

Die Vernunft in der Geschichte, ed. J. Hoffmeister (Hamburg, 1970), volume I of *Vorlesungen über die Philosophie der Weltgeschichte*. Cited as VG.

Lectures on the Philosophy of World History, trans. H.B. Nisbet (Cambridge, England, 1975).

History of Philosophy, trans. E.S. Haldane (London, 1892–95). Cited as HP.

Hegel's Political Writings, trans. T.M. Knox (Oxford, 1964). Cited as HPW.

Philosophy of History, trans. T. Sibree (New York, 1956).

[1] See, for example, Rudolf Haym, *Hegel and seine Zeit* (Leipzig, 1927), 45–46; Georg Lukács, *Der junge Hegel* (Frankfurt, 1973), I, 62, 135–36; and Jean Hyppolyte, *Genesis and Structure of the Phenomenology of Spirit* (Evanston, 1974), 27–34.

[2] See, for example, Hegel's critique of Kant's concept in his Lectures on the *History of Philosophy* XX, 352; HP III, 444–45. Also see Hegel's critique of empiricism, *Werke* XX, 79; HP III, 303.

[3] The definitive study of the origins of historicism is Friedrich Meinecke's *Die Entstehung des Historismus* (Munich, 1959). Unfortunately, Meinecke does not discuss Hegel. For a briefer discussion of Hegel's predecessors and Hegel himself, see R.G. Collingwood, *The Idea of History* (Oxford, 1980), 86–113.

[4] On the influence of Montesquieu, see *Werke* I, 60, 206, 263, 440; on the influence of Herder, see *Werke* I, 201, 215; XIII, 349; and XVIII, 21; and on the influence of Ferguson, see Rosenkranz, *G.W.F. Hegels Leben* (Berlin, 1844) 87.

[5] See *Werke* XVIII, 18–19, 49; and XX, 478–79; HP I, 29.

[6] See especially the new introduction to Hegel's *Positivity* essay, *Werke* I, 227–29; ETW, 167–81. For a study of the critical historical themes in Hegel's *Phenomenology*, see Judith Shklar, *Freedom and Independence: A Study of the Political Ideas of Hegel's Phenomenology of Mind* (Cambridge, England, 1976).

[7] Hegel stresses this doctrine in his *Lectures on the Philosophy of History*, *Werke* XII, 65–66; PH, 46. *Cf.* 52.

[8] See Hegel's *Lectures on the History of Philosophy*, *Werke* XVIII, 73–75; HP I, 53–54

[9] See Hegel's *Lectures on the History of Philosophy*, *Werke* XVIII, 20–28; HP I, 2–3.

[10] *Werke* XVIII, 25–27; HP I, 29–32.

[11] *Werke* XVIII, 54–55 *cf. Werke* XX, 506–9.

[12] *Cf. Werke* XVIII, 49, and XX, 478–79.

[13] See *Die deutsche Ideologie, Marx-Engels Gesamtausgabe* (Berlin: Dietz, 1973) III, 26–27, 39. Cf. Ergänzungsband I, 568–88.

[14] Here I disagree with Collingwood, *Idea of History*, p. 125, who sees Marx's fundamental difference with Hegel as his naturalism.

[15] On the importance of economics for the young Hegel, see Shlomo Avineri, *Hegel's Theory of the Modern State* (Cambridge, England, 1972), 132–54.

[16] *Werke* X, 43–199, §388–411.

[17] See the *Philosophy of History*, *Werke* XII, 52–53; PH, 45–46.

[18] This objection is made by Haym, *Hegel und seine Zeit*, 375–76, and by Meinecke, *Die Idee der Staatsräson in der Geschichte* (Munich & Berlin, 1929), 451–52. The same objection is implicit in the critique of those who accuse Hegel of legal positivism. This is the objection of Popper, *The Open Society and its Enemies* (London, 1945), 39, 62–63.

[19] See below, section VI, 294–95.

[20] The term "genetic fallacy" has received various definitions. The one I follow here is that of Morris Cohen and Ernest Nagel, *An Introduction to Logic and Scientific Method* (London, 1978), 388–90. For a criticism of the Hegelian and Marxist tradition on this score, see H.B. Acton, *The Illusion of the Epoch* (London, 1955) 108–9.

[21] See *Werke* XII, 11–20, 543–58. Also *Die Vernunft in der Geschichte*, pp. 3–27, and particularly 11–24.

[22] See W.H. Walsh, *An Introduction to the Philosophy of History* (London, 1967), 143–50.

[23] The *locus classicus* for this view is Benedetto Croce's *What is Living and What is Dead in the Philosophy of Hegel*, trans. Douglas Ainslie (London, 1915), 134–49.

[24] Herder, *Sämtliche Werke*, ed. B. Suphan (Berlin, 1877–1913), V, 503.

[25] This point has been argued in detail by W.H. Walsh, "Principle and Prejudice in Hegel's Philosophy of History," in *Hegel's Political Philosophy*, ed. Z.A. Pelczynski (Cambridge, England, 1971), 181–98.

[26] See *Concluding Unscientific Postscript* (Princeton, New Jersey, 1969), 100n.

[27] *Cf. Werke* VIII, 362–63, §205–6; and *Werke* VI, 458.

[28] The *locus classicus* for this criticism of Hegel is Haym's *Hegel und seine Zeit,* pp. 357–91. For a more-recent criticism of Hegel as a reactionary, see Popper, *The Open Society,* II, 27, 57–75.

[29] The *locus classicus* for the left-wing interpretation of Hegel's historicism is Engel's *Ludwig Feuerbach und der Ausgang der klassischen Philosophie,* MEGA XXI, 266–68.

[30] See, for example, the *Phenomenology, Werke* III, 431–41; *Philosophy of History, Werke* XII, 64–65; and the *Philosophy of Right, Werke* VII, 400–401, §258.

[31] See *Werke* I, 470–71; HPW, 152–53; *Werke* XI, HPW, 250–51, 273–74.

[32] For a more-detailed comparison of Burke and Hegel, see J-F Suter, "Burke, Hegel and the French Revolution," in *Hegel's Political Philosophy,* pp. 52–72.

[33] *Werke* IV, 506; HPW, 281–82.

14. Introduction to Marx

By the nineteenth century, the industrial revolution has created vast armies of industrial workers throughout Europe. Marx provides the working class with the means to challenge the ideological domination of the capitalist class, the *bourgeoisie*. He uses British political economy to produce an economic theory which proves that the worker is by definition exploited by the capitalist. He also uses Hegel's dialectic to reach an understanding of history according to which the final prevalence of the workers' over the *bourgeois* is certain.

The strongest part of Marx's theory is, arguably, his theory of surplus value. By interpreting an impressive volume of statistical and other economic data, Marx demonstrates that the worker is always paid less than what his labor is worth. Starting from the assumption of British political economists that the value of a product is determined by the amount of labor that goes into its production, Marx shows that the profit of the capitalist is the difference between the market value of the product and what the capitalist pays the worker. This difference is called surplus value.

The surplus value theory is historically important because it provided workers with an understanding of the way that capitalism worked. Also, despite the fact that parts of the theory have been severely criticized, the main concept behind it is very simple and hard to reject. It is self-evident that the capitalist will hire a worker only if he expects to make a profit out of his or her labor.

One very common misconception about Marx is that he advocates universal, absolute economic equality. This is not true. Marx envisages a society in which factories are run by workers' committees, representing all the workers, and where relative inequality of wealth may exist, but nobody has surplus value extracted out of their work. It was later that Marxists like Lenin came up with the idea of a centralized government enforcing Marxist principles. For Marx, the state was fundamentally an organization used by the ruling classes to perpetuate the subjection of workers, in other words an instrument of the *bourgeoisie*. In a socialist society it would disappear altogether and give its place to small, decentralized political associations.

One fundamental concept in Marx is the concept of class. People belong to a certain class depending on their role in production. If one owns means of production (for example a factory or a bank) one belongs to the *bourgeoisie*. If someone works as an industrial worker, he or she is a proletariat. Workers develop class consciousness due to the worsening of their position (unemployment, lower wages etc.). This consciousness may take a social-democratic form asking for better conditions, or a communist form asking for a total transformation of society. Marx endorses both forms. Lenin suggests that the second type of consciousness can be instilled into the workers only by a revolutionary party, like the communist party.

It is possible, however, for workers to be deceived by the ideological institutions of the *bourgeoisie* and the *bourgeoisie*-run state (church, schools, corporate-owned mass media) and act or vote against their real interests. Poor people, for example, may vote for conservative parties. For Marx, this is the phenomenon of 'false consciousness.' Actually, following Spinoza and Hegel, Marx argues that it is knowledge which will liberate the workers: the first step of the proletarians towards revolution is their realization of the fact that they are exploited. In the *Communist Manifesto* Marx emphasizes that it is the workers' grasp of their role in capitalism that will radicalize them. But it is only later, in the First Volume of the *Capital*, that he is able to explain precisely in what sense they are exploited by the capitalists.

Marx offers an understanding of history, according to which the locomotive of history is class struggle. Modes of production appear on the world scene, realize their full potential, and are then superseded by other modes of production. So, from the Asiatic mode of production (a bureaucracy in the service of a monarch or the priesthood), we move to Slave Ownership, then to Feudalism, to Capitalism and eventually, in the future, to Socialism. Socialism is different from other modes of production in that it does not involve class struggle. The workers take over political power, stop the extraction of surplus value from other human beings and therefore the capitalist class disappears. For Marx, this entails the complete and final supersession of all the contradictions of capitalism.

Every one of these modes of production is the dialectical negation of the previous one and the synthesis of the two modes that precede it. Socialism is the negation of capitalism; since capitalism is the negation of feudalism, socialism is also the negation of the negation of feudalism.

On the question of the order of reality, Marx has a theory which is called 'dialectical materialism.' External reality definitely exists, but has to be explained not through empirical observation, but through theory. Phenomena are not what they look like on the surface. For example, behind constitutional changes lies the dialectical historical process towards ever-developing modes of production.

Like Hegel, Marx does not have a moral theory *per se*. For him, morality is an instrument that the ruling class uses to perpetuate the submission of the other classes. Through education and control of information, they prevent the exploited class of thinking in a revolutionary way.

On a deeper level, however, Marx's crusade for the emancipation of the working class rests, implicitly, on a moral foundation. Although Marx quickly abandons the assumption—inspired by a Kantian viewpoint—that the workers are morally superior to the capitalists, their emancipation is a just, and therefore a moral, cause. This underlying assumption played a significant part in generating support for Marxist organizations.

What Marx offers instead of a moral theory is a theory of human emancipation, based on a specific understanding of human nature. Marx argues that all human beings should be not only permitted but also encouraged to fulfill their potential and achieve full intellectual development and freedom. This development and this freedom—which includes but goes beyond the freedoms dear to liberalism—cannot be achieved in capitalism, because the vast majority of human beings have to spend most of their waking time doing unrewarding work. This type of work and this type of social existence alienate them from their real nature and do not allow them to flourish as human beings: this is Marx's theory of alienation.

On the Jewish Question, a book review written by Marx in 1843, is a fascinating text which has sometimes been cited as evidence of Marx's anti-Semitism. We will discuss this issue in class.

The Communist Manifesto

Karl Marx and Friedrich Engels
Transcribed by Allen Lutins with assistance from Jim Tarzia

Manifesto of the Communist Party

[From the English edition of 1888, edited by Friedrich Engels]

A spectre is haunting Europe—the spectre of Communism. All the Powers of old Europe have entered into a holy alliance to exorcise this spectre: Pope and Czar, Metternich and Guizot, French Radicals and German police-spies.

Where is the party in opposition that has not been decried as Communistic by its opponents in power? Where is the Opposition that has not hurled back the branding reproach of Communism, against the more advanced opposition parties, as well as against its reactionary adversaries?

Two things result from this fact.

I. Communism is already acknowledged by all European Powers to be itself a Power.

II. It is high time that Communists should openly, in the face of the whole world, publish their views, their aims, their tendencies, and meet this nursery tale of the Spectre of Communism with a Manifesto of the party itself.

To this end, Communists of various nationalities have assembled in London, and sketched the following Manifesto, to be published in the English, French, German, Italian, Flemish and Danish languages.

I. Bourgeois and Proletarians

The history of all hitherto existing societies is the history of class struggles.

Freeman and slave, patrician and plebeian, lord and serf, guild-master and journeyman, in a word, oppressor and oppressed, stood in constant opposition to one another, carried on an uninterrupted, now hidden, now open fight, a fight that each time ended, either in a revolutionary re-constitution of society at large, or in the common ruin of the contending classes.

In the earlier epochs of history, we find almost everywhere a complicated arrangement of society into various orders, a manifold gradation of social rank. In ancient Rome we have patricians, knights, plebeians, slaves; in the Middle Ages, feudal lords, vassals, guildmasters, journeymen, apprentices, serfs; in almost all of these classes, again, subordinate gradations.

The modern bourgeois society that has sprouted from the ruins of feudal society has not done away with class antagonisms. It has but established new classes, new conditions of oppression, new forms of struggle in place of the old ones. Our epoch, the epoch of the bourgeoisie, possesses, however, this distinctive feature: it has simplified the class antagonisms. Society as a whole is more and more splitting up into two great hostile camps, into two great classes, directly facing each other: Bourgeoisie and Proletariat.

From the serfs of the Middle Ages sprang the chartered burghers of the earliest towns. From these burgesses the first elements of the bourgeoisie were developed.

The discovery of America, the rounding of the Cape, opened up fresh ground for the rising bourgeoisie. The East-Indian and Chinese markets, the colonisation of America, trade with the colonies, the increase in the means of exchange and in commodities generally, gave to commerce, to navigation, to industry, an impulse never before known, and thereby, to the revolutionary element in the tottering feudal society, a rapid development.

The feudal system of industry, under which industrial production was monopolised by closed guilds, now no longer sufficed for the growing wants of the new markets. The manufacturing system took its place. The guild-masters were pushed on one side by the manufacturing middle class; division of labour between the different corporate guilds vanished in the face of division of labour in each single workshop.

Meantime the markets kept ever growing, the demand ever rising. Even manufacture no longer sufficed. Thereupon, steam and machinery revolutionised industrial production. The place of manufacture was taken by the giant, Modern Industry, the place of the industrial middle class, by industrial millionaires, the leaders of whole industrial armies, the modern bourgeois.

Modern industry has established the world-market, for which the discovery of America paved the way. This market has given an immense development to commerce, to navigation, to communication by land. This development has, in its time, reacted on the extension of industry; and in proportion as industry, commerce, navigation, railways extended, in the same proportion the bourgeoisie developed, increased its capital, and pushed into the background every class handed down from the Middle Ages.

We see, therefore, how the modern bourgeoisie is itself the product of a long course of development, of a series of revolutions in the modes of production and of exchange.

Each step in the development of the bourgeoisie was accompanied by a corresponding political advance of that class. An oppressed class under the sway of the feudal nobility, an armed and self-governing association in the mediaeval commune; here independent urban republic (as in Italy and Germany), there taxable "third estate" of the monarchy (as in France), afterwards, in the period of manufacture proper, serving either the semi-feudal or the absolute monarchy as a counterpoise against the nobility, and, in fact, corner-stone of the great monarchies in general, the bourgeoisie has at last, since the establishment of Modern Industry and of the world-market, conquered for itself, in the modern representative State, exclusive political sway. The executive of the modern State is but a committee for managing the common affairs of the whole bourgeoisie.

The bourgeoisie, historically, has played a most revolutionary part.

The bourgeoisie, wherever it has got the upper hand, has put an end to all feudal, patriarchal, idyllic relations. It has pitilessly torn asunder the motley feudal ties that bound man to his "natural superiors," and has left remaining no other nexus between man and man than naked self-interest, than callous "cash payment." It has drowned the most heavenly ecstasies of religious fervour, of chivalrous enthusiasm, of philistine sentimentalism, in the icy water of egotistical calculation. It has resolved personal worth into exchange value, and in place of the numberless and feasible chartered freedoms, has set up that single, unconscionable freedom—Free Trade. In one word, for exploitation, veiled by religious and political illusions, naked, shameless, direct, brutal exploitation.

The bourgeoisie has stripped of its halo every occupation hitherto honoured and looked up to with reverent awe. It has converted the physician, the lawyer, the priest, the poet, the man of science, into its paid wage labourers.

The bourgeoisie has torn away from the family its sentimental veil, and has reduced the family relation to a mere money relation.

The bourgeoisie has disclosed how it came to pass that the brutal display of vigour in the Middle Ages, which Reactionists so much admire, found its fitting complement in the most slothful indolence. It has been the first to show what man's activity can bring about. It has accomplished wonders far surpassing Egyptian pyramids, Roman aqueducts, and Gothic cathedrals; it has conducted expeditions that put in the shade all former Exoduses of nations and crusades.

The bourgeoisie cannot exist without constantly revolutionising the instruments of production, and thereby the relations of production, and with them the whole relations of society. Conservation of the old modes of production in unaltered form, was, on the contrary, the first condition of existence for all earlier industrial classes. Constant revolutionising of production, uninterrupted disturbance of all social conditions, everlasting uncertainty and agitation distinguish the bourgeois epoch from all earlier ones. All fixed, fast-frozen relations, with their train of ancient and venerable prejudices and opinions, are swept away, all new-formed ones become antiquated before they can ossify. All that is solid melts into air, all that is holy is profaned, and man is at last compelled to face with sober senses, his real conditions of life, and his relations with his kind.

The need of a constantly expanding market for its products chases the bourgeoisie over the whole surface of the globe. It must nestle everywhere, settle everywhere, establish connexions everywhere.

The bourgeoisie has through its exploitation of the world-market given a cosmopolitan character to production and consumption in every country. To the great chagrin of Reactionists, it has drawn from under the feet of industry the national ground on which it stood. All old-established national industries have been destroyed or are daily being destroyed. They are dislodged by new industries, whose introduction becomes a life and death question for all civilised nations, by industries that no longer work up indigenous raw material, but raw material drawn from the remotest zones; industries whose products are consumed, not only at home, but in every quarter of the globe. In place of the old wants, satisfied by the productions of the country, we find new wants, requiring for their satis-faction the products of distant lands and climes. In place of the old local and national seclusion and self-sufficiency, we have intercourse in every direction, universal inter-dependence of nations. And as in material, so also in intellectual production. The intellectual creations of individual nations become common property. National one-sidedness and narrow-mindedness become more and more impossible, and from the numerous national and local literatures, there arises a world literature.

The bourgeoisie, by the rapid improvement of all instruments of production, by the immensely facilitated means of communication, draws all, even the most barbarian, nations into civilisation. The cheap prices of its commodities are the heavy artillery with which it batters down all Chinese walls, with which it forces the barbarians' intensely obstinate hatred of foreigners to capitulate. It compels all nations, on pain of extinction, to adopt the bourgeois mode of production; it compels them to introduce what it calls civilisation into their midst, i.e., to become bourgeois themselves. In one word, it creates a world after its own image.

The bourgeoisie has subjected the country to the rule of the towns. It has created enormous cities, has greatly increased the urban population as compared with the rural, and has thus rescued a consid-erable part of the population from the idiocy of rural life. Just as it has made the country dependent on the towns, so it has made barbarian and semi-barbarian countries dependent on the civilised ones, nations of peasants on nations of bourgeois, the East on the West.

The bourgeoisie keeps more and more doing away with the scattered state of the population, of the means of production, and of property. It has agglomerated production, and has concentrated property in a few hands. The necessary consequence of this was political centralisation. Independent, or but loosely connected provinces, with separate interests, laws, governments and systems of taxation, became lumped together into one nation, with one government, one code of laws, one national class-interest, one frontier and one customs-tariff. The bourgeoisie, during its rule of scarce one hundred years, has created more massive and more colossal productive forces than have all preceding generations together. Subjection of Nature's forces to man, machinery, application of chemistry to industry and agriculture, steam-navigation, railways, electric telegraphs, clearing of whole continents for cultivation, canalisation of rivers, whole populations conjured out of the ground—what earlier century had even a presentiment that such productive forces slumbered in the lap of social labour?

We see then: the means of production and of exchange, on whose foundation the bourgeoisie built itself up, were generated in feudal society. At a certain stage in the development of these means of production and of exchange, the conditions under which feudal society produced and exchanged, the feudal organisation of agriculture and manufacturing industry, in one word, the feudal relations of property became no longer compatible with the already developed productive forces; they became so many fetters. They had to be burst asunder; they were burst asunder.

Into their place stepped free competition, accompanied by a social and political constitution adapted to it, and by the economical and political sway of the bourgeois class.

A similar movement is going on before our own eyes. Modern bourgeois society with its relations of production, of exchange and of property, a society that has conjured up such gigantic means of production and of exchange, is like the sorcerer, who is no longer able to control the powers of the nether world whom he has called up by his spells. For many a decade past the history of industry and commerce is but the history of the revolt of modern productive forces against modern conditions of production, against the property relations that are the conditions for the existence of the bourgeoisie and of its rule. It is enough to mention the commercial crises that by their periodical return put on its trial, each time more threateningly, the existence of the entire bourgeois society. In these crises a great part not only of the existing products, but also of the previously created productive forces, are periodically destroyed. In these crises there breaks out an epidemic that, in all earlier epochs, would have seemed an absurdity—the epidemic of over-production. Society suddenly finds itself put back into a state of momentary barbarism; it appears as if a famine, a universal war of devastation had cut off the supply of every means of subsistence; industry and commerce seem to be destroyed; and why? Because there is too much civilisation, too much means of subsistence, too much industry, too much commerce. The productive forces at the disposal of society no longer tend to further the development of the conditions of bourgeois property; on the contrary, they have become too powerful for these conditions, by which they are fettered, and so soon as they overcome these fetters, they bring disorder into the whole of bourgeois society, endanger the existence of bourgeois property. The conditions of bourgeois society are too narrow to comprise the wealth created by them. And how does the bourgeoisie get over these crises? On the one hand inforced destruction of a mass of productive forces; on the other, by the conquest of new markets, and by the more thorough exploitation of the old ones. That is to say, by paving the way for more extensive and more destructive crises, and by diminishing the means whereby crises are prevented.

The weapons with which the bourgeoisie felled feudalism to the ground are now turned against the bourgeoisie itself.

But not only has the bourgeoisie forged the weapons that bring death to itself; it has also called into existence the men who are to wield those weapons—the modern working class—the proletarians. In proportion as the bourgeoisie, i.e., capital, is developed, in the same proportion is the proletariat, the modern working class, developed—a class of labourers, who live only so long as they find work, and who find work only so long as their labour increases capital. These labourers, who must sell themselves piece-meal, are a commodity, like every other article of commerce, and are consequently exposed to all the vicissitudes of competition, to all the fluctuations of the market.

Owing to the extensive use of machinery and to division of labour, the work of the proletarians has lost all individual character, and consequently, all charm for the workman. He becomes an append-age of the machine, and it is only the most simple, most monotonous, and most easily acquired knack, that is required of him. Hence, the cost of production of a workman is restricted, almost entirely, to the means of subsistence that he requires for his maintenance, and for the propagation of his race. But the price of a commodity, and therefore also of labour, is equal to its cost of production. In proportion therefore, as the repulsiveness of the work increases, the wage decreases. Nay more, in proportion as the use of machinery and division of labour increases, in the same proportion the burden of toil also increases, whether by prolongation of the working hours, by increase of the work exacted in a given time or by increased speed of the machinery, etc.

Modern industry has converted the little workshop of the patriarchal master into the great factory of the industrial capitalist. Masses of labourers, crowded into the factory, are organised like soldiers. As privates of the industrial army they are placed under the command of a perfect hierarchy of officers and sergeants. Not only are they slaves of the bourgeois class, and of the bourgeois State; they are daily and hourly enslaved by the machine, by the over-looker, and, above all, by the individual bourgeois manufacturer himself. The more openly this despotism proclaims gain to be its end and aim, the more petty, the more hateful and the more embittering it is.

The less the skill and exertion of strength implied in manual labour, in other words, the more modern industry becomes developed, the more is the labour of men superseded by that of women. Differences of age and sex have no longer any distinctive social validity for the working class. All are instruments of labour, more or less expensive to use, according to their age and sex.

No sooner is the exploitation of the labourer by the manufacturer, so far at an end, that he re-ceives his wages in cash, than he is set upon by the other portions of the bourgeoisie, the landlord, the shopkeeper, the pawnbroker, etc.

The lower strata of the middle class—the small tradespeople, shopkeepers, retired tradesmen generally, the handicraftsmen and peasants—all these sink gradually into the proletariat, partly because their diminutive capital does not suffice for the scale on which Modern Industry is carried on, and is swamped in the competition with the large capitalists, partly because their specialized skill is rendered worthless by the new methods of production. Thus the proletariat is recruited from all classes of the population.

The proletariat goes through various stages of development. With its birth begins its struggle with the bourgeoisie. At first the contest is carried on by individual labourers, then by the workpeople of a factory, then by the operatives of one trade, in one locality, against the individual bourgeois who directly exploits them. They direct their attacks not against the bourgeois conditions of production, but against the instruments of production themselves; they destroy imported wares that compete with their labour, they smash to pieces machinery, they set factories ablaze, they seek to restore by force the vanished status of the workman of the Middle Ages.

At this stage the labourers still form an incoherent mass scattered over the whole country, and broken up by their mutual competition. If anywhere they unite to form more compact bodies, this is not yet the consequence of their own active union, but of the union of the bourgeoisie, which class, in order to attain its own political ends, is compelled to set the whole proletariat in motion, and is moreover yet, for a time, able to do so. At this stage, therefore, the proletarians do not fight their enemies, but the enemies of their enemies, the remnants of absolute monarchy, the landowners, the non-industrial bourgeois, the petty bourgeoisie. Thus the whole historical movement is concentrated in the hands of the bourgeoisie; every victory so obtained is a victory for the bourgeoisie.

But with the development of industry the proletariat not only increases in number; it becomes concentrated in greater masses, its strength grows, and it feels that strength more. The various interests and conditions of life within the ranks of the proletariat are more and more equalised, in proportion as machinery obliterates all distinctions of labour, and nearly everywhere reduces wages to the same low level. The growing competition among the bourgeois, and the resulting commercial crises, make the wages of the workers ever more fluctuating. The unceasing improvement of machinery, ever more rapidly developing, makes their livelihood more and more precarious; the collisions between individual workmen and individual bourgeois take more and more the character of collisions between two classes. Thereupon the workers begin to form combinations (Trades Unions) against the bourgeois; they club together in order to keep up the rate of wages; they found permanent associations in order to make provision beforehand for these occasional revolts. Here and there the contest breaks out into riots.

Now and then the workers are victorious, but only for a time. The real fruit of their battles lies, not in the immediate result, but in the ever-expanding union of the workers. This union is helped on by the improved means of communication that are created by modern industry and that place the workers of different localities in contact with one another. It was just this contact that was needed to centralise the numerous local struggles, all of the same character, into one national struggle between classes. But every class struggle is a political struggle. And that union, to attain which the burghers of the Middle Ages, with their miserable highways, required centuries, the modern proletarians, thanks to railways, achieve in a few years.

This organisation of the proletarians into a class, and consequently into a political party, is continually being upset again by the competition between the workers themselves. But it ever rises up again, stronger, firmer, mightier. It compels legislative recognition of particular interests of the workers, by taking advantage of the divisions among the bourgeoisie itself. Thus the ten-hours' bill in England was carried.

Altogether collisions between the classes of the old society further, in many ways, the course of development of the proletariat. The bourgeoisie finds itself involved in a constant battle. At first with the aristocracy; later on, with those portions of the bourgeoisie itself, whose interests have become antagonistic to the progress of industry; at all times, with the bourgeoisie of foreign countries. In all these battles it sees itself compelled to appeal to the proletariat, to ask for its help, and thus, to drag it into the political arena. The bourgeoisie itself, therefore, supplies the proletariat with its own instruments of political and general education, in other words, it furnishes the proletariat with weapons for fighting the bourgeoisie.

Further, as we have already seen, entire sections of the ruling classes are, by the advance of industry, precipitated into the proletariat, or are at least threatened in their conditions of existence. These also supply the proletariat with fresh elements of enlightenment and progress.

Finally, in times when the class struggle nears the decisive hour, the process of dissolution going on within the ruling class, in fact within the whole range of society, assumes such a violent, glaring character, that a small section of the ruling class cuts itself adrift, and joins the revolutionary class, the class that holds the future in its hands. Just as, therefore, at an earlier period, a section of the nobility went over to the bourgeoisie, so now a portion of the bourgeoisie goes over to the proletariat, and in particular, a portion of the bourgeois ideologists, who have raised themselves to the level of comprehending theoretically the historical movement as a whole.

Of all the classes that stand face to face with the bourgeoisie today, the proletariat alone is a really revolutionary class. The other classes decay and finally disappear in the face of Modern Industry;

the proletariat is its special and essential product. The lower middle class, the small manufacturer, the shopkeeper, the artisan, the peasant, all these fight against the bourgeoisie, to save from extinction their existence as fractions of the middle class. They are therefore not revolutionary, but conservative. Nay more, they are reactionary, for they try to roll back the wheel of history. If by chance they are revolutionary, they are so only in view of their impending transfer into the proletariat, they thus defend not their present, but their future interests, they desert their own standpoint to place themselves at that of the proletariat.

The "dangerous class," the social scum, that passively rotting mass thrown off by the lowest layers of old society, may, here and there, be swept into the movement by a proletarian revolution; its conditions of life, however, prepare it far more for the part of a bribed tool of reactionary intrigue.

In the conditions of the proletariat, those of old society at large are already virtually swamped. The proletarian is without property; his relation to his wife and children has no longer anything in common with the bourgeois family-relations; modern industrial labour, modern subjection to capital, the same in England as in France, in America as in Germany, has stripped him of every trace of national character. Law, morality, religion, are to him so many bourgeois prejudices, behind which lurk in ambush just as many bourgeois interests.

All the preceding classes that got the upper hand, sought to fortify their already acquired status by subjecting society at large to their conditions of appropriation. The proletarians cannot become masters of the productive forces of society, except by abolishing their own previous mode of appropriation, and thereby also every other previous mode of appropriation. They have nothing of their own to secure and to fortify; their mission is to destroy all previous securities for, and insurances of, individual property.

All previous historical movements were movements of minorities, or in the interests of minorities. The proletarian movement is the self-conscious, independent movement of the immense majority, in the interests of the immense majority. The proletariat, the lowest stratum of our present society, cannot stir, cannot raise itself up, without the whole superincumbent strata of official society being sprung into the air.

Though not in substance, yet in form, the struggle of the proletariat with the bourgeoisie is at first a national struggle. The proletariat of each country must, of course, first of all settle matters with its own bourgeoisie.

In depicting the most general phases of the development of the proletariat, we traced the more or less veiled civil war, raging within existing society, up to the point where that war breaks out into open revolution, and where the violent overthrow of the bourgeoisie lays the foundation for the sway of the proletariat.

Hitherto, every form of society has been based, as we have already seen, on the antagonism of oppressing and oppressed classes. But in order to oppress a class, certain conditions must be assured to it under which it can, at least, continue its slavish existence. The serf, in the period of serfdom, raised himself to membership in the commune, just as the petty bourgeois, under the yoke of feudal absolutism, managed to develop into a bourgeois. The modern laborer, on the contrary, instead of rising with the progress of industry, sinks deeper and deeper below the conditions of existence of his own class. He becomes a pauper, and pauperism develops more rapidly than population and wealth. And here it becomes evident, that the bourgeoisie is unfit any longer to be the ruling class in society, and to impose its conditions of existence upon society as an over-riding law. It is unfit to rule because it is incompetent to assure an existence to its slave within his slavery, because it cannot help letting him sink into such a state, that it has to feed him, instead of being fed by him. Society can no longer live under this bourgeoisie, in other words, its existence is no longer compatible with society.

The essential condition for the existence, and for the sway of the bourgeois class, is the formation and augmentation of capital; the condition for capital is wage-labour. Wage-labour rests exclusively on competition between the laborers. The advance of industry, whose involuntary promoter is the bourgeoisie, replaces the isolation of the labourers, due to competition, by their revolutionary combination, due to association. The development of Modern Industry, therefore, cuts from under its feet the very foundation on which the bourgeoisie produces and appropriates products. What the bourgeoisie, therefore, produces, above all, is its own grave-diggers. Its fall and the victory of the proletariat are equally inevitable.

II. Proletarians and Communists

In what relation do the Communists stand to the proletarians as a whole?

The Communists do not form a separate party opposed to other working-class parties.

They have no interests separate and apart from those of the proletariat as a whole.

They do not set up any sectarian principles of their own, by which to shape and mould the proletarian movement.

The Communists are distinguished from the other working-class parties by this only: (1) In the national struggles of the proletarians of the different countries, they point out and bring to the front the common interests of the entire proletariat, independently of all nationality. (2) In the various stages of development which the struggle of the working class against the bourgeoisie has to pass through, they always and everywhere represent the interests of the movement as a whole.

The Communists, therefore, are on the one hand, practically, the most advanced and resolute section of the working-class parties of every country, that section which pushes forward all others; on the other hand, theoretically, they have over the great mass of the proletariat the advantage of clearly understanding the line of march, the conditions, and the ultimate general results of the proletarian movement.

The immediate aim of the Communist is the same as that of all the other proletarian parties: formation of the proletariat into a class, overthrow of the bourgeois supremacy, conquest of political power by the proletariat.

The theoretical conclusions of the Communists are in no way based on ideas or principles that have been invented, or discovered, by this or that would-be universal reformer. They merely express, in general terms, actual relations springing from an existing class struggle, from a historical movement going on under our very eyes. The abolition of existing property relations is not at all a distinctive feature of Communism.

All property relations in the past have continually been subject to historical change consequent upon the change in historical conditions.

The French Revolution, for example, abolished feudal property in favour of bourgeois property.

The distinguishing feature of Communism is not the abolition of property generally, but the abolition of bourgeois property. But modern bourgeois private property is the final and most complete expression of the system of producing and appropriating products, that is based on class antagonisms, on the exploitation of the many by the few.

In this sense, the theory of the Communists may be summed up in the single sentence: Abolition of private property.

We Communists have been reproached with the desire of abolishing the right of personally acquiring property as the fruit of a man's own labour, which property is alleged to be the groundwork of all personal freedom, activity and independence.

Hard-won, self-acquired, self-earned property! Do you mean the property of the petty artisan and of the small peasant, a form of property that preceded the bourgeois form? There is no need to abolish that; the development of industry has to a great extent already destroyed it, and is still destroying it daily.

Or do you mean modern bourgeois private property?

But does wage-labour create any property for the labourer? Not a bit. It creates capital, i.e., that kind of property which exploits wage-labour, and which cannot increase except upon condition of begetting a new supply of wage-labour for fresh exploitation. Property, in its present form, is based on the antagonism of capital and wage-labour. Let us examine both sides of this antagonism.

To be a capitalist, is to have not only a purely personal, but a social status in production. Capital is a collective product, and only by the united action of many members, nay, in the last resort, only by the united action of all members of society, can it be set in motion.

Capital is, therefore, not a personal, it is a social power.

When, therefore, capital is converted into common property, into the property of all members of society, personal property is not thereby transformed into social property. It is only the social character of the property that is changed. It loses its class-character.

Let us now take wage-labour.

The average price of wage-labour is the minimum wage, i.e., that quantum of the means of subsistence, which is absolutely requisite in bare existence as a labourer. What, therefore, the wage-labourer appropriates by means of his labour, merely suffices to prolong and reproduce a bare existence. We by no means intend to abolish this personal appropriation of the products of labour, an appropriation that is made for the maintenance and reproduction of human life, and that leaves no surplus wherewith to command the labour of others. All that we want to do away with, is the miserable character of this appropriation, under which the labourer lives merely to increase capital, and is allowed to live only in so far as the interest of the ruling class requires it.

In bourgeois society, living labour is but a means to increase accumulated labour. In Communist society, accumulated labour is but a means to widen, to enrich, to promote the existence of the labourer.

In bourgeois society, therefore, the past dominates the present; in Communist society, the present dominates the past. In bourgeois society capital is independent and has individuality, while the living person is dependent and has no individuality.

And the abolition of this state of things is called by the bourgeois, abolition of individuality and freedom! And rightly so. The abolition of bourgeois individuality, bourgeois independence, and bourgeois freedom is undoubtedly aimed at.

By freedom is meant, under the present bourgeois conditions of production, free trade, free selling and buying.

But if selling and buying disappears, free selling and buying disappears also. This talk about free selling and buying, and all the other "brave words" of our bourgeoisie about freedom in general, have a meaning, if any, only in contrast with restricted selling and buying, with the fettered traders of the Middle Ages, but have no meaning when opposed to the Communistic abolition of buying and selling, of the bourgeois conditions of production, and of the bourgeoisie itself.

You are horrified at our intending to do away with private property. But in your existing society, private property is already done away with for nine-tenths of the population; its existence for the few is solely due to its non-existence in the hands of those nine-tenths. You reproach us, therefore, with intending to do away with a form of property, the necessary condition for whose existence is the non-existence of any property for the immense majority of society.

In one word, you reproach us with intending to do away with your property. Precisely so; that is just what we intend.

From the moment when labour can no longer be converted into capital, money, or rent, into a social power capable of being monopolised, i.e., from the moment when individual property can no longer be transformed into bourgeois property, into capital, from that moment, you say individuality vanishes.

You must, therefore, confess that by "individual" you mean no other person than the bourgeois, than the middle-class owner of property. This person must, indeed, be swept out of the way, and made impossible.

Communism deprives no man of the power to appropriate the products of society; all that it does is to deprive him of the power to subjugate the labour of others by means of such appropriation.

It has been objected that upon the abolition of private property all work will cease, and universal laziness will overtake us.

According to this, bourgeois society ought long ago to have gone to the dogs through sheer idleness; for those of its members who work, acquire nothing, and those who acquire anything, do not work. The whole of this objection is but another expression of the tautology: that there can no longer be any wage-labour when there is no longer any capital.

All objections urged against the Communistic mode of producing and appropriating material products, have, in the same way, been urged against the Communistic modes of producing and appropriating intellectual products. Just as, to the bourgeois, the disappearance of class property is the disappearance of production itself, so the disappearance of class culture is to him identical with the disappearance of all culture.

That culture, the loss of which he laments, is, for the enormous majority, a mere training to act as a machine.

But don't wrangle with us so long as you apply, to our intended abolition of bourgeois property, the standard of your bourgeois notions of freedom, culture, law, etc. Your very ideas are but the outgrowth of the conditions of your bourgeois production and bourgeois property, just as your jurisprudence is but the will of your class made into a law for all, a will, whose essential character and direction are determined by the economical conditions of existence of your class.

The selfish misconception that induces you to transform into eternal laws of nature and of reason, the social forms springing from your present mode of production and form of property—historical relations that rise and disappear in the progress of production—this misconception you share with every ruling class that has preceded you. What you see clearly in the case of ancient property, what you admit in the case of feudal property, you are of course forbidden to admit in the case of your own bourgeois form of property.

Abolition of the family! Even the most radical flare up at this infamous proposal of the Communists.

On what foundation is the present family, the bourgeois family, based? On capital, on private gain. In its completely developed form this family exists only among the bourgeoisie. But this state of things finds its complement in the practical absence of the family among the proletarians, and in public prostitution.

The bourgeois family will vanish as a matter of course when its complement vanishes, and both will vanish with the vanishing of capital.

Do you charge us with wanting to stop the exploitation of children by their parents? To this crime we plead guilty.

But, you will say, we destroy the most hallowed of relations, when we replace home education by social.

And your education! Is not that also social, and determined by the social conditions under which you educate, by the intervention, direct or indirect, of society, by means of schools, etc.? The Communists have not invented the intervention of society in education; they do but seek to alter the character of that intervention, and to rescue education from the influence of the ruling class.

The bourgeois clap-trap about the family and education, about the hallowed co-relation of parent and child, becomes all the more disgusting, the more, by the action of Modern Industry, all family ties among the proletarians are torn asunder, and their children transformed into simple articles of commerce and instruments of labour.

But you Communists would introduce community of women, screams the whole bourgeoisie in chorus.

The bourgeois sees in his wife a mere instrument of production. He hears that the instruments of production are to be exploited in common, and, naturally, can come to no other conclusion than that the lot of being common to all will likewise fall to the women.

He has not even a suspicion that the real point is to do away with the status of women as mere instruments of production.

For the rest, nothing is more ridiculous than the virtuous indignation of our bourgeois at the community of women which, they pretend, is to be openly and officially established by the Communists. The Communists have no need to introduce community of women; it has existed almost from time immemorial.

Our bourgeois, not content with having the wives and daughters of their proletarians at their disposal, not to speak of common prostitutes, take the greatest pleasure in seducing each other's wives.

Bourgeois marriage is in reality a system of wives in common and thus, at the most, what the Communists might possibly be reproached with, is that they desire to introduce, in substitution for a hypocritically concealed, an openly legalised community of women. For the rest, it is self-evident that the abolition of the present system of production must bring with it the abolition of the community of women springing from that system, i.e., of prostitution both public and private.

The Communists are further reproached with desiring to abolish countries and nationality.

The working men have no country. We cannot take from them what they have not got. Since the proletariat must first of all acquire political supremacy, must rise to be the leading class of the nation, must constitute itself the nation, it is, so far, itself national, though not in the bourgeois sense of the word.

National differences and antagonisms between peoples are daily more and more vanishing, owing to the development of the bourgeoisie, to freedom of commerce, to the world-market, to uniformity in the mode of production and in the conditions of life corresponding thereto.

The supremacy of the proletariat will cause them to vanish still faster. United action, of the leading civilised countries at least, is one of the first conditions for the emancipation of the proletariat.

In proportion as the exploitation of one individual by another is put an end to, the exploitation of one nation by another will also be put an end to. In proportion as the antagonism between classes within the nation vanishes, the hostility of one nation to another will come to an end.

The charges against Communism made from a religious, a philosophical, and, generally, from an ideological standpoint, are not deserving of serious examination.

Does it require deep intuition to comprehend that man's ideas, views and conceptions, in one word, man's consciousness, changes with every change in the conditions of his material existence, in his social relations and in his social life?

What else does the history of ideas prove, than that intellectual production changes its character in proportion as material production is changed? The ruling ideas of each age have ever been the ideas of its ruling class.

When people speak of ideas that revolutionise society, they do but express the fact, that within the old society, the elements of a new one have been created, and that the dissolution of the old ideas keeps even pace with the dissolution of the old conditions of existence.

When the ancient world was in its last throes, the ancient religions were overcome by Christianity. When Christian ideas succumbed in the 18th century to rationalist ideas, feudal society fought its death battle with the then revolutionary bourgeoisie. The ideas of religious liberty and freedom of conscience merely gave expression to the sway of free competition within the domain of knowledge.

"Undoubtedly," it will be said, "religious, moral, philosophical and juridical ideas have been modified in the course of historical development. But religion, morality, philosophy, political science, and law, constantly survived this change."

"There are, besides, eternal truths, such as Freedom, Justice, etc. that are common to all states of society. But Communism abolishes eternal truths, it abolishes all religion, and all morality, instead of constituting them on a new basis; it therefore acts in contradiction to all past historical experience."

What does this accusation reduce itself to? The history of all past society has consisted in the development of class antagonisms, antagonisms that assumed different forms at different epochs.

But whatever form they may have taken, one fact is common to all past ages, viz., the exploitation of one part of society by the other. No wonder, then, that the social consciousness of past ages, despite all the multiplicity and variety it displays, moves within certain common forms, or general ideas, which cannot completely vanish except with the total disappearance of class antagonisms.

The Communist revolution is the most radical rupture with traditional property relations; no wonder that its development involves the most radical rupture with traditional ideas.

But let us have done with the bourgeois objections to Communism.

We have seen above, that the first step in the revolution by the working class, is to raise the proletariat to the position of ruling as to win the battle of democracy.

The proletariat will use its political supremacy to wrest, by degrees, all capital from the bourgeoisie, to centralise all instruments of production in the hands of the State, i.e., of the proletariat organised as the ruling class; and to increase the total of productive forces as rapidly as possible.

Of course, in the beginning, this cannot be effected except by means of despotic inroads on the rights of property, and on the conditions of bourgeois production; by means of measures, therefore, which appear economically insufficient and untenable, but which, in the course of the movement, outstrip themselves, necessitate further inroads upon the old social order, and are unavoidable as a means of entirely revolutionising the mode of production.

These measures will of course be different in different countries.

Nevertheless in the most advanced countries, the following will be pretty generally applicable.

1. Abolition of property in land and application of all rents of land to public purposes.
2. A heavy progressive or graduated income tax.
3. Abolition of all right of inheritance.
4. Confiscation of the property of all emigrants and rebels.
5. Centralisation of credit in the hands of the State, by means of a national bank with State capital and an exclusive monopoly.
6. Centralisation of the means of communication and transport in the hands of the State.
7. Extension of factories and instruments of production owned by the State; the bringing into cultivation of waste-lands, and the improvement of the soil generally in accordance with a common plan.
8. Equal liability of all to labour. Establishment of industrial armies, especially for agriculture.

9. Combination of agriculture with manufacturing industries; gradual abolition of the distinction between town and country, by a more equable distribution of the population over the country.
10. Free education for all children in public schools. Abolition of children's factory labour in its present form. Combination of education with industrial production, &c., &c.

When, in the course of development, class distinctions have disappeared, and all production has been concentrated in the hands of a vast association of the whole nation, the public power will lose its political character. Political power, properly so called, is merely the organised power of one class for oppressing another. If the proletariat during its contest with the bourgeoisie is compelled, by the force of circumstances, to organise itself as a class, if, by means of a revolution, it makes itself the ruling class, and, as such, sweeps away by force the old conditions of production, then it will, along with these conditions, have swept away the conditions for the existence of class antagonisms and of classes generally, and will thereby have abolished its own supremacy as a class.

In place of the old bourgeois society, with its classes and class antagonisms, we shall have an association, in which the free development of each is the condition for the free development of all.

III. Socialist and Communist Literature

1. REACTIONARY SOCIALISM

A. Feudal Socialism

Owing to their historical position, it became the vocation of the aristocracies of France and England to write pamphlets against modern bourgeois society. In the French revolution of July 1830, and in the English reform agitation, these aristocracies again succumbed to the hateful upstart. Thenceforth, a serious political contest was altogether out of the question. A literary battle alone remained possible. But even in the domain of literature the old cries of the restoration period had become impossible.

In order to arouse sympathy, the aristocracy were obliged to lose sight, apparently, of their own interests, and to formulate their indictment against the bourgeoisie in the interest of the exploited working class alone. Thus the aristocracy took their revenge by singing lampoons on their new master, and whispering in his ears sinister prophecies of coming catastrophe.

In this way arose Feudal Socialism: half lamentation, half lampoon; half echo of the past, half menace of the future; at times, by its bitter, witty and incisive criticism, striking the bourgeoisie to the very heart's core; but always ludicrous in its effect, through total incapacity to comprehend the march of modern history.

The aristocracy, in order to rally the people to them, waved the proletarian alms-bag in front for a banner. But the people, so often as it joined them, saw on their hindquarters the old feudal coats of arms, and deserted with loud and irreverent laughter.

One section of the French Legitimists and "Young England" exhibited this spectacle.

In pointing out that their mode of exploitation was different to that of the bourgeoisie, the feudalists forget that they exploited under circumstances and conditions that were quite different, and that are now antiquated. In showing that, under their rule, the modern proletariat never existed, they forget that the modern bourgeoisie is the necessary offspring of their own form of society.

For the rest, so little do they conceal the reactionary character of their criticism that their chief accusation against the bourgeoisie amounts to this, that under the bourgeois regime a class is being developed, which is destined to cut up root and branch the old order of society.

What they upbraid the bourgeoisie with is not so much that it creates a proletariat, as that it creates a revolutionary proletariat.

In political practice, therefore, they join in all coercive measures against the working class; and in ordinary life, despite their high falutin phrases, they stoop to pick up the golden apples dropped from the tree of industry, and to barter truth, love, and honour for traffic in wool, beetroot-sugar, and potato spirits.

As the parson has ever gone hand in hand with the landlord, so has Clerical Socialism with Feudal Socialism.

Nothing is easier than to give Christian asceticism a Socialist tinge. Has not Christianity declaimed against private property, against marriage, against the State? Has it not preached in the place of these, charity and poverty, celibacy and mortification of the flesh, monastic life and Mother Church? Christian Socialism is but the holy, water with which the priest consecrates the heart-burnings of the aristocrat.

B. Petty-Bourgeois Socialism

The feudal aristocracy was not the only class that was ruined by the bourgeoisie, not the only class whose conditions of existence pined and perished in the atmosphere of modern bourgeois society. The mediaeval burgesses and the small peasant proprietors were the precursors of the modern bourgeoisie. In those countries which are but little developed, industrially and commercially, these two classes still vegetate side by side with the rising bourgeoisie.

In countries where modern civilisation has become fully developed, a new class of petty bourgeois has been formed, fluctuating between proletariat and bourgeoisie and ever renewing itself as a supplementary part of bourgeois society. The individual members of this class, however, are being constantly hurled down into the proletariat by the action of competition, and, as modern industry develops, they even see the moment approaching when they will completely disappear as an independent section of modern society, to be replaced, in manufactures, agriculture and commerce, by overlookers, bailiffs and shopmen.

In countries like France, where the peasants constitute far more than half of the population, it was natural that writers who sided with the proletariat against the bourgeoisie, should use, in their criticism of the bourgeois regime, the standard of the peasant and petty bourgeois, and from the standpoint of these intermediate classes should take up the cudgels for the working class. Thus arose petty-bourgeois Socialism. Sismondi was the head of this school, not only in France but also in England.

This school of Socialism dissected with great acuteness the contradictions in the conditions of modern production. It laid bare the hypocritical apologies of economists. It proved, incontrovertibly, the disastrous effects of machinery and division of labour; the concentration of capital and land in a few hands; overproduction and crises; it pointed out the inevitable ruin of the petty bourgeois and peasant, the misery of the proletariat, the anarchy in production, the crying inequalities in the distribution of wealth, the industrial war of extermination between nations, the dissolution of old moral bonds, of the old family relations, of the old nationalities.

In its positive aims, however, this form of Socialism aspires either to restoring the old means of production and of exchange, and with them the old property relations, and the old society, or to cramping the modern means of production and of exchange, within the framework of the old property relations that have been, and were bound to be, exploded by those means. In either case, it is both reactionary and Utopian.

Its last words are: corporate guilds for manufacture, patriarchal relations in agriculture.

Ultimately, when stubborn historical facts had dispersed all intoxicating effects of self-deception, this form of Socialism ended in a miserable fit of the blues.

C. German, or "True," Socialism

The Socialist and Communist literature of France, a literature that originated under the pressure of a bourgeoisie in power, and that was the expression of the struggle against this power, was introduced into Germany at a time when the bourgeoisie, in that country, had just begun its contest with feudal absolutism.

German philosophers, would-be philosophers, and beaux esprits, eagerly seized on this literature, only forgetting, that when these writings immigrated from France into Germany, French social conditions had not immigrated along with them. In contact with German social conditions, this French literature lost all its immediate practical significance, and assumed a purely literary aspect. Thus, to the German philosophers of the eighteenth century, the demands of the first French Revolution were nothing more than the demands of "Practical Reason" in general, and the utterance of the will of the revolutionary French bourgeoisie signified in their eyes the law of pure Will, of Will as it was bound to be, of true human Will generally.

The world of the German literate consisted solely in bringing the new French ideas into harmony with their ancient philosophical conscience, or rather, in annexing the French ideas without deserting their own philosophic point of view.

This annexation took place in the same way in which a foreign language is appropriated, namely, by translation.

It is well known how the monks wrote silly lives of Catholic Saints over the manuscripts on which the classical works of ancient heathendom had been written. The German literate reversed this process with the profane French literature. They wrote their philosophical nonsense beneath the French original. For instance, beneath the French criticism of the economic functions of money, they wrote "Alienation of Humanity," and beneath the French criticism of the bourgeois State they wrote "dethronement of the Category of the General," and so forth.

The introduction of these philosophical phrases at the back of the French historical criticisms they dubbed "Philosophy of Action," "True Socialism," "German Science of Socialism," "Philosophical Foundation of Socialism," and so on.

The French Socialist and Communist literature was thus completely emasculated. And, since it ceased in the hands of the German to express the struggle of one class with the other, he felt conscious of having overcome "French one-sidedness" and of representing, not true requirements, but the requirements of truth; not the interests of the proletariat, but the interests of Human Nature, of Man in general, who belongs to no class, has no reality, who exists only in the misty realm of philosophical fantasy.

This German Socialism, which took its schoolboy task so seriously and solemnly, and extolled its poor stock-in-trade in such mountebank fashion, meanwhile gradually lost its pedantic innocence.

The fight of the German, and especially, of the Prussian bourgeoisie, against feudal aristocracy and absolute monarchy, in other words, the liberal movement, became more earnest.

By this, the long wished-for opportunity was offered to "True" Socialism of confronting the political movement with the Socialist demands, of hurling the traditional anathemas against liberalism, against representative government, against bourgeois competition, bourgeois freedom of the press, bourgeois legislation, bourgeois liberty and equality, and of preaching to the masses that they had nothing to gain, and everything to lose, by this bourgeois movement. German Socialism forgot, in the nick of time, that the French criticism, whose silly echo it was, presupposed the existence of modern bourgeois society, with its corresponding economic conditions of existence, and the political constitution adapted thereto, the very things whose attainment was the object of the pending struggle in Germany.

To the absolute governments, with their following of parsons, professors, country squires and officials, it served as a welcome scarecrow against the threatening bourgeoisie.

It was a sweet finish after the bitter pills of floggings and bullets with which these same governments, just at that time, dosed the German working-class risings.

While this "True" Socialism thus served the governments as a weapon for fighting the German bourgeoisie, it, at the same time, directly represented a reactionary interest, the interest of the German Philistines. In Germany the petty-bourgeois class, a relic of the sixteenth century, and since then constantly cropping up again under various forms, is the real social basis of the existing state of things.

To preserve this class is to preserve the existing state of things in Germany. The industrial and political supremacy of the bourgeoisie threatens it with certain destruction; on the one hand, from the concentration of capital; on the other, from the rise of a revolutionary proletariat. "True" Socialism appeared to kill these two birds with one stone. It spread like an epidemic.

The robe of speculative cobwebs, embroidered with flowers of rhetoric, steeped in the dew of sickly sentiment, this transcendental robe in which the German Socialists wrapped their sorry "eternal truths," all skin and bone, served to wonderfully increase the sale of their goods amongst such a public. And on its part, German Socialism recognised, more and more, its own calling as the bombastic representative of the petty-bourgeois Philistine.

It proclaimed the German nation to be the model nation, and the German petty Philistine to be the typical man. To every villainous meanness of this model man it gave a hidden, higher, Socialistic interpretation, the exact contrary of its real character. It went to the extreme length of directly opposing the "brutally destructive" tendency of Communism, and of proclaiming its supreme and impartial contempt of all class struggles. With very few exceptions, all the so-called Socialist and Communist publications that now (1847) circulate in Germany belong to the domain of this foul and enervating literature.

2. CONSERVATIVE, OR BOURGEOIS, SOCIALISM

A part of the bourgeoisie is desirous of redressing social grievances, in order to secure the continued existence of bourgeois society.

To this section belong economists, philanthropists, humanitarians, improvers of the condition of the working class, organisers of charity, members of societies for the prevention of cruelty to animals, temperance fanatics, hole-and-corner reformers of every imaginable kind. This form of Socialism has, moreover, been worked out into complete systems.

We may cite Proudhon's Philosophie de la Misere as an example of this form.

The Socialistic bourgeois want all the advantages of modern social conditions without the struggles and dangers necessarily resulting therefrom. They desire the existing state of society minus its revolutionary and disintegrating elements. They wish for a bourgeoisie without a proletariat. The bourgeoisie naturally conceives the world in which it is supreme to be the best; and bourgeois Socialism develops this comfortable conception into various more or less complete systems. In requiring the proletariat to carry out such a system, and thereby to march straightway into the social New Jerusalem, it but requires in reality, that the proletariat should remain within the bounds of existing society, but should cast away all its hateful ideas concerning the bourgeoisie.

A second and more practical, but less systematic, form of this Socialism sought to depreciate every revolutionary movement in the eyes of the working class, by showing that no mere political reform, but only a change in the material conditions of existence, in economic relations, could be of any advantage to them. By changes in the material conditions of existence, this form of Socialism, however, by no means understands abolition of the bourgeois relations of production, an abolition that can be effected only by a revolution, but administrative reforms, based on the continued existence of these relations;

reforms, therefore, that in no respect affect the relations between capital and labour, but, at the best, lessen the cost, and simplify the administrative work, of bourgeois government.

Bourgeois Socialism attains adequate expression, when, and only when, it becomes a mere figure of speech.

Free trade: for the benefit of the working class. Protective duties: for the benefit of the working class. Prison Reform: for the benefit of the working class. This is the last word and the only seriously meant word of bourgeois Socialism.

It is summed up in the phrase: the bourgeois is a bourgeois—for the benefit of the working class.

3. CRITICAL-UTOPIAN SOCIALISM AND COMMUNISM

We do not here refer to that literature which, in every great modern revolution, has always given voice to the demands of the proletariat, such as the writings of Babeuf and others.

The first direct attempts of the proletariat to attain its own ends, made in times of universal excitement, when feudal society was being overthrown, these attempts necessarily failed, owing to the then undeveloped state of the proletariat, as well as to the absence of the economic conditions for its emancipation, conditions that had yet to be produced, and could be produced by the impending bourgeois epoch alone. The revolutionary literature that accompanied these first movements of the proletariat had necessarily a reactionary character. It inculcated universal asceticism and social levelling in its crudest form.

The Socialist and Communist systems properly so called, those of Saint-Simon, Fourier, Owen and others, spring into existence in the early undeveloped period, described above, of the struggle between proletariat and bourgeoisie (see Section 1. Bourgeois and Proletarians).

The founders of these systems see, indeed, the class antagonisms, as well as the action of the decomposing elements, in the prevailing form of society. But the proletariat, as yet in its infancy, offers to them the spectacle of a class without any historical initiative or any independent political movement.

Since the development of class antagonism keeps even pace with the development of industry, the economic situation, as they find it, does not as yet offer to them the material conditions for the emancipation of the proletariat. They therefore search after a new social science, after new social laws, that are to create these conditions.

Historical action is to yield to their personal inventive action, historically created conditions of emancipation to fantastic ones, and the gradual, spontaneous class-organisation of the proletariat to the organisation of society specially contrived by these inventors. Future history resolves itself, in their eyes, into the propaganda and the practical carrying out of their social plans.

In the formation of their plans they are conscious of caring chiefly for the interests of the working class, as being the most suffering class. Only from the point of view of being the most suffering class does the proletariat exist for them.

The undeveloped state of the class struggle, as well as their own surroundings, causes Socialists of this kind to consider themselves far superior to all class antagonisms. They want to improve the condition of every member of society, even that of the most favoured. Hence, they habitually appeal to society at large, without distinction of class; nay, by preference, to the ruling class. For how can people, when once they understand their system, fail to see in it the best possible plan of the best possible state of society?

Hence, they reject all political, and especially all revolutionary, action; they wish to attain their ends by peaceful means, and endeavour, by small experiments, necessarily doomed to failure, and by the force of example, to pave the way for the new social Gospel.

Such fantastic pictures of future society, painted at a time when the proletariat is still in a very undeveloped state and has but a fantastic conception of its own position correspond with the first instinctive yearnings of that class for a general reconstruction of society.

But these Socialist and Communist publications contain also a critical element. They attack every principle of existing society. Hence they are full of the most valuable materials for the enlightenment of the working class. The practical measures proposed in them—such as the abolition of the distinction between town and country, of the family, of the carrying on of industries for the account of private individuals, and of the wage system, the proclamation of social harmony, the conversion of the functions of the State into a mere superintendence of production, all these proposals, point solely to the disappearance of class antagonisms which were, at that time, only just cropping up, and which, in these publications, are recognised in their earliest, indistinct and undefined forms only. These proposals, therefore, are of a purely Utopian character.

The significance of Critical-Utopian Socialism and Communism bears an inverse relation to historical development. In proportion as the modern class struggle develops and takes definite shape, this fantastic standing apart from the contest, these fantastic attacks on it, lose all practical value and all theoretical justification. Therefore, although the originators of these systems were, in many respects, revolutionary, their disciples have, in every case, formed mere reactionary sects. They hold fast by the original views of their masters, in opposition to the progressive historical development of the proletariat. They, therefore, endeavour, and that consistently, to deaden the class struggle and to reconcile the class antagonisms. They still dream of experimental realisation of their social Utopias, of founding isolated "phalansteres," of establishing "Home Colonies," of setting up a "Little Icaria"—duodecimo editions of the New Jerusalem—and to realise all these castles in the air, they are compelled to appeal to the feelings and purses of the bourgeois. By degrees they sink into the category of the reactionary conservative Socialists depicted above, differing from these only by more systematic pedantry, and by their fanatical and superstitious belief in the miraculous effects of their social science.

They, therefore, violently oppose all political action on the part of the working class; such action, according to them, can only result from blind unbelief in the new Gospel.

The Owenites in England, and the Fourierists in France, respectively, oppose the Chartists and the Reformistes.

IV. Position of the Communists in Relation to the Various Existing Opposition Parties

Section II has made clear the relations of the Communists to the existing working-class parties, such as the Chartists in England and the Agrarian Reformers in America.

The Communists fight for the attainment of the immediate aims, for the enforcement of the momentary interests of the working class; but in the movement of the present, they also represent and take care of the future of that movement. In France the Communists ally themselves with the Social-Democrats, against the conservative and radical bourgeoisie, reserving, however, the right to take up a critical position in regard to phrases and illusions traditionally handed down from the great Revolution.

In Switzerland they support the Radicals, without losing sight of the fact that this party consists of antagonistic elements, partly of Democratic Socialists, in the French sense, partly of radical bourgeois.

In Poland they support the party that insists on an agrarian revolution as the prime condition for national emancipation, that party which fomented the insurrection of Cracow in 1846.

In Germany they fight with the bourgeoisie whenever it acts in a revolutionary way, against the absolute monarchy, the feudal squirearchy, and the petty bourgeoisie.

But they never cease, for a single instant, to instil into the working class the clearest possible recognition of the hostile antagonism between bourgeoisie and proletariat, in order that the German workers may straightaway use, as so many weapons against the bourgeoisie, the social and political conditions that the bourgeoisie must necessarily introduce along with its supremacy, and in order that, after the fall of the reactionary classes in Germany, the fight against the bourgeoisie itself may immediately begin.

The Communists turn their attention chiefly to Germany, because that country is on the eve of a bourgeois revolution that is bound to be carried out under more advanced conditions of European civilisation, and with a much more developed proletariat, than that of England was in the seventeenth, and of France in the eighteenth century, and because the bourgeois revolution in Germany will be but the prelude to an immediately following proletarian revolution.

In short, the Communists everywhere support every revolutionary movement against the existing social and political order of things.

In all these movements they bring to the front, as the leading question in each, the property question, no matter what its degree of development at the time.

Finally, they labour everywhere for the union and agreement of the democratic parties of all countries.

The Communists disdain to conceal their views and aims. They openly declare that their ends can be attained only by the forcible overthrow of all existing social conditions. Let the ruling classes tremble at a Communistic revolution. The proletarians have nothing to lose but their chains. They have a world to win.

WORKING MEN OF ALL COUNTRIES, UNITE!

On *The Jewish Question*

Karl Marx

I

Bruno Bauer,
The Jewish Question,
Braunschweig, 1843

The German Jews desire emancipation. What kind of emancipation do they desire? *Civic*, *political* emancipation.

Bruno Bauer replies to them: No one in Germany is politically emancipated. We ourselves are not free. How are we to free you? You Jews are *egoists* if you demand a special emancipation for yourselves as Jews. As Germans, you ought to work for the political emancipation of Germany, and as human beings, for the emancipation of mankind, and you should feel the particular kind of your oppression and your shame not as an exception to the rule, but on the contrary as a confirmation of the rule.

Or do the Jews demand the same status as *Christian subjects of the state*? In that case, they recognize that the *Christian state* is justified and they recognize, too, the regime of general oppression. Why should they disapprove of their special yoke if they approve of the general yoke? Why should the German be interested in the liberation of the Jew, if the Jew is not interested in the liberation of the German?

The *Christian* state knows only *privileges*. In this state, the Jew has the privilege of being a Jew. As a Jew, he has rights which the Christians do not have. Why should he want rights which he does not have, but which the Christians enjoy?

In wanting to be emancipated from the Christian state, the Jew is demanding that the Christian state should give up its *religious* prejudice. Does he, the Jew, give up *his* religious prejudice? Has he, then, the right to demand that someone else should renounce his religion?

By its very nature, the Christian state is incapable of emancipating the Jew; but, adds Bauer, by his very nature the Jew cannot be emancipated. So long as the state is Christian and the Jew is Jewish, the one is as incapable of granting emancipation as the other is of receiving it.

The Christian state can behave towards the Jew only in the way characteristic of the Christian state—that is, by granting privileges, by permitting the separation of the Jew from the other subjects, but making him feel the pressure of all the other separate spheres of society, and feel it all the more intensely because he is in *religious* opposition to the dominant religion. But the Jew, too, can behave towards the state only in a Jewish way—that is, by treating it as something alien to him, by counterposing his imaginary nationality to the real nationality, by counterposing his illusory law to the real law, by deeming himself justified in separating himself from mankind, by abstaining on principle from taking part in the historical movement, by putting his trust in a future which has nothing in common with the future of mankind in general, and by seeing himself as a member of the Jewish people, and the Jewish people as the chosen people.

213

On what grounds, then, do you Jews want emancipation? On account of your religion? It is the mortal enemy of the state religion. As citizens? In Germany, there are no citizens. As human beings? But you are no more human beings than those to whom you appeal.

Bauer has posed the question of Jewish emancipation in a new form, after giving a critical analysis of the previous formulations and solutions of the question. What, he asks, is the *nature* of the Jew who is to be emancipated and of the Christian state that is to emancipate him? He replies by a critique of the Jewish religion, he analyzes the *religious* opposition between Judaism and Christianity, he elucidates the essence of the Christian state—and he does all this audaciously, trenchantly, wittily, and with profundity, in a style of writing what is as precise as it is pithy and vigorous.

How, then, does Bauer solve the Jewish question? What is the result? The formulation of a question is its solution. The critique of the Jewish question is the answer to the Jewish question. The summary, therefore, is as follows:

We must be emancipated ourselves before we can emancipate others.

The most rigid form of the opposition between the Jew and the Christian is the *religious* opposition. How is an opposition resolved? By making it impossible. How is *religious* opposition made impossible? By *abolishing religion*. As soon as Jew and Christian recognize that their respective religions are no more than *different stages in the development of the human mind*, different snake skins cast off by *history*, and that man is the snake who sloughed them, the relation of Jew and Christian is no longer religious but is only a critical, *scientific*, and human relation. *Science*, then, constitutes their unity. But, contradictions in science are resolved by science itself.

The *German* Jew, in particular, is confronted by the general absence of political emancipation and the strongly marked Christian character of the state. In Bauer's conception, however, the Jewish question has a universal significance, independent of specifically German conditions. It is the question of the relation of religion to the state, of the *contradiction between religious constraint and political emancipation*. Emancipation from religion is laid down as a condition, both to the Jew who wants to be emancipated politically, and to the state which is to effect emancipation and is itself to be emancipated.

> "Very well," it is said, and the Jew himself says it, "the Jew is to become emancipated not as a Jew, not because he is a Jew, not because he possesses such an excellent, universally human principle of morality; on the contrary, the *Jew* will retreat behind the *citizen* and be a *citizen*, although he is a Jew and is to remain a Jew. That is to say, he is and remains a *Jew*, although he is a *citizen* and lives in universally human conditions: his Jewish and restricted nature triumphs always in the end over his human and political obligations. The *prejudice* remains in spite of being outstripped by *general* principles. But if it remains, then, on the contrary, it outstrips everything else."
>
> "Only sophistically, only apparently, would the Jew be able to remain a Jew in the life of the state. Hence, if he wanted to remain a Jew, the mere appearance would become the essential and would triumph; that is to say, his *life in the state* would be only a semblance or only a temporary exception to the essential and the rule." ("The Capacity of Present-Day Jews and Christians to Become Free," *Einundzwanzig Bogen*, pp. 57)

Let us hear, on the other hand, how Bauer presents the task of the state.

> "France," he says, "has recently shown us" (Proceedings of the Chamber of Deputies, December 26, 1840) "in the connection with the Jewish question—just as it has continually done in all other *political* questions—the spectacle of a life which is free, but which revokes its freedom by law, hence declaring it to be an appearance, and on the other hand contradicting its free laws by its action." (*The Jewish Question*, p. 64)

"In France, universal freedom is not yet the law, the Jewish question too has *not* yet been solved, because legal freedom—the fact that all citizens are equal—is restricted in actual life, which is still dominated and divided by religious privileges, and this lack of freedom in actual life reacts on law and compels the latter to sanction the division of the citizens, who as such are free, into oppressed and oppressors." (p. 65)

When, therefore, would the Jewish question be solved for France?

"The Jew, for example, would have ceased to be a Jew if he did not allow himself to be prevented by his laws from fulfilling his duty to the state and his fellow citizens, that is, for example, if on the Sabbath he attended the Chamber of Deputies and took part in the official proceedings. Every *religious privilege*, and therefore also the monopoly of a privileged church, would have been abolished altogether, and if some or many persons, or even the overwhelming majority, still believed themselves bound to fulfil religious duties, this fulfilment ought to be left to them as a purely private matter." (p. 65)

"There is no longer any religion when there is no longer any privileged religion. Take from religion its exclusive power and it will no longer exist." (p. 66)

"Just as M. Martin du Nord saw the proposal to omit mention of Sunday in the law as a motion to declare that Christianity has ceased to exist, with equal reason (and this reason is very well founded) the declaration that the law of the Sabbath is no longer binding on the Jew would be a proclamation abolishing Judaism." (p. 71)

Bauer, therefore, demands, on the one hand, that the Jew should renounce Judaism, and that mankind in general should renounce religion, in order to achieve *civic* emancipation. On the other hand, he quite consistently regards the *political* abolition of religion as the abolition of religion as such. The state which presupposes religion is not yet a true, real state.

"Of course, the religious notion affords security to the state. But to what state? To what kind of state?" (p. 97)

At this point, the *one-sided* formulation of the Jewish question becomes evident.

It was by no means sufficient to investigate: Who is to emancipate? Who is to be emancipated? Criticism had to investigate a third point. It had to inquire: *What kind of emancipation* is in question? What conditions follow from the very nature of the emancipation that is demanded? Only the criticism of *political emancipation* itself would have been the conclusive criticism of the Jewish question and its real merging in the "*general question of time.*"

Because Bauer does not raise the question to this level, he becomes entangled in contradictions. He puts forward conditions which are not based on the nature of *political* emancipation itself. He raises questions which are not part of his problem, and he solves problems which leave this question unanswered. When Bauer says of the opponents of Jewish emancipation: "Their error was only that they assumed the Christian state to be the only true one and did not subject it to the same criticism that they applied to Judaism" (op. cit., p. 3), we find that his error lies in the fact that he subjects to criticism *only* the "Christian state," not the "state as such," that he does not investigate the *relation of political emancipation to human emancipation* and, therefore, puts forward conditions which can be explained only by uncritical confusion of political emancipation with general human emancipation. If Bauer asks the Jews: Have you, from your standpoint, the right to want *political emancipation*? we ask the converse question: Does the standpoint of *political* emancipation give the right to demand from the Jew the abolition of Judaism and from man the abolition of religion?

The Jewish question acquires a different form depending on the state in which the Jew lives. In Germany, where there is no political state, no state as such, the Jewish question is a purely *theological* one. The Jew finds himself in *religious* opposition to the state, which recognizes Christianity as its basis. This state is a theologian *ex professo*. Criticism here is criticism of theology, a double-edged criticism—criticism of Christian theology and of Jewish theology. Hence, we continue to operate in the sphere of theology, however much we may operate *critically* within it.

In France, a *constitutional* state, the Jewish question is a question of constitutionalism, the question of the *incompleteness of political emancipation*. Since the semblance of a state religion is retained here, although in a meaningless and self-contradictory formula, that of a *religion of the majority*, the relation of the Jew to the state retains the *semblance* of a religious, theological opposition.

Only in the North American states—at least, in some of them—does the Jewish question lose its *theological* significance and become a really *secular* question. Only where the political state exists in its completely developed form can the relation of the Jew, and of the religious man in general, to the political state, and therefore the relation of religion to the state, show itself in its specific character, in its purity. The criticism of this relation ceases to be theological criticism as soon as the state ceases to adopt a theological attitude toward religion, as soon as it behaves towards religion as a state—*i.e., politically*. Criticism, then, becomes criticism of the political state. At this point, where the question ceases to be theological, Bauer's criticism ceases to be critical.

> "In the United States there is neither a state religion nor a religion declared to be that of the majority, nor the predominance of one cult over another. The state stands aloof from all cults." (*Marie ou l'esclavage aux Etats-Unis, etc.,* by G. de Beaumont, Paris, 1835, p. 214)
>
> Indeed, there are some North American states where "the constitution does not impose any religious belief or religious practice as a condition of political rights." (op. cit., p. 225)
>
> Nevertheless, "in the United States people do not believe that a man without religion could be an honest man." (op. cit., p. 224)

Nevertheless, North America is pre-eminently the country of religiosity, as Beaumont, Tocqueville, and the Englishman Hamilton unanimously assure us. The North American states, however, serve us only as an example. The question is: What is the relation of complete political emancipation to religion? If we find that even in the country of complete political emancipation, religion not only exists, but displays a fresh and vigorous vitality, that is proof that the existence of religion is not in contradiction to the perfection of the state. Since, however, the existence of religion is the existence of defect, the source of this defect can only be sought in the nature of the state itself. We no longer regard religion as the *cause*, but only as the manifestation of secular narrowness. Therefore, we explain the religious limitations of the free citizen by their secular limitations. We do not assert that they must overcome their religious narrowness in order to get rid of their secular restrictions, we assert that they will overcome their religious narrowness once they get rid of their secular restrictions. We do not turn secular questions into theological ones. History has long enough been merged in superstition, we now merge superstition in history. The question of the relation of political emancipation to religion becomes for us the question of the relation of political emancipation to human emancipation. We criticize the religious weakness of the political state by criticizing the political state in its secular form, apart from its weaknesses as regards religion. The contradiction between the state and a particular religion, for instance Judaism, is given by us a human form as the contradiction between the state and *particular* secular elements; the contradiction between the state and religion in general as the contradiction between the state and its presuppositions in general.

The political emancipation of the Jew, the Christian, and, in general, of religious man, is the emancipation of the *state* from Judaism, from Christianity, from religion in general. In its own form, in the manner characteristic of its nature, the state as a state emancipates itself from religion by emancipating itself from the state religion—that is to say, by the state as a state not professing any religion, but, on the contrary, asserting itself as a state. The *political* emancipation from religion is not a religious emancipation that has been carried through to completion and is free from contradiction, because political emancipation is not a form of *human* emancipation which has been carried through to completion and is free from contradiction.

The limits of political emancipation are evident at once from the fact that the state can free itself from a restriction without man being really free from this restriction, that the state can be a *free state* [pun on word Freistaat, which also means republic] without man being a *free man.* Bauer himself tacitly admits this when he lays down the following condition for political emancipation:

> "Every religious privilege, and therefore also the monopoly of a privileged church, would have been abolished altogether, and if some or many persons, or even the overwhelming majority, still believed themselves bound to fulfil religious duties, this fulfilment ought to be left to them as a purely private matter." [*The Jewish Question*, p. 65]

It is possible, therefore, for the *state* to have emancipated itself from religion even if the *overwhelming majority* is still religious. And the overwhelming majority does not cease to be religious through being religious in private.

But, the attitude of the state, and of the republic [free state] in particular, to religion is, after all, only the attitude to religion of the *men* who compose the state. It follows from this that man frees himself through the *medium* of the state, that he frees himself politically from a limitation when, in contradiction with himself, he raises himself above this limitation in an abstract, limited, and partial way. It follows further that, by freeing himself politically, man frees himself in a roundabout way, through an intermediary, although an essential intermediary. It follows, finally, that man, even if he proclaims himself an atheist through the medium of the state—that is, if he proclaims the state to be atheist— still remains in the grip of religion, precisely because he acknowledges himself only by a roundabout route, only through an intermediary. Religion is precisely the recognition of man in a roundabout way, through an intermediary. The state is the intermediary between man and man's freedom. Just as Christ is the intermediary to whom man transfers the burden of all his divinity, all his religious constraint, so the state is the intermediary to whom man transfers all his non-divinity and all his human constraint.

The political elevation of man above religion shares all the defects and all the advantages of political elevation in general. The state as a state annuls, for instance, private property, man declares by political means that private property is abolished as soon as the property qualification for the right to elect or be elected is abolished, as has occurred in many states of North America. Hamilton quite correctly interprets this fact from a political point of view as meaning:

> "the masses have won a victory over the property owners and financial wealth." [Thomas Hamilton,
> *Men and Manners in America*, 2 vols, Edinburgh, 1833, p. 146.]

Is not private property abolished in idea if the non-property owner has become the legislator for the property owner? The property qualification for the suffrage is the last political form of giving recognition to private property.

Nevertheless, the political annulment of private property not only fails to abolish private property but even presupposes it. The state abolishes, in its own way, distinctions of birth, social rank, education, occupation, when it declares that birth, social rank, education, occupation, are non-political distinctions, when it proclaims, without regard to these distinctions, that every member of the nation is an *equal* participant in national sovereignty, when it treats all elements of the real life of the nation from the standpoint of the state. Nevertheless, the state allows private property, education, occupation, to *act* in *their* way—*i.e.*, as private property, as education, as occupation, and to exert the influence of their *special* nature. Far from abolishing these real distinctions, the state only exists on the presupposition of their existence; it feels itself to be a political state and asserts its universality only in opposition to these elements of its being. Hegel, therefore, defines the relation of the political state to religion quite correctly when he says:

> "In order [. . .] that the state should come into existence as the self-knowing, moral reality of the mind, its distraction from the form of authority and faith is essential. But this distinction emerges only insofar as the ecclesiastical aspect arrives at a separation within itself. It is only in this way that the state, above the particular churches, has achieved and brought into existence universality of thought, which is the principle of its form" (Hegel's *Philosophy of Right*, 1st edition, p. 346).

Of course! Only in this way, *above* the *particular* elements, does the state constitute itself as universality.

The perfect political state is, by its nature, man's species-life, as opposed to his material life. All the preconditions of this egoistic life continue to exist in civil society outside the sphere of the state, but as qualities of civil society. Where the political state has attained its true development, man—not only in thought, in consciousness, but in reality, in life—leads a twofold life, a heavenly and an earthly life: life in the political community, in which he considers himself a communal being, and life in civil society, in which he acts as a private individual, regards other men as a means, degrades himself into a means, and becomes the plaything of alien powers. The relation of the political state to civil society is just as spiritual as the relations of heaven to earth. The political state stands in the same opposition to civil society, and it prevails over the latter in the same way as religion prevails over the narrowness of the secular world—*i.e.*, by likewise having always to acknowledge it, to restore it, and allow itself to be dominated by it. In his most immediate reality, in civil society, man is a secular being. Here, where he regards himself as a real individual, and is so regarded by others, he is a fictitious phenomenon. In the state, on the other hand, where man is regarded as a species-being, he is the imaginary member of an illusory sovereignty, is deprived of his real individual life and endowed with an unreal universality.

Man, as the adherent of a *particular* religion, finds himself in conflict with his citizenship and with other men as members of the community. This conflict reduces itself to the *secular* division between the *political* state and *civil society*. For man as a *bourgeois* [i.e., as a member of civil society, "bourgeois society" in German], "life in the state" is "only a semblance or a temporary exception to the essential and the rule." Of course, the *bourgeois*, like the Jew, remains only sophistically in the sphere of political life, just as the *citoyen* ['citizen' in French, *i.e.*, the participant in *political* life] only sophistically remains a Jew or a *bourgeois*. But, this sophistry is not personal. It is the *sophistry of the political state* itself. The difference between the merchant and the citizen [*Staatsbürger*], between the day-laborer and the citizen, between the landowner and the citizen, between the merchant and the citizen, between the *living individual* and the *citizen*. The contradiction in which the religious man finds himself with the political man is the same contradiction in which the bourgeois finds himself with the *citoyen*, and the member of civil society with his *political lion's skin*.

This secular conflict, to which the Jewish question ultimately reduces itself, the relation between the political state and its preconditions, whether these are material elements, such as private property, etc., or spiritual elements, such as culture or religion, the conflict between the general interest and private interest, the schism between the political state and civil society—these secular antitheses Bauer allows to persist, whereas he conducts a polemic against their religious expression.

> "It is precisely the basis of civil society, the need that ensures the continuance of this society and guarantees its necessity, which exposes its existence to continual dangers, maintains in it an element of uncertainty, and produces that continually changing mixture of poverty and riches, of distress and prosperity, and brings about change in general." (p. 8)

Compare the whole section: "Civil Society" (pp. 8–9), which has been drawn up along the basic lines of Hegel's philosophy of law. Civil society, in its opposition to the political state, is recognized as necessary, because the political state is recognized as necessary.

Political emancipation is, of course, a big step forward. True, it is not the final form of human emancipation in general, but it is the final form of human emancipation within the hitherto existing world order. It goes without saying that we are speaking here of real, practical emancipation.

Man emancipates himself *politically* from religion by banishing it from the sphere of public law to that of private law. Religion is no longer the spirit of the state, in which man behaves—although in a limited way, in a particular form, and in a particular sphere—as a species-being, in community with other men. Religion has become the spirit of *civil society*, of the sphere of egoism, of *bellum omnium contra omnes*. It is no longer the essence of *community*, but the essence of *difference*. It has become the expression of man's *separation* from his *community*, from himself and from other men—as it was originally. It is only the abstract avowal of specific perversity, *private whimsy*, and arbitrariness. The endless fragmentation of religion in North America, for example, gives it even *externally* the form of a purely individual affair. It has been thrust among the multitude of private interests and ejected from the community as such. But one should be under no illusion about the limits of political emancipation. The division of the human being into a *public man* and a *private man*, the *displacement* of religion from the state into civil society, this is not a stage of political emancipation but its completion; this emancipation, therefore, neither abolished the *real* religiousness of man, nor strives to do so.

The *decomposition* of man into Jew and citizen, Protestant and citizen, religious man and citizen, is neither a deception directed *against* citizenhood, nor is it a circumvention of political emancipation, it is *political emancipation itself*, the *political* method of emancipating oneself from religion. Of course, in periods when the political state as such is born violently out of civil society, when political liberation is the form in which men strive to achieve their liberation, the state can and must go as far as the *abolition of religion*, the *destruction* of religion. But it can do so only in the same way that it proceeds to the abolition of private property, to the maximum, to confiscation, to progressive taxation, just as it goes as far as the abolition of life, the *guillotine*. At times of special self-confidence, political life seeks to suppress its prerequisite, civil society and the elements composing this society, and to constitute itself as the real species-life of man, devoid of contradictions. But, it can achieve this only by coming into *violent* contradiction with its own conditions of life, only by declaring the revolution to be permanent, and, therefore, the political drama necessarily ends with the re-establishment of religion, private property, and all elements of civil society, just as war ends with peace.

Indeed, the perfect Christian state is not the so-called *Christian* state—which acknowledges Christianity as its basis, as the state religion, and, therefore, adopts an exclusive attitude towards other religions. On the contrary, the perfect Christian state is the *atheistic* state, the *democratic* state, the state which relegates religion to a place among the other elements of civil society. The state which is still theological, which still officially professes Christianity as its creed, which still does not dare to proclaim itself *as a state*, has, in its *reality* as a state, not yet succeeded in expressing the *human* basis—of which Christianity is the high-flown expression—in a *secular, human* form. The so-called Christian state is simply nothing more than a non-state, since it is not Christianity as a religion, but only the *human background* of the Christian religion, which can find its expression in actual human creations.

The so-called Christian state is the Christian negation of the state, but by no means the political realization of Christianity. The state which still professes Christianity in the form of religion, does not yet profess it in the form appropriate to the state, for it still has a religious attitude towards religion—that is to say, it is not the *true implementation* of the human basis of religion, because it still relies on the *unreal, imaginary* form of this human core. The so-called Christian state is the *imperfect* state, and the Christian religion is regarded by it as the *supplementation* and *sanctification* of its imperfection. For the Christian state, therefore, religion necessarily becomes a *means*; hence, it is a *hypocritical* state. It makes a great difference whether the *complete* state, because of the defect inherent in the general *nature* of the state, counts religion among its *presuppositions*, or whether the *incomplete* state, because of the defect inherent in its *particular existence* as a defective state, declares that religion is its basis. In the latter case, religion becomes *imperfect politics*. In the former case, the imperfection even of consummate *politics* becomes evident in religion. The so-called Christian state needs the Christian religion in order to complete itself *as a state*. The democratic state, the real state, does not need religion for its political completion. On the contrary, it can disregard religion because in it the human basis of religion is realized in a secular manner. The so-called Christian state, on the other hand, has a political attitude to religion and a religious attitude to politics. By degrading the forms of the state to mere semblance, it equally degrades religion to mere semblance.

In order to make this contradiction clearer, let us consider Bauer's projection of the Christian state, a projection based on his observation of the Christian-German state.

> "Recently," says Bauer, "in order to prove the *impossibility* or *non-existence* of a Christian state, reference has frequently been made to those sayings in the Gospel with which the [present-day] state *not only does not* comply, but *cannot possibly comply, if it does not want to dissolve itself completely* [as a state]." "But the matter cannot be disposed of so easily. What do these Gospel sayings demand? Supernatural renunciation of self, submission to the authority of revelation, a turning-away from the state, the abolition of secular conditions. Well, the Christian state demands and accomplishes all that. It has assimilated the *spirit of the Gospel*, and if it does not reproduce this spirit in the same terms as the Gospel, that occurs only because it expresses this spirit in political forms, *i.e.*, in forms which, it is true, are taken from the political system in this world, but which in the religious rebirth that they have to undergo become degraded to a mere semblance. This is a turning-away from the state while making use of political forms for its realization." (p. 55)

Bauer then explains that the people of a Christian state is only a non-people, no longer having a will of its own, but whose true existence lies in the leader to whom it is subjected, although this leader by his origin and nature is alien to it—*i.e.*, given by God and imposed on the people without any co-operation on its part. Bauer declares that the laws of such a people are not its own creation, but are actual revelations, that its supreme chief needs privileged intermediaries with the people in the strict sense, with the masses, and that the masses themselves are divided into a multitude of particular groupings which are formed and determined by chance, which are differentiated by their interests, their particular passions and prejudices, and obtain permission as a privilege, to isolate themselves from one another, etc. (p. 56)

However, Bauer himself says:

"Politics, if it is to be nothing but religion, ought not to be politics, just as the cleaning of saucepans, if it is to be accepted as a religious matter, ought not to be regarded as a matter of domestic economy." (p. 108)

In the Christian-German state, however, religion is an "economic matter" just as "economic matters" belong to the sphere of religion. The domination of religion in the Christian-German state is the religion of domination.

The separation of the "spirit of the Gospel" from the "letter of the Gospel" is an *irreligious* act. A state which makes the Gospel speak in the language of politics—that is, in another language than that of the Holy Ghost—commits sacrilege, if not in human eyes, then in the eyes of its own religion. The state which acknowledges Christianity as its supreme criterion, and the *Bible* as its *Charter*, must be confronted with the *words* of Holy Scripture, for every word of Scripture is holy. This state, as well as the *human rubbish* on which it is based, is caught in a painful contradiction that is insoluble from the standpoint of religious consciousness when it is referred to those sayings of the Gospel with which it "not only does not comply, but *cannot possibly comply, if it does not want to dissolve itself completely as a state."* And why does it not want to dissolve itself completely? The state itself cannot give an answer either to itself or to others. In its *own consciousness*, the official Christian state is an *imperative*, the realization of which is unattainable, the state can assert the reality of its existence only by lying to itself, and therefore always remains in its own eyes an object of doubt, an unreliable, problematic object. Criticism is, therefore, fully justified in forcing the state that relies on the Bible into a mental derangement in which it no longer knows whether it is an *illusion* or a *reality*, and in which the infamy of its *secular* aims, for which religion serves as a cloak, comes into insoluble conflict with the sincerity of its *religious* consciousness, for which religion appears as the aim of the world. This state can only save itself from its inner torment if it becomes the police agent of the Catholic Church. In relation to the church, which declares the *secular* power to be its servant, the state is powerless, the secular power which claims to be the rule of the religious spirit is powerless.

It is, indeed, *estrangement* which matters in the so-called Christian state, but not *man*. The only man who counts, the king, is a being specifically different from other men, and is, moreover, a religious being, directly linked with heaven, with God. The relationships which prevail here are still relationships dependent of *faith*. The religious spirit, therefore, is still not really secularized.

But, furthermore, the religious spirit cannot be *really* secularized, for what is it in itself but the *non-secular* form of a stage in the development of the human mind? The religious spirit can only be secularized insofar as the stage of development of the human mind of which it is the religious expression makes its appearance and becomes constituted in its *secular* form. This takes place in the democratic state. Not Christianity, but the *human basis* of Christianity is the basis of this state. Religion remains the ideal, non-secular consciousness of its members, because religion is the ideal form of the *stage of human development* achieved in this state.

The members of the political state are religious owning to the dualism between individual life and species-life, between the life of civil society and political life. They are religious because men treat the political life of the state, an area beyond their real individuality, as if it were their true life. They are religious insofar as religion here is the spirit of civil society, expressing the separation and remoteness of man from man. Political democracy is Christian since in it man, not merely one man but everyman, ranks as *sovereign*, as the highest being, but it is man in his uncivilized, unsocial form, man in his fortuitous existence, man just as he is, man as he has been corrupted by the whole organization of our society, who has lost himself, been alienated, and handed over to the rule of inhuman conditions and elements—in short, man who is not yet a *real* species-being. That which is a creation of fantasy, a dream, a postulate of Christianity, *i.e.*, the sovereignty of man—but man as an alien being different from the real man—becomes, in democracy, tangible reality, present existence, and secular principle.

In the perfect democracy, the religious and theological consciousness itself is in its own eyes the more religious and the more theological because it is apparently without political significance, without worldly aims, the concern of a disposition that shuns the world, the expression of intellectual narrow-mindedness, the product of arbitrariness and fantasy, and because it is a life that is really of the other world. Christianity attains, here, the *practical* expression of its universal-religious significance in that the most diverse world outlooks are grouped alongside one another in the form of Christianity and still more because it does not require other people to profess Christianity, but only religion in general, any kind of religion (cf. Beaumont's work quoted above). The religious consciousness revels in the wealth of religious contradictions and religious diversity.

We have, thus, shown that political emancipation from religion leaves religion in existence, although not a privileged religion. The contradiction in which the adherent of a particular religion finds himself involved in relation to his citizenship is only *one aspect* of the universal *secular contradiction between the political state and civil society*. The consummation of the Christian state is the state which acknowledges itself as a state and disregards the religion of its members. The emancipation of the state from religion is not the emancipation of the real man from religion.

Therefore, we do not say to the Jews, as Bauer does: You cannot be emancipated politically without emancipating yourselves radically from Judaism. On the contrary, we tell them: Because you can be emancipated politically without renouncing Judaism completely and incontrovertibly, *political emancipation* itself is not *human* emancipation. If you Jews want to be emancipated politically, without emancipating yourselves humanly, the half-hearted approach and contradiction is not in you alone, it is inherent in the *nature* and *category* of political emancipation. If you find yourself within the confines of this category, you share in a general confinement. Just as the state *evangelizes* when, although it is a state, it adopts a Christian attitude towards the Jews, so the Jew *acts politically* when, although a Jew, he demands civic rights.

[*]

But, if a man, although a Jew, can be emancipated politically and receive civic rights, can he lay claim to the so-called *rights of man* and receive them? Bauer *denies* it.

"The question is whether the Jew as such, that is, the Jew who himself admits that he is compelled by his true nature to live permanently in separation from other men, is capable of receiving the *universal rights of man* and of conceding them to others."

"For the Christian world, the idea of the rights of man was only discovered in the last century. It is not innate in men; on the contrary, it is gained only in a struggle against the historical traditions in which hitherto man was brought up. Thus the rights of man are not a gift of nature, not a legacy from past history, but the reward of the struggle against the accident of birth and against the privileges which up to now have been handed down by history from generation to generation. These rights are the result of culture, and only one who has earned and deserved them can possess them."

"Can the Jew really take possession of them? As long as he is a Jew, the restricted nature which makes him a Jew is bound to triumph over the human nature which should link him as a man with other men, and will separate him from non-Jews. He declares by this separation that the particular nature which makes him a Jew is his true, highest nature, before which human nature has to give way."

"Similarly, the Christian as a Christian cannot grant the rights of man." (p. 19, 20)

According to Bauer, man has to sacrifice the *"privilege of faith"* to be able to receive the universal rights of man. Let us examine, for a moment, the so-called rights of man—to be precise, the rights of man in their authentic form, in the form which they have among those who *discovered* them, the North Americans and the French. These rights of man are, in part, *political* rights, rights which can only be exercised in community with others. Their content is participation in the *community*, and specifically in the *political* community, in the *life of the state*. They come within the category of *political freedom*, the category of *civic rights*, which, as we have seen, in no way presuppose the incontrovertible and positive abolition of religion—nor, therefore, of Judaism. There remains to be examined the other part of the rights of man—the *droits d'homme*, insofar as these differ from the *droits d'citoyen*.

Included among them is freedom of conscience, the right to practice any religion one chooses. The *privilege of faith* is expressly recognized either as a *right of man* or as the consequence of a right of man, that of liberty.

> *Déclaration des droits de l'droits et du citoyen*, 1791, Article 10: "No one is to be subjected to annoyance because of his opinions, even religious opinions." "The freedom of every man to practice the religion of which he is an adherent."
>
> *Declaration of the Rights of Man*, etc., 1793, includes among the rights of man, Article 7: "The free exercise of religion." Indeed, in regard to man's right to express his thoughts and opinions, to hold meetings, and to exercise his religion, it is even stated: "The necessity of proclaiming these rights presupposes either the existence or the recent memory of despotism." Compare the Constitution of 1795, Section XIV, Article 354.
>
> *Constitution of Pennsylvania*, Article 9, § 3: "All men have received from nature the imprescriptible right to worship the Almighty according to the dictates of their conscience, and no one can be legally compelled to follow, establish, or support against his will any religion or religious ministry. No human authority can, in any circumstances, intervene in a matter of conscience or control the forces of the soul."
>
> *Constitution of New Hampshire*, Article 5 and 6: "Among these natural rights some are by nature inalienable since nothing can replace them. The rights of conscience are among them." (Beaumont, op. cit., pp. 213, 214)

Incompatibility between religion and the rights of man is to such a degree absent from the concept of the rights of man that, on the contrary, a man's right to be religious, in any way he chooses, to practise his own particular religion, is expressly included among the rights of man. The *privilege of faith* is a *universal right of man*.

The *droits de l'homme*, the rights of man, are, as such, distinct from the *droits du citoyen*, the rights of the citizen. Who is *homme* as distinct from *citoyen*? None other than the *member of civil society*. Why is the member of civil society called "man," simply man; why are his rights called the *rights of man*? How is this fact to be explained? From the relationship between the political state and civil society, from the nature of political emancipation.

Above all, we note the fact that the so-called rights of man, the *droits de l'homme* as distinct from the *droits du citoyen*, are nothing but the rights of a *member of civil society*—i.e., the rights of egoistic man, of man separated from other men and from the community. Let us hear what the most radical Constitution, the Constitution of 1793, has to say:

Declaration of the Rights of Man and of the Citizen. Article 2. "These rights, etc., (the natural and imprescriptible rights) are: equality, liberty, security, property."

What constitutes liberty?

> Article 6. "Liberty is the power which man has to do everything that does not harm the rights of others," or, according to the *Declaration of the Rights of Man* of 1791: "Liberty consists in being able to do everything which does not harm others."

Liberty, therefore, is the right to do everything that harms no one else. The limits within which anyone can act *without harming* someone else are defined by law, just as the boundary between two fields is determined by a boundary post. It is a question of the liberty of man as an isolated monad, withdrawn into himself. Why is the Jew, according to Bauer, incapable of acquiring the rights of man?

> "As long as he is a Jew, the restricted nature which makes him a Jew is bound to triumph over the human nature which should link him as a man with other men, and will separate him from non-Jews."

But, the right of man to liberty is based not on the association of man with man, but on the separation of man from man. It is the *right* of this separation, the right of the *restricted* individual, withdrawn into himself.

The practical application of man's right to liberty is man's right to *private property*.

What constitutes man's right to private property?

> Article 16. (Constitution of 1793): "The right of property is that which every citizen has of enjoying and of disposing at his discretion of his goods and income, of the fruits of his labor and industry."

The right of man to private property is, therefore, the right to enjoy one's property and to dispose of it at one's discretion (*à son gré*), without regard to other men, independently of society, the right of self-interest. This individual liberty and its application form the basis of civil society. It makes every man see in other men not the realization of his own freedom, but the *barrier* to it. But, above all, it proclaims the right of man

> "of enjoying and of disposing at his discretion of his goods and income, of the fruits of his labor and industry."

There remains the other rights of man: *égalité* and *sûreté*.

Equality, used here in its non-political sense, is nothing but the equality of the *liberté* described above—namely: each man is to the same extent regarded as such a self-sufficient monad. The Constitution of 1795 defines the concept of this equality, in accordance with this significance, as follows:

> Article 3 (Constitution of 1795): "Equality consists in the law being the same for all, whether it protects or punishes."

And security?

> Article 8 (Constitution of 1793): "Security consists in the protection afforded by society to each of its members for the preservation of his person, his rights, and his property."

Security is the highest social concept of civil society, the concept of *police*, expressing the fact that the whole of society exists only in order to guarantee to each of its members the preservation of his person, his rights, and his property. It is in this sense that Hegel calls civil society "the state of need and reason."

The concept of security does not raise civil society above its egoism. On the contrary, security is the *insurance* of egoism.

None of the so-called rights of man, therefore, go beyond egoistic man, beyond man as a member of civil society—that is, an individual withdrawn into himself, into the confines of his private interests and private caprice, and separated from the community. In the rights of man, he is far from being conceived as a species-being; on the contrary, species-like itself, society, appears as a framework external to the individuals, as a restriction of their original independence. The sole bond holding them together is natural necessity, need and private interest, the preservation of their property and their egoistic selves.

It is puzzling enough that a people which is just beginning to liberate itself, to tear down all the barriers between its various sections, and to establish a political community, that such a people solemnly proclaims (*Declaration* of 1791) the rights of egoistic man separated from his fellow men and from the community, and that indeed it repeats this proclamation at a moment when only the most heroic devotion can save the nation, and is therefore imperatively called for, at a moment when the sacrifice of all the interest of civil society must be the order of the day, and egoism must be punished as a crime. (*Declaration of the Rights of Man*, etc., of 1793.) This fact becomes still more puzzling when we see that the political emancipators go so far as to reduce citizenship, and the *political community*, to a mere means for maintaining these so-called rights of man, that, therefore, the *citoyen* is declared to be the servant of egotistic *homme*, that the sphere in which man acts as a communal being is degraded to a level below the sphere in which he acts as a partial being, and that, finally, it is not man as *citoyen*, but man as private individual [*bourgeois*] who is considered to be the *essential* and *true* man.

> "The aim of all political association is the preservation of the natural and imprescriptible rights of man." (*Declaration of the Rights, etc.*, of 1791, Article 2.)
>
> "Government is instituted in order to guarantee man the enjoyment of his natural and imprescriptible rights." (*Declaration*, etc., of 1793, Article 1.)

Hence, even in moments when its enthusiasm still has the freshness of youth and is intensified to an extreme degree by the force of circumstances, political life declares itself to be a mere *means*, whose purpose is the life is civil society. It is true that its revolutionary practice is in flagrant contradiction with its theory. Whereas, for example, security is declared one of the rights of man, violation of the privacy of correspondence is openly declared to be the order of the day. Whereas "unlimited freedom of the press" (Constitution of 1793, Article 122) is guaranteed as a consequence of the right of man to individual liberty, freedom of the press is totally destroyed, because "freedom of the press should not be permitted when it endangers public liberty." ("Robespierre jeune," *Historie parlementaire de la Révolution française* by Buchez and Roux, vol. 28, p. 159.) That is to say, therefore: The right of man to liberty ceases to be a right as soon as it comes into conflict with *political* life, whereas in theory political life is only the guarantee of human rights, the rights of the individual, and therefore must be abandoned as soon as it comes into contradiction with its *aim*, with these rights of man. But, practice is merely the exception, theory is the rule. But even if one were to regard revolutionary practice as the correct presentation of the relationship, there would still remain the puzzle of why the relationship is turned upside-down in the minds of the political emancipators and the aim appears as the means, while the means appears as the aim. This optical illusion of their consciousness would still remain a puzzle, although now a psychological, a theoretical puzzle.

The puzzle is easily solved.

Political emancipation is, at the same time, the *dissolution* of the old society on which the state alienated from the people, the sovereign power, is based. What was the character of the old society? It can be described in one word—*feudalism*. The character of the old civil society was *directly political*—that is to say, the elements of civil life, for example, property, or the family, or the mode of labor, were raised to the level of elements of political life in the form of seigniory, estates, and corporations. In this form, they determined the relation of the individual to the *state as a whole—i.e.*, his *political* relation, that is, his relation of separation and exclusion from the other components of society. For that organization of national life did not raise property or labor to the level of social elements; on the contrary, it completed their *separation* from the state as a whole and constituted them as *discrete* societies within society. Thus, the vital functions and conditions of life of civil society remained, nevertheless, political, although political in the feudal sense—that is to say, they secluded the individual from the state as a whole and they converted the *particular* relation of his corporation to the state as a whole into his general relation to the life of the nation, just as they converted his particular civil activity and situation into his general activity and situation. As a result of this organization, the unity of the state, and also the consciousness, will, and activity of this unity, the general power of the state, are likewise bound to appear as the *particular* affair of a ruler isolated from the people, and of his servants.

The political revolution which overthrew this sovereign power and raised state affairs to become affairs of the people, which constituted the political state as a matter of *general* concern, that is, as a real state, necessarily smashed all estates, corporations, guilds, and privileges, since they were all manifestations of the separation of the people from the community. The political revolution thereby *abolished* the *political character of civil society*. It broke up civil society into its simple component parts; on the one hand, the *individuals*; on the other hand, the *material* and *spiritual* elements constituting the content of the life and social position of these individuals. It set free the political spirit, which had been, as it were, split up, partitioned, and dispersed in the various blind alleys of feudal society. It gathered the dispersed parts of the political spirit, freed it from its intermixture with civil life, and established it as the sphere of the community, the *general* concern of the nation, ideally independent of those particular elements of civil life. A person's *distinct* activity and distinct situation in life were reduced to a merely individual significance. They no longer constituted the general relation of the individual to the state as a whole. Public affairs as such, on the other hand, became the general affair of each individual, and the political function became the individual's general function.

But, the completion of the idealism of the state was at the same time the completion of the materialism of civil society. Throwing off the political yoke meant at the same time throwing off the bonds which restrained the egoistic spirit of civil society. Political emancipation was, at the same time, the emancipation of civil society from politics, from having even the *semblance* of a universal content.

Feudal society was resolved into its basic element—*man*, but man as he really formed its basis—*egoistic* man.

This *man*, the member of civil society, is thus the basis, the precondition, of the *political* state. He is recognized as such by this state in the rights of man.

The liberty of egoistic man and the recognition of this liberty, however, is rather the recognition of the *unrestrained* movement of the spiritual and material elements which form the content of his life.

Hence, man was not freed from religion, he received religious freedom. He was not freed from property, he received freedom to own property. He was not freed from the egoism of business, he received freedom to engage in business.

The establishment of the political state and the dissolution of civil society into independent individuals—whose relation with one another on *law*, just as the relations of men in the system of estates and guilds depended on *privilege*—is accomplished by one and the same act. Man as a member of civil society, unpolitical man, inevitably appears, however, as the *natural* man. The "rights of man" appears as "natural rights," because conscious activity is concentrated on the *political* act. Egoistic man is the passive result of the dissolved society, a result that is simply found in existence, an object of immediate certainty, therefore a *natural* object. The political revolution resolves civil life into its component parts, without revolutionizing these components themselves or subjecting them to criticism. It regards civil society, the world of needs, labor, private interests, civil law, as the basis of its existence, as a precondition not requiring further substantiation and therefore as its *natural* basis. Finally, man as a member of civil society is held to be man in his sensuous, individual, *immediate* existence, whereas *political* man is only abstract, artificial man, man as an allegorical, juridical person. The real man is recognized only in the shape of the egoistic individual, the true man is recognized only in the shape of the abstract citizen.

Therefore, Rousseau correctly described the abstract idea of political man as follows:

> "Whoever dares undertake to establish a people's institutions must feel himself capable of changing, as it were, human nature, of transforming each individual, who by himself is a complete and solitary whole, into a part of a larger whole, from which, in a sense, the individual receives his life and his being, of substituting a limited and mental existence for the physical and independent existence. He has to take from man his own powers, and give him in exchange alien powers which he cannot employ without the help of other men."

All emancipation is a *reduction* of the human world and relationships to *man himself.*

Political emancipation is the reduction of man, on the one hand, to a member of civil society, to an *egoistic*, *independent* individual, and, on the other hand, to a *citizen*, a juridical person.

Only when the real, individual man re-absorbs in himself the abstract citizen, and as an individual human being has become a *species-being* in his everyday life, in his particular work, and in his particular situation, only when man has recognized and organized his "own powers" as *social* powers, and, consequently, no longer separates social power from himself in the shape of *political* power, only then will human emancipation have been accomplished.

II
Bruno Bauer,
"The Capacity of Present-day Jews and Christians to Become Free,"
Einundzwanzig Bogen aus der Schweiz, pp. 56–71

It is in this form that Bauer deals with the relation between the Jewish and the Christian religions, and also with their relation to criticism. Their relation to criticism is their relation "to the capacity to become free."

The result arrived at is:

> "The Christian has to surmount only one stage, namely, that of his religion, in order to give up religion altogether,"

and therefore become free.

> "The Jew, on the other hand, has to break not only with his Jewish nature, but also with the development towards perfecting his religion, a development which has remained alien to him." (p. 71)

Thus, Bauer here transforms the question of Jewish emancipation into a purely religious question. The theological problem as to whether the Jew or the Christian has the better prospect of salvation is repeated here in the enlightened form: which of them is *more capable of emancipation*. No longer is the question asked: Is it Judaism or Christianity that makes a man free? On the contrary, the question is now: Which makes man freer, the negation of Judaism or the negation of Christianity?

> "If the Jews want to become free, they should profess belief not in Christianity, but in the dissolution of Christianity, in the dissolution of religion in general, that is to say, in enlightenment, criticism, and its consequences, free humanity." (p. 70)

For the Jew, it is still a matter of a profession of faith, but no longer a profession of belief in Christianity, but of belief in Christianity in dissolution.

Bauer demands of the Jews that they should break with the essence of the Christian religion, a demand which, as he says himself, does not arise out of the development of Judaism.

Since Bauer, at the end of his work on the Jewish question, had conceived Judaism only as crude religious criticism of Christianity, and therefore saw in it "merely" a religious significance, it could be foreseen that the emancipation of the Jews, too, would be transformed into a philosophical-theological act.

Bauer considers that the *ideal*, abstract nature of the Jew, his *religion*, is his *entire* nature. Hence, he rightly concludes:

> "The Jew contributes nothing to mankind if he himself disregards his narrow law," if he invalidates his entire Judaism. (p. 65)

Accordingly, the relation between Jews and Christians becomes the following: the sole interest of the Christian in the emancipation of the Jew is a general human interest, a *theoretical* interest. Judaism is a fact that offends the religious eye of the Christian. As soon as his eye ceases to be religious, this fact ceases to be offensive. The emancipation of the Jew is, in itself, not a task for the Christian.

The Jew, on the other hand, in order to emancipate himself, has to carry out not only his own work, but also that of the Christian—*i.e.*, the *Critique of the Evangelical History of the Synoptics* and the *Life of Jesus*, etc.

> "It is up to them to deal with it: they themselves will decide their fate; but history is not to be trifled with." (p. 71)

We are trying to break with the theological formulation of the question. For us, the question of the Jew's capacity for emancipation becomes the question: What particular *social* element has to be overcome in order to abolish Judaism? For the present-day Jew's capacity for emancipation is the relation of Judaism to the emancipation of the modern world. This relation necessarily results from the special position of Judaism in the contemporary enslaved world.

Let us consider the actual, worldly Jew—not the *Sabbath Jew*, as Bauer does, but the *everyday Jew*.

Let us not look for the secret of the Jew in his religion, but let us look for the secret of his religion in the real Jew.

What is the secular basis of Judaism? *Practical* need, *self-interest*. What is the worldly religion of the Jew? *Huckstering*. What is his worldly God? *Money*.

Very well then! Emancipation from *huckstering* and *money*, consequently from practical, real Judaism, would be the self-emancipation of our time.

An organization of society which would abolish the preconditions for huckstering, and therefore the possibility of huckstering, would make the Jew impossible. His religious consciousness would be dissipated like a thin haze in the real, vital air of society. On the other hand, if the Jew recognizes that this *practical* nature of his is futile and works to abolish it, he extricates himself from his previous development and works for *human emancipation* as such and turns against the supreme practical expression of human self-estrangement.

We recognize in Judaism, therefore, a general *anti-social* element of the *present time*, an element which through historical development—to which in this harmful respect the Jews have zealously contributed—has been brought to its present high level, at which it must necessarily begin to disintegrate.

In the final analysis, the *emancipation of the Jews* is the emancipation of mankind from *Judaism*. The Jew has already emancipated himself in a Jewish way.

> "The Jew, who in Vienna, for example, is only tolerated, determines the fate of the whole Empire by his financial power. The Jew, who may have no rights in the smallest German state, decides the fate of Europe. While corporations and guilds refuse to admit Jews, or have not yet adopted a favorable attitude towards them, the audacity of industry mocks at the obstinacy of the material institutions." (Bruno Bauer, *The Jewish Question*, p. 114)

This is no isolated fact. The Jew has emancipated himself in a Jewish manner, not only because he has acquired financial power, but also because, through him and also apart from him, *money* has become a world power and the practical Jewish spirit has become the practical spirit of the Christian nations. The Jews have emancipated themselves insofar as the Christians have become Jews.

Captain Hamilton, for example, reports:

> "The devout and politically free inhabitant of New England is a kind of *Laocoön* who makes not the least effort to escape from the serpents which are crushing him. *Mammon* is his idol which he adores not only with his lips but with the whole force of his body and mind. In his view the world is no more than a Stock Exchange, and he is convinced that he has no other destiny here below than to become richer than his neighbor. Trade has seized upon all his thoughts, and he has no other recreation than to exchange objects. When he travels he carries, so to speak, his goods and his counter on his back and talks only of interest and profit. If he loses sight of his own business for an instant it is only in order to pry into the business of his competitors."

Indeed, in North America, the practical domination of Judaism over the Christian world has achieved as its unambiguous and normal expression that the *preaching of the Gospel* itself and the Christian ministry have become articles of trade, and the bankrupt trader deals in the Gospel just as the Gospel preacher who has become rich goes in for business deals.

> "The man who you see at the head of a respectable congregation began as a trader; his business having failed, he became a minister. The other began as a priest but as soon as he had some money at his disposal he left the pulpit to become a trader. In the eyes of very many people, the religious ministry is a veritable business career." (Beaumont, op. cit., pp. 185, 186.)

According to Bauer, it is

> "a fictitious state of affairs when in theory the Jew is deprived of political rights, whereas in practice he has immense power and exerts his political influence *en gros*, although it is curtailed *en détail*." (*Die Judenfrage*, p. 114)

The contradiction that exists between the practical political power of the Jew and his political rights is the contradiction between politics and the power of money in general. Although theoretically the former is superior to the latter, in actual fact politics has become the serf of financial power.

Judaism has held its own *alongside* Christianity, not only as religious criticism of Christianity, not only as the embodiment of doubt in the religious derivation of Christianity, but equally because the practical Jewish spirit, Judaism, has maintained itself and even attained its highest development in Christian society. The Jew, who exists as a distinct member of civil society, is only a particular manifestation of the Judaism of civil society.

Judaism continues to exist not in spite of history, but owing to history.

The Jew is perpetually created by civil society from its own entrails.

What, in itself, was the basis of the Jewish religion? Practical need, egoism.

The monotheism of the Jew, therefore, is in reality the polytheism of the many needs, a polytheism which makes even the lavatory an object of divine law. ***Practical need*, *egoism***, is the principle of *civil society*, and as such appears in pure form as soon as civil society has fully given birth to the political state. The god of *practical need and self-interest* is *money*.

Money is the jealous god of Israel, in face of which no other god may exist. Money degrades all the gods of man—and turns them into commodities. Money is the universal self-established *value* of all things. It has, therefore, robbed the whole world—both the world of men and nature—of its specific value. Money is the estranged essence of man's work and man's existence, and this alien essence dominates him, and he worships it.

The god of the Jews has become secularized and has become the god of the world. The bill of exchange is the real god of the Jew. His god is only an illusory bill of exchange.

The view of nature attained under the domination of private property and money is a real contempt for, and practical debasement of, nature; in the Jewish religion, nature exists, it is true, but it exists only in imagination.

It is in this sense that [in a 1524 pamphlet] Thomas Münzer declares it intolerable

> "that all creatures have been turned into property, the fishes in the water, the birds in the air, the plants on the earth; the creatures, too, must become free."

Contempt for theory, art, history, and for man as an end in himself, which is contained in an abstract form in the Jewish religion, is the real, conscious standpoint, the virtue of the man of money. The species-relation itself, the relation between man and woman, etc., becomes an object of trade! The woman is bought and sold.

The *chimerical* nationality of the Jew is the nationality of the merchant, of the man of money in general.

The groundless law of the Jew is only a religious caricature of groundless morality and right in general, of the purely *formal* rites with which the world of self-interest surrounds itself.

Here, too, man's supreme relation is the *legal* one, his relation to laws that are valid for him not because they are laws of his own will and nature, but because they are the *dominant* laws and because departure from them is *avenged*.

Jewish Jesuitism, the same practical Jesuitism which Bauer discovers in the Talmud, is the relation of the world of self-interest to the laws governing that world, the chief art of which consists in the cunning circumvention of these laws.

Indeed, the movement of this world within its framework of laws is bound to be a continual suspension of law.

Judaism could not develop further as a *religion*, could not develop further theoretically, because the world outlook of practical need is essentially limited and is completed in a few strokes.

By its very nature, the religion of practical need could find its consummation not in theory, but only in *practice*, precisely because its truth is practice.

Judaism could not create a new world; it could only draw the new creations and conditions of the world into the sphere of its activity, because practical need, the rationale of which is self-interest, is passive and does not expand at will, but *finds* itself enlarged as a result of the continuous development of social conditions.

Judaism reaches its highest point with the perfection of civil society, but it is only in the *Christian* world that civil society attains perfection. Only under the dominance of Christianity, which makes *all* national, natural, moral, and theoretical conditions *extrinsic* to man, could civil society separate itself completely from the life of the state, sever all the species-ties of man, put egoism and selfish need in the place of these species-ties, and dissolve the human world into a world of atomistic individuals who are inimically opposed to one another.

Christianity sprang from Judaism. It has merged again in Judaism.

From the outset, the Christian was the theorizing Jew, the Jew is, therefore, the practical Christian, and the practical Christian has become a Jew again.

Christianity had only in semblance overcome real Judaism. It was too *noble-minded*, too spiritualistic to eliminate the crudity of practical need in any other way than by elevation to the skies.

Christianity is the sublime thought of Judaism, Judaism is the common practical application of Christianity, but this application could only become general after Christianity as a developed religion had completed *theoretically* the estrangement of man from himself and from nature.

Only then could Judaism achieve universal dominance and make alienated man and alienated nature into *alienable*, vendible objects subjected to the slavery of egoistic need and to trading.

Selling [*verausserung*] is the practical aspect of alienation [*Entausserung*]. Just as man, as long as he is in the grip of religion, is able to objectify his essential nature only by turning it into something *alien*, something fantastic, so under the domination of egoistic need he can be active practically, and produce objects in practice, only by putting his products, and his activity, under the domination of an alien being, and bestowing the significance of an alien entity—money—on them.

In its perfected practice, Christian egoism of heavenly bliss is necessarily transformed into the corporal egoism of the Jew, heavenly need is turned into world need, subjectivism into self-interest. We explain the tenacity of the Jew not by his religion, but, on the contrary, by the human basis of his religion—practical need, egoism.

Since in civil society the real nature of the Jew has been universally realized and secularized, civil society could not convince the Jew of the *unreality* of his *religious* nature, which is indeed only the ideal aspect of practical need. Consequently, not only in the Pentateuch and the Talmud, but in present-day society we find the nature of the modern Jew, and not as an abstract nature but as one that is in the highest degree empirical, not merely as a narrowness of the Jew, but as the Jewish narrowness of society.

Once society has succeeded in abolishing the *empirical* essence of Judaism—huckstering and its preconditions—the Jew will have become *impossible*, because his consciousness no longer has an object, because the subjective basis of Judaism, practical need, has been humanized, and because the conflict between man's individual-sensuous existence and his species-existence has been abolished.

The *social* emancipation of the Jew is the *emancipation of society from Judaism*.

15. Introduction to John Stuart Mill

John Stuart Mill is a British philosopher and roughly a contemporary of Marx. He is known for his political essay *On Liberty*, in which he argues for the widest possible freedom of thought and speech. Mill believes that the political choices that people make are determined by self-interest. He accepts classical liberal doctrine, but he is ahead of his time in warning that democratic government may on occasion conflict with individual freedoms.

But the most lasting contribution of John Stuart Mill to philosophy is his moral theory of Utilitarianism, which eventually emerged as the principal alternative to duty ethics. Utilitarianism was introduced by another English philosopher, Jeremy Bentham, in the late eighteenth century, but it became popular in Mill's version. In his essay *Utilitarianism*, Mill agrees with Kant that there is a supreme normative ethical principle, but argues that it is experience, not intuition, which gives us knowledge of this principle.

For Mill, the supreme normative principle takes the form:

> Actions are right in proportion as they tend to promote happiness; wrong as they tend to produce the reverse of happiness.

By happiness Mill means pleasure, but he rates intellectual pleasures higher than sensual ones. He claims that all human beings tend to do this, because they have an inherent sense of decency.

Mill also argues that, since there can be no other way to prove that general happiness is desirable, the only way to prove this is to demonstrate that people desire it. This proof takes the form:

> If X is the only thing desired, then X is the only thing that ought to be desired. General happiness is the only thing desired. Therefore, general happiness is the only thing that ought to be desired.

Utilitarianism was very successful in some areas, such as economics. Cost-benefit analysis, for example, is based on the notion of Utilitarianism. Nevertheless, this theory has been severely criticized on several points. If something is desired, does it follow that it ought to be desired? If I desire a triple hamburger, but I know it is bad for my heart condition, ought I to desire it? Moreover, is it possible to know what makes other people happy? Utilitarianism also appears to disregard considerations of justice (Mill writes the fifth part of *Utilitarianism* to address this criticism, but with rather limited success). Finally, under certain circumstances, Utilitarianism sanctions the flagrant violation of individual rights. All these issues constitute serious question marks hanging over the utility of Utilitarianism.

Utilitarianism

John Stuart Mill

Chapter IV
Of What Sort of Proof the Principle of Utility is Susceptible

It has already been remarked, that questions of ultimate ends do not admit of proof, in the ordinary acceptation of the term. To be incapable of proof by reasoning is common to all first principles; to the first premises of our knowledge, as well as to those of our conduct. But the former, being matters of fact, may be the subject of a direct appeal to the faculties which judge of fact—namely, our senses, and our internal consciousness. Can an appeal be made to the same faculties on questions of practical ends? Or by what other faculty is cognizance taken of them?

Questions about ends are, in other words, questions what things are desirable. The utilitarian doctrine is, that happiness is desirable, and the only thing desirable, as an end; all other things being only desirable as means to that end. What ought to be required of this doctrine—what conditions is it requisite that the doctrine should fulfil—to make good its claim to be believed?

The only proof capable of being given that an object is visible, is that people actually see it. The only proof that a sound is audible, is that people hear it: and so of the other sources of our experience. In like manner, I apprehend, the sole evidence it is possible to produce that anything is desirable, is that people do actually desire it. If the end which the utilitarian doctrine proposes to itself were not, in theory and in practice, acknowledged to be an end, nothing could ever convince any person that it was so. No reason can be given why the general happiness is desirable, except that each person, so far as he believes it to be attainable, desires his own happiness. This, however, being a fact, we have not only all the proof which the case admits of, but all which it is possible to require, that happiness is a good: that each person's happiness is a good to that person, and the general happiness, therefore, a good to the aggregate of all persons. Happiness has made out its title as *one* of the ends of conduct, and consequently one of the criteria of morality.

But it has not, by this alone, proved itself to be the sole criterion. To do that, it would seem, by the same rule, necessary to show, not only that people desire happiness, but that they never desire anything else. Now it is palpable that they do desire things which, in common language, are decidedly distinguished from happiness. They desire, for example, virtue, and the absence of vice, no less really than pleasure and the absence of pain. The desire of virtue is not as universal, but it is as authentic a fact, as the desire of happiness. And hence the opponents of the utilitarian standard deem that they have a right to infer that there are other ends of human action besides happiness, and that happiness is not the standard of approbation and disapprobation.

But does the utilitarian doctrine deny that people desire virtue, or maintain that virtue is not a thing to be desired? The very reverse. It maintains not only that virtue is to be desired, but that it is to be desired disinterestedly, for itself. Whatever may be the opinion of utilitarian moralists as to the original conditions by which virtue is made virtue; however they may believe (as they do) that actions and dispositions are only virtuous because they promote another end than virtue; yet this being granted, and it having been decided, from considerations of this description, what *is* virtuous, they not only place virtue at the very head of the things which are good as means to the ultimate end, but they also recognise as a psychological fact the possibility of its being, to the individual, a good in itself, without looking to any end beyond it; and hold, that the mind is not in a right state, not in a state conformable to Utility, not in the state most conducive to the general happiness, unless it does love virtue in this manner—as a thing desirable in itself, even although, in the individual instance, it should not produce those other desirable consequences which it tends to produce, and on account of which it is held to be virtue. This opinion is not, in the smallest degree, a departure from the Happiness principle. The ingredients of happiness are very various, and each of them is desirable in itself, and not merely when considered as swelling an aggregate. The principle of utility does not mean that any given pleasure, as music, for instance, or any given exemption from pain, as for example health, are to be looked upon as means to a collective something termed happiness, and to be desired on that account. They are desired and desirable in and for themselves; besides being means, they are a part of the end. Virtue, according to the utilitarian doctrine, is not naturally and originally part of the end, but it is capable of becoming so; and in those who love it disinterestedly it has become so, and is desired and cherished, not as a means to happiness, but as a part of their happiness.

To illustrate this farther, we may remember that virtue is not the only thing, originally a means, and which if it were not a means to anything else, would be and remain indifferent, but which by association with what it is a means to, comes to be desired for itself, and that too with the utmost intensity. What, for example, shall we say of the love of money? There is nothing originally more desirable about money than about any heap of glittering pebbles. Its worth is solely that of the things which it will buy; the desires for other things than itself, which it is a means of gratifying. Yet the love of money is not only one of the strongest moving forces of human life, but money is, in many cases, desired in and for itself; the desire to possess it is often stronger than the desire to use it, and goes on increasing when all the desires which point to ends beyond it, to be compassed by it, are falling off. It may be then said truly, that money is desired not for the sake of an end, but as part of the end. From being a means to happiness, it has come to be itself a principal ingredient of the individual's conception of happiness. The same may be said of the majority of the great objects of human life—power, for example, or fame; except that to each of these there is a certain amount of immediate pleasure annexed, which has at least the semblance of being naturally inherent in them; a thing which cannot be said of money. Still, however, the strongest natural attraction, both of power and of fame, is the immense aid they give to the attainment of our other wishes; and it is the strong association thus generated between them and all our objects of desire, which gives to the direct desire of them the intensity it often assumes, so as in some characters to surpass in strength all other desires. In these cases the means have become a part of the end, and a more important part of it than any of the things which they are means to. What was once desired as an instrument for the attainment of happiness, has come to be desired for its own sake. In being desired for its own sake it is, however, desired as part of happiness. The person is made, or thinks he would be made, happy by its mere possession; and is made unhappy by failure to obtain it. The desire of it is not a different thing from the desire of happiness, any more than the love of music, or the desire of health. They are included in happiness. They are some of the elements of which the desire of happiness is made up. Happiness is not an abstract idea, but a concrete whole; and these are some of its parts. And the utilitarian standard sanctions and approves their being so. Life would be a poor thing, very ill provided with sources of happiness, if there were not this provision of nature, by which things originally indifferent, but conducive to, or otherwise associated with, the satisfaction of our primitive desires, become in themselves sources of pleasure more valuable than the primitive pleasures, both in permanency, in the space of human existence that they are capable of covering, and even in intensity. Virtue, according to the utilitarian conception, is a good of this description. There was no original desire of it, or motive to it, save its conduciveness to pleasure, and especially to protection from pain. But through the association thus formed, it may be felt a good in itself, and desired as such with as great intensity as any other good; and with this difference between it and the love of money, of power, or of fame, that all of these may, and often do, render the individual noxious to the other members of the society to which he belongs, whereas there is nothing which makes him so much a blessing to them as the cultivation of the disinterested, love of virtue. And consequently, the utilitarian standard, while it tolerates and approves those other acquired desires, up to the point beyond which they would be more injurious to the general happiness than promotive of it, enjoins and requires the cultivation of the love of virtue up to the greatest strength possible, as being above all things important to the general happiness.

It results from the preceding considerations, that there is in reality nothing desired except happiness. Whatever is desired otherwise than as a means to some end beyond itself, and ultimately to happiness, is desired as itself a part of happiness, and is not desired for itself until it has become so. Those who desire virtue for its own sake, desire it either because the consciousness of it is a pleasure, or because the consciousness of being without it is a pain, or for both reasons united; as in truth the pleasure and pain seldom exist separately, but almost always together, the same person feeling pleasure in the degree of virtue attained, and pain in not having attained more. If one of these gave him no pleasure, and the other no pain, he would not love or desire virtue, or would desire it only for the other benefits which it might produce to himself or to persons whom he cared for.

We have now, then, an answer to the question, of what sort of proof the principle of utility is susceptible. If the opinion which I have now stated is psychologically true—if human nature is so constituted as to desire nothing which is not either a part of happiness or a means of happiness, we can have no other proof, and we require no other, that these are the only things desirable. If so, happiness is the sole end of human action, and the promotion of it the test by which to judge of all human conduct; from whence it necessarily follows that it must be the criterion of morality, since a part is included in the whole.

And now to decide whether this is really so; whether mankind do desire nothing for itself but that which is a pleasure to them, or of which the absence is a pain; we have evidently arrived at a question of fact and experience, dependent, like all similar questions, upon evidence. It can only be determined by practised self-consciousness and self-observation, assisted by observation of others. I believe that these sources of evidence, impartially consulted, will declare that desiring a thing and finding it pleasant, aversion to it and thinking of it as painful, are phenomena entirely inseparable, or rather two parts of the same phenomenon; in strictness of language, two different modes of naming the same psychological fact: that to think of an object as desirable (unless for the sake of its consequences), and to think of it as pleasant, are one and the same thing; and that to desire anything, except in proportion as the idea of it is pleasant, is a physical and metaphysical impossibility.

So obvious does this appear to me, that I expect it will hardly be disputed: and the objection made will be, not that desire can possibly be directed to anything ultimately except pleasure and exemption from pain, but that the will is a different thing from desire; that a person of confirmed virtue, or any other person whose purposes are fixed, carries out his purposes without any thought of the pleasure he has in contemplating them, or expects to derive from their fulfilment; and persists in acting on them, even though these pleasures are much diminished, by changes in his character or decay of his passive sensibilities, or are outweighed by the pains which the pursuit of the purposes may bring upon him. All this I fully admit, and have stated it elsewhere, as positively and emphatically as any one. Will, the active phenomenon, is a different thing from desire, the state of passive sensibility, and though originally an offshoot from it, may in time take root and detach itself from the parent stock; so much so, that in the case of an habitual purpose, instead of willing the thing because we desire it, we often desire it only because we will it. This, however, is but an instance of that familiar fact, the power of habit, and is nowise confined to the case of virtuous actions. Many indifferent things, which men originally did from a motive of some sort, they continue to do from habit. Sometimes this is done unconsciously, the consciousness coming only after the action: at other times with conscious volition, but volition which has become habitual, and is put into operation by the force of habit, in opposition perhaps to the deliberate preference, as often happens with those who have contracted habits of vicious or hurtful indulgence. Third and last comes the case in which the habitual act of will in the individual instance is not in contradiction to the general intention prevailing at other times, but in fulfilment of it; as in the case of the person of confirmed virtue, and of all who pursue deliberately and consistently any determinate end. The distinction between will and desire thus understood, is an authentic and highly important psychological fact; but the fact consists solely in this—that will, like all other parts of our constitution, is amenable to habit, and that we may will from habit what we no longer desire for itself, or desire only because we will it. It is not the less true that will, in the beginning, is entirely produced by desire; including in that term the repelling influence of pain as well as the attractive one of pleasure. Let us take into consideration, no longer the person who has a confirmed will to do right, but him in whom that virtuous will is still feeble, conquerable by temptation, and not to be fully relied on; by what means can it be strengthened? How can the will to be virtuous, where it does not exist in sufficient force, be implanted or awakened? Only by making the person *desire* virtue—by making him think of it in a pleasurable light, or of its absence in a painful one. It is by associating the doing right with pleasure, or the doing wrong with pain, or by eliciting and impressing and bringing home to the person's experience the pleasure naturally involved in the one or the pain in the other, that it is possible to call forth that will to be virtuous, which, when confirmed, acts without any thought of either pleasure or pain. Will is the child of desire, and passes out of the dominion of its parent only to come under that of habit. That which is the result of habit affords no presumption of being intrinsically good; and there would be no reason for wishing that the purpose of virtue should become independent of pleasure and pain, were it not that the influence of the pleasurable and painful associations which prompt to virtue is not sufficiently to be depended on for unerring constancy of action until it has acquired the support of habit. Both in feeling and in conduct, habit is the only thing which imparts certainty; and it is because of the importance to others of being able to rely absolutely on one's feelings and conduct, and to oneself of being able to rely on one's own, that the will to do right ought to be cultivated into this habitual independence. In other words, this state of the will is a means to good, not intrinsically a good; and does not contradict the doctrine that nothing is a good to human beings but in so far as it is either itself pleasurable, or a means of attaining pleasure or averting pain.

But if this doctrine be true, the principle of utility is proved. Whether it is so or not, must now be left to the consideration of the thoughtful reader.